Weaving

Shirley E. Held

Iowa State University

Weaving

A Handbook for Fiber Craftsmen

HOLT, RINEHART AND WINSTON, INC.
*New York   Chicago   San Francisco   Atlanta
Dallas   Montreal   Toronto   London   Sydney*

To my parents, who taught me to observe
and appreciate my environment

Editor Dan W. Wheeler
Production editor Rita Gilbert
Picture editor Joan Curtis
Designer Marlene Rothkin Vine
Illustrator Ronald Gilbert

Acknowledgment is made to Paul R. Reynolds, Inc.,
for permission to reproduce an illustration from
Needleweaving: Easy As Embroidery by Esther Warner Dendel.
Copyright © 1972 by Countryside Press.

Preface

Weaving is the age-old, ageless art and process of forming lengths of strandlike materials into an interlacement or structured web capable of giving practical service and immense pleasure to both hand and eye. My purpose in writing about it has been to offer for students and those generally fascinated by handcrafted objects enough basic information to enable them to have a functional understanding and a developed appreciation of the substances usable for warp and weft and of the tools, equipment, and techniques needed to fashion a woven article.

My procedure has been to commence with a brief review of the history of the fiber crafts as they developed in the East and the West and among peoples at all stages of cultural evolution. Not only does a recapitulation of the genesis and progress of a technology like weaving help to clarify the logic of its functions, it also provides an opportunity to reproduce examples of the most ambitious and appealing works ever accomplished in the form, whose extraordinary beauty may well be the most effective teacher the student of weaving could have. From this vantage point I have proceeded into a detailed discussion of fibers, yarns, and the instrumentation available for weaving fabrics on a loom. In this passage appear entire chapters on drafting, on weaves that are loom-controlled and on those subject to control by the weaver, and on ways to finish a woven textile. Subsequently, the focus moves to such techniques of fabric construction as pile weaving, weaving on simple looms, and the nonloom processes of macramé, sprang, netting, plaiting and braiding, spool and slot knitting, God's-eye, and card weaving. Especially important to the weaver concerned for controlling his work and its effect on completion are handspinning, the coloring of yarns with natural dyestuffs, and printing by the ikat and silk screen methods. These constitute the subject of an entire section composed of several chapters. Building on the foundation laid in earlier discussions, a final section opens up the possibilities offered by design based on an analysis of such elements and principles as form, line, space, texture, color, and light, in addition to proportion, balance, emphasis, and rhythm. Stressing the need for each weaver to develop his own individual sensibility into an original creative force, this material is applied to the capabilities peculiar to work on looms and then explored in the experiments and innovations achieved by modern masters of weaving.

Supplementing the text are appendices on common drafts for the four-harness loom, record-keeping, sources of materials and equipment, selected yarn designations, and metric conversion tables. Further aids to the beginning weaver can be found in the bibliography and notes and in a terminal glossary. Throughout the book I have made every effort to define terms clearly and accurately on their initial introduction into the text and within the context of their usage.

Because I find weaving more interesting as a means of creative visual expression than as a technology, I and the editors have been eager for the book's visual dimension to be as full and complete as the prose explanations given in the text. But to make technology an efficient servant of expressive intentions, we have taken great care, in both text and illustrations, to develop each process step by step and to move systematically from the simple to the complex. One device for accomplishing this has been the development of samplers, which lead the weaver sequentially through a wide selection of basic loom-controlled and weaver-controlled variations.

By providing demonstrations of a range of related fabric processes, I have hoped to indicate how the various types of yarn interlacement both resemble and depart from one another. With this understanding, the weaver can experiment with techniques and recombine them to achieve entirely new and personal variations. Among all the processes can be found those requiring little equipment and only small investment in order to commence creative work. The nonloom techniques especially permit the accomplishment of inventive weaving wherever expensive and complicated equipment cannot be employed. The chapter on drafting teaches the weaver how to turn imagination into controlled production. Elsewhere, weaving is shown to have sufficient versatility to yield not only yardage but also products as various in form as sculpture and loom-constructed garments.

The presentation guides the weaver through the decision-making process and the planning routine necessary for weaving a designed project. Yarn quantity and suitability, the identification of an appropriate form of fabric construction, and loom set-up are all considered in relation to the article the weaver wishes to achieve. In this context appear sample projects and for them the basic information concerning form, size, and organic development on the loom suitable to the creation of webs capable of fulfilling their intended purposes.

Above all, I have attempted to help the weaver visualize the project as he would wish it to exist after the web has been cut from the loom. Thus, all the time that specific help is given for individual procedures, the process of analysis emphasizes the complete problem. And since the success of an original design can be measured only in terms of the satisfaction it gives on completion, some special attention has been drawn to methods of finishing woven products.

There is no single way to perform a task in weaving. The procedures described here are mostly classic, assuring a certain reliable standard of success, but also sterility if the weaver does not use them to develop an idiomatic expression altogether his own. The inch-by-inch, yarn-by-yarn descriptions of techniques are meant to serve as safeguards for the beginner. Once the weaver has mastered them and discovered their mystery, he should proceed with daring, even to the extent of making himself vulnerable to the educational experience of mistakes. Often, misadventures in art can be transformed into remarkable and thrilling discoveries.

A book on weaving, especially one that addresses itself to the history of the process, would not be complete without its considering the phenomenon of the revival of handweaving in the present century. In our time, the fiber crafts are immensely popular, and out of the great activity in weaving have emerged master designers, equal to any whose works appear in historical collections. The presence of their powerful forms can be found in the avant-garde ranks of modern art as well as in industrial production. As a salute to its significance, the fiber art of the 20th century is the subject of the final chapter.

Before all others, I want to thank my students, who have tested these ideas, both in class and in their use of a preliminary edition of *Weaving,* and given me the benefit of their response to the experiment. Whatever the effectiveness of this final edition, much of its teachability will be owing to their eagerness to test and be tested. Among my former students I wish to cite Dee A. Dreezen for the contribution she made of her typing skills. My friend James D. Okey had the patience to read through a draft of the manuscript and the astuteness to provide a searching commentary on its content and organization. I am grateful to Carolyn Saul Logan for several valuable illustrations of Peruvian textiles. Dr. Margaret Warning and Dr. Agatha Huepenbecker made it possible for me to exploit the riches to be found in the historical textile collection maintained at Iowa State University. To Alice Adams, weaver and sculptor, and to Professors Bernard Kester of the University of California in Los Angeles, Jack Arends of Northern Illinois University, and Evelyn DeGraw of the University of Kansas, both I and my readers owe a debt of gratitude, for we are the beneficiaries of the massive critical review that they made of the manuscript, saving us from the confusion and embarrassment of a number of faults and failures. Museums, collectors, and weavers themselves have been immensely generous in providing illustrations, and I am pleased to have an opportunity to express thanks. Professor Donald Cyr of Southern Connecticut State College and Ms. Kate Edgerton of Edgerton's Handcrafts prepared the superb photographs now illustrating the chapters on dyeing and spinning. Dan Wheeler and the staff for the art books at Holt, Rinehart and Winston steered the project along the treacherous course leading to publication. Rita Gilbert went over every line of the manuscript, and her contributions were virtually those of an author. Joan Curtis collected the illustrations and brought to the task both a substantial knowledge of and a joy in the subject matter. Marlene Vine prepared the stunning and appropriate design, while Ronald Gilbert put it all together in a layout that makes text and illustrations function in a close, visual relationship. It was he who executed the line drawings and developed for them a uniquely suitable and consistent style. All these have my warmest appreciation, as does my family, who long endured the obsession that the making of an illustrated book becomes for its author.

Ames, Iowa   S.E.H.
February 1973

Contents

Preface   v

I THE HISTORY
OF FABRIC CONSTRUCTION   1

1 *The Origins of Fabric*   3

The Need for Fabric
The Inspiration for Fabric Construction
Early Construction Techniques
Primitive Materials
Evidences of Prehistoric Weaving

2 *The Evolution of Nonloom Processes*   10

Matting
Felting
Netting
Basketry
Twining
Sprang
Macramé
Lacemaking

3 *Handweaving of the Past: The First Six Millennia*   25

The Ancient Middle East
The Classical World
Early Weaving in the Far East: Pre-Buddhist China
The Christian World: Alexandria and Byzantium
The Moslem Conquest

ix

4 Handweaving of the Past: Europe, the Far East, and the New World — 45

The Middle Ages in Europe
Pre-Columbian America
The Meeting of East and West: China and Japan
Europe in Renaissance
The Baroque Period in Europe
The American Settlers
The Industrial Revolution

5 Twentieth-century Handweaving — 70

William Morris
The Bauhaus
The Revival of Handweaving in the United States
The Craft Revival in the Southern Highlands

II HANDWEAVING ON THE LOOM — 77

6 Materials for Weaving — 79

Fiber Classification
Fiber Characteristics
Weaving Yarns
Nonyarn Materials

7 Tools and Equipment — 90

The Loom
Other Equipment

8 Preparation for Weaving — 108

Yarn Calculations
Winding the Warp
Dressing the Loom
An Alternate Method for Dressing the Loom
The Tie-up
The Weaving Process

9 Drafting — 136

The Threading Draft
The Tie-up Draft
The Treadling Draft
The Weave Draft
The Comprehensive Draft
Deriving the Weave Draft

10 *Loom-controlled Weaves* 140

The Basic Weaves
Loom-controlled Weaves: A Sampler
Double Weaves
Brocade

11 *Weaver-controlled Weaves* 156

Lace Weaves
Lace Weaves: A Sampler
Warp Wrapping
Pattern Double Weave
Laid-in Weaves
Tapestry

12 *Finishing Procedures* 180

Edge Finishes
Functional Finishes

III OTHER CONSTRUCTION METHODS 187

13 *Pile Weaves* 189

Low-pile Weaves: Chaining, Twining, Soumak
High-pile Weaves: Looping, Rug Knots,
   Rya and Flossa, Corduroy, Hooking

14 *Simple Looms* 209

The Backstrap Loom
Permanent Frame Looms
Reusable Frame Looms

15 *Nonloom Techniques* 221

Macramé
Sprang
Netting
Plaiting and Braiding
Spool and Slot Knitting
God's-eye
Card Weaving

IV SPINNING AND COLORING 245

16 *Handspinning* 247

A History of Spinning
Materials for Spinning

Equipment
Planning the Yarn
Fiber Preparation
The Spinning Process
Yarn Design

17 *Yarn Dyeing*

268

A History of Dyes
The Dyeing Process
Natural Dyestuffs

18 *Yarn Printing*

290

Ikat
Silk Screen

V DESIGN IN FABRIC CONSTRUCTION   299

19 *Elements and Principles of Design*

301

Design Elements: Shape, Line, Space, Texture,
  Color and Light
Design Principles: Proportion, Balance, Emphasis, Rhythm

20 *Designing for the Loom*

315

Design Decisions
Planning Specific Items
The Profile Draft
Weave Analysis

21 *The Contemporary Fiber Craftsman*

327

Innovations in Fiber Craft
The Professional Weaver
Weaving: Art and Craft

Appendices

347

Appendix A	Common Drafts for the Four-harness Loom	349
Appendix B	Records	350
Appendix C	Sources of Materials and Equipment	352
Appendix D	Selected Yarn Designations	354
Appendix E	Metric Conversion Tables	357

Bibliography	358
Notes to the Text	361
Glossary	362
Index	367
Photographic Sources	372

part one
THE HISTORY OF FABRIC CONSTRUCTION

1
The Origins of Fabric

And the eyes of them both were opened, and they knew that they were naked; and they sewed fig leaves together, and made themselves aprons.

Unto Adam also and to his wife did the Lord God make coats of skins, and clothed them.

Genesis 3:7, 21

Weaving is one of the oldest crafts—and arts—practiced by man. In the very early stages of man's development weaving satisfied two of his most essential needs: those of clothing and shelter. Moreover, the creation of fabric is inextricably bound with man's quest for the third basic need—food, for when primitive man made the transition from a food-gathering to a food-producing way of life, he learned to use the hair from the animals he domesticated and the fruits of the crops he cultivated to construct garments and dwellings.

THE NEED FOR FABRIC
Shelter

Second only to the requirement for bodily sustenance is the need for shelter—from the elements and from predators, both animal and human. Even before prehistoric man emerged from the caves he learned to devise ways of making those crude abodes more comfortable and secure. He discovered that by laying an animal skin on the floor he could diminish the dampness, thus making the cave somewhat warmer. By hanging a pelt in the entryway he could inhibit the passage of inclement weather and wild animals.

When man's horizons expanded and he began to wander in search of more plentiful food supplies, he developed the technique of creating simple shelters, first by covering branches with animal skins and subsequently by plaiting, twining, knotting, or interweaving branches or grasses to erect freestanding structures. Such crude "houses," although temporary, had to be assembled quickly and securely. A method was devised whereby rigid poles made of tree branches were set in the ground, and flexible materials were twined around them at right angles. In warmer regions, a somewhat more permanent abode could be fashioned from baked mud, with a door of woven branches or rushes (Fig. 1). Animal skins were still put to use as door coverings and as "rugs" to insulate the earthen floor. They were

3

slit into strips to make cords or binders. Where skins were not abundant or desirable, man learned to adapt the same methods he had used for constructing his shelter to making other useful items. A rough fabric could be attached by its ends to the walls of his dwelling for a suspended sleeping bag—a hammock. At first these hammocks served principally as cradles for the young, but later they were built with sufficient strength to support the weight of a full-grown man or woman, thus providing a far more satisfactory arrangement than sleeping on the damp ground. Once the technique of fabric construction had been mastered, it could be applied to an endless variety of products—carriers for food and equipment, blankets, and, of course, body coverings.

Clothing

Authorities have long debated the initial impetus that led man to clothe his body. As the species

homo sapiens evolved, the thick mat of hair that had covered the body gradually disappeared, and denuded man was impelled to don artificial coverings. Was it a quest for protection from the elements, a desire for power and prestige, or simple modesty that made him take this step? Most writers agree that, although virtually every culture we know has employed some sort of clothing (albeit a tiny loincloth), modesty was a later development. Only after the wearing of clothes had become commonplace did man acquire his vanity and the feeling that nudity was shameful. Furthermore, since the earliest civilizations were established in the warm regions of the earth, clothing was not essential for comfort or for protection from the elements. It seems likely, then, that clothing first developed in a display of power, to frighten the enemy or to demonstrate the skill of the hunter, who adorned himself with furs as a testament to his success in the hunt. Later, rudimentary textiles were substituted for the pelts, and clothing became a means of gaining social approval. The increasing popularity of clothing led to a heightened demand for textiles, which in turn stimulated weaving. As variety in fabric patterns emerged, tribes began to engage in an exchange of designs.

The Aesthetic Impulse

It is believed that variety in design and the desire for enhancement of the created object followed closely upon the invention of fabric. One historian considers the pursuit of the aesthetic to be a condition of civilization. He writes: "When fear is overcome, curiosity and constructiveness are free, and man passes by natural impulse towards the understanding and embellishment of life."[1]

Documenting this hypothesis are examples from primitive cultures of mats, fishing nets, and baskets in which several materials, such as grasses, rushes, sinews, or strips of skin, have been combined, indicating that man has always had an interest in color and design. He selected grasses with different natural colors and com-

1. Mud hut with basketry door, Africa.

---

[1] All notes to the text can be found in a special section on page 361.

left: 2. SWEENIE WILLIS, a Choctaw from Mississippi. Mat. 1965. River cane (natural and walnut-dyed), plaited; 4'11" × 3'11". U.S. Department of the Interior, Indian Arts and Crafts Board.

below: 3. Oriole's nest.

bined them to create patterns (Fig. 2). Later, he added colors by dyeing or painting the fibers or strips of skin with berries, nuts, or other natural materials. Thus it seems that even when the business of survival occupied all his waking hours and life was precarious at best, man still found time to supersede mere functionalism and create beautiful objects.

THE INSPIRATION
FOR FABRIC CONSTRUCTION

Man has always been observant of and influenced by nature's creatures, their forms and behavior as well as their products. Thus, we can assume that birds, animals, and insects have helped to provide him with ideas that could be adapted for fashioning coverings for his body, tools for capturing food, and carriers for goods or for the young. For example, man has devoted considerable attention to the spider's method of spinning its web and the way in which birds build their nests (Fig. 3). A sturdy, intricate nest such as that of the oriole may well have inspired early man to construct his shelters in similar manner. A beaver's dam could have suggested barricades for capturing fish and small game. And it is not too farfetched to imagine that the opossum and other animals with pouches for transporting their young might have sparked the idea for the pa-

poose carrier of the American Indian. Many skills that the animals possess by virtue of their instinct man must learn by imitation.

EARLY CONSTRUCTION TECHNIQUES

Wattling or twining is probably the oldest of the preweaving construction techniques. The process was employed for linking rushes along the banks of streams in order to snare fish, as well as for creating the framework of shelters. This was followed by thatching, braiding or looping, knotting, and netting—all procedures that could be applied to readily available materials in their natural state.

Matted and felted fabrics, both of which are produced by pounding rather than interlacing, undoubtedly preceded weaving. Matting was developed in tropical areas. The bark of a tree is cut into thin layers, soaked, and then beaten until it takes the form of a mat. The resultant fabric is called *tapa cloth* (Pl. 1, p. 21).

Historians theorize that man developed the idea for felting after observing the natural matting that occurs when a sheep's wool is left unsheared for an extended period of time. He saw the same tendency toward matting in the fur pelts he wore for clothing. The skins were worn fur side in for comfort, and the combination of body heat and perspiration, plus the friction that was created by rubbing against the body, caused the wool to become permanently matted, forming a tough, resilient fabric. Later, man learned to apply heat, moisture, and pressure by artificial means to create quite serviceable cloth.

Both plaiting techniques and basketry are believed to have been employed earlier than weaving. One authority considers plaiting to have been the precursor of the primitive harness loom of the American Indian. Basketry is actually a limited form of weaving. It was an essential development during prehistoric man's wandering period, since he required carriers for his food and equipment. When a waterproof container was needed, the basket was lined with clay, much as some birds incorporate mud into their nests to hold the sticks together. It is generally agreed that pottery was invented when such a clay-lined basket accidentally fell into the fire.

Once the technique of basketry had been mastered, the underlying principle of weaving was within man's grasp. At first it was accomplished by simple means. Perhaps the rushes or reeds were laid out on the ground and the more limber vegetable fibers were interlaced over and under the rushes. Only when man began to choose more flexible materials for the *warps*—the lengthwise strips—did he require some device to hold the warps rigid during the weaving process. The first loom most likely consisted of two stakes between which one set of fibers was stretched. The earliest woven textiles were used to cover tent poles and were placed on the ground inside the shelter to serve as a floor covering.

The introduction of the loom was followed quickly by the need for spinning. Spinning made possible the use of a greater variety of fibers, many of which were too short in their natural state to be woven. Although some materials could be extended by knotting their ends together, spinning was a much more satisfactory method and greatly enlarged the repertoire of the weaver. Spindle whorls unearthed in archae-ological digs indicate that spinning was done during the Paleolithic Age in Europe.

PRIMITIVE MATERIALS

Although it is difficult to determine just which fibers were used by prehistoric man, it seems evident that he employed all the obvious materials in his environment: hemp, leaf fibers, hair, wool, strips of fur, and sinew. Human hair, deer hair, and the hair from dogs, cattle, and apes were all used to spin weaving yarns. One culture of prehistoric Denmark epitomized the maxim "waste not, want not" by making total use of the cow. The animal supplied both food and drink, the horn served as a drinking vessel as well as a musical instrument, the skin and sinews could yield material for garments, and the bones were made into sewing needles. Finally, the cow's tail was cut before winter and used as a strainer for milk (Fig. 4). By spring the tail had regrown, long enough for chasing flies. Tail hair was also spun into coarse yarn and made into a mesh. Even today cow's hair is a weaving staple in this area, commonly made into the backing for rya rugs.

Cotton fibers and wool became usable with the invention of spinning. It is believed that spinning was developed first among peoples who employed vegetable fibers for fabric construction, because evidence indicates that cotton and flax were spun earlier than wool. Cotton yarns were produced in India as early as 3500 B.C., and spun linen was available by 2000 B.C., although the fiber had been used in Egypt prior to that time by twining the strands. Wool became accessible with the domestication of sheep, a feat that was accomplished in Afghanistan and Iran by Neolithic times.

EVIDENCES OF PREHISTORIC WEAVING

It is challenging, to say the least, to obtain accurate information about a craft whose origins date back perhaps 35,000 years. Much of our understanding of very early fabric making is based on conjecture. Nevertheless, scientists have been quite successful in piecing together scraps of evidence from a variety of sources, including archae-ological findings, written and painted records,

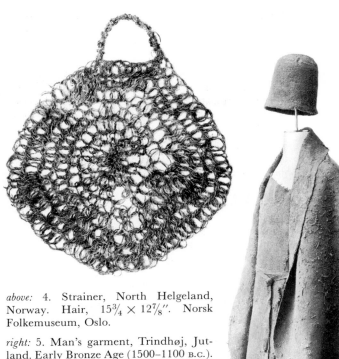

above: 4. Strainer, North Helgeland, Norway. Hair, 15¾ × 12⅞″. Norsk Folkemuseum, Oslo.

right: 5. Man's garment, Trindhøj, Jutland. Early Bronze Age (1500–1100 B.C.). National Museum of Copenhagen.

far right: 6. Pile rug, Scythian, from Tomb No. 5 at Pazyryk, Siberia. 5th–4th century B.C. c. 6′ square. The Hermitage, Leningrad.

patterns on clay vessels, and modern-day societies that operate on a primitive level. The first of these sources is, of course, the most reliable.

Archaeological Findings

The archaeologist seeking the remains of a long history of fabric construction has an unusually difficult task because of the impermanence of the material. Dampness, mildew, moths, fire, and chemicals in the soil all serve to destroy animal and vegetable fibers, so that very few remnants of early woven goods survive. Fortunately, certain areas in the world have climatic conditions that are more favorable to the preservation of textiles. Among these are the extremely cold northern part of Siberia, the boglands of Scandinavia, the hot, arid Sahara region, and the Andes and coastal plains of Peru.

Remnants of woven fabric dating possibly from 5000 B.C. have been found in the tombs of

Egypt, sealed under conditions ideal to preservation. One of the richest lodes of archaeological evidence for prehistoric weaving has been uncovered in the region of the Swiss Lake Dwellers, a culture dating to about 2500 B.C. Here scientists have discovered textile scraps, spinning whorls, and other artifacts that indicate an advanced capability for spinning and weaving during the Stone Age. The robe illustrated in Figure 5 was unearthed in Trindhøj, Jutland. It is one of seven complete garments found in oak coffin graves in the Danish boglands and is believed to date from the beginning of the Early Bronze Age (1500–1100 B.C.), before the funerary custom changed to cremation.

Until 1949 it had been believed that the oldest existing rugs dated from the 3rd century of the Christian era. However, in that year a Soviet expedition uncovered an ice-bound grave in Pazyryk in the Altai and made an amazing discovery (Fig. 6). The grave contained a wool rug,

left: 7. Black-figure lekythos, Greece, with image of vertical warp-weighted loom. c. 560 B.C. Terra cotta, height 6¾". Metropolitan Museum of Art, New York (Fletcher Fund, 1931).

below: 8. Funerary model of a weaver's workshop from Girga, Egypt, 12th Dynasty (c. 19th century B.C.), containing a simple horizontal loom and upright pegs for warping. Stuccoed and painted wood, height 8¾". Metropolitan Museum of Art, New York (anonymous gift, 1930).

bottom: 9. Neolithic pottery with weave imprint, found in the Thames near Mortlake. Terra cotta, height 5¼". British Museum, London.

approximately 6 feet square and almost perfectly preserved. The rug, which is dated to the 4th or 5th century B.C., was created by Scythian nomads, who were highly skilled craftsmen. It is less than $\frac{1}{10}$ inch thick and has 230 knots per square inch. The design consists of central squares with rosettes and a five-band border containing rows of winged griffins, grazing elk, and horsemen. Since the carpet exhibits such an advanced technical prowess, it can be safely assumed that the method was in use from at least the 1st millenium B.C.

Clues from Other Art Forms

Where fabric remains are not available, the historian must rely on peripheral evidence from other sources. He can examine the pictures made by ancient peoples to get an idea of the tools they used (Fig. 7). Wall paintings in tombs at Beni Hassan show weavers and spinners at work, and a model room recovered by archaeologists provides a three-dimensional illustration of a weaving shop in ancient Egypt (Fig. 8).

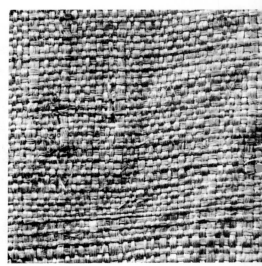

left: 10. Shirt, Minahasa, Sumatra. Collected before 1887. Bamboo fiber, knotted to increase length; height 3'11". Tropical Museum, Amsterdam.

below: 11. Detail of the shirt reproduced in Figure 10.

Such pictures also convey the artist's version of the garments worn by his fellows.

After about the 5th century B.C. the archaeologist has additional help from written records—accounts kept by weavers' guilds and tradesmen, as well as the writings of contemporary historians. Both Herodotus and Pliny have left us good descriptions of weaving in the ancient world.

In their excavations archaeologists often come upon bits of early pottery showing textile imprints (Fig. 9). Long after the fabric itself has disintegrated, the fired clay endures to preserve a record of the weaves employed.

Primitive Societies Today

In a world that sends men traveling to the Moon it is hard to believe that Stone Age societies still exist in remote parts of the globe, but this is indeed the case. There are groups of people living in isolated areas who still practice the most primitive manipulations of materials, using the crudest forms of equipment. This is true of some tribes in Central and South America, as well as in Africa and Southeast Asia. By studying such societies it is possible to project their pattern of development in fabric construction onto their ancient counterparts.

In Southeast Asia bamboo fibers serve to make cloth for sacks, sails, and decorated garments (Fig. 10). Young stems of bamboo are harvested, slit lengthwise, and soaked for the bast fibers. Further preparation occurs by chewing, much as the bast fibers of banana trees are separated. Once knotted together, the relatively short fibers thus obtained can be employed as yarns and subsequently woven on primitive looms (Fig. 11).

Since before the advent of recorded history textiles have served men in a multitude of ways. They not only protect him from extremes of temperature but they also are identified with his ideas about himself. For thousands of years fabrics have symbolized man's power, authority, humanity, social position, success on the battlefield, spiritual attitudes, economic position, and the adoration of his own body.

The Evolution of Nonloom Processes 2

And when she could not longer hide him, she took for him an ark of bulrushes, and daubed it with slime and with pitch, and put the child therein; and she laid it in the flags by the river's brink.

Exodus 2:3

With two exceptions the techniques described in this chapter predated the invention of the loom. Long before man discovered the advantages of weaving flexible materials through a set of stretched warps he had devised various methods for interlocking fibers or strands to create usable fabric. The oldest of these processes were in use during the Stone Age; the last to be considered—lacemaking—is new relative to the long history of fabric construction, having achieved its fullest development only in the 16th century.

MATTING

Fabric made from pounded bark is usually associated with Hawaii and the South Sea Islands, but much tapa cloth was also produced in Africa, Southeast Asia, and Central and South America. It is almost exclusively a product of the tropical regions: one rarely finds examples of the technique outside the equatorial zone bounded by the 25th parallels.

The preferred material for tapa cloth is the bark of the paper mulberry tree, colored light tan in its natural state. Although lightweight, soft, pliable, and attractive, the best tapa does not have great durability as a principal characteristic. Worn or damaged tapa fabric can be repaired by pounding in new bark, but the result is never satisfactory.

Tapa was most frequently used for clothing, both utilitarian and ceremonial. The Rio Negro Indians of Brazil made splendid dance masks that covered the entire body, and masks fashioned of tapa have appeared in many other cultures (Fig. 12). The people of the Admiralty Islands produced lavish dance skirts decorated with seeds, shells, and feathers. Bedding was another common end-product. Immense sheets, often more decorative than serviceable, were made in

Hawaii by felting strips of tapa cloth together. The fabric also served for funeral wrappings and for architectural adornment.

Despite the attractiveness of the natural tan color of bark cloth, the fabric was often dyed, usually in earth tones of red, brown, and black (Pl. 1, p. 21). The practice of stamping or pressing dye-soaked leaves or flowers into the cloth was widespread. Tahitian tapa became famous for its imprinted leaf patterns in crimson on yellow cloth. In some regions natural colors were rubbed directly into the fabric. Another common method of decorating bark cloth involved sewing strips of the fabric together in predetermined patterns. The Bushongo of Africa stitched alternating triangles of white and gray tapa into an allover geometric design.

Because of its poor strength, little utilitarian tapa cloth is made today. Almost invariably, bark cloth disappears once weaving has been introduced into a society. However, the manufacture of tapa cloth is still practiced as an art form in Polynesia, primarily for the tourist trade.

above: 12. Helmet mask from the Elema tribe, Gulf of Papua area, New Guinea. Collected by F. E. Williams before 1940. Bark cloth, paint, and raffia; height 37¾″. Museum of Primitive Art, New York.

right: 13. Wetting and rolling wool fibers to make felt, Mongolia.

FELTING

Felting involves the interlocking of loose fibers by a process that combines heat, moisture, and pressure. In the colder regions of the world felting took the place of matting as an early method of fabric construction. The best raw material for felt is sheep's wool, but the hair from many other animals—and even human hair—can be successfully felted.

It is possible to study primitive methods for making felt, because these same techniques are still in use today in Central Asia (Fig. 13). The wool is first laid in layers on a large mat, the top layer comprising the highest quality of wool. When the desired thickness has been attained, it can be bound with grease or with a mixture of oil and water. The entire mat is then rolled tightly like a jelly roll, unrolled, and rerolled from the opposite end. This process continues for four or five hours. Finally, the matted wool is washed and dried, then dampened and stretched on the mat to dry in the sun.

Today these same steps are accomplished at high speed by sophisticated felting machines, and manufacturers have found ways to incorporate a certain percentage of nonfelting materials—such as rayon—into the finished product. Despite the prevalence of woven fabrics, felt remains much sought after because of its unique characteristics. Since there is no grain line, felt will not ravel or tear. An excellent insulator against cold, shock, and sound, it can also be shaped easily.

Historians believe that the earliest felt garments were caps and hoods, probably because

14. Hood, Nazca culture, Peru. Felted human hair, width 13½″. Museum of the American Indian, Heye Foundation, New York.

15. *Eagle-Griffin Attacking an Ibex,* from the Pazyryk tombs, Siberia. 5th–4th century B.C. Appliquéd dyed felt. The Hermitage, Leningrad.

felt could be readily molded to the shape of the head (Fig. 14). By the time of the Romans felt had more varied applications. One of Caesar's armies was equipped with felt breastplates, tunics, boots, and socks. Even Roman slaves wore felt, in the form of skullcaps to cover their shaved heads. Shops unearthed at Pompeii appear to have specialized in the production of felt hats and gloves.

The use of felt was not limited to Western civilizations. The nomads of Siberia worked delicate appliqués in dyed felts (Fig. 15). Chinese historical records indicate that their warriors went to battle with felt shields, clothing, and hats. The popularity of felt for warfare is not surprising when one considers its nontearing qualities, which would have impeded, to some extent, the penetration of missiles.

Perhaps the most ingenious use of felt was and still is made by the nomadic Mongols of Central Asia, who construct huge tents known as *yourtas* or *yurts* from felted goat hair (Fig. 16). For this purpose goat hair has proved more practical than wool, owing to its superior ability to contract when wet and expand when dry. Thus, the yurt is watertight in rain yet breathes in dry weather.

Modern uses for felt extend from the cradle to the grave, from diapers to shrouds. Felt is widely used in curtains, handkerchiefs, bandages, napkins, place mats, and numerous other products.

16. Exterior of a felt yurt, Mongolia.

NETTING

Netting is a looping and knotting technique done on a single continuous strand. It is also a rudimentary form of lacemaking. Netting produces an openwork fabric suitable for carrying or for fishing and trapping wild game. Prehistoric man used nets for just these purposes, and the descendants of primitive nets can be seen today on the fishing boats that set out each morning from coastal towns.

The ancient Egyptians used nets for garments, often in the form of an openwork tunic worn over a solid fabric. A related technique—though not really a netting process at all—was Egyptian leatherwork netting. A piece of leather was slit in rows to form an open pattern. The result was a fabric that could be lifted as a unit but at the same time could be stretched sideways to cover a larger area than the original piece of leather.

Netting served a variety of utilitarian purposes in the New World. The Indians of Peru made slings for carrying their babies, as well as caplike head coverings (Fig. 17). A waterproof cape could be constructed from a net foundation, with straw or tied leaves interlaced with the net.

In medieval Europe nets of exquisite beauty were made, often for purely decorative purposes. The Cid reportedly presented the Sultan of Persia with a tunic of netting. Five centuries later, when Charles V of Spain (1500–58) led his armies on an expedition against Tunis, his horses were equipped with trappings of gold and scarlet silk net over crimson cloth. Nevertheless, the popularity of nets for hunting and other utilitarian purposes continued. The Emperor Charles is said to have instituted a chase form of hunting with nets, because game was rather scarce in the area. A large section of land would be enclosed by yarn nets, and, since the animals could not escape to high ground, they were captured by the hunter (Fig. 18). In the late 18th century a fashionable Spanish lady's wardrobe included an upper skirt made of knotted net finished at the bottom with tassels (Fig. 19).

Today modern industry produces nets of great strength, often using space-age fibers. Such is the pervasiveness of netted materials, they are taken for granted: fish nets, hair nets, tennis nets, net curtains—an endless variety of functional ob-

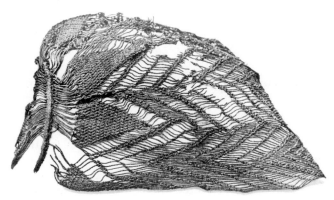

above: 17. Cap, central coast, Peru. Netted cotton worked in a symmetrical pattern of knots. Collection Fritz Iklé, St. Gall, Switzerland.

below: 18. Woodcut illustrating hunting with nets. From *Libro de la monteria* by Gonzalo Argote y Molina, Seville, 1582. Library of the Hispanic Society of America, New York.

19. FRANCISCO DE GOYA. *Queen Maria Luisa.* Late 18th century. Oil on canvas, 6'8¼" × 4'1¼". Museo di Capodimonte, Naples.

left: 20. TED HALLMAN. *Albe's Tree.* c. 1970. Interlaced yarns, $9 \times 4\frac{1}{2} \times 4'$. Courtesy the artist.

center: 21. Wappo gift basket, Napa County, California. 19th century (?). Coiled basketry with feathers and abalone shell. M. H. de Young Memorial Museum, San Francisco.

right: 22. Egyptian basketry boat, detail of a limestone relief in the tomb of Mereruka at Saqqara. 6th Dynasty (c. 2300 B.C.).

jects. However, the aesthetic possibilities of netting have not been ignored, for a number of artist-craftsmen have experimented with the technique (Fig. 20).

BASKETRY

Basketry is the process of making objects from various semirigid vegetable materials, such as grasses, rushes, reeds, and sticks. Known throughout the world, the technique has been practiced in one region or another for at least eleven thousand years. So versatile is the basket construction that it has been applied to containers and carrying vessels of every kind, cooking utensils, hats, sandals, mats, fish traps, armor, furniture, and even boats.

There exist two principal methods of basketry. In *coiled basketry* a foundation of grasses or other materials is coiled upon itself and then the coils are fastened together. Thus, coiled baskets usually have round or oval shapes. For *woven basketry* two sets of strips—a warp and a crosswise *weft*—are interlaced, usually at right angles to one another. It was the latter technique that led to the development of weaving, for when the use of more flexible materials became desirable, a

crude loom had to be devised to hold the warps rigid. Many kinds of decoration have been applied to baskets. The most obvious involves the use of different colored grasses or reeds, often one color for the warp and a contrasting color for the weft. In highly developed basketry richly patterned weaves can be created (Fig. 2). Some cultures have incorporated shells, beads, or feathers into their basketwork, either woven in during the construction or attached to the outside of the completed basket (Fig. 21).

Baskets found in the western region of the United States have been dated between 9000 and 7000 B.C., and the level of technical mastery in these examples indicates that the method had been practiced for a considerable time before that period. Evidence suggests that basketry developed in Eurasia even earlier.

The ancient Egyptians employed basketry to construct a wide variety of objects, including canoelike fishing boats bound together with papyrus (Fig. 22). Numerous Biblical references, including the story of Moses quoted at the beginning of this chapter, attest to the widespread use of basketry throughout the ancient Middle East, and the Greeks and Romans continued this reliance on baskets for containers and carriers.

By far the highest development in the art of basketry was attained by the so-called primitive cultures, notably the Indians of the western regions of North America. The Pomo, Wappo, Pima, and Tulare tribes are especially renowned for the beauty of their coiled baskets, in which the colorful geometric designs express the shape of the object (Fig. 23).

During the Middle Ages in Europe the basket makers were organized into guilds, whose rules prevailed until the end of the 18th century. Basketry objects and furniture were popular throughout the 18th and 19th centuries, and several designers have adapted this ancient technique to strikingly modern forms in our own era (Fig. 24).

TWINING

Twining differs from basketry in a number of respects. One or both of the sets of strands may be flexible, and consequently the product is more pliable, though not so soft as a woven fabric. A frame or *warp-weighted loom* (Fig. 149) is often used; that is, the warp threads are suspended from a rod of some kind and weighted at the bottom to hold them in position. In twining, each weft is a double strand. One strand passes in front of the warp and the other strand behind it; then the two strands are twisted together before continuing to the next warp thread or set of threads. In many cases the warp is completely covered by the weft. Twining served as the link between basketry and true weaving: Man had learned to weave with the aid of a simple frame, but he had not yet produced a soft, drapable fabric from flexible materials.

The oldest extant twined fabrics were discovered in Asia Minor and date from about 6500 B.C. These remnants exhibit a fairly rudimentary grasp of the principles of twining and indicate that the skill had been only recently acquired. Far more developed was the twining practiced by the Indians of ancient America. Fabrics dating from approximately 2500 B.C. have been found on the northern coast of Peru. It is apparent that twining coexisted for a time with weaving, but after their weaving became sufficiently expert, the Peruvian Indians abandoned twining.

Unlike most other groups, the Maori of New Zealand used no frame for their twining, but simply held the strands in the lap and manipulated them with the hands. The women wore shaped garments made entirely of twined fabric. Taaniko weaving (Fig. 25), a highly sophisticated

above left: 23. Pomo storage basket, California. 19th century. Coiled basketry. Museum of the American Indian, Heye Foundation, New York.

left: 24. WOLFRAM KRANK. *Vase with Outriding Strings.* 1969. Woven raffia and reed, height 15″. From *Objects: USA*, Johnson Wax Collection of Contemporary Crafts, Racine, Wisconsin.

above: 25. Maori taaniko border, New Zealand. Before 1920. Flax. American Museum of Natural History, New York.

The Evolution of Nonloom Processes   15

right: 26. Chilkat blanket, Alaska. c. 1875. Mountain goat's wool on cedar-bark fiber, 3 × 6′. Museum of the American Indian, Heye Foundation, New York.

below: 27. Chilkat warp-weighted loom with partly woven legging, Alaska. c. 1880. Width of loom 18″. Museum of the American Indian, Heye Foundation, New York.

variation of pattern twining, was in common use when James Cook first visited New Zealand in the latter part of the 18th century.

The Indians of North America were especially ingenious in adapting local materials to the requirements of twining. The cliff dwellers of the Southwest, for example, employed yucca for twining their carrier bands. The bags and pouches of the Plains Indians were twined from cornhusks, stems of rushes, the bast fibers of trees, or buffalo yarn. In each area of the world the natives learned to utilize raw materials indigenous to that region.

Most striking of all twined fabrics were the famous Chilkat blankets (Fig. 26), actually large ceremonial robes made by the Tlingit Indians of Alaska. The blankets typically combined a stylized animal form flanked by symmetrical abstract shapes and human heads, all of which formed the family crest of a particular clan. The

Chilkat tribe used a warp-weighted loom (Fig. 27) for their intricate three-strand twining. The warp threads, which were completely covered by the twining, consisted of mountain goat hair spun around strands of bark from the yellow cedar tree. The pattern-carrying weft was made only of goat hair dyed in shades of black, white, green, and yellow. Elaborately designed and meticulously executed, Chilkat blankets often required a whole year's work for a single garment to be produced. Very few of the blankets still exist, for the Tlingit customarily cremated them with their dead chief.

SPRANG

Sprang is a technique that involves a set of stretched parallel yarns twisted upon one another. There is no weft, or crosswise thread. The warps are twisted to form a lacelike pattern and then secured at the center, so that the two ends of the meshwork become absolutely symmetrical. Sprang is extremely elastic in all directions. In order for the design to be visible, the yarns must be held taut.

Sprang is sometimes called *knotless netting* or *Egyptian plaitwork*. A very ancient technique, remnants of such meshwork have been found in the Danish boglands, in the Swiss Lake region, and in Peru. Of these, the oldest examples come from the Bronze Age burial grounds in Denmark. The prehistoric Danes used sprang for a variety of utilitarian objects, such as stockings, cloaks, head coverings, mittens, strainers (Fig. 4), and dish cloths. Often, pig bristles or horsehair served as the yarn. Sprang was also known to the ancient Egyptians and to the Copts (Fig. 28).

Many primitive cultures, including the Eskimos and the Australian aborigines, used sprang to make carrying bags and hammocks. The Indians of northwestern North America produced blankets and garments from sprang, using strips of rabbit skin for the yarns. The strips were cut about ¼ inch wide and then twisted so that the outer surface showed only the animal's hair.

In medieval Europe sprang was employed primarily for making women's bonnets (Fig. 29). In fact, sprang bonnets were a part of the native costume of Yugoslav women until modern times.

In most parts of the world, knitting, crocheting, and weaving have replaced sprang. Like tapa cloth, sprang usually disappears when a culture masters the art of weaving. However, the Indians of Mexico still use the technique to make hammocks and market bags (often for international export), and at least one commune in the United States supports itself by the manufacture of sprang hammocks.

In recent years a number of craftsmen have experimented with sprang for decorative pieces. Foremost among them is Peter Collingwood, the noted English weaver, who has created some exceptionally effective wall hangings (Fig. 30). In an age of multiple media, it is to be expected that sprang will be incorporated with other techniques to broaden the range of handcraftsmen.

MACRAMÉ

The concept of knotting is so elementary that it hardly seems to qualify as a technique. However, for prehistoric man the idea that he could tie two short strands of fiber together to make a longer strand was a giant step in his development. The oldest known examples of knotted fabrics are nets originally made for catching wild game (Fig. 31).

right: 31. *Hunting with Net,* Assyrian relief from the North Palace of Ashurbanipal at Ninevah. 668–626 B.C. British Museum, London.

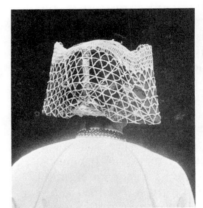
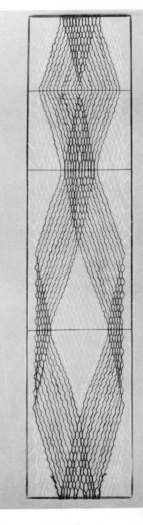

top left: 28. Coptic sprangwork cap or bag. A.D. 4th–5th century. Linen, 15¼ × 9½". Textile Museum Collection, Washington, D.C.

above left: 29. Sprang bonnet worn by the women of Trg in Croatia. The "Jalba" fabric is mounted on a framework to maintain its shape.

above right: 30. PETER COLLINGWOOD. Screen of double-twist sprang. 1966. Horsehair and monofilament nylon in a copper frame, 6′ × 1′3″. Victoria & Albert Museum, London.

Macramé is a specialized form of knotting perfected by the Arabs perhaps as early as the 7th century. Like sprang, it involves only one set of strands, a vertical warp. However, in the case of macramé, the strands can move either vertically or horizontally, so that the effect of a weft is created. Only two simple knots form the basis of macramé, but they can be combined in endless variations to achieve diversified effects.

The word *macramé* comes from the Arabic *migramah*, meaning fringe, and the technique was apparently first used for a decorative fringe on towels. In the 8th century the conquering Moors carried the knowledge of macramé into Spain, whence it spread to France and Italy. In medieval Europe macramé was used widely in decorative fringes or tassels for ecclesiastical vestments (Fig. 32). The banners carried in procession on holy days were often embellished with macramé, as were special altar cloths. Instead of merely hemming the edges of the cloth, weavers would knot the warp ends into elaborate patterns. The work was extremely fine and came to be known as *macramé lace*. Gold and silver threads were often included for special enrichment. The costume of the squire and the trappings of his horse provided another opportunity for decoration. Bed curtains, face towels, purses, veils, headdresses, pillows, and gloves were all considered appropriate subjects for macramé fringes.

The art of macramé declined after the 17th century, only to be revived in the mid-19th century under several different circumstances. Victorian Europe worked macramé fringes on table coverings, lampshades, umbrellas, baby carriages, clerical vestments, and accessories (Fig. 33). The craft became a staple of Latin America and to this day is taught to school children in several South American countries. However, it was among sailors, away at sea for months at a time, that macramé reached a pinnacle of popularity (Fig. 34). Knotting came naturally to these seamen, for it was a part of their everyday work on the ship's riggings. In their leisure hours they demonstrated remarkable ingenuity in finding surfaces to embellish with macramé, or as they called it, *square knotting*. Unfortunately, few of these knotted articles have survived, for the sailors typically sold them or gave them away as soon as they reached port. But it was in this way that the knowledge of macramé spread,

above left: 32. Macramé tassels, France. 16th–17th century. Silk and gilt thread, length of each 8″. Metropolitan Museum of Art, New York (Rogers Fund, 1908).

above right: 33. Victorian side pocket of macramé knots. From *Sylvia's Book of Macramé Lace,* c. 1882–85.

below: 34: Sailor's sampler of traditional knotting and braiding. 48 × 30″. Mariner's Museum, Newport News, Va.

much as the invading Moors had introduced the craft to Europe centuries earlier.

Toward the end of the 19th century macramé again declined and virtually disappeared. Then, in the mid-1960s the craft enjoyed another renaissance. Craftsmen interested in structural design in fabrics have explored the possibilities of knotting in both two- and three-dimensional forms and have even experimented with large sculptural constructions (Pl.2, p. 22).

LACEMAKING

Lace is an intricate twisting of fine threads done in such a way as to form a pattern. It is a descendant of netting, knotting, and plaitwork, as well as of *cutwork embroidery,* in which the cloth backing of an embroidered piece is cut away to leave only the stitched areas. An entire piece of fabric may be composed of lace, or the lacework may serve as an edging for a woven cloth. There are essentially three types of lace: needle or point lace, bobbin lace, and decorated nets.

Needle lace (Fig. 35) is probably the oldest variety and was inspired by cutwork embroidery. It is composed of stitches and knots made with a single yarn in a needle. Most needle lace construction derives from the buttonhole stitch. The pattern to be worked is drawn on a small piece of parchment or paper, and the latter attached to cloth for support. After the pattern has been outlined in a foundation thread *couched* (that is, tacked down with thread) to the backing, the design is then worked inside the foundation. Cutting the couching threads removes the finished lace from the parchment and cloth.

Bobbin lace is worked with several individual yarns each wrapped around a bobbin—a short

36. JAN VERMEER. *The Lacemaker.* 1660s(?). Oil on canvas, $9\frac{5}{16} \times 8\frac{3}{16}''$. Louvre, Paris.

stick with a spool at the end. It is sometimes called *bone lace,* because many bobbins were made of bone, or *pillow lace,* because a pillow is used as a support in constructing the lace. The introduction of the bobbin made it possible for quantities of yarn to be worked simultaneously without the problem of tangling. A paper or parchment pattern is first laid over the pillow, and marking needles are inserted at strategic points in the design. With a bobbin held in each hand, the threads are twisted, crossed, or plaited (Fig. 36) and cast around the marking needles

to build a firm network of lace. Bobbin lace can be further subdivided into two types, straight lace and free lace. *Straight lace* (Fig. 37), as the name implies, is a strip of lace such as might be used for a border or inset. It sometimes requires a vast number of bobbins: as many as three or four hundred might be used to produce a complex pattern only 3 or 4 inches wide. All the threads are attached at the top of the pillow and allowed to hang down over the pattern. The yarns are worked down to the bottom of the pattern and then reestablished at the top to begin the repeat. *Free lace* (Fig. 38) can take any form the lacemaker wishes. It is worked over a round pillow so that the pillow can be turned to follow the pattern. Far fewer bobbins are required for free lace—seldom more than twenty or thirty.

The third category of lace, *decorated net,* consists of patterns darned or embroidered with the chain stitch on a net structure ranging from coarse to extremely fine (Fig. 39). It is less common than needle lace and bobbin lace.

To the extent that lacemaking traces its ancestry to plaitwork and netting, the technique has been known for a very long time. Rods that may have served as bobbins have been found in Etruscan graves in Italy, thus dating them well before the Christian era. However, true lace can be said to have been invented in 16th-century

Plate 1. Tapa cloth, Fiji. c. 1830–52. Collected by Captain Ben Wallis. Peabody Museum of Salem, Mass.

Plate 2. CLAIRE ZEISLER. *Red Wednesday*. 1969. Knotted jute, height 36″.
Courtesy Ruth Kaufmann Gallery, New York.

left: 40. Bobbins with Romayne-type carving used for lace-making in gold and silver thread. Early 16th century. Boxwood. City Museum & Art Gallery, Birmingham, England (Pinto Collection).

below: 41. Lacemaking in 18th-century France, from Diderot's *Encyclopedie,* 1753. *Fig. 1:* the lacemaker; *Fig. 2:* another worker pricks the lace, which is placed on a bit of green awning material stretched on the cushion; *Fig. 3:* an empty spindle; *Fig. 4:* a full spindle and the pin to which one attaches it by means of a loop of thread; *Fig. 5:* a so-called "cushion," actually a cylindrical piece of wood; *Fig. 6:* frame for holding the cushion; *Fig. 7:* frame with the cushion in place; *Fig. 8:* a half-case of horn or reed; *Fig. 9:* coarse pins with heads of diamond or Spanish wax.

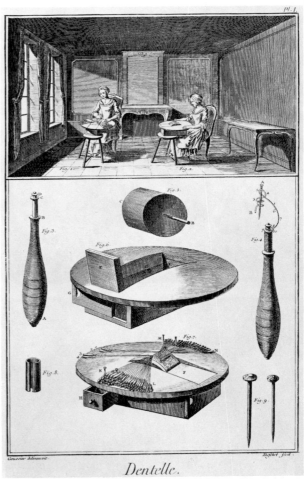

Dentelle.

Venice, when the *punto in aria*—the stitch drawn freely in the air—broke free of older embroidery methods. The first lace patterns were based on embroidery designs, but as early as 1530 a book of patterns intended specifically for lace was published in Italy. By 1557 a collection of bobbin lace patterns had appeared in print. Originally, Venice specialized in needle laces, while Milan and Genoa were better known for their bobbin lace. In time, Flanders took the lead in the production of bobbin lace, with important manufacturies at Bruges, Mechelin, Brussels, and Valenciennes. Gold and silver threads were often used for the construction of 16th-century bobbin laces. Unfortunately, few specimens of these sumptuous laces still exist, for they were later melted down and sold for the precious metal. During the same luxurious period highly decorated bobbins were made of carved wood and ivory (Fig. 40). In the latter half of the 16th century Spain set the fashion for wearing apparel throughout Europe, and the high Spanish collar or ruff greatly increased the demand for lace.

Lacemaking was introduced into France in the 17th century, when the French government, under the leadership of Colbert, imported workers from Italy and Flanders. A lace center was established at Alençon, where needle laces, primarily, were made. Chantilly and Cluny, among other cities, produced bobbin lace. Closely supervised by the state (Fig. 41), the French lace industry worked by such high standards that France dominated Europe in lacemaking until the end of the 19th century.

During the Industrial Revolution machines were introduced that could duplicate very closely the fine handmade laces. In fact, as early as 1769 Robert Frost of Nottingham invented a machine on which he made plain lacy webbing. To date no machine can fabricate the buttonhole stitch, which is the basis of needle laces, but bobbin lace can be copied quite faithfully. With these developments it seemed, for a time, that the traditional lace industry was doomed. However, a small market for handmade lace remained, and the art of lacemaking has endured in most of the well-known centers into the 20th century. Today one can still find lacemakers in Spain, Italy, Ireland, England, Finland, Belgium, and Czech-

below: 42. MARIAN POWYS. *Fawns.* c. 1930. Devon pillow lace. Collection Peter P. Grey, Blauvelt, N.Y.

bottom: 43. MARIE VAŇKOVÁ. *Space Lace Form,* detail. 1970. Pillow lace; height 13′, diameter 1′7½″. International Biennial of Tapestries, Lausanne, 1971.

right: 44. LUBA KREJCI. Panel. 1965. Lace, 17½ × 13¾″. Collection Maureen O'Connor, New York.

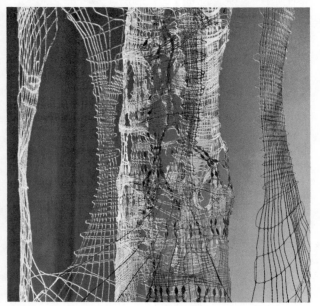

oslovakia. Marian Powys, who studied in Brussels, was considered by many to be the foremost lacemaker ever to have worked in the United States (Fig. 42).

Some of the more inspired contemporary lacework is currently being done in Czechoslovakia. Marie Vaňková of Prague constructs in bobbin lace works that are both delicate in structure and massive in scale (Fig. 43). Luba Krejci achieved international prominence during the 1960s with her unconventional designs for free lace (Fig. 44). Krejci's work combines a background in traditional lacemaking—acquired at the School of Applied Art in Brno—with a contemporary tendency toward simplification of form. She works her design figures on a weblike structural ground almost as fine as a spider's web. The result is as different from a 16th-century lace collar as a Picasso is from a Vermeer.

It should be clear from the foregoing discussion that the sum of man's knowledge in the textile arts need not overshadow its individual parts. Although man has developed highly sophisticated machines and techniques for the production of fabric, the old methods are still open to restatement. Skilled, imaginative craftsmen throughout the world are proving this today.

3 Handweaving of the Past: The First Six Millennia

And thou shalt make a hanging for the door of the tent, of blue, and purple, and scarlet, and fine twined linen, wrought with needlework.

Exodus 26:36

Weaving is the process by which two sets of threads of any substance are interlaced at right angles to form a continuous web. Although simple weaving can be done with the fingers alone, virtually every culture with a tradition of weaving has devised some kind of frame to facilitate the interlacing of the yarns. This chapter, therefore, traces the history of techniques that are usually associated with the loom, primarily weaving and tapestry. The process of weaving is treated fully in Part II; however, in order to better understand the discussion that follows, the reader should be familiar with certain terms peculiar to the craft. The *web* referred to above is the product of the loom—the fabric or other material that the weaver creates. As noted in Chapter 1, the *warp* threads or *ends* are the lengthwise yarns, which are set up first on the loom. The *weft* yarns—also called *pick, woof,* or *filler*—are the crosswise intersecting yarns. The finished edge at either side of the web is referred

to as the *selvedge* (or *selvage*). A *tapestry* can be defined as a woven cloth in which the pattern-carrying weft yarns, for the most part, are visible on the surface, for they are closely packed on a less-concentrated warp. This definition will assume more meaning in the context of Chapter 11, in which the tapestry technique is explained in detail.

The terms warp and weft have acquired symbolic meaning in the Orient. In China the word for "warp" also means "king."

The elements of weaving have assumed a profound symbolic meaning. The warp firmly attached to the frame of the loom symbolizes the immutable forces of the world while the weft, which moves lightly to and fro between the warp threads, stands for the transient affairs of men. Other symbolic meanings are derived from the cross formed by the linking of warp and weft.

In Indian symbolism the horizontal threads of the weft stand for the stages of the individual life, while his super-individual, external existence is represented by the vertical threads of the warp. Finally the warp threads of the fabric symbolize the male principle (*Purusha*) and the weft indicates the female (*Prarriti*).[1]

It is often said that there is "nothing new under the Sun." Many of the most splendid and complicated weaves had their origins in antiquity, so it is extremely useful for the weaver to have some background knowledge of a craft almost as old as man himself.

THE ANCIENT MIDDLE EAST

Egypt

Like most accounts of the development of man's art and civilization, our history of weaving starts along the banks of the Nile, where the highly sophisticated culture we call ancient Egypt began to take form more than five thousand years ago. Weaving undoubtedly was practiced in many parts of the ancient world at a very early date, but in Egypt, with its hot, dry climate, evidence of this accomplishment has been preserved (Fig. 45). Remnants of fabrics found in the areas of Fayum and Badari in the Nile Valley have been dated as early as 5000 B.C. These fabrics are of a plain weave—a simple one-up-one-down weave (Figs. 235, 247)—as were all textiles

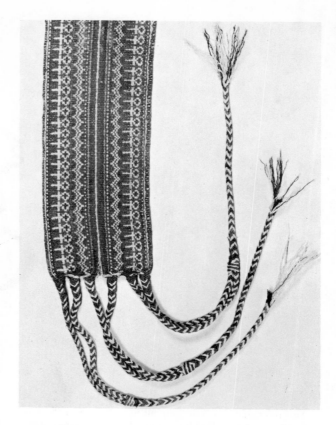

woven in the Middle East until roughly 2500 B.C. They are made of linen, and this preference for the product of the flax plant prevailed throughout the era of Egyptian civilization.

Although the Egyptians knew and certainly wore wool, they did not regard it with high esteem. Sheep and goat herders belonged to the lowest stratum of Egyptian society, and, similarly, the wool from the animals they tended was considered profane. Garments of wool are rarely found in Egyptian tombs. The Egyptian legal code contained sumptuary laws that restricted the use of wool. Members of the priesthood were forbidden to wear wool clothing next to their bodies and were required to remove all woolen garments before entering a temple.

Cotton was cultivated widely in Egypt, and many excellent examples of cotton textiles have

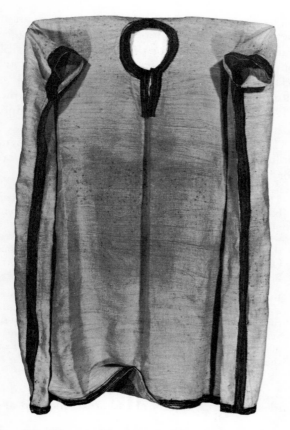

left: 45. Tunic edged with colored braid, Amenophis III–IV, Tomb of Kha, Thebes. 18th Dynasty, 1405–1352 B.C. Turin Museum.

above: 46. Girdle of Ramses III, Egypt. c. 1200 B.C. Linen, overall length 17′. City of Liverpool Museums, England.

been unearthed in tombs. However, the finest linen was reserved for royal garments (Fig. 46) and for mummy wrappings (Fig. 47), which were woven during the lifetime of the individual. During the First Dynasty (c. 3000 B.C.) mummy cloths with as many as 160 warps and 120 wefts per inch were made. (By comparison, fine modern cambric has 70 warps and 70 wefts per inch.) Silk was not introduced into Egypt until the Christian era.

Spinning and weaving were the province of women, and slave girls were often employed to help the free weavers. *Tablet weaving* (also known as *card weaving*, Figs. 446–452) preceded conventional loom weaving. Subsequently, the Egyptians developed a warp-weighted loom similar to that used throughout the ancient world (Fig. 7). Pictorial representations of yarn spinning and weaving during the period of the Middle Kingdom (2133–1991 B.C.) have been found in the tombs at Beni Hassan (Fig. 48). The horizontal frame loom that was ultimately adopted by the Egyptians is almost identical to the common floor loom in use today.

right: 47. Mummy cloth fragments, Egypt. Plain-weave linen. Textile and Clothing Department Collection, Iowa State University, Ames. The fragment at lower right is coated with paint on an earthlike material, and is probably an outer wrapping.

below: 48. *Women Weaving and Spinning,* tempera copy after an Egyptian wall painting from the reign of Se'n Wosret II, 12th Dynasty (c. 19th century B.C.). Metropolitan Museum of Art, New York.

The Egyptians were skilled dyers and are known to have employed acids and salts. Threads were often dyed before weaving, so that elaborate, patterned effects could be achieved on the loom (Fig. 49). The art of embroidery was also practiced to a high degree of perfection, and the earliest known embroidered fabrics have been found in Egypt. However, both polychrome textiles and embroidery were considered by the Egyptians to be alien to their taste; they were reserved for offerings to specific deities, such as the cat goddess Bast. Appliqué with leather and beads was known, and tapestry was common.

This high level of expertise in all facets of textile art continued until the decline of Egypt toward the end of the second millennium B.C., only to be revived again several centuries later with the Copts (see pp. 35–37).

Mesopotamia

At the same time that the Egyptian civilization was developing along the banks of the Nile, another culture, equally remarkable, flourished between the Tigris and the Euphrates in the land known as Mesopotamia. This area, dominated successively by the Sumerians, the Babylonians, and the Assyrians, was renowned in the ancient world for the quality of the textiles produced.

Wool was more highly regarded in Mesopotamia than in Egypt and was, in fact, the main fiber employed. The wealth of the nomadic peoples was measured by the size of their flocks. Nevertheless, sumptuary laws did exist in Mesopotamia, as in Egypt and Palestine, which prohibited the use of wool next to the body.

Evidence indicates that the Sumerians had developed a weaving industry by the 3rd millennium B.C. Archaeologists have uncovered clay

below left: 49. Tapestry-woven rug with lotus pattern, from the tomb of Kha, Thebes. 18th Dynasty (c. 14th century B.C.). Linen, $25\frac{5}{8} \times 19\frac{3}{4}''$. Museo Egizio, Turin.

below: 50. *Woman Holding Aryballus,* Sumerian, from Tello. c. 2100 B.C. Alabaster, height $7\frac{5}{8}''$. Louvre, Paris.

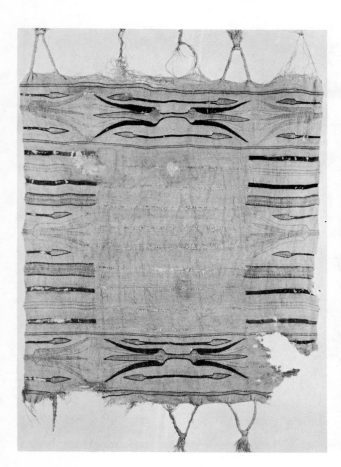

tablets, some dated as early as 2200 B.C., which served as account books for the weavers. The robes favored by the kings and priests of Sumeria consisted of many overlapping layers of fringe, apparently in imitation of the fur pelts worn by their Stone Age ancestors. The women's garments (Fig. 50), also tiers of fringe, were cut and sewn to form a round neckline and a cape effect.

The Babylonian culture, which superseded the Sumerian about 1800 B.C., also placed great emphasis on weaving. Not only were the weavers highly skilled, but they specialized as well, with each of the craftsman responsible for a particular kind of cloth. The Babylonian weavers' guild embraced the canvas weaver, the cloth weaver, the wool weaver, and the weaver who employed a variety of yarns. Even more important to the Babylonians was the art of embroidery. From Mesopotamia and from Phrygia to the west, the knowledge of embroidery spread to the entire Mediterranean world. According to Pliny, Babylonian embroideries enjoyed such great esteem that the technique was generally called "Babylonian."

The invading Assyrians adopted much of the culture of Babylon, including the art of embroidery. The Assyrians were equally energetic in propagating the weaving industry, and Queen Semiramis, who conquered Egypt, was responsible for establishing many cotton manufactures along the Nile River. The sumptuary laws regarding wool remained in effect through the period of Assyrian domination. The Greek historian Herodotus wrote: "For their dress the Assyrians wear a linen tunic. Over this they put a garment of wool." However, the most rigid restrictions on wool were enforced by the Hebrew people.

The Hebrews

Despite the dearth of surviving examples, we know more about the weaving practiced by the Hebrew peoples than about that of any other ancient race, thanks to detailed accounts in the Old Testament. In the 13th century B.C., during the period of the New Kingdom in Egypt and the domination of the Assyrians in Mesopotamia, Moses led the children of Israel out of captivity. The Book of Exodus contains meticulous instructions about the tabernacle that was to be built in the Promised Land:

Moreover thou shalt make the tabernacle with ten curtains of fine twined linen, and blue, and purple, and scarlet: with cherubim of cunning work shalt thou make them.

The length of one curtain shall be eight and twenty cubits, and the breadth of one curtain four cubits: and every one of the curtains shall have one measure. The five curtains shall be coupled together one to another; and the other five curtains shall be coupled one to another.

And thou shalt make loops of blue upon the edge of the one curtain from the selvedge in the coupling; and likewise shalt thou make in the uttermost edge of another curtain, in the coupling of the second.

Fifty loops shalt thou make in the edge of the curtain that is in the coupling of the second; that the loops may take hold one of another.

And thou shalt make curtains of goats' hair to be a covering upon the tabernacle: eleven curtains shalt thou make.

The length of one curtain shall be thirty cubits, and the breadth of one curtain four cubits: and the eleven curtains shall be all of one measure.

And thou shalt couple five curtains by themselves, and six curtains by themselves, and shalt double the sixth curtain in the forefront of the tabernacle.

And thou shalt make a covering for the tent of rams' skins dyed red, and a covering of badgers' skins.

And thou shalt make a veil of blue, and purple, and scarlet, and fine twined linen of cunning work: with cherubim shalt it be made.

And thou shalt hang it upon four pillars of shittim wood overlaid with gold: their hooks shall be of gold, upon the four sockets of silver.

And thou shalt hang up the veil under the taches, that thou mayest bring in thither within the veil the ark of the testimony: and the veil shall divide unto you between the holy place and the most holy.

Exodus 26:1–5, 7–9, 14, 31–33

Fragments of wool and linen fabrics dating from as early as 3000 B.C. have been found in Palestine. Cotton was available by the time of Solomon (968–937 B.C.), having been imported from Egypt, but wool constituted the most common fiber. Considered choice, white wool was reserved for the finest weaving. The inferior, coarse wools, or mixtures of black wool and camel hair, were used for making tents and nets. However, garments of mixed fibers were absolutely proscribed. The Book of Deuteronomy (22:11) instructs that: "Thou shalt not wear a garment of divers sorts, as of woolen and linen together." In fact, such fabrics had to be transported to market on sticks to prevent their touching the bodies of the carriers. Only garments of pure linen could be worn by the high priest entering the holy of holies. Thus, God described to Moses the clothing that was to be prepared for Aaron and his sons:

And these are the garments which they shall make: a breastplate, and an ephod, and a robe, and a broidered coat, a mitre, and a girdle: and they shall make holy garments for Aaron thy brother, and his sons, that he may minister unto me in the priest's office.

And they shall take gold, and blue, and purple, and scarlet, and fine linen.

And they shall make the ephod of gold, of blue, and of purple, of scarlet, and fine twined linen, with cunning work.

It shall have the two shoulderpieces thereof joined at the two edges thereof; and so it shall be joined together.

And the curious girdle of the ephod, which is upon it, shall be of the same, according to the work thereof; even of gold, of blue, and purple, and scarlet, and fine twined linen.

And thou shalt make the breastplate of judgment with cunning work: after the work of the ephod thou shalt make it; of gold, of blue, and of purple, and of scarlet, and of fine twined linen, shalt thou make it.

Foursquare it shall be being doubled; a span shall be the length thereof, and a span shall be the breadth thereof.

And beneath upon the hem of it thou shalt make pomegranates of blue, and of purple, and of scarlet, round about the hem thereof; and bells of gold between them round about.

And thou shalt put it on a blue lace, that it may be upon the mitre; upon the forefront of the mitre it shall be.

And thou shalt embroider the coat of fine linen, and thou shalt make the mitre of fine linen, and thou shalt make the girdle of needlework.

Exodus 28:4–8, 15–16, 33, 37, 39

The Old Testament mentions three types of weavers: the weavers of plain weaves, the weavers of multicolor materials, and the "art-weavers," who embroidered figures on fabrics for clothing and curtains. Joseph's coat of many colors is believed to have been woven in narrow strips that were later sewn together, but garments generally were woven in a single piece. The ends of the warps often served to connect the new web with cloth already woven. The Hebrew weavers were subject to a number of special regulations. "The weaver shall not sing at work, in his ear he wears a woolen plug and smears his fingers with fat or oil. He binds the threads when broken and works the weft through the warps with his fingers."[2]

In Palestine spinning was the work of women and even considered by law to be the woman's property. In the event of a divorce, all yarns that had been made by the wife on her spindle remained in her possession. Hebrew law declared that: "Married women should not spin in the street nor in the open, certainly not at night by the light of the moon."[3] If a woman were to spin outdoors, it would necessitate revealing her arms, and this might be cause for divorce.

right: 51. *Archers with Embroidered Robes,* frieze from an Achaemenid palace, Susa. 5th century B.C. Glazed tile. Louvre, Paris.

It is known that the ancient Hebrews were capable of producing very complex yarns. Jewish law tells of yarns of as many as 28 ply—that is, 28 single strands twisted together. According to tradition, the curtain of the last Temple was woven from 24- and 72-ply yarns. The Hebrews used both gold and silver threads in their weaving, and, as is evident from the Biblical descriptions, they had a knowledge of dyeing techniques.

above: 52. *Penelope at the Loom,* detail of an Attic red-figure skyphos, Greece. 5th century B.C. Terra cotta. Chiusi Museum, Italy.

The Persian Empire

In the 6th century B.C. the Persians, under the leadership of Darius I and Xerxes, built an empire far larger than any of its predecessors in the ancient world. At its height the Persian Empire extended from Greece and Egypt in the west to the borders of India in the east.

The textile arts were valued highly in ancient Persia, and testament to this can still be seen in the architectural sculpture of the great cities of Persepolis and Susa (Fig. 51). Tapestry weaving was particularly important and became even more so in the 6th century of the Christian era, when silk culture was introduced from China (see p. 37). Exquisite silk tapestries that have seldom been equalled in richness of color and pattern were made during the period of the Sassanian dynasty (A.D. 226–637). These tapestries (Pl. 3, p. 39) were widely exported to both the Byzantine and the Roman worlds. They were later to have a profound effect on European, Byzantine, Islamic, and even Chinese art. The Persians are also credited with production of the first velvets, which were similarly exported to all parts of the ancient world.

As commerce increased, Persia became the crossroads for trade routes between Europe and the Far East. European merchants brought home not only the spices and silks of the Orient but design concepts acquired in Persia along the way. This influence lasted until the middle of the 7th century, when Persia was swept up in the all-encompassing tide of Islam.

THE CLASSICAL WORLD

Greece

That the ancient Greeks were accomplished weavers we know primarily from written and pictorial records, for no examples of their craft survive. The most famous episode involving weaving in Classical Greece is in the legend of Penelope, wife of Odysseus and universal symbol of constancy (Fig. 52). Although Odysseus had been away on his voyage for many years and was presumed lost, Penelope continued to refuse the many suitors who pressed for her hand in marriage. As her excuse she explained that, before she could remarry, she must complete a winding sheet for her father-in-law. By day she would sit at her loom and weave, and at night she would unravel all the work she had done. Eventually, the suitors began to realize that her progress was unusually slow, and she was forced to finish the shroud and urged to choose a new husband. However, Odysseus returned in the nick of time, routed the suitors singlehandedly, and reclaimed his devoted wife.

Representations of Penelope show her at work on a warp-weighted loom (Figs. 7, 149), and this is apparently the type that was employed throughout the ancient world. For her fiber she might have chosen wool or linen, for both were common in Greece, although at the time Homer composed his epic, linen was preferred by the Ionians, while the northern Dorians favored wool. Later, wool exclusively was used for men's garments throughout Greece, while *byssus,* a very fine linen, was the material for women's dresses. Silk was also available, for it had been introduced from China perhaps as early as 1000 B.C. Cotton, grown abundantly in India during this period, would have been known to the Greeks from the writings of Herodotus: "There are trees growing wild which produce a kind of wool better then sheep's wool in beauty and quality, which the Indians use for making their clothes."[4]

The Greeks were accomplished in embroidery and tapestry weaving—in fact, in all the decorative textile arts then known. Their mastery in the fields of architecture, sculpture, painting, and pottery making tends to overshadow their other skills. However, were it not for the absence of surviving examples, they might be equally renowned for their work in fabric.

Rome

The mighty empire of the Romans absorbed all the cultures previously discussed, with the exception of the Persian. Egyptians, Mesopotamians, Hebrews, Phoenicians, Greeks—all eventually came under the domination of Imperial Rome. Thus, the accumulated expertise in weaving techniques acquired by various groups was at the disposal of the Romans.

The free Roman citizenry did very little weaving, considering it to be beneath them. Fabrics were imported from Greece, or else Greek and other slaves were employed in the weaving of cloth. There were, of course, exceptions to this rule. We are told that: "Except for special occasions, Caesar Augustus wore common clothes for the house, made by his sister, wife, daughter, or granddaughters."[5] Columella considered weaving to be an essential task of the estate:

Nowadays when wives so generally give way to luxury and idleness that they do not deign to carry the burden of manufacturing wool, but disdain clothing that costs

53. Sign from the shop of Vecilius Verecundus, cloth merchant of Pompeii. Before A.D. 79.

great sums and is bought at a whole year's income, we had to appoint stewardesses on the farm to perform the offices of the matron. On rainy and cold days when the slavewomen cannot do farm work in the open, let the wool be ready-combed and prepared beforehand so that they may busy themselves at spinning and weaving, and the steward's wife may exact the usual amount of work. It will do no harm if clothing is spun at home for the stewards, overseers, and the better class of slaves so that the owner's accounts may bear the less burden.[6]

It was the custom in aristocratic Roman households to employ slaves for the exclusive purpose of spinning, weaving, and making garments for the members of the family. Those who could not afford the luxury of a personal weaver relied on the groups of free tradesmen who sold their wares in shops. The weavers of Pompeii apparently lived in a particular district of the town. Frescoes on the entrance pillars of one building depict the interior of the factory (Fig. 53), showing four felters at the table, three weavers at their looms, and the proprietor displaying finished wares. In Rome itself the weavers, spinners, and dyers were organized into a guild, which had its headquarters in the Temple of Minerva Medica. So highly organized was its membership that it reminds one of a modern trade union. There were dues, guild regulations, individual and group privileges, and even a widows' fund.

Each weaving center produced a distinctive type of fabric. For example, the Po Valley and parts of Gaul supplied the city of Rome with the woolen fabric used for togas and tunics. Padua specialized in expensive carpets and elaborate textiles, while the rougher fabrics that clothed the workmen and slaves came from Gaul. Until the beginning of the Christian era the principal fibers were linen and wool, with linen used primarily in underclothing. For a particularly lavish effect, wealthy Romans might don a garment into which gold threads had been woven. Agrippina, the wife of Emperor Claudius (A.D. 41–57) reportedly owned a robe made entirely of gold.

Toward the end of the 1st century B.C. silk came into vogue, first in mixtures with linen or cotton and later in the form of pure silk fabrics. It is said that the Emperor Heliogabalus (A.D. 218–222) was the first to wear garments all of silk. In order to weave with silk the Romans imported fabrics from China, then painstakingly unraveled and rewove them. This factor partially explains the very high cost of silk in Rome: in A.D. 16 a pound of silk was sold for 12 ounces of gold. Later, the supply of silk became more plentiful and the price declined. However, the tedious process of unraveling the fiber was still necessary, for the secrets of *sericulture*—the cultivation of the silkworm and production of silk—were locked in China until the 6th century.

EARLY WEAVING IN THE FAR EAST: PRE-BUDDHIST CHINA

It is customary to think of the "cradles of civilization" in terms of the Nile River Valley in Egypt and the plains between the Tigris and the Euphrates in Mesopotamia. However, by the 3rd millennium B.C. two other great cultures were flourishing in the valleys of the Indus of India and the Yellow River of China. Many written records—including that of Herodotus—attest to the knowledge of weaving in ancient India, but no concrete evidence of this skill prior to the 7th century A.D. has survived. Much more is known about the evolution of the textile arts in China.

The history of weaving in China centers almost exclusively around the one commodity deemed most precious in the West: silk. A number of legends are told about the discovery of silk, but the most famous concerns the Chinese empress Hsi-Ling-shi. Emperor Huang-Ti, who reigned sometime during the 27th century B.C., had become increasingly worried about a blight that was gradually destroying the royal mulberry grove, and so he asked his empress to study the problem. Hsi-Ling-shi noticed that the mulberry leaves were being consumed by hundreds of tiny white worms, which would then crawl from the leaves to the stem and spin pale, glossy cocoons. She took several of the cocoons into her apartments for further investigation, and accidentally dropped one into a basin of hot water. In water, the cocoon separated into a delicate network of fibers, and the empress discovered that she could draw a thin, continuous filament into the air. The more she drew out the filament, the smaller the cocoon became. Thus, Hsi-Ling-shi stumbled upon a technique that would be jealously sought after by the rest of the world—and just as jealously guarded by the Chinese—for almost three thousand years. Not until about A.D. 300 did

above left: 54. KITAGAWA UTAMARO, Japan. *Reeling of Silk.* 18th century. Woodcut. Textile Museum Collection, Washington, D.C.

above right: 55. KITAGAWA UTAMARO, Japan. *Weaving of Silk.* 18th century. Woodcut. Textile Museum Collection, Washington, D.C.

Japan learn the secret, and sericulture finally reached the West only in the 6th century.

With the introduction of silk, the Chinese had no need for spinning; a filament from a single cocoon frequently measures more than 1000 yards. The weavers would merely soften the cocoon and unravel the filament, after which it would be ready for the loom (Figs. 54, 55).

The earliest surviving silk textiles date from the end of the Eastern Chou Dynasty (771–256 B.C.). They are extremely fine, indicating a long period of development in the textile arts. The pair of silk mitts in Figure 56 suggest mastery of the ikat technique of dyeing (see Chap. 18).

56. Woven mitts, found at Ch'ang-sha, Hunan Province, China. Late Eastern Chou Period, c. 3rd century B.C. Silk with warp pattern and plain weave, length 8¼". Cooper-Hewitt Museum of Decorative Arts and Design, Smithsonian Institution, New York.

Highly complex figurative weaves were produced during the Han Dynasty (206 B.C.–A.D. 220), some with stylized natural motifs and others with an overall lozenge pattern (Figs. 57–59).

According to tradition, Buddhism was introduced into China in A.D. 68. By the 3rd century Buddhist elements had begun to appear in Chinese art, just as, in the West, the Christian influence had started to manifest itself.

THE CHRISTIAN WORLD: ALEXANDRIA AND BYZANTIUM

The Copts

During the first three centuries of the Christian era, when the new religion was beginning to take hold throughout the disintegrating Roman Empire, numerous converts were made in Egypt, then still under the domination of Imperial Rome. Among the first to embrace the Christian faith were members of a peasant class known as the Copts, who traced their ancestry back directly to the ancient Egyptians. The word *Copt* is actually of Arab derivation and did not come into use until the Moslem conquest in the 7th century. However, the group to which it applied was clearly identifiable some several hundred years earlier. Records tell of Coptic martyrs to Christianity in the middle of the 3rd century, when the religion was still proscribed throughout the Empire. A Coptic version of the Bible was prepared during the same period. By the 5th century Christianity had become dominant in Egypt; it remained so until the Arab conquest.

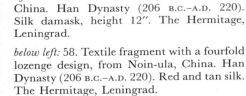

left: 57. *Mountains and Birds,* from Noin-ula, China. Han Dynasty (206 B.C.–A.D. 220). Silk damask, height 12″. The Hermitage, Leningrad.

below left: 58. Textile fragment with a fourfold lozenge design, from Noin-ula, China. Han Dynasty (206 B.C.–A.D. 220). Red and tan silk. The Hermitage, Leningrad.

below: 59. Gauze fragment with a pattern of triple lozenges on a ground of small lozenges, from Noin-ula, China. Han Dynasty (206 B.C.–A.D. 220). Cream-colored silk, 3⅛ × 2″. Philadelphia Museum of Art.

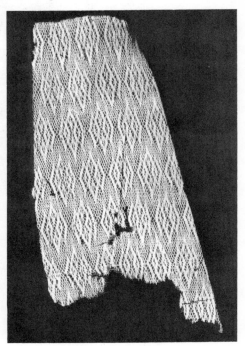

Coptic art is particularly distinguished for its splendid textiles (Fig. 60). The Copts' mastery of weaving was recognized early by the Romans, who made some attempt to regulate the craft. The lease of a house to a weaver in A.D. 246 reads: "It shall not be permitted to weave in the house except in the gateway more than three webs, but if I wish to weave garments for my own use, I have the right to weave up to four webs."[7]

Early Coptic textiles show the influence of the flowing naturalism and refined taste of later Greek art, but from the 3rd century until the 6th—when Coptic art achieved its highest development—the tendency was increasingly toward abstract, highly stylized forms. Since the Copts were primarily a peasant class, they rejected the cosmopolitan styles of the cities in favor of a more provincial, "Oriental" mode. Stylized animals, the tree of life, the acanthus leaf, palmettes, and floral designs were all characteristic motifs. In the 5th century Christian elements began to appear, and a rich iconography emerged (Pl. 4, p. 39).

The Copts were especially skilled at tapestry weaving. They formed their tapestries in the manner of a mosaic, combining many small pieces of simple weaving in different colors. The best known of their forms is the so-called *medallion*, a woolen insert, usually circular but sometimes square, woven into the linen garments as they were being made (Fig. 61). The medallions were often applied to clothing at the shoulders, knees, and other points of wear. Medallions also appeared in curtains and church hangings (Fig. 62). Tapestry weaves with *pile* (that is, with protruding strands of wool) were invented in Coptic Egypt (Fig. 63).

With the assistance of the Copts, the Arabs conquered Egypt in 627, and this event marked the beginning of a decline in Coptic art. The Coptic weavers were pressed into the service of the Moslem caliphs, with the result that Islamic motifs intermingled with Coptic forms (Fig. 71). Under the Arabs the Copts performed some remarkable feats of weaving. One woven tent is described as having been so large that it required a train of seventy camels to haul the tent and its furnishings.

Despite their domination by the forces of Mohammed, the Copts never intermarried with their conquerors, so they retained the charac-

above: 60. Segment of a tunic, with design of confronted gazelles with suckling young flanking a tree of life, from Egypt. 8th century. Silk, $8\frac{3}{4} \times 9''$. Cleveland Museum of Art (purchase from the J. H. Wade Fund).

below: 61. Coptic tunic, probably from Tuna (Ashmunein). 6th–7th century. Undyed wool with clavi and orbiculi tapestry woven in colors, $5'5\frac{5}{8}'' \times 3'5''$. Metropolitan Museum of Art, New York (gift of Maurice Nahman, 1912).

left: 62. Panel of a curtain with a large central medallion, Coptic. 4th–5th century. Black wool border on undyed loop-weave linen ground, 25½ × 20″. Cooper-Hewitt Museum of Decorative Arts and Design, Smithsonian Institution, New York.

above: 63. Coptic *Head.* Loop weave in wool, height 6″. Collection Norman Ives, New Haven, Conn.

below: 64. Monks presenting Chinese silkworm eggs to the Byzantine Emperor Justinian I. Etching by PHILIPPE GALLE after a painting by JOHANNES STRADANUS (1536–1605).

teristics of their race—traceable to ancient Egypt—into the modern era. The prevalence of Coptic forms in Egyptian woolens endured until the 12th century.

The Byzantine Empire

In A.D. 323 the Roman Emperor Constantine decided to move the capital of the Empire to the city of Byzantium, renaming it Constantinople. With the western portions of the Empire weakening and subject to periodic barbarian invasions, the power of the eastern capital gradually increased, so that by the 5th century it is possible to speak of a "Byzantine" Empire, distinct in culture, tastes, and particularly in art, from the Roman west.

The weaving of Byzantium, like that of China, focuses primarily on silk. In A.D. 552 the Emperor Justinian succeeded in penetrating the wall of secrecy that had protected the Chinese monopoly of sericulture for three thousand years. Two Nestorian monks concealed silkworm eggs in a

hollow walking cane and smuggled them out of China. The monks brought the eggs to Constantinople and gave them to Justinian (Fig. 64), along with some mulberry leaves—also smuggled out—to feed the silk larvae when they hatched. Justinian appointed a special caretaker for the

left: 65. *Samson and the Lion,* Byzantine, from Alexandria. 6th–7th century. Silk compound twill, $37\frac{3}{8} \times 15\frac{7}{8}''$. Dumbarton Oaks Collection, Washington, D.C.

above: 66. Byzantine textile with elephant pattern, from the tomb of Charlemagne. c. 1000. Silk, $5'3\frac{3}{4}'' \times 4'4''$. Cathedral Museum, Aachen.

below: 67. *The Sudarium of St. Germanus,* Byzantine. c. 1000. Silk serge with purple, height of each eagle $29\frac{1}{4}''$. Church of St. Eusebius, Auxerre.

precious eggs and at the same time began to import silks from abroad, presumably to serve as models for his own weavers. Subsequently Constantinople became a major center for the manufacture of silk textiles. State workshops, in which most of the weavers were women, supported a thriving commerce in silks.

Animals seem to play an important role in Byzantine textiles. Among the most famous silks made in the workshops of Constantinople are: that from the 7th century showing Samson struggling with a lion (Fig. 65); the splendid 10th-century elephant weave from the tomb of Charlemagne, placed there about two hundred years after the Emperor's death (Fig. 66); and the majestic purple eagle textiles (Fig. 67), probably reserved for the emperor himself and for other members of the nobility.

Unlike Coptic Egypt, Byzantium withstood the onslaughts of Islam. Constantinople remained preeminent in textiles well into the 14th century.

top: Plate 3. *Cock,* Sassanian. c. 600. Silk twill, diameter of medallion 10¼″. Museo Cristiano, Vatican.

above: Plate 4. *Sacrifice of Isaac,* Coptic. 7th century. Tapestry, 4⅝ x 10⅛″. Musée Historique des Tissus, Lyons.

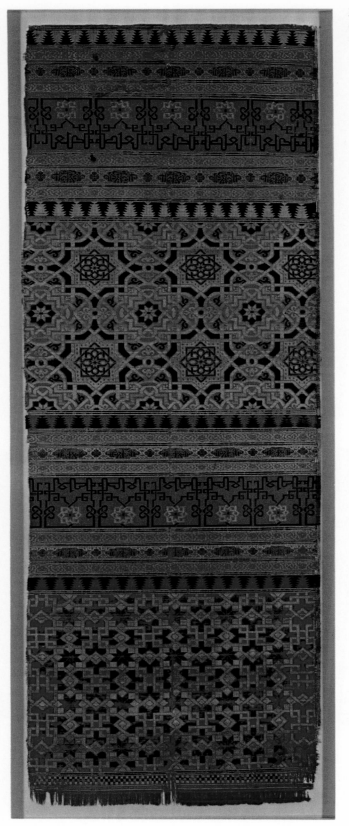

Plate 5. Textile, Hispano-Moresque. 15th century. Silk, 40⅜ x 14¾". Metropolitan Museum of Art, New York (Fletcher Fund, 1929).

Plate 7. Funerary mantle, Paracas Necropolis, Peru. 1st century B.C.–A.D. 1st century. Wool plain weave and embroidery, 9' x 3'9". Brooklyn Museum, New York.

THE MOSLEM CONQUEST

When the Prophet Mohammed died at Medina in 632, the religion he had preached—Islam—was known only in the Arabian peninsula. Within one hundred years his followers had conquered all the land as far east as the Indus River, the entire northern coast of Africa, all of Spain, and even parts of southern France. They carried with them not only the word of Allah but a political system, a language, and a culture that amalgamated the Oriental elements of its origins with the most refined tastes and skills of the conquered nations. We can thus speak of *Islamic* weaving as that practiced by Arab craftsmen as well as by native artisans in all the lands under the domination of the Caliphate.

Islamic decoration in the arts tended to be highly abstract and geometric, partially because of the Koranic ban on representations of the human form. When animal forms did appear, they were usually stylized and purely decorative in character (Fig. 68). Another prohibition concerned the use of silk, which in the early Islamic period was considered too luxurious for clothing. Wool, cotton, and linen were the preferred materials, but these were often enriched with silk borders or bands (Fig. 69). Gradually, the silk bands became wider and wider, and laws were passed regarding the amount of silk that could be added to a garment. In time the ban was forgotten, and the weaving of silk textiles became a profitable industry throughout the Islamic world.

Persia fell to the Arabs in the first decade after Mohammed's death, and the invaders thus became heir to the rich heritage of Sassanian weaving (Pl. 3, p. 39). Recognizing, perhaps, the artistry of Sassanian tapestries—or perhaps their commercial importance—the caliphs never enforced the injuction against silk weaving in Persia. Therefore, the Sassanian silk industry continued without interruption after the conquest

left: 68. Egypto-Arabic tapestry fragment. 8th century. Colored wools on undyed linen warp, 20 × 4½″. Metropolitan Museum of Art, New York (gift of George D. Pratt, 1933).

below: 69. Egypto-Arabic textile fragment. 10th–11th century. Undyed linen with tapestry band in colored silks, 10⅛ × 7½″. Metropolitan Museum of Art, New York (Rogers Fund, 1909).

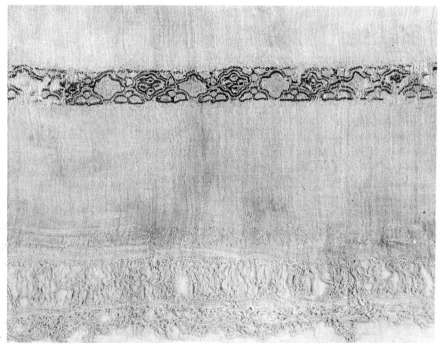

(Fig. 70). There was, however, a gradual change in style, as the more abstract Moslem forms, including the Kufic script, began to dominate. In the service of the Caliphate, the Buyids, descendants of the Sassanians, established textile workshops known as *tirāz* in Baghdad and other major cities. The *tirāz* were responsible for producing a garment called a *khil'at,* which the ruler would present to individuals who had achieved distinction.

With the conquest of Egypt the Arabs inherited a second great cultural tradition—from the Copts. *Tirāz* were established in several Egyptian cities, and the textile industries flourished. The transition to the Islamic decorative styles cannot have been too difficult for the Copts, so abstract were their own artistic forms. Many textiles produced in Egypt under Moslem domination incorporated elaborate Arabic calligraphy (Fig. 71).

When Islam reached Spain in the early part of the 8th century, it subjugated a people who had been under the influence of the Byzantine Empire and thus of Byzantine culture. Nevertheless, so thoroughly was the Moorish aesthetic absorbed into Spanish art that it remained a visible presence until the 15th century. Spanish textiles of the Islamic period incorporate the Kufic script and other Arab motifs, and Spanish silks were reputed to be as fine as those woven in Persia.

The explusion of the Arabs from Spain began in the 10th century, but many Arab craftsmen stayed in Spain and continued to work in their accustomed modes. This period of Spanish art— from the Christian reconquest to the final explusion of all the Moors in 1492—is referred to as *Hispano-Moresque.* The most characteristic textiles from this era are in the "Alhambra" style (Pl. 5, p. 40)—geometric plait-band patterns based on designs found in the stucco and tile of that remarkable palace at Granada.

The decline in power of the Islamic empire corresponded in time to the emergence of the European kingdoms. From this point, with a few digressions, the history of weaving can be traced in Christian Europe.

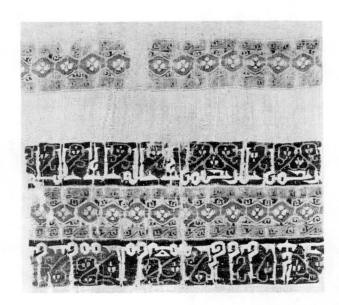

4 *Handweaving of the Past: Europe, the Far East, and the New World*

THE MIDDLE AGES IN EUROPE

Until medieval times families supplied all their textile needs from fabrics made in the home (Fig. 72). When they produced more than they required, the extra cloth would be paid to their feudal lords as part of their taxes. The lord would then mark each piece of fabric with his personal brand and sell it in the local market. The brand might be a symbolic representation of the baron's name or castle or, in the case of a monastery, the patron saint. Since the brands readily identified the source of the fabric, they became a guarantee of quality, a kind of trademark.

Certain fabrics became so important to barter and payment that they served as a currency in themselves. This was true particularly of *wadmal* (Fig. 73), a woolen fabric woven in Scandinavia and in England. Wadmal was commonly made into clothing, sails, and bedding, but in standardized measure—2 by 20 ells (an ell equals 45

72. Women carding, spinning, and weaving wool. From a 15th-century illuminated manuscript. British Museum, London.

Weavers on the Continent had formed guilds even before the Norman Conquest in 1066, but England was slower to accept the new associations. King John (1154–89) reportedly required all weavers to leave London; nevertheless, by the 12th century the Weavers' Guild, the oldest of the English guilds, had been organized. The manufacture of woolen cloth introduced England to industry and commerce. It also created a number of new occupations, not only weaver and spinner but cloth merchant as well. The manufacture of cloth required that a considerable amount of money be tied up for quite a long time. Consequently, the cloth merchants were of necessity among the wealthiest citizens of the town.

The guilds served a twofold purpose: They helped the artisan by eliminating unfair competition and by enabling him to buy his raw materials at wholesale prices; on the other hand, the standards set by the guilds protected the consumer. Until this time quality of workmanship had been a variable factor. The guild standards ensured the purchaser of high quality at a fair price. King Henry I of England (1100–35) is credited with establishing the standard yard measurement—the length of his own arm. Such universal measures were essential to weavers who were merchandising their cloth. Many of the controls introduced by cloth inspectors were intended as a gauge for assessing fines, so they benefitted the consumer only indirectly. These regulations governed the length and width of fabric, the number of warp yarns, and the evenness of dyeing. In France a law of 1258 prohibited the weaving of tapestry by artificial light, which might cause poor workmanship. Tapestry weaving was also forbidden to women.

One of the most common fabrics used by the peasant class during this period was *fustian,* a cloth originally woven in Fustat (present-day Cairo). In many ways similar to wadmal, fustian had a linen warp and a coarse cotton weft. It was woven in a twill (Figs. 238–242), with a low pile formed by protruding loops of weft yarn on one side.

inches)—lengths of wadmal took the place of legal tender. Woolen and linen fabrics were also used as currency in Germany and the Slavic region. In fact, the word "pay" in the Slavic language derives from a term for "woven fabric."

The nobles could afford more variety and luxury in their textiles. Trade with the Middle East had long been in effect, and in the 13th century Marco Polo opened the lucrative trade routes to China and India. The more exotic goods from the East were made available to the feudal lords through annual fairs, which were held as early as the reign of Charlemagne (768–814). At the fairs the Frankish nobles (and the peasants, too, of course) "could rub elbows with the Venetian, Syrian, and Jewish merchants . . . and occasionally with Mongolian Avars from the plains of Hungary."[2]

Before the development of towns, weaving was exclusively women's work. Monasteries and convents often provided space for the weavers and spinners to work. As the manufacture of cloth gradually moved out of the home and into the workshop, weaving came more and more into the province of men, and guilds were established.

At the opposite end of the social spectrum, *cloth of gold,* a rich brocade ornamented with gold yarns, was much sought by European royalty throughout the medieval and Renaissance periods (Fig. 98). It was woven in the Middle East, probably in Persia, from yarns produced by winding the solid metal leaf around a core of silk or cotton. Cloth of gold was in particular demand for ceremonial occasions, such as coronations. Everything imaginable would be draped extravagantly with this exquisite fabric—horses, banners, canopies, the stage, the throne, the banquet hall, and, of course, the king himself.

The art of tapestry weaving was practiced in many parts of Europe by the 11th century. However, until the Renaissance, the production of fine silks and brocades achieved commercial importance only in Italy.

France

The most famous tapestry dating from the Middle Ages—perhaps the most famous textile of all time—is not really a tapestry at all. A remarkable work of embroidery measuring 231 feet in length, the *Bayeux Tapestry* (Fig. 74) was made to cover the masonry frieze of Bayeux Cathedral. Its 79 panels, worked in wool on a coarse linen cloth, depict the conquest of Saxon England by William of Normandy, culminating in the Battle of Hastings in 1066. The tapestry is much like an enormous book, for its scenes are read, for the most part, from left to right, following the sequence of events. The episode illustrated, *Harold Swearing Oath,* is from the first segment of the narrative, in which Earl Harold of Wessex apparently pledged himself to support William's claim to the English throne upon the death of Edward the Confessor. After Edward's death,

however, Harold had himself crowned king, whereupon William cited the oath as a pretext for leading his armies across the Channel. No effort is spared to make the tapestry's message abundantly clear, from the Latin inscriptions that accompany each episode, to the presence of symbolic beasts along the top border. In this case, the inclusion of the fox and crow, the wolf and stork, and the ewe, goat, and cow with a lion all signify Harold's potential treachery.

The *Bayeux Tapestry* is thought to have been commissioned shortly after the Norman Conquest by Odon of Conteville, Count of Kent and Bishop of Bayeux, for display in the recently completed nave of Bayeux Cathedral. Incorrectly attributed in the 18th century to the consort of William the Conqueror, the work is still popularly known as "The Tapestry of Queen Mathilda."

Conventional tapestries, in which the figures were woven into the cloth rather than applied to it, served a functional as well as a decorative purpose during the Middle Ages. They were often made as large wall coverings for the cold, dismal "great halls" of castles and churches. In addition to cutting drafts, the tapestries created a feeling of warmth. Only in the earliest times did tapestries hang directly on the walls. Later, they provided a corridor, used by the servants, between the hanging and the wall.

Tapestry weaving was flourishing in Paris in the 13th century, but it did not reach its pinnacle until the latter part of the 14th. In the Middle Ages, for the first time, it is possible to ascribe certain textiles to the hand of a known artisan.

below: 74. *Harold Swearing Oath,* detail of *Bayeux Tapestry.* c. 1073–88. Wool embroidery on linen; height 20″, overall length 231′. Town Hall, Bayeux.

Three French master-weavers dominated the field: Jacques Dourdin (active c. 1380–1407) wove allegorical and chivalric subjects, as well as pastoral and hunting scenes; Pierre de Beaumetz (active c. 1383–1412) specialized in religious and mythological themes; and Nicolas Bataille (active c. 1363–1400) drew his subjects from heraldry and religion. Bataille's masterpiece was the *Apocalypse* (Fig. 75), a series of seven hangings commissioned by Louis d'Anjou. Records indicate that the tapestry, which was paid for (and presumably underway) in 1377, was inspired by an illuminated manuscript lent by Louis' brother, King Charles V. Each of the seven panels was 65½ feet long, and, when hung in series, the backgrounds alternated between red and turquoise. The figures are drawn in a rather coarse weave with approximately twenty colors. In spite of these limited technical means, the subjects are portrayed with great sensitivity and linear clarity.

Another monumental tapestry series of the period depicts the *Nine Heroes* (Fig. 76), a theme that was very popular in the 14th century, largely because of the mystical connotations of three and three times three. The roster includes three pagan heroes (Hector, Alexander, and Julius Caesar), three Hebrew heroes (David, Joshua, and Judas Maccabeus), and three Christian heroes (Arthur, Charlemagne, and Godfrey of Bouillon). Several of the tapestries bear the arms of that formidable patron of the arts Jean, Duc de Berry, also brother of Charles V, although it is not certain that they actually belonged to him. A number of similarities between the *Heroes* and the *Apocalypse* suggest that Bataille's workshop was responsible for the for-

mer as well as the latter, but this, too, cannot be proved. Because the composition of the *Nine Heroes* is much more complex, the series is dated a bit later than the *Apocalypse,* about 1390.

It is often assumed that all the splendid medieval tapestries were designed to be hung on the wall, where they could be admired in all their beauty. This is far from the case. The very large pieces, such as the *Nine Heroes* and the *Apocalypse* could scarcely be put anywhere else, but many smaller tapestries served as table covers, window curtains, bench covers, or even nonspecific textiles that could be put to use wherever the need arose. On commission from Philip the Bold, duke of Burgundy (yet another brother of King Charles), Nicolas Bataille wove tapestry mule blankets and a garment for the nobleman's favorite leopard.

The Hundred Years' War had a devastating effect on the French tapestry industry. With much of France, including Paris, lost to the English, the weaving workshops were disbanded.

Flanders

In the Early Middle Ages the city of Arras established itself as a major textile center, and it held that position for several hundred years. By the 14th century both the weaving and the tapestry workshops had attained so large a scale that they could almost be called factories. These workshops flourished under the patronage of such discriminating clients as the French court and the dukes of Burgundy. The tapestry industry had close connections with its counterpart in Paris. Jacques Dourdin, one of the French master-weavers and merchants, was a citizen of Arras.

Most of our knowledge of early Flemish tapestry weaving comes from contemporary documents, for little has been preserved. These records describe extravagant representations of themes then popular in France: religious and heroic subjects, battle scenes, and legends of love. One of the few remaining examples of medieval Flemish tapestry is the *Saga of Jourdain de Blaye* (Fig. 77), a work of the late 14th century.

Norway

The Norwegians have been skilled at figural weaving since Viking times. Among the items uncovered at the 9th-century Oseberg ship-burial

below: 77. *Saga of Jourdain de Blaye,* Arras. c. 1400. Wool tapestry, 10′9″ × 12′6″. Museo Civico, Padua.

site are figure weaves of great richness and imagination (Fig. 78). However, the most important surviving example of early tapestry weaving in Norway dates from three centuries later. The *Baldishol Tapestry* (Pl. 6, p. 41) is a fragment of a bench cover depicting the months of April ("Prilis," a bearded and robed figure) and May ("Ivis," a knight in armor). It is woven in six colors, with geometric and other decorative motifs covering the entire surface. In many respects—the flatness of the figures and space, the presence of heraldic beasts—it is similar to the *Bayeux Tapestry* (Fig. 74) of the previous century.

Italy

When the great Islamic Empire fell into decline, its position of importance in the production of fine textiles, particularly silks, was ceded to Italy. The revival of the textile arts came earliest in Sicily, which had been under Moslem domination in the 10th century. Before the Moslem conquest Sicily had been first Roman and then Byzantine; afterward it was successively Norman, Swabian, and Spanish. This curious mélange of influences was naturally reflected in the textiles. A specialty of the Sicilian workshops was the weaving of borders made from gold thread. These ornamental borders were exported to all parts of Europe.

It would be impossible to discuss the history of weaving in Europe without mention of Lucca, the most important textile center of the Middle Ages. By the 14th century there were about three

above: 78. Textile from the Oseberg Burial Ship, Norway. A.D. 830. Tapestry. University Museum of Antiquities, Oslo.

right: 79. *Falcons with Prey,* Lucca. 14th century. Silk brocade, 26 × 7″. Museum of Fine Arts, Boston (Helen and Alice Colburn Fund).

thousand looms operating in Lucca alone, and commercial offices had been established in many European and Middle Eastern cities. (One Luccan silk merchant, Giovanni Arnolfini, has been immortalized in Jan van Eyck's famous portrait, now in London's National Gallery.) In addition to the domestic production, fine textiles were imported from Persia, Syria, Egypt, and eastern Asia. Silk weaving (Fig. 79) remained an important industry in Lucca until the 18th century.

The city of Venice was second only to Lucca in both weaving and commerce. Venetian merchants had close contact with textile centers in Byzantium and the Middle East, with the result that Byzantine and Islamic motifs were adopted by local craftsmen. In 1269 Marco Polo, with his father and uncle, set out from Venice on an overland route to the Far East, arriving in the Chinese capital of Pekin two years later. Marco remained in the service of Kublai Khan for seventeen years. When he finally returned to Venice, he related tales of unimaginable wealth to be found in the East, and as a result of his journey, direct importation of silk from China was begun. Some of the Oriental silk that reached medieval Europe took the form of fine cloth woven on Chinese looms; the remainder was raw silk that the Italians themselves processed into fabric, frequently combining the silk with a certain amount of linen fiber in order to produce a more durable textile.

The travels of the Polo family, and the memoirs published by Marco upon his return to Venice, awakened Europeans to the riches that existed beyond their own world. It was this quest for exotic treasure that led them, ultimately, to the shores of the Americas.

PRE-COLUMBIAN AMERICA

Archaeologists and art historians have long debated whether the textile arts flowered spontaneously among the tribes that inhabited Central and South America before the arrival of the *conquistadores,* or whether some previously unsuspected contact existed between these groups and the ancient peoples of the Middle East, by which weaving knowledge was transmitted. The voyages of Thor Heyerdahl opened the *possibility* that Egyptian or other Mediterranean sailors, in their fragile papyrus boats, managed to cross the Atlantic and land in Latin America. Furthermore, a number of authorities have pointed to the striking similarity between the textiles of ancient Peru and those of Egypt. In 1889 William Holmes, writing for the Smithsonian Institution, declared of Peruvian fabrics:

> The grade of culture represented by this work would seem to be very high, considering American products only, but its equivalent in old world culture must be sought in remote ages. This is shown in a striking manner when we place the more delicate pieces of Peruvian work beside fabrics taken from the mummies of ancient Egypt. In quality of fabric, method of construction, color and style of embellishment, the correspondence is indeed remarkable. The close analogy, so far as my observation extends, is with some Egyptian fabrics of the first few centuries of the Christian era.[3]

In any event, one can say that a very high level of expertise in all the textile arts was achieved by the tribes who inhabited the Americas from the pre-Christian era to the 16th century.

The Pueblo Indians of what is now the southwestern United States had developed the art of weaving cotton to a fairly advanced degree by A.D. 700. They also employed fibers from the yucca plant, and, for cold-weather protection, the chiefs wore wraps made from strips of rabbit skins interlaced with the yucca warps. For their bedding the Pueblos made thick cotton sheets and blankets woven from feathers. Over the centuries the art of weaving declined among the Pueblos and eventually disappeared altogether. Fortunately, their techniques and decorative styles were passed along to a neighboring tribe, the Navajo, who later applied the same methods to wool after the Spaniards introduced sheep in the 17th century.

From surviving pottery, sculpture, and painting, archaeologists have deduced that the Indians of Mexico and Central America were also adept at weaving, but of their craft nothing remains. However, thanks to the special preserving qualities of the climate, a fabulous wealth of woven textiles has been unearthed in the coastal plains of Peru.

Most of the textiles found in Peru have come from tombs, for it was the custom among the Indians to wrap the bodies of their dead and to provide them with an array of new clothing for use in the afterlife. Agave fiber, cotton, and wool

below: 80. Head ornament, Nazca Valley, Peru. c. 2500 B.C. Cotton or agave and feathers, 11 × 8″. Collection the author.

right: 81. *Paracas Textile,* Cabeza Larga, south coast of Peru. Late 1st century B.C.–A.D. early 1st century. Woven cotton with loop stitch border of wool, 5′5″ × 1′8″. Brooklyn Museum, New York (John T. Underwood Memorial Fund).

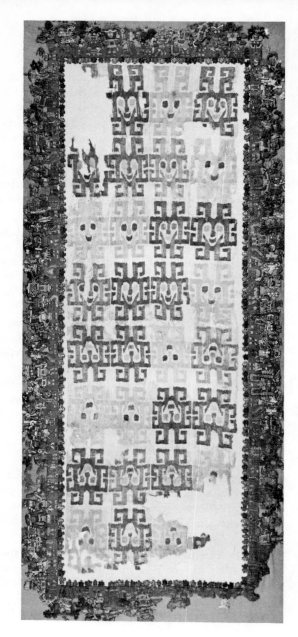

from the llama, the alpaca, and the vicuña were their principal materials; silk and linen were never available. Often, fibers were combined: the warps were of cotton, and wool, which readily accepted the natural dyes, served as the pattern-carrying weft. Reds were obtained from cochineal, yellow from ocherous earth, brown from vegetable juices, and blue and green from indigo.

The oldest Peruvian fabrics known date from the preceramic period, that is, before 1200 B.C. The example in Figure 80 has a braided fringe terminating in tiny feathers. By the Experimenter Period (400 B.C.–A.D. 400) the range of the Peruvian fabric maker had grown impressive indeed, despite the fact that his loom consisted of little more than two sticks. Stripes, abstract designs, and even figures were woven into cloth through the use of colored wefts. Figure 81 illus-

trates a shawl so fabulous that for many years after its discovery it was called simply *The Paracas Textile.* The central portion, patterned with stylized faces, is of loosely woven wool on cotton, while the elaborate border (Fig. 82) consists of a procession of figures—warriors, serpents, mythological beasts—worked in a loop stitch that resembles knitting. Many textiles were elaborately painted in an allover design, often consisting of stylized figures crowded one atop the other (Fig. 83). The embroiderer's repertoire was astonishing, as evidenced by the sampler reproduced in

Figure 84. Human forms, birds, animals, fish, monsters, and abstract patterns of various kinds were all at his command.

The most striking textiles from this period are the Paracas funerary mantles (Pl. 7, p. 42). These were wrapped around mummies before burial, and interspersed between the layers of the mantle were ponchos, headbands, and ceremonial gear that the deceased might require. (When archaeologists excavated the tombs, it often took them weeks to unwrap these burial bundles.) Measuring about 3 yards by 1 yard, the mantles are of plain cloth embroidered all over with free-floating human or animal forms—cat demons, fish, butterfly gods, birds, men, or combinations of various elements.

below: 82. Detail of Figure 81, *Paracas Textile.*

right: 83. Painted textile fragment, Nazca, southern Peru. c. A.D. 300–500. Linen, 34 × 23½″. Staatliche Museum für Völkerkunde, Munich.

below right: 84. Sampler, Nazca, south coast of Peru. 100 B.C.–A.D. 200. Wool and cotton, 42 × 28½″. Museum of Primitive Art, New York.

The following period—A.D. 400 to 1000—is aptly termed the "Age of the Mastercraftsmen." Not only in textiles, but in pottery, metalwork, and other crafts the Peruvian artist reached a pinnacle of achievement. Paracas burial mantles were still made, and they were often accompanied by matched sets of shirts, ponchos, and shawls with the same overall polychrome embroidery. During this period the cultural center shifted from the Paracas peninsula on the coast to Tiahuanaco on the shores of Lake Titicaca in modern Bolivia. The Tiahuanaco style emphasized tapestry weaves characterized by straight, rectilinear, strongly outlined forms, as in the sleeveless shirt reproduced in Figure 85.

The period between 1000 and 1438 witnessed a decline in the pan-Peruvian Tiahuanaco style and the emergence of regional styles—Chancay, Chimu, and Ica (Figs. 86, 87). The three styles have in common a more lighthearted, even humorous approach and a preference for stylized animal forms. A number of fabric innovations were perfected during this era, including the complicated feather textiles (Fig. 88). After weaving a fine cloth, the craftsman sewed in tiny bird's feathers, selected for their color.

The mighty empire of the Incas (1438–1532) demarcates the last great period in the art of pre-Columbian Peru. Most of the surviving textiles from this culture are articles of clothing, particularly the shirt or *cuzma*. They are characterized by bright, contrasting colors and rigidly geometric forms—crosses, lozenges, spirals, me-

above: 85. Poncho-shirt, Tiahuanaco, south coast of Peru. A.D. 800–1100. Interlocking tapestry weave in cotton and wool, 3′6″ × 7′4″. Art Institute of Chicago (purchase, Buckingham Fund).

below: 86. Hanging, Chancay, central coast of Peru. 1000–1450. Wool and cotton, 6′4″ × 8′5″. Museum of Primitive Art, New York.

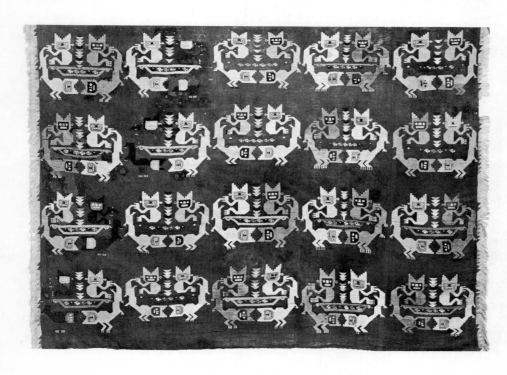

above: 87. Shirt, Ica, south coast of Peru. 1000–1450. Wool and cotton. Museum of Primitive Art, New York.

below: 88. Feather mantle, Chancay, north coast of Peru. 1000–1300. 45 × 44½″. Nelson Gallery-Atkins Museum, Kansas City (Nelson Fund).

above: 89. Sleeveless checkerboard shirt, Inca, Peru. 1438–1532. Tapestry weave in alpaca wool, 34 × 31″. Museum of Fine Arts, Boston (William Francis Warden Fund).

anders, and checkerboards (Fig. 89). Inca weaving was, in a sense, a refinement of all that had gone before—a purification of form combined with a mastery of technique.

In 1527 a small band of Spaniards led by Francisco Pizarro landed in Peru. The Incas welcomed their European visitors, and for five years the two groups coexisted peacefully. Then, in 1532 Pizarro seized the ruling Inca and established Spanish colonial government. The art of the Indians, so different from that of Europe, was either ignored or destroyed.

THE MEETING OF EAST AND WEST: CHINA AND JAPAN

China

Unlike Pizarro, Marco Polo knew full well the value of the textiles and other works of art he encountered in the Chinese court. Almost immediately fine silks from China began to appear in the churches and royal houses of Europe. Among the first of these was a gold brocaded silk vestment used as a burial garment for Pope Benedict XI, who died in 1304 (Fig. 90). Apart from stylistic differences, Chinese gold textiles can be distinguished from those made in the Middle East and in Europe because the precious metal was applied to thin strips of leather.

Silk tapestries had been popular in China since the Sung Dynasty (960–1279), when they were fashioned after contemporary painting styles (Fig. 91). By the Ming Dynasty (1368–1644) tapestry weaving had become an art in its own right. The *K'o-ssu* silks of that period (Pl. 8, p. 59) were often copies of lost paintings, but

above: 90. Dalmatic, Chinese, said to be from the tomb of Pope Benedict XI (d. 1304). Silk and gold brocade with embroidery. San Domenico, Perugia.

below: 91. Panel, from Ku K'ai-Chih Roll, China. Sung Dynasty (960–1279). K'o-ssu (silk tapestry), 7 × 9½". British Museum, London.

opposite: 92. *Emperor's Dragon Medallion,* China. Ming Dynasty (1368–1644). Silk with embroidery and couched gold, diameter 12". Metropolitan Museum of Art, New York (anonymous gift, 1946).

they were never direct imitations. Instead, the original design was reinterpreted in the idiom of the tapestry technique, with soft colors and flattened forms. Tapestries also served for court robes, furnishing fabrics, and accessories.

The borrowing of designs from one art form to another was quite common under the Ming Dynasty. It has been established that many patterns on the famous Ming porcelains were adapted from silk embroidery and brocades. Typical forms included phoenixes, lions, peacocks, storks, flying fish, and dragons (Fig. 92).

The Chinese were exceptionally proficient in the manufacture of velvets. In the 17th century the most sumptuous velvets had alternately cut and uncut pile, which enhanced the quality of reflected light. Pile carpets (Fig. 93), often featuring Buddhist and Taoist images, also date from this period. The most unusual were the "pillar" carpets, meant to be hung around a column.

Japan

The origins of Japanese art are most often traced to the Asuka Period, beginning with the introduction of Buddhism from China in A.D. 552. From written records it is known that the Japanese were already skilled in the production of fine silks, damasks, brocades, and embroideries (Fig. 94). By the Nara Period (645–794) the government had become so stratified that elaborate

above: 93. Pile rug, China. 18th century. Wool and cotton, 8′8″ × 5′3″. Textile Museum Collection, Washington, D.C.

below: 94. *Ban* (Buddhist ritual pendant,) detail, Japan. Asuka Period (552–645). Silk ikat. Tokyo National Museum.

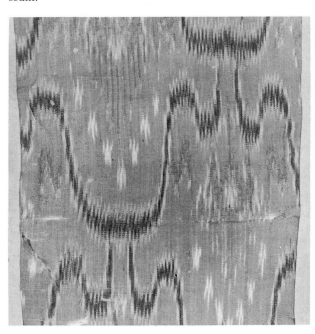

above: 95. Brocade fragment, detail, Japan. Nara Period (646–793). Silk, 18 × 12¼″. Tokyo National Museum (Shoso-in Collection).

right: 96. Noh robe for female role, Japan. Early 17th century. Kara-ori (brocade) in silk. Metropolitan Museum of Art, New York (purchase, 1932, Joseph Pulitzer Bequest).

below right: 97. Fragment of a kosode, Japan. Edo Period (1615–1868). Silk embroidery, 22¾ × 12½″. Tokyo National Museum.

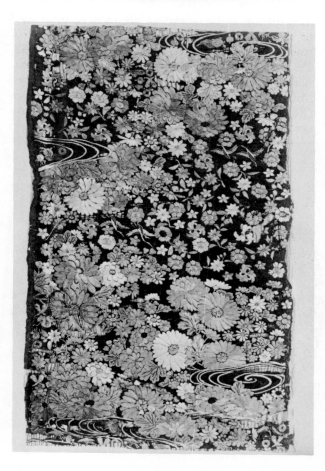

rules of dress were instituted. Each official rank was assigned a particular color and pattern of clothing, and this, of course, greatly stimulated the weaving and dyeing industries. Brocades (Fig. 95), called *nishiki*, were especially ornate, with patterns woven in either the warp or the weft. Silk textiles were most highly prized, but cotton and hemp were also employed. The textile industries continued to flourish during the Heian Period (794–1185). Rich and diversified colors were important, and silk was the principal fiber.

During the Kamakura and Muromachi periods weaving declined, and the most elegant fabrics were imported from China—the textiles referred to as *meibutsu-gire,* or "famous materials." The Momoyama Period (1573–1615) revived the textile arts most splendidly in the costumes of the *Noh* theater (Fig. 96). The more extravagant costumes were painted or embroidered, but a few simple and lovely gold brocades survive. Everyday clothing among members of the *samurai* class reflected the tendency toward greater luxury. Both sexes wore a one-piece kimono called a *kosode,* decorated with bright, large-scale designs.

The tastes of the Edo Period (1615–1868) were, if possible, even more lavish. The *kosode* (Fig. 97)

Plate 8. Fragment of a panel, China. Ming Dynasty (1368–1644). K'o-ssu (silk tapestry) with gold thread, 6'6" x 2'2". Cleveland Museum of Art (J. H. Wade Collection).

Plate 9. CHARLES LEBRUN design, executed at Gobelins. *Marriage of Louis XIV of France and the Infanta Marie-Thérèse of Spain,* from the series *The Life of the King.* 1665–80. Wool, silk, and gold thread; 16′3″ x 31′5″. Palace at Versailles.

was adopted by all levels of society, and longer sleeves and wider *obi* (sashes) were fashionable in women's dress. Printing and dyeing rather eclipsed woven patterns, because the former were capable of stronger effects. During this period Kyoto was the center of the textile industry, but many other cities and towns became famous for their individual styles. Some of these local manufacturies are in operation to this day.

Both the Portuguese and the Spanish Jesuits reached Japan in 1542, with the result that a few Japanese textiles were introduced to Europe. However, it was the Dutch, arriving half a century later, who instigated active trade between Europe and Japan.

EUROPE IN RENAISSANCE

The fantastic rebirth of arts and sciences that engulfed Europe in the centuries following what we call the "Middle Ages" did not occur simultaneously on all parts of the Continent. It came first to Italy and Flanders, then spread later to Spain, France, England, and Germany. However, for purposes of discussion it is convenient to label as "Renaissance" the period between 1400 and 1600—an era made fabulous by the Medici in Florence, the art patron popes in Rome, Ferdinand and Isabella of Spain, Francis I of France, and Henry VIII of England.

Weaving shared in the enormous popularity enjoyed by all the arts. In both quantity and quality, the product of the Renaissance looms rivals that of any other age, with the possible exception of our own. To satisfy the tastes of wealthy clients, a number of opulent fabrics were developed. Velvets—plain, cut, embroidered, appliquéd, brocaded—were much sought for garments and clerical vestments. Silk brocades, enriched with gold and silver threads, served as clothing, upholstery fabrics, wall coverings, and draperies. Furthermore, the nobility no longer held a monopoly on elegant fabrics, for a newly prosperous bourgeoisie competed in the demand for iridescent taffetas, fine silks, and damasks.

Cloth of gold (see p. 47) remained popular for festive and ceremonial occasions. In 1520 a historic meeting took place on a plain in Normandy, when Henry VIII of England joined Francis I of France for two weeks of diplomacy, feasting, tournaments, and regal one-upmanship.

So splendid were the trappings of the two monarchs, so lavish the entertainments they planned for one another, that the meeting place was called the Field of the Cloth of Gold (Fig. 98).

Tapestry weaving, in particular, reached the quintessence of its form; indeed, the Renaissance and early Baroque periods have been termed "the golden age of tapestry." Among those who could afford it, the fashion of the day called for rooms hung entirely with intricate, highly decorated tapestries. One can get some idea of the expense involved in keeping up this fashion from the fact that *The Story of Alexander the Great* reproduced in Figure 100 was acquired by Philip the Good, duke of Burgundy, for the extraordinary sum of five thousand gold pieces.

During the Renaissance nearly every region of Europe had its tapestry weavers, but in the production of large-scale epic tapestries the supremacy of Flanders was unchallenged.

Flanders

For the first half of the 15th century Arras maintained its prominent position in the field of tapestry weaving. Its closest rival was the neighboring city of Tournai, and after about 1450 the balance gradually shifted in favor of the latter, which had captured that most enviable prize— the patronage of the dukes of Burgundy.

below: 98. Anonymous. *The Field of the Cloth of Gold.* 16th century. Oil on canvas. Royal Collection, London.

Throughout the period the two cities had very close artistic and commercial ties, so it is often difficult to attribute a particular work to one or another. But most authorities agree that the splendid *Annunciation* in Figure 99 was woven in Arras.

The Story of Alexander the Great (Fig. 100) was created in the workshop of Pasquier Grenier (d. 1493), the most famous merchant-weaver of Tournai. The manufactures had, by this time, been organized on an industrial level; their products attained monumentality in both scale and concept. One has only to list the titles of major tapestry series to understand their epic nature: *The History of the Sacrament, The History of St. Peter, The History of Julius Caesar.*

After a hundred years of leadership, Tournai declined as a tapestry capital. In the latter half of the 15th century wealthy patrons had begun to turn to Brussels, where the style of weaving was more closely oriented toward painting. A characteristic of many Brussels tapestries is the segmenting of narrative episodes in an architectural setting reminiscent of wooden altar pieces. The extravagant use of gold threads in these works inspired the name *tapis d'or* ("cloth of gold"). Such tapestries were considered precious works of art and intended purely for decoration; they no longer had a functional role.

Among the more prominent merchant-weavers in early 16th-century Brussels were Pieter Pannemaker and Pieter van Aelst. Van Aelst was responsible for executing *The Acts of the Apostles* (Fig. 101), for which Raphael prepared the cartoons (Fig. 102). The tapestry was woven for the Sistine Chapel and completed in 1519, seven years after Michelangelo had finished the ceiling frescoes. In style it is more indicative of Italian painting than of northern textile art, for Raphael emphasized a sense of mass and three-dimensional space, both of which had previously been minimal in tapestry decoration.

Flemish tapestries of the Renaissance are so magnificent that they tend to overshadow the other textile arts; however, simple weaving was

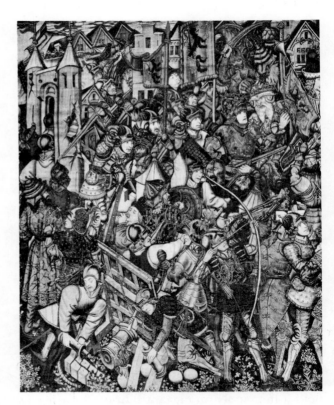

left: 99. MELCHIOR BROEDERLANI or follower, Arras (?). *Annunciation.* Early 15th century. Wool and metal thread, 11'4" × 9'6". Metropolitan Museum of Art, New York (gift of Harriet Barnes Pratt, 1949, in memory of her husband, Harold Irving Pratt).

above: 100. Workshop of PASQUIER GRENIER, Tournai. *The Story of Alexander the Great,* detail. Mid-15th century. Tapestry weave in wool, silk, and gold and silver threads; 13'7" × 32'4" overall. Galleria Doria Pamphili, Rome.

also a highly profitable industry during that period. The Counter-Reformation had driven many craftsmen out of France, and in the 15th century Flanders became the European center for wool weaving. Exquisite damasks, often with complicated figural designs (Fig. 103), also came from Flemish looms.

England

Many of the Protestant weavers who emigrated from France during the Counter-Reformation also settled in England, where they became part of a thriving enterprise. Queen Elizabeth I made the weaving industry the basis for England's trade and the establishment of her merchant marine. Ships laden with English fabrics reached ports throughout the Mediterranean, and their captains were charged with selling the entire cargo in a lot. If this proved impossible, foreign

top left: 101. Pieter van Aelst, after a design by Raphael. *The Miraculous Draught of Fishes,* from *The Acts of the Apostles.* 1516–19. Tapestry weave in wool, silk, and gold threads; 15′11″ × 16′7″. Vatican Museum.

above left: 102. Raphael. Cartoon for *The Miraculous Draught of Fishes.* 1515–16. Watercolor, 10′5½″ × 13′1″. Victoria & Albert Museum, London (on loan from H. M. the Queen).

above: 103. *Annunciation,* Flanders. c. 1500. Linen damask, 3′11½″ × 2′6¾″. Victoria & Albert Museum, London.

merchants were encouraged to buy at least one item for their own use. The most desirable customer was Spain, which would pay in the gold she was draining from her recently conquered territories in the New World. In time English woolens for bed covers, cushions, draperies, and hangings became stylish in Europe, replacing the much more expensive silk.

In 1510, under the direction of William Sheldon of Weston House, a series of county

above: 104. Sheldon tapestry map of Worcestershire, detail. 1588. Wool, 12′3″ × 16′ overall. Collection Bodleian Library, Oxford, presently at the Victoria & Albert Museum, London.

maps were woven in tapestry. The example in Figure 104 shows a portion of the tapestry map of Worcestershire—a charming mixture of geographical representation and decorative design.

France

No single tapestry center comparable to Arras or Tournai existed in France during the Renaissance. Some writers have suggested that most French tapestry weaving of the period was accomplished by itinerant craftsmen who moved from town to town, setting up their looms whenever they found a patron. Consequently, it is almost impossible to determine where a particular tapestry was woven.

The Hunt of the Unicorn (Fig. 105), a series of seven tapestries depicting a favorite Renaissance theme, is among the works whose exact origins are unknown. Five of the tapestries were almost certainly woven to celebrate the marriage of Anne of Brittany to Louis XII of France in 1499, and the other two may have been added to the series a decade and a half later in honor of the wedding of Anne's daughter. The *Unicorn* tapestries have much in common with contemporary production in Tournai, so they may actually have been woven in that city, or at least by a weaver familiar with the Flemish style.

Italy and Spain

Most of the sumptuous velvets used in clothing and ecclesiastical vestments were woven in Italy and Spain. Venice and Florence in particular specialized in the production of rich cut velvets, in which the height of the pile was varied to create a "carved" effect. Several Italian painters, including Pisanello and Jacopo Bellini, designed patterns for cut velvet. A favorite motif in Italy was the pomegranate (Fig. 106), while in Spain, still influenced by the Hispano-Moresque tradition, the pomegranate often appeared side by side with the Turkish tulip and arabesque (Fig. 107). All the refined techniques for fabric ornamentation were brought to bear in the design of

left: 105. *The Unicorn in Captivity* from *The Hunt of the Unicorn,* Franco-Flemish. c. 1500. Tapestry weave, 12′ × 8′3″. Metropolitan Museum of Art, New York (gift of John D. Rockefeller, Jr., 1937).

clerical vestments. The more elaborate garments consisted of cut and voided velvet, heavily appliquéd in silk and metallic threads (Fig. 108).

Until the 16th century the great patrons of Italy commissioned their tapestries in the North, for the art of tapestry weaving was not well established. In 1546 Cosimo I de' Medici contracted with Nicolaus Carcher, a Flemish weaver, to organize a tapestry works in Florence. A number of Florentine painters—notably Pontormo and Agnolo Bronzino—contributed cartoons. Carcher had also set up a workshop in Ferrara, but its production was short-lived. On the whole, tapes-

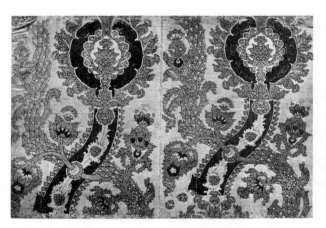

left: 106. Altar frontal, detail with pomegranate motif, Florence. Late 15th century. Voided velvet with brocade. Museo Poldi Pezzoli, Milan.

below left: 107. AGNOLO BRONZINO. *Eleanora of Toledo and Her Son Giovanni de'Medici.* c. 1550. Oil on canvas, 45¼ × 37¼". Uffizi Gallery, Florence.

above: 108. Ecclesiastical cape, Spain. c. 1438. Velvet with ferronnière design embroidered in couched gold thread and embroidered orphreys, height 4'8½". Metropolitan Museum of Art, New York (Cloisters Collection, Purchase, 1953).

try weaving was never a significant industry in either Italy or Spain, for the textile manufacture of both countries was dominated by the cut velvets and, especially in Italy, the fine silks.

THE BAROQUE PERIOD IN EUROPE

In its original usage the word "baroque" connoted something bizarre, grotesque, and distorted; however, as applied to the arts, especially music and the visual arts, *baroque* has come to designate the dynamic, opulent, curvilinear style prevalent in Europe between 1600 and 1750.

Flanders

Just as Raphael had left his mark on the tapestry style of 16th-century Brussels, another great master of painting—Peter Paul Rubens—exercised enormous influence on 17th-century production

65

in that city. In the very early part of the century the most popular subjects had been small hunting scenes; Rubens set out to restore the monumental character of tapestry weaving. To this end he designed a number of tapestry series all with epic themes and powerful figures. *The History of Constantine* (Figs. 109, 110), commissioned by Louis XIII, illustrates Rubens' preference for heroic figures in the foreground, with a minimum of background interest. The implied analogy between Louis and Constantine obviously served to glorify the king. Many sets of these tapestries exist, for it was common in the 17th century for several different workshops throughout Europe to copy the same design, with minor alterations. Rubens continued to prepare sketches for the tapestry ateliers of Brussels and France until his death in 1640.

below left: 109. Anonymous weaver, after a design by PETER PAUL RUBENS. *The Battle of Constantine,* from *The History of Constantine.* 17th century. Tapestry. Mobilier National, Paris.

bottom left: 110. PETER PAUL RUBENS. *Battle of Constantine and Licinius.* 1622. Oil on panel, 14 × 22½″. Nelson Gallery-Atkins Museum, Kansas City (Nelson Fund).

above: 111. *Culture of Silkworms in France.* 1602. Engraving, Bibliothèque Nationale, Paris.

below: 112. Wall panel with scenes of silk manufacture, from France. Second half of 18th century. Silk brocade *chinoiserie,* 4′11″ × 2′6¼″. Musée Historique des Tissus, Lyons.

France

During the 17th century France assumed the position long held by Italy in the production of fine silks. The silk manufactures at Lyons had been established in the mid-15th century, but for approximately two hundred years their output consisted mainly of copies from Italian imports. Then, under the sponsorship of Henry IV (1589–1610) and Louis XIV (1643–1715) the French weaving industry received the stimulus it needed to dominate all Europe.

As part of his program for revitalizing the French economy, Henry IV introduced silk cultivation to France (Fig. 111). The promulgation of the Edict of Nantes in 1598, which granted religious freedom to the Huguenots, enabled many Protestant weavers to return to France. However, most crucial to the success of the weaving industry was the founding in Paris, in 1667, of the Manufacture Royale des Meubles de la Couronne, a state-subsidized workshop planned by Louis XIV and expedited by his minister Colbert. Originally, the Manufacture Royale included cabinetmakers, goldsmiths, and engravers, and it incorporated the famous Gobelins tapestry works. Although a government superintendent controlled the workshop's operation, artistic activity was under the direction of the painter Charles Lebrun.

The silk ateliers were prolific in their output of clothing, wall hangings, and upholstery. Improved looms enabled the weavers to use an immense number of colors—as many as 1800, all derived from natural dyestuffs, were available by the 18th century—and to achieve unusual effects. After the establishment of the royal manufactury, only domestic silks were obtainable throughout France. The radiant example set by the French court greatly stimulated exportation, as did the sumptuous representation of French silks in paintings by such masters as Watteau.

A special category of silk textiles were the *chinoiseries* (Fig. 112), westernized adaptations of the Chinese silks that circulated throughout Europe during the latter part of the 17th century. It is said that Madame de Pompadour personally directed the design of *chinoiseries* in Lyons.

Over a period of three years the most important tapestry centers of France were granted royal recognition. In 1664 the title Manufacture Royale de Tapisserie was conferred upon the workshops at Beauvais, and the same honor was bestowed upon the Aubusson factory the following year. In both towns production consisted mainly of *verdures,* small tapestries featuring trees and foliage. The Gobelins workshops of Paris, organized under the royal manufactury in 1667, held the monopoly on crown commissions, with the inevitable result that much of their output was designed to glorify the Sun King, Louis XIV. Typical examples were *Royal Palaces* and *The Life of the King* (Pl. 9, p. 60), both completed under the direction of Lebrun in about 1680.

The textile and tapestry workshops were severely affected by the French Revolution of 1789. Silk production was brought to a virtual standstill, and only tapestries featuring patriotic themes were permitted. However, a different kind of revolution—that caused by the invention of mechanical weaving devices—would have much more spectacular implications for the entire weaving industry.

THE AMERICAN SETTLERS

In the 17th century weaving was still a common household chore in rural parts of Europe. Consequently, the settlers who traveled to the American colonies brought with them a tradition of home weaving. They also brought their looms and their patterns, for contact with the mother country was uncertain at best, and the colonists had to be entirely self-sufficient. At first each family satisfied all its own textile needs, from clothing to blankets to bed and table linens. Later, traveling weavers or *journeymen*—the term "journey" meaning a day's work—supplied the scattered colonists with goods they could not produce themselves. "Like other itinerant workmen of the day, the wandering weaver was welcomed by the isolated family, for he carried the tattle of the countryside, and the early weaver soon acquired a towering reputation as a gossip. . . . When he came with his pattern book of drafts it was most exciting. There was the task of selecting the design for the coverlet to go into the daughter's hope chest."[4]

Raw materials were a constant problem to the colonists. The most abundant fiber was linen, for the early settlers had brought flax seeds with them, and their crops achieved success in most parts of the colonies. Cotton was scarce, because it could not be cultivated in the northern regions, and the cotton industry in the South did not become significant until the 1830s. Wool presented even greater difficulties. Columbus had carried sheep to the New World on his second voyage in 1493, but this was of little use to the settlers in the thirteen colonies. The Revolution halted the flow of wool from England, after which small quantities were purchased from Spain. However, not until the 19th century, when George Washington encouraged the importation of Merino sheep, did wool become plentiful.

As the settlements grew increasingly permanent and ships called more frequently at colonial ports, some fabrics from Europe began to filter in, but only the wealthiest families could afford them. By 1638 the first textile factory in America had been established in the Massachusetts Bay Colony by one Ezekiel Rogers. Later, William Penn himself introduced the textile industry to Pennsylvania, when he rented a house ("at 40 pounds a year, at the southwest corner of Ninth and Market Streets"[5]) to be used for the manufacture of cloth. In time, most colonies had a small factory, and there were professional weavers in every community who produced wool blankets, linen and flannel sheets, fustian (called "thick-sett," see p. 47), and striped linsey-woolsey for everyday clothing.

Written accounts of the infant weaving industry are scarce, but they do exist. A certain Deborah Morton of New Jersey, and her descendants, kept such a record book for a hundred years. The Mortons were proprietors of a professional weaving shop. Despite the tiny salaries their employees received, they were still charged for the shuttles and candles they used. In 1801 one of Deborah's daughters was married to Richard Longstreet, Jr., who was paid 17s, 7½d (perhaps $3.00) for weaving 23 yards of "cloath" at 9d (10 to 15 cents) per yard.[6]

Notwithstanding the growing number of professional weavers, a large percentage of the textiles were still produced in the home. In 1810 more than ten thousand looms existed in the Ohio country alone. Virtually all yarn, even that provided to journeyman weavers, was homespun. "When Phebe Davis married in 1797 her dowry included two slaves, blue china for the dining room, spinning wheels and winding reels."[7] In

top: 113. Woven coverlet, from Preston Hollow, N.Y. 1800. Tabby weave with weft float pattern in blue and white, wool and linen; 6'10" × 5'9". Art Institute of Chicago.

above: 114. ABRAM WILLIAM VAN DOREN. Coverlet, from Oakland County, Mich. 1845. Wool and cotton in red and white double weave, 6'4" × 7'4". Art Institute of Chicago (Dr. F. Gunsaulus Collection).

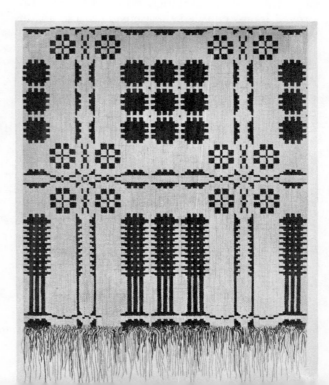

affluent families the slaves did the weaving, but the spinning and winding of yarn were still considered the task of the housewife.

Of the early textiles that have been preserved, the most common item is the coverlet (Figs. 113, 114). Woven on simple looms, usually with a natural linen warp and a colored wool weft, these beautiful fabrics display an amazing intricacy and a very high level of craftsmanship. The coverlet in Figure 115 is a form of double cloth (see pp. 152–55), with two warp threads and two weft threads woven together at points where the design areas meet. The pattern is called "Nine Snowballs with Pine Tree Border."

The Industrial Revolution reached America very shortly after it had taken hold in England. With the coming of the machines, a factory system developed, and home weaving virtually ceased.

THE INDUSTRIAL REVOLUTION

Insofar as the textile industry was concerned, the Industrial Revolution commenced in 1764, with the historic introduction of James Hargreaves' spinning jenny. This rather crude invention was superseded within fifteen years by Samuel Crompton's spinning mule, which, tended by one worker, could match the output of two hundred hand spinners. On a hand-operated loom a single weaver could produce about 8 yards of fabric a day, and eight hand spinners were kept busy supplying the yarn he consumed. The spinning mule and the new power looms that came into use at the end of the century dramatically accelerated the rate of production. Incensed at the loss of their jobs, many handweavers and spinners rebelled. Machines were smashed, and at one point a factory containing four hundred power looms was burned. But the new system was so profitable that the workers could not possibly reverse the trend. With the rebels hanged or deported, the machines clanked on.

An immediate result of this mechanical revolution was the emergence of a factory system.

Workers were taken out of their homes or shops and herded together in huge plants. The craftsman who had once taken pride in his work, had seen a project through from beginning to end, was now reduced to an automaton, occasionally pushing a lever or tying a broken thread. It was soon discovered that women and children would work more cheaply than men, and these unfortunate creatures were forced to spend mercilessly long hours—often as many as eighteen hours a day—under ghastly conditions (Fig. 116).

Despite the vast quantity of textiles produced, a price was paid in the marked deterioration of quality. The machines could operate best when conditions were standardized, so that thousands of yards of identical material were manufactured. The resultant fabric might be technically perfect, but the human touch of the weaver disappeared forever. Furthermore, the increasing complexity of the looms tempted entrepreneurs, like children with new toys, to experiment with more and more highly decorated fabrics.

The Industrial Revolution proceeded most rapidly in England, where the product of the weaving mills stimulated trade and fed an expanding economy. By 1864, just a century after the invention of the spinning jenny, handweaving in England was almost a forgotten craft.

opposite: 115. Double-cloth coverlet, Florida. Early 19th century. Linen, 8′ × 8′8″. Private collection.

right: 116. *Love Conquered Fear,* engraving showing women and children laborers in a textile mill, from a London publication of April 20, 1839. British Museum, London.

Twentieth-century Handweaving 5

The true root and basis of all Art lies in the handicrafts.
*Catalogue of the Arts and Crafts
Exhibition Society, 1888*

By the end of the 19th century public interest in the handcrafts had all but vanished from the industrialized nations of the world. The machine was king: its products were bigger, better, more uniform; they could be manufactured faster and much more cheaply than old-fashioned handmade goods. Artists, writers, and musicians competed to outdo one another in eulogizing the age of technology. Half a century later the crafts were once again flourishing. Weaving, ceramics, jewelry making, needlecraft—in fact, *all* the hand processes, including a few that had been out of vogue for hundreds of years—were more popular than ever before.

Many writers have attempted to explain this fantastic resurrection. The most common theory postulates an aesthetic reaction to an overstandardized environment, a world in which one's house, furniture, car, clothing, and personal effects look much like everyone else's. Combined with this is a growing dismay at shoddy workmanship. A machine cannot take pride in its job;

it cannot be held accountable if its product falls apart the first time it is used. In increasing numbers people are seeking the handcrafted object— the slight irregularities, the meticulous care of execution, the burst of inspiration that give evidence of humanity.

WILLIAM MORRIS

The roots of this 20th-century craft revival must be sought in the latter part of the 19th, when a few individuals began to speak out against the machine. William Morris (1834–96) was trained as a painter and architect. In 1857 he set out to furnish his first studio in London. To Morris' shock he found that, even by assembling the best of the industrial products then available, he could not possibly construct an environment suitable for painting magnificent pictures. An artist, Morris theorized, surrounded by poorly built and grossly overdecorated objects, would ultimately see his own ideals corrupted. Consequently, in 1861 Morris took the initiative in organizing the firm of Morris, Marshall & Faulkner, Fine Art Workmen in Painting, Carving, Furniture, and the Metals. The company designed and manufactured chairs "such as Barbarossa might have sat in," strong, functional tables, carpeting, stained glass, and metal objects—all in the highest possible standards of taste and craftsmanship. Morris also designed fabrics, wallpaper, and tapestries, a splendid example of which is the *Woodpecker* (Pl. 10, p. 93), woven at Merton Abbey in 1885.

For the rest of his life Morris wrote and lectured extensively in an attempt to popularize his ideas. Moreover, Morris, who was a Socialist, did not merely seek an elitist concept of excellence. He believed that well-designed and well-crafted objects should be within the reach of even the poorest individual, that the public could be educated to good taste as well as bad. "What business," he wrote, "have we with art at all unless all can share it?"[1]

A direct outgrowth of Morris' preaching was the Arts and Crafts Movement in England. As part of their campaign to restore the handcrafts, followers of the movement sought out native craftsmen in areas of continental Europe where the Industrial Revolution had not completely taken over. The peasant class of Sweden, Norway, and Denmark were still producing handwoven articles for their daily needs on their own looms, and these skilled weavers taught their methods to the students from England. To this day the Scandinavian countries have an enormous influence on the design of handcrafted—and to some extent mass-produced—items throughout the world.

THE BAUHAUS

Not all the proponents of excellence in design and construction wished to abolish the machine. Many people believed, instead, that the machine could be harnessed, that sound workmanship and good taste were not incompatible with mass production. The most ambitious statement of this ideal was developed in the Bauhaus.

The Bauhaus School of Design was founded in 1919 in Weimar, Germany. Its stated aim was to "create a new guild of craftsmen, without the class distinctions which raise an arrogant barrier between craftsman and artist."[2] To this end, studies were organized on a workshop basis, and the medieval guild roles of "master," "journeyman," and "apprentice" substituted for those of teacher and student. The original director of the Bauhaus was the architect Walter Gropius, whose belief that "form follows function" became gospel for his adherents (see p. 302).

The weaving workshop was the first to be fairly well organized. Its co-masters were Hélène Börner and Georg Muche, but many resident painters supplied ideas and designs for the weavers.

Increasing pressure from the government, which accused the school of subversion and even Bolshevism, forced the Bauhaus, in 1924, to move to Dessau. There, under the direction of Gunta Stölzl (Fig. 117), the weaving workshop achieved its first commercial success. Systematic training in weaving and dyeing techniques was undertaken, and the course of study was aimed

117. Gunta Stölzl. Slit Gobelin wall hanging. 1927–28. Linen warp, cotton weft; 4'7" × 3'7". Bauhaus-Archiv, Darmstadt (on permanent loan from the Carpet Association of Wuppertal).

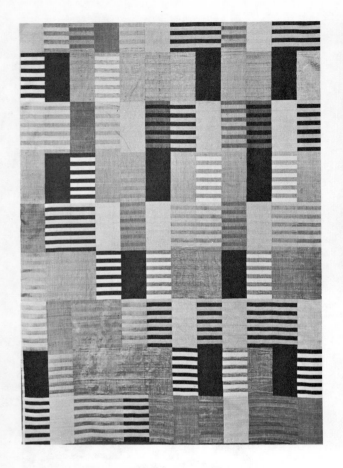

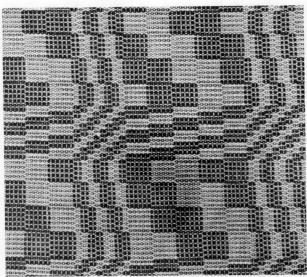

left: 118. ANNI ALBERS. Bauhaus tapestry. 1926. Silk, 6 × 4′. Busch-Reisinger Museum, Harvard University, Cambridge, Mass. (purchase, Germanic Museum Association).

above: 119. MARY MEIGS ATWATER. *Crackle Weave,* detail. Six-strand floss on three-ply cotton warp, 10 × 12″ overall. Southern California Handweavers' Guild, Los Angeles (Mary Meigs Atwater Memorial Collection).

ultimately at design for industry. Many of the weavers, including Otti Berger and Anni Albers (Fig. 118), did, in fact, have their textile designs mass-produced by German manufacturers.

On April 11, 1933, the Gestapo occupied the Bauhaus. Attempts to reconcile the ideals of the school with those of the new regime were doomed to failure, and in July of 1933 the Bauhaus was closed. To the incalculable good fortune of the American crafts movement, the great majority of the faculty and students emigrated to the United States.

THE REVIVAL OF HANDWEAVING IN THE UNITED STATES

American interest in handweaving began to reassert itself in the latter part of the 1920s. One of the pioneers in this movement was Mary Atwater (1878–1956), who as a bride arrived in a remote Montana mining town shortly after the

turn of the century. Recreational opportunities for women were limited in that isolated community, so as a diversion Atwater taught herself to weave. She had been shown an heirloom coverlet belonging to one of the townspeople, and this inspired her to try her own designs (Fig. 119). Soon she began to share her newly acquired knowledge with other women in the town. Her interest in pre-Columbian textiles was awakened when she accompanied her husband on a series of business trips to Central and South America. There she had an opportunity to examine the ancient fabrics and record their patterns.

During World War I Atwater served as an occupational therapist for injured servicemen, which experience encouraged her to write a book about the possibilities of weaving in rehabilitation. Later, she organized the first weavers' guild in the United States. As a service to her members she developed *Shuttlecraft Bulletin,* at the time the only magazine written expressly for handweavers. Her research in Early American fabrics made it possible for modern weavers to understand and copy the traditional patterns for their own adaptation.

Until the 1940s pattern weaving, based on old coverlets and other Colonial designs, was the prevalent style in the United States. Women collected weaving patterns like cooking recipes, and sometimes guarded them just as jealously. However, during and after World War II the trend shifted to an interest in texture created with the simplest weaves. To some extent the new fashion was stimulated by the influx of Bauhaus expatriates.

Anni Albers, with her husband Josef, the noted painter and colorist, came to the United States in the thirties. Like many of her compatriots, she taught for a time at Black Mountain College in North Carolina. Since then, her influence has been exercised through extensive lecturing and through her books.

Although Albers' early training emphasized design for industry, she is very much a master of the hand loom. For her, the two are never incompatible: "I have made no distinction between the craftsman designer, the industrial designer, and the artist—because the fundamental, if not the specific, considerations are the same,

left: 120. ANNI ALBERS. *With Verticals.* 1946. 5'1" × 3'10½". Collection Robert Pottinger, Chicago.

above: 121. LILI BLUMENAU. *Transparent and Opaque.* 1958. Braided ribbon and fine rayon, 7' × 2'9". From *Objects: USA,* Johnson Wax Collection of Contemporary Crafts, Racine, Wis.

I believe, for those who work with the conscience and apperception of the artist."[3] Albers is essentially an analytical weaver, concentrating on the elements—linear, coloristic, textural—that are combined in creating a textile (Fig. 120).

Another German-trained craftsman, Lili Blumenau, has had a comparable influence on the spread of handweaving in the United States. Until the early 1950s the main product of the handloom was yardage. Blumenau's métier was the titled wall hanging—the woven object as a discrete work of art expressing her thoughts and ideas (Fig. 121). She has been active in virtually every phase of the crafts movement, as teacher, author, museum curator, lecturer, and industrial designer.

Much of the current interest in vivid colors and unusual materials can be traced to the work of Dorothy Liebes, a California-born weaver-designer who has often been referred to as "America's first lady of the loom." Trained as a painter, Liebes turned to weaving when she realized that the standard of excellence she sought could best be attained in fiber. Her early inspiration was drawn from the vibrant Oriental colors and patterns she found in San Francisco's Chinatown (Pl. 11, p. 94), and bright lacquer red has become a mainstay of her repertoire. Incredible as it seems, she was among the first of her generation to combine blue and green in a textile—a daring color scheme that seemed to many a violation of color theory.

In her search for exciting textures, Liebes experimented with leather strips, ticker tape, tape measures, and especially metallic yarns, including pure gold. Her best-known textiles exhibit a striking glitter effect derived also from the early Chinese influence. Perhaps her most important contribution was in raising the quality of design in mass-produced, moderately priced fabrics (see p. 334 and Fig. 557).

As more and more individuals were attracted to the crafts, the number of organizations and publications specifically dedicated to their needs began to grow. The American Crafts Council (originally named the American Craftsmen's Council) was founded in 1943, chiefly through the efforts of Mrs. Aileen Vanderbilt Webb. The council's stated aim was to "stimulate interest in the work of handcraftsmen." To this end the ACC has been instrumental in reteaching the techniques of age-old crafts, as well as newer ones, and in helping craftsmen to market their goods. Membership is open to any interested person. The council also operates the Museum of Contemporary Crafts in New York, which develops a year-round program of craft and craft-related exhibitions. In recent years the

122. GRAU-GARRIGA. *Ecumenisme.* 1969. Tapestry of wool, cotton, and jute, with pile; 10'11¼" × 13'1 1/16". Courtesy Arras Gallery, New York. (See also Fig. 303.)

The production of yardage, accomplished much more efficiently by power looms, has declined, and there is a new emphasis on wall hangings, garments, rugs, and sculptural constructions. The tapestry technique was revived in the late fifties, at first as a medium for copying paintings. Artists commissioned to prepare the designs executed their cartoons in terms of paint on canvas. Later, tapestry weaving earned respect as an art form in its own right.

Many contemporary artists refuse to limit themselves to a single technique or even a single craft (Fig. 122), for only by combining two or more yarn-interlacement methods (for example, weaving and netting) or two or more media (weaving and ceramics) can they achieve the expression they seek.

THE CRAFT REVIVAL IN THE SOUTHERN HIGHLANDS

It is easy to forget that not all parts of the world have been touched equally by the Industrial Revolution. There are, indeed, sections of the United States, the most heavily industrialized nation on earth, where the machine age has gone virtually unnoticed. The mountain regions of the Virginias, the Carolinas, Maryland, Kentucky, Tennessee, Georgia, and Alabama—known collectively as the Southern Highlands—constitute such a special area. There, daily life has changed but little over the last three hundred years. Long isolated in their remote mountain homes, inaccessible to any railroad, jet plane, or superhighway, the Appalachian peoples have learned to be almost totally self-sufficient. The folk handcrafts passed down from generation to generation satisfy their daily needs for woven fabrics, baskets, pottery utensils, and wooden objects (Fig. 123). They also provide a form of recreation, particularly for the women. According to the Works Progress Administration *Guide to North Carolina* (1939), "Colonial handicrafts have survived in North Carolina despite the flood of machine-made products from the factories. The influence of tradition, poverty, isolation, and

craftsmen in nearly every state have formed their own branch organizations. These groups conduct exhibitions, fairs, seminars, competitions, and many other activities on a local level. The World Crafts Council, launched in 1964 and now affiliated with the UNESCO branch of the United Nations, helps to bring craftsmen from all parts of the world closer together.

The American Crafts Council publishes *Craft Horizons,* a bi-monthly magazine that reports current happenings in all craft areas, both nationally and internationally. *Handweaver & Craftsman* was established in 1950 to serve artisans working in fiber. According to Jack Lenor Larsen, "The magazine became a two-way street, an open-ended line of communication for not only philosphy and techniques but also reality."[4] Larsen called its founder and longtime editor Mary Alice Smith "a one-woman crusade for weaving in particular and anti-institutionalism in general."[5] Such dedicated individuals have contributed to the growing prestige of all the handcrafts.

Since the 1940s the output of the handloom has changed considerably. New materials—nylon, rayon, plastics, metallics—have broadened the resources of the weaver immeasurably.

right: 124. Child's dress made from precut materials by the craftsman's cooperatives in the Southern Highlands. Distributed to major retail outlets through Mountain Artisans, Charleston, W. Va.

some steady local markets have served to keep alive these native skills."

The Southern Highland Handicraft Guild was first organized in 1930 to aid local craftsmen in establishing a broader market for their goods. In recent years interested outsiders have encouraged the mountain women to turn their household crafts into cottage industries. Woven fabrics, patchwork, and other fiber products (Fig. 124) have begun to appear in fashionable shops in the large cities, where their meticulous craftsmanship and exquisite designs fetch handsome prices from a sophisticated clientele.

The example of the Southern Highlands is symptomatic of a trend evident in all the crafts. Folk handcrafts from all parts of the world are being explored by contemporary artists who seek a fresh outlook in their own work. This fact explains the current interest in macramé, sprang, twining, patchwork (in essence a form of collage), and many other techniques. To a very real extent, the future of the handcrafts lies in the past.

part two
HANDWEAVING ON THE LOOM

6 *Materials for Weaving*

Yarn is to the weaver what clay is to the potter,
metal to the jeweler, and wood to the cabinet-
maker: the raw material that is needed to make
the finished product. In the case of weaving, the
character of a textile depends to a large extent
on the properties of the yarns chosen for a specific project (Pl. 12, p. 94).

All yarns are composed of *fibers,* either the
natural fibers derived from living and growing
things or the man-made fibers extruded from the
spinnerette. Until the 20th century most weaving
was confined to the four major fibers—cotton,
linen, wool, and silk (Figs. 125–128). However,
since the 1930s fiber manufacturers have introduced a vast number of synthetic materials,
many of which are suitable for handweaving.
Furthermore, in their search for new modes of
expression, contemporary craftsmen have begun
to show an interest in less common fibers (such
as jute, sisal, and hemp), materials used by primitive man (such as feathers, grasses, and rushes),
and totally nonfibrous materials (such as wire

125–128. *Photomicrographs of the four principal fibers, in longitu-
dinal view.*

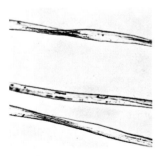

125. Cotton.

126. Linen.

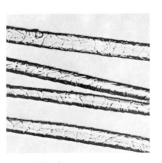

127. Wool.

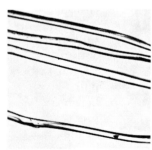

128. Silk.

and plastic). The suitability of a material for weaving is limited only by its appropriateness to the project for which it is intended. Before a weaver can feel adequately prepared to work, he should have at hand a wide range of yarns and other materials—providing a variety of color, size, texture, and fiber—from which to select.

FIBER CLASSIFICATION

Considering the myriad fibers on today's market, it is essential, in order to avoid confusion, that some means of classification be established. Many different systems have been proposed, but the most common is based on the source of each individual fiber. The simplest breakdown separates the natural from the man-made fibers; under each of these broad categories one can isolate several important subdivisions. In the outline that follows, the synthetic fibers are identified by their *generic* or family names, plus a few of the more common *trade* names used by individual manufacturers (the latter distinguished by an initial capital letter).

Until recent years it was common to differentiate between *synthetic* fibers—those created in the laboratory but composed partly of vegetable materials—and *man-made* fibers, which contain no natural ingredients. However, in the last decade the textile industry has expressed a preference for the term "man-made" and avoided the word "synthetic," which to many connotes artificiality and an inferior product. In this text the terms are used synonymously to embrace all nonnatural fibers, regardless of their composition.

Natural fibers

Vegetable (cellulosic) fibers
1. seed hairs
   a. cotton
   b. kapok
   c. milkweed
   d. cattail
2. bast (stem) fibers
   a. flax
   b. hemp
   c. jute
   d. ramie
   e. bamboo
3. leaf fibers
   a. sisal
   b. yucca
   c. abaca (Manila hemp)
   d. raffia (palm leaf)
   e. piña (pineapple)
   f. reed
   g. grass
4. fruit fibers
   a. coir (coconut)
5. bark and root
   a. broom
   b. cedar

Animal (protein) fibers
1. hair fibers
   a. wool
   b. cashmere (Tibetan goat)
   c. mohair (Angora goat)
   d. llama
   e. alpaca
   f. vicuña
   g. camel hair
   h. cow hair
   i. horse hair
   j. dog hair
   k. rabbit hair
   l. bristle hair
   m. buffalo hair
   n. beard hair
   o. reindeer hair
2. internal animal parts
   a. sinews
   b. intestines
3. animal secretions
   a. silk

Mineral fibers
1. asbestos
2. metal
   a. aluminum
   b. gold
   c. silver

Man-made fibers

Cellulosic fibers
1. rayon
2. high-wet-modulus rayon

Modified cellulosic fibers
1. acetate

a. secondary acetate (Celanese, Chrom-
   spun, etc.)
b. triacetate (Arnel)

Protein fibers
1. azlon

Synthesized fibers
1. condensation polymer fibers
   a. nylon
   b. polyester (Dacron, etc.)
2. addition polymer fibers
   a. anidex
   b. acrylic (Acrilan, Orlon, etc.)
   c. modacrylic (Dynel, Verel, etc.)
   d. nytril
   e. olefin
   f. saran
   g. vinal
   h. vinyon
3. elastomers
   a. spandex
   b. rubber

Mineral fibers
1. glass

FIBER CHARACTERISTICS

It is often necessary for a weaver to know in advance how a particular fiber will behave both on and off the loom—how much it will stretch or sag, whether it is flammable, how readily it will accept dyes, and so forth. If a heavy wall hanging is woven from relatively elastic fibers, the entire composition may stretch out of shape merely from its own weight. Such foreknowledge is especially important for industrial designers and for those handweavers involved in executing large-scale commissions. For example, a theater curtain made of flammable materials would probably be rejected on the basis of local fire laws. The table (below) lists several of the more common fibers used for handweaving and the qualities associated with each *in its natural state.* Various finishes can be applied to the fibers, markedly altering their properties.

WEAVING YARNS

The properties of a yarn are affected by several factors, including the origin, size, and texture of the fiber, the type of yarn construction, the time

Fiber Characteristics				
Fiber	*Strength*	*Elasticity*	*Receptiveness to dyes*	*Flammability*
cotton	medium	low	good	high
linen	high	low	good	high
hemp	high	low	difficult to bleach, but will accept bright or dark dyes	high
jute	medium	low	difficult to bleach, but will accept bright or dark dyes	high
wool	low	medium to high	excellent	medium
silk	medium to high	medium	good	medium
rayon	varies with type	medium	good	high
nylon	high	high	poor	medium

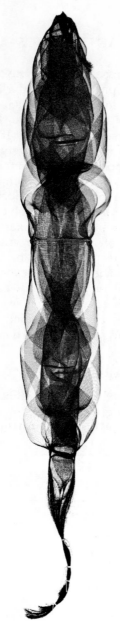

left: 129. KAY SEKIMACHI. *Nagare III*. 1968. Handwoven monofilament, 7'4" × 1'1". Courtesy Lee Nordness Galleries, New York.

Yarn Construction

Yarns can be composed of either filament or staple fibers. *Filament fibers* are those that are measured in yards or even miles, primarily the man-made fibers, which can be extruded in an infinite unbroken length from the machines. Among the natural fibers, only silk is classified as a filament fiber, since the unraveled cocoon sometimes measures up to 3000 yards. Yarns made from filament fibers are either *monofilament*—consisting of a single continuous strand—or *multifilament*—composed of two or more filaments twisted together. Some fibers, such as nylon, lend themselves to monofilament weaving (Fig. 129).

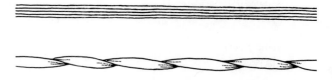

above: 130. Yarns are subjected to varying degrees of twist, depending upon the nature of the fiber involved and the use to which the yarn will be put. *top to bottom:* roving or untwisted yarn, low-twist yarn, crepe or high-twist yarn.

below: 131. A ply yarn is composed of two or more single yarns twisted together; a cable or cord yarn consists of two or more plies twisted together. *top to bottom:* singles yarn, 2-ply yarn, cord.

and method of coloring, and the presence or absence of a finish. A cotton yarn, for example, may be composed of short or long fibers; it can be given high or low twist, or constructed to achieve certain novelty effects; it can be dyed by the manufacturer or by the craftsman, in the latter case before or after weaving; it can be mercerized (treated with caustic soda) or left in its natural state. All these variables will influence the behavior of a yarn on the loom and its appearance in the finished project.

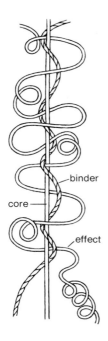

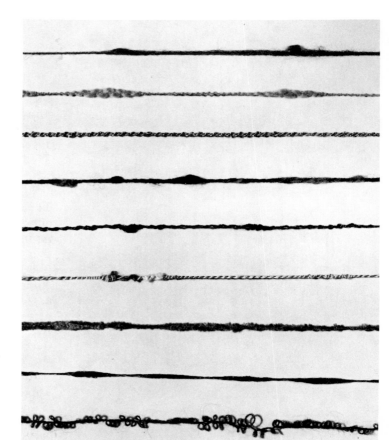

above: 132. Many novelty yarns are composed of three parts: a core yarn, an effect yarn, and a binder that holds the effect yarn in place.

right: 133. Novelty yarns are characterized by spaced irregularities of size, twist, or effect. *top to bottom:* slub, ratiné, bouclé, nub, seed, corkscrew, chenille, flake, loop.

Staple fibers are measured in inches or fractions of inches and must be spun to produce a thread. All natural fibers except silk are staple length, and occasionally short ends of silk from broken cocoons are spun to create a staple yarn. In addition, most synthetic fibers can be cut apart and spun in the usual manner. *Long-staple* yarns are considered top quality. They are sturdier, more lustrous, and capable of being spun tighter, thus rendering them fine and smooth. Cotton is divided into three staple lengths: long staple (roughly, greater than an inch), short staple, and waste or *linters* (fibers picked directly from the seeds). Linters are used primarily in the manufacture of rayon. Hair staple fibers vary from 1 to 15 inches in length. Coarse wools and Angora goat hair are the longest, while fine wools, such as Merino, are usually about 5 to 6 inches long. The most luxurious hairs, including cashmere and vicuña, are shorter. Woolen yarns are spun from short, uncombed fibers; worsted yarns are composed of longer wool fibers that have been *combed,* or straightened (pp. 258-259). Flax fibers for linen are classified as either *line* (greater than 12 inches) or *tow* (less than 12 inches). Sometimes an intermediate grade—*demi-line*—is recognized.

Most yarns, both filament and staple, are given a certain amount of twist in order to hold the fibers together. The degree of twist required depends upon the particular fiber (Fig. 130); it varies from no twist at all (*roving*) to high twist (*crepe*). When two or more yarns are twisted together, the result is known as a *ply* (Fig. 131). A 2-ply yarn, for example, is composed of two single yarns plied together. A *cable* or *cord* yarn is even more complicated: it results from two or more *plies* twisted together. Many *novelty yarns* are ply yarns consisting of a *core,* a *decorative* or *effect yarn,* and a *binder* (Fig. 132). They are characterized by spaced irregularities of size, twist, or effect (Fig. 133). Among the more common novelty yarns are:

pet warp), nubby (bouclé), velvety (chenille), shiny (monofilament rayon), or dull (spun silk).

Metallics, such as gold and silver, are produced in sheets, then cut into fine, flat strips.

Dyes and Finishes

The fiber composition of a yarn has a marked effect on the degree to which it will accept a dye. As indicated in the table, most natural fibers are dye receptive; however, animal and vegetable fibers will often absorb dyes at different rates. Therefore, if fibers of varying composition, such as silk (protein) and linen (cellulose) are spun or twisted together, the resulting yarn will not dye evenly. Some man-made fibers cannot be dyed at all, and so color must be introduced into the chemical solution before the fibers are extruded. A complete discussion of yarn dyeing appears in Chapter 17.

In recent decades scientists have developed a great many chemical finishes to enhance fiber properties. While most of these are intended for use on completed fabrics, a few can be applied to yarns. *Mercerization* improves the luster, dyeability, and strength of cotton. (*Perle* cotton is a ply yarn twisted from two single mercerized yarns.) Wool yarns can be treated with mothproofing compounds or with finishes designed to retard shrinkage. Other finishes introduce luster, stretch, or resistance to fire. Before purchasing a yarn, the weaver should be aware of the finishes employed in its manufacture.

Yarn Properties

Despite the wide variety of "miracle" fibers available, most handweavers still rely heavily on the basic four: wool, linen, cotton, and silk (Fig. 135). Wool yarns may bear special labels that indicate the previous life of the fiber. *Virgin wool* is new wool that has never before been made into yarn. Included in this category is *lamb's wool,* which has been clipped from sheep less than eight months old. *Reprocessed wool* has been reclaimed from fabric scraps that were never used,

Slub yarns, which are left untwisted at different intervals to produce bulky areas (Fig. 134);

Ratiné and *guimpe yarns,* in which a bulky yarn is looped around a core yarn, with the two held in place by a binder;

Bouclé yarns, similar to ratiné and guimpe, but with wider spacing between the loops;

Nub or *knob yarns,* in which the decorative yarn is wrapped repeatedly around the core yarn at a given point to form an enlarged segment;

Seed yarns, which have smaller nubs;

Corkscrew yarns, created by twisting together yarns of different diameters, sizes, or fiber content, or by varying the speed or direction in which the yarns are twisted;

Chenille yarns, narrow strips cut from a special fabric;

Flake yarns, to which small tufts of fiber have been added at irregular intervals;

Loop yarns, in which a curling effect yarn is held in place around a core by a binder yarn.

In addition to these standard designations, yarns are often subjectively described as smooth (car-

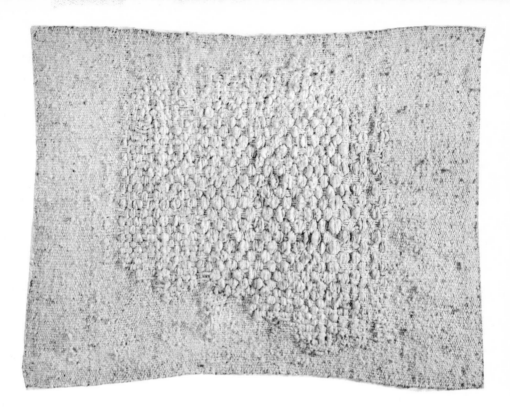

perhaps from remnants of material cut for sewing. The fabric is shredded and respun into yarn. *Reused wool* or *shoddy* is wool reclaimed from used fabric, such as rags or second-hand clothing. Both reused wool and reprocessed wool are lower in quality—notably in strength—than virgin wool. In most cases they are not worth the time and energy expended in a handwoven project.

Silk yarns, too, fall into different categories. *Tussah silk,* also called *wild silk,* is obtained from the cocoons of uncultivated silkworms found in India and Assam. The fiber has a pale brown tint. *Raw silk* has not been degummed, so it still contains the sericin secreted by the insect. Raw silk yarns produce a fabric that is rather stiff and has a tendency to waterspot. A *thrown silk* yarn is a ply yarn into which twist has been inserted. It is not as lustrous as the original silk filament.

For centuries man has been intrigued with the idea of incorporating fireproof asbestos into textiles. According to one legend, Charlemagne took great delight in astonishing his guests by throwing a tablecloth woven from asbestos into the fire and then removing it unharmed. The functional fireplace illustrated in Figure 136 shows one possible, if slightly eccentric, application of the fiber to handweavers.

above: 135. SHEILA HICKS. *White Letter.* 1962. Plain-weave wool with four-side selvedge finish, 38 × 47½″. Museum of Modern Art, New York (gift of Knoll Associates).

below: 136. BONNIE MACGILCHRIST. *Soft Fireplace.* 1970. Handwoven bands of asbestos fiber, 12 × 3′. Courtesy California Design XI, Pasadena, Calif.

The earliest synthetic fibers were developed in an attempt to imitate the natural fibers. In fact, when rayon was introduced in the latter half of the 19th century, it was called "artificial silk" and was not given a proper name of its own until 1924. Serious research in man-made fibers was undertaken during the 1930s, but it was not until World War II, when the supply of silk was cut off and the demand for fibers in military applications was enormous, that experimentation became reality. After the war, the new fibers were made available to the general public, and acceptance was immediate. Instead of trying to simulate the natural fibers, manufacturers stressed the *superior* qualities of their product. For example, nylon, which is nonabsorbent, has practical applications for rainwear and other items in which water resistance is important. Its mothproof quality has fostered the development of coarse, heavy yarns for carpeting. Nylon possesses far greater elasticity than silk or wool, so it is often used in stretch yarns.

Serious competition from man-made fibers has prompted the manufacturers of natural yarns to reassess their potential. As a result, the usefulness of natural fibers has been greatly extended, chiefly through the development of new finishes.

Yarn Sizes

At present there is no widely accepted uniform system for measuring yarn size or *count;* different standards are applied to the various fibers.

Filament yarns—that is, silk and all the man-made fibers—are measured in deniers (Fig. 137), a *denier* being equivalent to the weight in grams of 9000 meters of yarn. A 30-denier yarn is three times as large as a 10 denier. Thus, in dealing with filament yarns, the greater the number, the *coarser* the yarn.

Staple fiber yarns reverse this process: the greater the number, the *finer* the yarn (Fig. 138). Such yarns are measured according to the number of *hanks* required to make 1 pound of yarn. A hank of *cotton* equals 840 yards. Therefore, the coarsest cotton singles yarn is labeled 1s, since one hank alone will weigh a pound. A 3s yarn would be one-third as coarse, and so on. Ply yarns are designated by two numbers separated by a slash. A yarn marked 5/3, for instance, is a *size* 5, *3-ply* yarn.

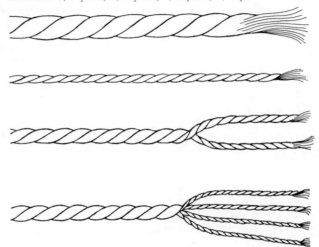

above: 137. Filament-fiber yarns, including silk and most synthetics, are measured in deniers; the greater the number, the coarser the yarn. *top to bottom:* 1-denier yarn, 3-denier yarn.

below: 138. For staple-fiber yarns, the greater the number, the finer the yarn. The numerator in the fraction indicates the singles yarn size, the denominator the ply number. *top to bottom:* 1/1 yarn, 4/1 yarn, 4/2 yarn, 8/4 yarn.

The same system pertains to other spun yarns, except that the unit of measure varies. A hank of *worsted* yarn equals 560 yards; a hank of *woolen* yarn equals 300 yards when indicated in cuts, 1600 yards when indicated in runs; a hank of *spun silk* equals 840 yards. For *linen* yarns the unit of measure is a *lea,* equivalent to 300 yards.

NONYARN MATERIALS

The contemporary handweaver is by no means restricted to the use of classic yarns. He is free to experiment with many different kinds of nonfibrous materials, both natural and synthetic, in order to achieve the expression he seeks. Corn husks, cattails, seed pods, horsehair, seaweed, river cane, feathers (Fig. 139), grasses (Fig. 140), and pine needles are only a few of the possibilities among the natural materials.

Native materials vary according to the geographical region and the season of the year in which they are collected (Fig. 141). Some of

above: 139. Dominic Di Mare. *Sculptural Form.* 1966. Linen, jute, wool, and feathers; 7' × 5'10" × 1'10". From *Objects: USA,* Johnson Wax Collection of Contemporary Crafts, Racine, Wis.

above right: 140. Thelma Becherer. Wall hanging, detail. 1961. Velon plastic warp, three types of Long Island grass heads in weft; 5' × 1'9". Courtesy Hadassah Rothgart, New York.

right: 141. Many native materials can be incorporated in a weaving.

Materials for Weaving   87

these, such as common milkweed, are best harvested in late summer or fall, while others can be gathered at any time. Native materials must be dried thoroughly before they can be used in order to shrink them and to prevent mold. Drying away from light will help to preserve the color. Before weaving, the materials should be remoistened to make them pliable. Cattails, grasses, and similar plants can be treated with glycerin to maintain their suppleness. A coating of clear plastic will retard insect damage. A few suggestions for gathering and handling native materials are listed below.

Corn husks can be gathered in any season, but if they are collected at the normal harvesting time, they are already dried. They can be used in their natural state or dyed. The inner husks are most desirable. To restore their pliability, the dried husks should be placed for several hours in a sealed plastic bag to which some moisture has been added. During the weaving process the cloth beam of the loom must be protected from dampness with newspapers or plastic. The woven fabric cannot be left too long on the loom, for the corn husks will mildew.

Cattails must be gathered as soon as possible after they have reached optimum size. Small heads will be found in late June or early July.

Rushes should be harvested during the summer months, before they grow brown and brittle.

left: 142. MILDRED FISCHER. *Elokuu.* 1967. Linen yarns and transparent celanese strips, 4'7" × 2'6". Courtesy the artist.

above: 143. ED ROSSBACH. *Construction with Newspaper and Plastic.* 1968. Polyethylene film, polyethylene twine, and newsprint; 40 × 30". Courtesy the artist.

Sedges are recognized by their triangular stems. For weaving purposes they are best collected in summer.

Grasses suitable for weaving include wheat, rye, oats, timothy, tall reed grass, sweet vernal grass, and bromegrass. Most will accept dyes. The grains should be collected when they are ripe (in July), before they are combined or broken by baling.

Milkweed is usable in either the swamp or the common form.

Dogbane provides a fiber from its inner bark. It is best gathered in summer.

Willow shoots can be harvested either in spring or in fall. If white shoots are desired, they should be gathered in the spring, after the sap begins to flow and the buds swell. Shoots harvested in the fall will be tan.

Blue stem grass (original Illinois prairie grass) is best collected in the fall.

Feathers of many sorts, including white chicken or turkey feathers, will accept dyes. Pheasant feathers have an interesting variety of colors in their natural state.

Pine needles can be gathered at any time of the year. It is best to remove them directly from the tree, but the brown needles on the ground are satisfactory. The long-leaved needles of the southeastern United States have more character and are easier to work with than the shorter Midwestern needles.

In order to fulfill the requirements of a special project, the handweaver may have recourse to an endless variety of synthetic materials. Among these are wire, nails, strips of Plexiglas or acetate (Fig. 142), plastic, newspaper (Fig. 143), beads, chain, and ceramic pieces. No material, regardless of its size, shape, composition, color, or degree of rigidity, can be conclusively eliminated as a possibility for weaving.

7

Tools and Equipment

It takes a beginner that doesn't know a thing won't work to come up with something that's just right.

Berta Frey

Weaving can be accomplished without any tools at all. Primitive man learned to weave long before he had invented the loom. However, it is a tedious business, and the outcome may not be very satisfactory. The contemporary handweaver has at his disposal a wide variety of precision looms and other equipment to aid the weaving process and encourage professional results.

THE LOOM

In its most elementary form the loom consists of a framework to hold the warp yarns rigid while the weft is interlaced. Despite the complexity of modern looms, only two refinements, essentially, have been added to this simple structure: a *shedding* device, to raise or lower certain warp threads so that the weft can be inserted; and a *beating* device, to push the weft into position. A loom is like a piano: one must *learn* to play it, and only when its full potential is understood can the weaver feel free to create. Few looms come equipped with operating instructions, and often they lack directions for assembly. Therefore, even the beginning weaver must be thoroughly familiar with the parts of a loom and their functions. Once mastered, the individual elements should be easily recognizable on any loom.

Parts of the Basic Loom

Figure 144 is a diagram of the basic loom with each of its parts indicated.

The Frame   The frame is the superstructure of the loom. It holds the warp yarns in tension and supports the moving parts of the loom. Among its components are:

1. The *warp beam,* which stores the warp until it is needed. The warp beam is equipped with a *ratchet* to hold it stationary, thus regulating the tension of the warp yarns. When additional warp is needed, the weaver releases the ratchet and rolls the warp beam forward.
2. The *back beam,* a rigid beam that supports the warp and maintains its horizontal position.
3. The *breast beam,* an equivalent support at the front of the loom.
4. The *cloth beam,* which stores the web after it has been woven. The cloth beam also has a

ratchet, which maintains warp tension when a section of completed web is to be taken up onto the cloth beam.

5. The *castle*, the uppermost part of the loom, which supports the harnesses.

The Shedding Mechanism The shedding mechanism incorporates all the parts necessary to create a *shed*, the space between spread warps through which the weft is thrown. It includes:

1. The *heddles* (Fig. 145), vertical cords or strips of metal. Each has an *eye* in the center, and an individual warp yarn is threaded through each eye. Occasionally, two or more yarns are passed through a single heddle. In aluminum or steel heddles the length of the eye varies from $\frac{1}{4}$ to $\frac{1}{2}$ inch; if linen cord is used to make heddles, the opening can be as large as the weaver requires.

It sometimes happens that an extra heddle is required in the middle of a harness, perhaps because the weaver has made an error in threading. In this case, a *corrective heddle* (Fig. 145) can be snapped into place, or a string heddle can be added. To make a string heddle one uses a piece of linen carpet warp 3 or 4 inches longer than twice the height of the heddle frame. The cord is looped over the bottom of the frame (Fig. 146), tied in an overhand knot at the bottom and top of the eye, and then knotted securely on the top of the frame. The string should be fairly taut, so that the eye will remain in line with those of the other heddles. The extra length of cord is trimmed off.

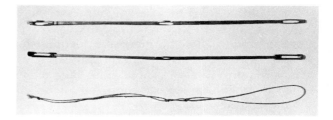

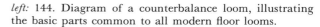

left: 144. Diagram of a counterbalance loom, illustrating the basic parts common to all modern floor looms.

above: 145. A heddle is a knotted cord or strip of metal with an eye in the center through which an individual warp yarn—or occasionally more than one yarn—is threaded before weaving. *Top to bottom:* metal heddle; corrective heddle, which can be snapped in place in the center of a harness without disturbing the adjacent heddles; string heddle.

below: 146. A string heddle is made from linen carpet warp looped over the bottom of the harness, tied in an overhand knot at the bottom and top of the eye, and knotted securely over the top of the harness.

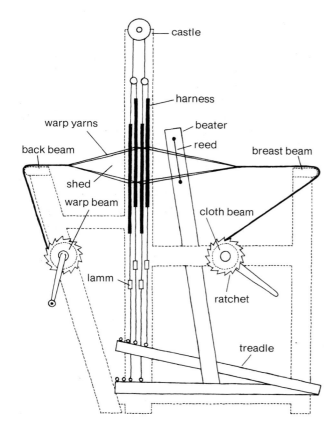

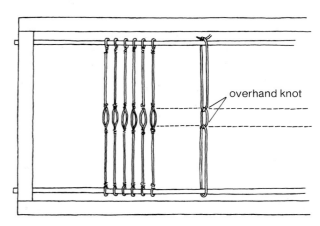

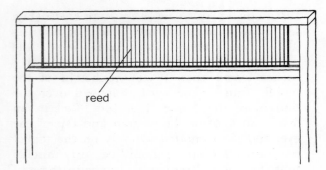

147. The beater of the loom, with a reed in position.

2. The *harnesses* or *heddle frames,* which support the heddles. The number of harnesses on a given loom controls the complexity of weaves it can produce. Two harnesses are adequate for plain weave, while an elaborate pattern weave may require twenty or more. Four- and eight-harness looms are most commonly used by handweavers.
3. The *treadles,* foot levers that raise and lower the harnesses.
4. The *lamms,* bars that connect the harnesses to the treadles.

The Beating Mechanism   The beating mechanism (Fig. 147) orders the warp yarns, regulates their density, and packs the weft yarns into position. It has two parts:

1. The *reed,* a comblike device, parallel to the harnesses, through which the warp yarns are threaded after they leave the heddles. Its function is to keep the warp yarns perfectly aligned. The spaces in the reed are called *dents.* They vary in concentration from four per inch to forty or more.
2. The *beater,* a framework that holds the reed. It is attached to either the top or the bottom of the loom by a pair of uprights, which allow it to swing freely. After each new shot of weft

yarn has been passed through the shed, the beater is pulled against the web in such a way that the reed packs the new weft against the previous one.

Evolution of the Loom

When weaving was accomplished entirely by hand, rushes were laid lengthwise on the ground and lifted alternately to allow the weft to be threaded across. The first improvement on this system was a method of holding the warp yarns taut. Primitive man undoubtedly drove two stakes into the ground and stretched his warp between them. Such a "loom" was eminently portable—or even disposable—a serious consideration for the nomadic peoples of the Stone Age. A variation on this simple device was the Solomon Islands hand loom (Fig. 148), a slit piece of wood held apart by two vertical wooden props and tied at the ends to prevent further separation. The warp was a continuous bast fiber wound around the center section of the loom. A crude needle assisted the weaver's fingers in inserting the weft threads at right angles to the stretched warp.

The Warp-weighted Loom   The vertical warp-weighted loom was an outgrowth of the twining process (pp. 15–16). It appeared first in Egypt during the second millennium B.C. and was eventually adopted by the Swiss Lake Dwellers, the Greeks, the Romans, the Scandinavians, and the Indians of North and South America (Figs. 7, 27, 48, 52). The loom consisted of a horizontal beam—supported at either end by a vertical post—around which the warp threads were tied. As a rule, each warp yarn or group of yarns was weighted at the bottom with a stone

below: 148. The Solomon Islands hand loom, a very simple loom with no heddles or harnesses.

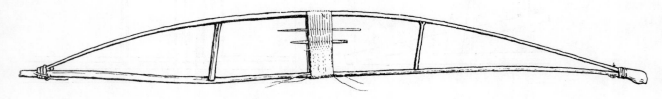

Plate 10. WILLIAM MORRIS design, executed at Merton Abbey by Morris & Company. *The Woodpe*cker. 1885. Wool tapestry, 9'7" x 5'. William Morris Gallery, London.

left: Plate 11. DOROTHY LIEBES. Hand-woven blinds, detail. 1952. Rayon, cotton, and braided metallic yarns, with Oriental reeds and painted wood dowels. Courtesy Museum of Contemporary Crafts, New York.

below: Plate 12. MAGDALENA ABAKAN-OWICZ. *Abakan Red III*. 1968–71. Sisal tapestry, 9 x 12 x 9′. Courtesy the artist.

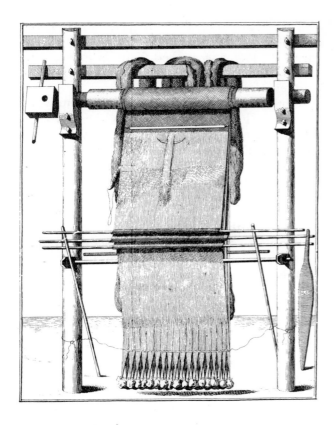

left: 149. Vertical warp-weighted loom used in 18th-century Iceland. From Olaus Olavius, *Oeconomisk Reise igiennem de nordvestlige, nordlige, og nordostlige Kanter af Island,* Dresden and Leipzig, 1780.

Uprights were constructed from available timber at the new location. Warp-weighted looms are probably still used in isolated parts of Lapland and in other remote areas.

The Backstrap Loom   Among the simplest of horizontal looms is the backstrap loom (Fig. 377), in which the warp yarns are held taut between a tree or other fixed object and the body of the weaver (pp. 209–213). A strap or band attached to the loom is passed around the weaver's waist in such a way that tension in the warp yarns can be controlled by a simple shift of weight. Originally, weaving was done with the fingers alone, but more advanced backstrap looms employ heddle rods and separators to create the shed, as well as a beater stick to pack the weft yarns into position. The backstrap loom was common among the Indians of Peru during the pre-Inca period (Fig. 150). It is still used by native peoples

or a piece of metal. A shed rod and a heddle rod facilitated changing of the shed. In the Greek version of the loom (Fig. 52) weaving proceeded from the top downward, and the warp beam revolved, so that as sections of web were completed, they could be rolled up over the beam. Herodotus referred to the making of cloth by "pushing the woof upwards." Both the Romans and the New Kingdom Egyptians (Fig. 48) used a type of loom in which the warp yarns were weighted by another horizontal beam at the bottom. Weaving proceeded upwards, and the weft was beat into place by a comb that was the ancestor of our modern-day reed.

The Icelandic loom illustrated in Figure 149 is an 18th-century version of the Greek warp-weighted loom. It is equipped with three heddle rods and two shed rods. When the shed was to be changed, a heddle rod was lifted to raise selected warp yarns, and the movable shed rod was inserted, followed by a bobbin containing the weft yarn. Such a loom was quite practical for the nomadic Lapps. When they moved, they carried only the warp beam and heddle rods.

below: 150. Pottery from the pre-Inca period, Peru, with representations of weaving on the backstrap loom. British Museum, London.

or lowered alternately to change the shed. A reed controlled the horizontal spacing of the warp yarns. Pit looms were used in India for weaving cotton. They are the ancestor of the modern counterbalance loom (Fig. 158).

Another type of horizontal ground loom is the *tripod loom* (Fig. 153), still used by the natives of Liberia for weaving their narrow bands of country cloth. This loom provides a more efficient method for separating the warps: it is equipped with string heddles and a reed beater. The tripod supports the heddle frames, while tension in the warp is maintained by a stake driven into the ground at either end. When sticks, performing as treadles, are attached to the heddle frames, the tripod loom functions much like a more complex counterbalance loom.

Horizontal Frame Looms   The horizontal frame loom was known in ancient Egypt, but it may have been invented in China much earlier. Although many refinements have been added over the centuries, in operating principle it was identical to the common floor loom used today. A complex version of the horizontal frame loom—with treadle-operated harnesses, a reed beater, and a movable warp beam—appeared in

of Southeast Asia and the Americas, including the Navajo of Arizona and New Mexico and the Indians of Mexico (Fig. 151).

Horizontal Ground Looms   It is not known precisely when the horizontal ground loom was developed. Such a loom provides for a fixed support at *both* ends of the warp, thus freeing the weaver physically from the loom. One version was the *pit loom* (Fig. 152), so called because it was designed to be placed over a pit dug in the ground. The weaver sat on the ground at a level with the loom, while his feet, in the pit, operated the treadles. Each warp yarn had its own heddle. The heddles were divided into two groups and suspended from two shafts, which could be raised

above: 151. Backstrap weaving of belts and bands, Tetelcingo, Morelos, Mexico.

right: 152. The pit loom, as used in India, one form of horizontal ground loom.

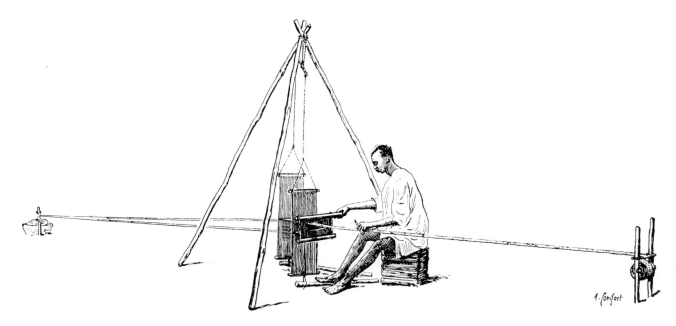

Europe by the 13th century, but its mechanisms must have been perfected long before. Hans Holbein's conception of *Penelope at the Loom* (Fig. 154) suggests the type of instrument employed by Renaissance weavers. Even after the Industrial Revolution much cloth was woven on the horizontal frame loom in nonindustrialized parts of Europe (Fig. 155).

above: 153. The tripod loom, used in various parts of Africa for making narrow bands of cloth.

below left: 154. HANS HOLBEIN THE YOUNGER. *Penelope at the Loom,* marginal drawing in *Moraiae Encomium (Praise of Folly)* by Desiderius Erasmus. 1515. Kunstmuseum, Basel.

below right: 155. LUDWIG VOGEL. *Two Women Weaving in the "Schachental," Canton of Uri, Switzerland.* 19th century. Pencil drawing, $8\frac{7}{8} \times 8\frac{3}{8}$″. Swiss National Museum, Zurich.

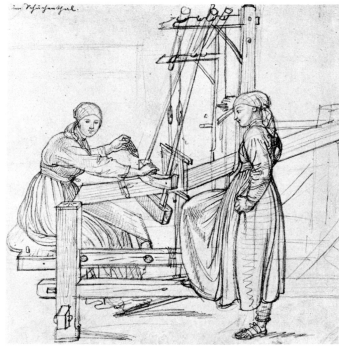

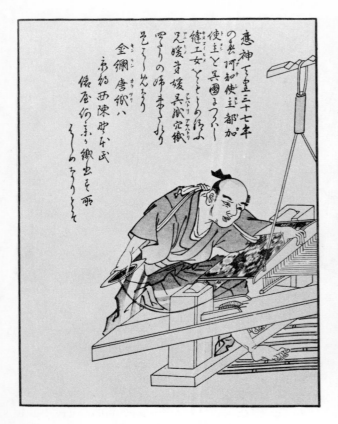

The Draw Loom   The draw loom was invented in China about the time of the birth of Christ. As the Japanese print in Figure 156 illustrates, it was a two-man loom: the master weaver manipulated the heddle frames and threw the shuttle, while his assistant (the *drawboy*), stationed at the top of the loom, controlled individual warp yarns, independent of the heddle frames. This system permitted amazing intricacy of pattern. Each warp yarn was attached to a cord run through a comber board to the top of the loom. On command from the weaver, the drawboy, in marionettelike fashion, could raise any warp or group of warps, thus providing infinite variety in the shed.

Along with the knowledge of sericulture, the draw loom migrated westward. All the elaborate pattern weaves of the Renaissance and Baroque periods were created on a European version of the draw loom. Until 1733 the maximum fabric width was about 22 inches, but in that year John and Robert Kay introduced the fly shuttle, which made it possible to weave fabrics in

greater widths. The Kays' invention also speeded the weaving process considerably. The draw loom was used in Europe until the end of the 18th century, when it was replaced by the Jacquard loom.

The Jacquard Loom   When a new device has been introduced, it is not unusual for one individual's name to become associated with it, even though many people may have contributed their ingenuity. Such was the case with the Jacquard loom, the first pattern loom to operate successfully on a mechanized basis. As far back as 1725 Basile Bonchon had experimented with perforated paper as a means of selecting the cords to be raised on a draw loom. In 1745, Jacques de Vaucanson improved the mechanism by adding a *griffe*, a metal bar that could be cranked up or down, carrying with it those wires selected by

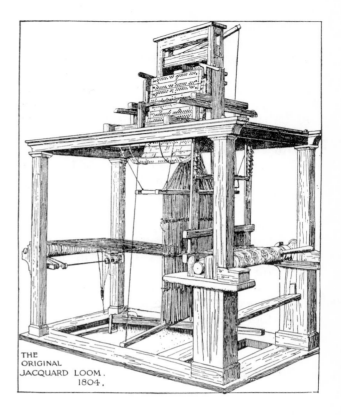

THE ORIGINAL JACQUARD LOOM. 1804.

Bonchon's perforations. Vaucanson is also credited with placing the entire apparatus on the top of the loom, a position it still occupies today.

Joseph Marie Jacquard was born in 1752 at Lyons, France. His first textile innovation seems to have been a machine for weaving net, which captured the prize in a London competition. Jacquard thought little of his invention and forgot about it, until he was suddenly arrested on orders from Napoleon. He was taken to Paris and charged with, in effect, technological blasphemy, for having pretended "to do that which God Almighty cannot do, tie a knot in a stretched string." To clear himself of the charge, Jacquard built a model of his machine. This so impressed his interrogators that he was asked to examine a loom—probably one built on Vaucanson's principle—that had failed to weave satisfactorily certain rich fabrics intended for the Emperor's personal use. Jacquard succeeded in correcting the flaws, and in 1806 the French government accepted what came to be known as the Jacquard loom (Fig. 157). The French weavers, on the other hand, did not take kindly to the appearance of yet another machine that would eliminate their jobs. Upon his return to Lyons, Jacquard was greeted with such hostility that on three occasions he barely escaped with his life. His machine was destroyed, and, in his own words, "the wood was sold as wood and the iron as iron while the inventor was delivered over to universal ignominy."[1] Jacquard died in poverty in 1834. Inevitably, the advantages of mechanized pattern weaving soon overwhelmed the weavers' objections. The loom ultimately brought great prosperity to the city of Lyons.

The Jacquard loom operates on the same principle as a player piano or a modern computer. Each warp yarn is connected, by means of a cord or *lease,* to a metal needle. A series of cards, one for each weft shot, are punched with holes in a preordained pattern. The cards are then arranged in sequence and laced together to pass through the machine. As each card comes into position, only those needles corresponding to the holes in the card are released, thus raising the warp yarns attached to those particular needles to create a shed. Any combination of warp yarns can be raised. The weft is shot through, the card moves on, and a new card takes its place for the next shed. When all the cards are used, the series begins again and the pattern is repeated.

Compared to the draw loom, the Jacquard loom is astonishingly fast. The huge industrial models are capable of 160 weft shots per minute. Furthermore, once the shedding sequence has been determined and the cards arranged in order, operation is completely automatic. The Jacquard loom is used for damasks, brocades, brocatelles, and patterned ribbons.

Modern Hand Looms

Three types of looms are in common use among handweavers today. Of these, two are floor looms, equipped with treadles connected to the harnesses. The weaver thus controls the changing of the shed with his feet, leaving his hands free to throw the shuttle and beat the weft.

The harnesses in a *counterbalance loom* (Fig. 158) operate in tandem: as one harness is raised, the connecting harness is lowered. Thus, to create any shed, *all* the warp yarns must depart from the horizontal—some above it and some below. As a rule, counterbalance looms are available with either two harnesses or four, but some have six or eight.

With a *jack loom* (Fig. 159) each harness functions independently; when one set of harnesses is raised, the others remain stationary. Jack looms are made with four harnesses or more.

A *table loom* (Fig. 160) requires that all weaving operations be performed with the hands. In place of treadles, the table loom has a set of levers connected to the harnesses, so that in order to change the shed, the weaver must drop the shuttle and manipulate a lever at the side of the loom or on the castle. Most table looms have either two or four harnesses, but some have as many as twenty.

Selecting a Loom

A loom is the most elaborate and costly piece of equipment a weaver must purchase. It is a lifetime investment, for a sturdy and well-constructed loom should give efficient service for decades. There are many factors to be weighed in buying a loom. Perhaps the most compelling are the space available, the cost, and—most important—the kind of work the weaver intends to do. The craftsman interested primarily in finger weaves will probably select a tapestry loom (Fig. 300). It is cheaper, requires less floor space, and will perform satisfactorily for a number of techniques. However, once this possibility has been eliminated, several variables must be considered.

Type of Loom The weaver who expects to have only one loom should—if space and money permit—select a floor loom. Table looms are perfectly adequate for weaving samples that are later to be worked up on a floor loom, but the necessity of dropping the shuttle to change the shed makes it difficult to achieve rhythm in weaving. Of course, if one's space is very limited, or if portability is desirable, the table loom may be the best choice.

There are certain differences in performance between a counterbalance loom and a jack. The counterbalance loom is quite efficient when one is treadling two harnesses against two, but it is

158. Leclerc 4-harness counterbalance floor loom. On a counterbalance loom, the harnesses operate in tandem; as one harness is raised, the connecting harness is lowered.

below: 160. Artcraft 4-harness table loom.

less so when only one harness or three are to be raised. In the latter event, the jack loom is easier to operate. Therefore, the weaver may find himself slightly hampered when he attempts a more complicated weave on the counterbalance loom.

Number of Harnesses   Most handweavers find that four or eight harnesses are sufficient for the kinds of projects they will undertake. Plain weave requires only a two-harness loom, but, naturally, the more intricate the weave, the greater the number of harnesses one must have. The craftsman who is interested in experimenting with elaborate patterns would not select a counterbalance loom. Some four-harness jack looms have space for adding another set of four when money permits. Such a loom is highly practical for the weaver who anticipates expanding his horizons.

In addition to pattern complexity, the number of harnesses also affects the density of a potential fabric. For example, if a very dense—that is, a very tightly woven—fabric is to be constructed from relatively fine yarns, a great many warp yarns, and therefore a great many heddles, would be required. A two-harness loom might not be able to accommodate the necessary heddles.

Distribution of the warp yarns onto several harnesses also lessens the weight on each treadle. A four-harness loom should have six treadles, while an eight-harness should be equipped with at least twelve.

Width of the Web   The size of a loom is designated not by its overall dimensions but by the maximum width of the fabric that can be woven upon it. In other words, a 36-inch loom can produce a web up to 36 inches wide, but the framework of the loom might measure anywhere from 42 inches to 48 inches across. Loom sizes vary from 20 to 60 inches, with a 32-inch maximum for table looms. A web greater than 45 inches in width requires considerable strength on the part of the weaver merely to depress the treadles and throw the shuttle.

Cost   It is always folly to economize on the price of a loom. When buying a loom, particularly a first loom, the weaver should invest in the finest one he can afford. A good machine, made by a nationally or internationally known manufacturer, will almost invariably prove more satisfactory than a bargain, for in the latter case standard parts may be impossible to obtain.

A jack loom is more expensive than a counterbalance loom, which in turn is more expensive than a table loom of the same size. The price, as a rule, is directly related to the loom width and the number of harnesses.

Patterns are available from which the weaver can construct his own loom, but this is seldom advisable. Even a fine wood craftsman might have difficulty in achieving the correct balance and proportion of parts that is essential to smooth operation. Furthermore, the cost of labor and materials almost equals that of a readymade commercial loom.

Some of the major loom manufacturers are listed in Appendix C.

Type of Beater   Depending on the way the loom is constructed, the beater may pivot from either the top or the bottom. Weavers disagree about which type is easier to handle, but the balance seems to be slightly in favor of the type that swings from the bottom of the loom. One can develop a comfortable rhythm with either version.

The beater should have a removable reed, so that other sizes can be substituted if necessary. Most looms are equipped with a fifteen-dent reed—that is, fifteen dents to the inch. For extremely fine or coarse yarns, a different size may be more convenient. Reed sizes range from four dents per inch to thirty or more, but the average weaver has little occasion to use a reed with a greater concentration of dents than fifteen or twenty per inch.

Many looms are equipped with a *shuttle race,* a horizontal extension at the base of the reed along which the shuttle can travel. This accessory is particularly helpful when the warp yarns are widely spaced, for it prevents the shuttle from falling through to the floor.

Type of Frame   A good loom should be constructed from close-grained hardwood with a smooth surface. Folding looms are practical when space is at a premium—many can be collapsed even when threaded—or when portability is desirable, but they are, of course, not as sturdy as rigid looms.

Heddle threading is easier and more comfortable when the breast beam is removable, for the weaver can then sit closer to the harnesses. The distance between the breast beam and the harnesses should be at least 18 inches to ensure a clean shed and even tension.

Some looms have sectional warp beams, with pegs at 2-inch intervals (Fig. 203). This arrangement is more flexible than a plain beam, since the sectional beam can be used for both standard and sectional warping (see pp. 121–122). Warp beams smaller than 1/2 yard in circumference are impractical. The ratchet wheel releases on the warp and cloth beams should be within easy reach.

When buying a loom, the weaver should, if possible, check the balance of the shed. In a counterbalance loom the rising and sinking warps should form the same angle with the horizontal. This helps to maintain an even tension in the warp.

Kind of Heddles   Steel heddles are preferable to linen ones, because they are more durable and they slip more easily along the heddle frame. In order to accommodate various yarn sizes, the heddle eye should be at least 1/2 inch long. The heddles ought to be detachable from the harness.

OTHER EQUIPMENT

Loom Accessories

Loom Bench   A loom bench (Fig. 161) is not essential, but it is usually more comfortable than a stool, because its height is appropriate to that of the loom. Many loom benches have slanted tops, which in addition to being comfortable encourage the weaver to lean into his work.

A *rug shuttle* is designed to hold a quantity of rug yarn or other heavy weft material.

The *ski shuttle,* a new Scandinavian rug shuttle, is also useful for bulky yarns.

The *boat shuttle,* which contains a bobbin (or, in some cases, two separate bobbins), is most commonly used by handweavers. It is satisfactory for fine weft yarns and adapts well to continuous treadling of the loom, as for yardage, because the yarn is doled out automatically from the bobbin. Bobbins can be made of paper and tape, but purchased bobbins of plastic, metal, wood, or cardboard are more efficient, since they are specially designed to prevent the yarn from falling off the ends.

A *throw shuttle* with a spool is similar in operation to the boat shuttle but will hold a greater quantity of yarn.

Tapestry bobbins, which take the place of a conventional shuttle in finger weaving, are similar to the bobbins used by lacemakers—that is, a shaped dowel form. Flat plastic bobbins for tapestry can also be purchased. If desired, the yarn holders normally used for knitting can serve as

Shuttles   There are many types and sizes of shuttles, each designed to carry the weft yarn for a particular kind of web (Fig. 162). A shuttle containing a *bobbin,* on which the yarn is wound, is more convenient for most textiles, since the yarn unreels smoothly as it is needed. However, in an emergency, a simple flat shuttle can be made from a thin wood strip, a tongue depressor, or tough cardboard.

A *flat* or *stick shuttle* is convenient for bulky yarn or for a narrow web, but it does not release the yarn automatically.

above: 161. Gilmore loom bench.

below: 162. Shuttles are available in various designs to accommodate the weft yarn for different kinds of weaving. *Top to bottom:* flat or stick shuttle, rug shuttle, ski shuttle, open boat shuttle, closed boat shuttle, sword beater.

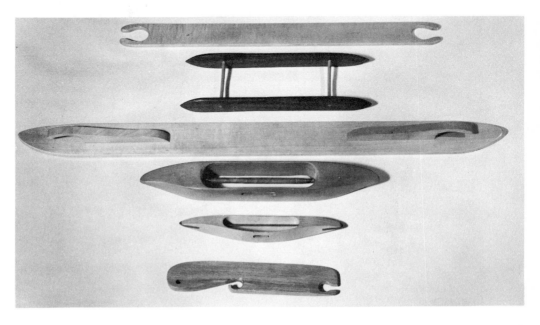

tapestry bobbins, or a bobbin can be made from ½-inch dowel cut into 3 or 4-inch lengths and tapered to a blunt point at one end.

Bobbin Winder   Hand-cranked and electric bobbin winders (Figs. 163, 164) are available to fill the bobbins in a boat shuttle. They can also be used to split a spool of warp yarn into several temporary spools. When guiding the yarn onto an electric winder, it is wise to wrap a small piece of cloth around the yarn to avoid friction burns.

Stretcher   The stretcher (Fig. 165), also called a *temple*, is used to maintain a consistent width in the fabric, particularly for yardage or rugs.

Heddle Transfer Rods   Thin, pliable steel rods called heddle transfer rods are used for adding and removing heddles from the frames. They also make it possible to store the heddles in an organized manner for easy reuse.

Warping Aids

Warping Frame   A *warping frame* or *warping reel* (Figs. 166–168) is required for measuring the warp yarns. Reels are available in both horizontal and vertical models.

Warping Paddle   Warping paddles (Fig. 169) have a series of holes or parallel slots and holes.

below: 163. Swedish hand-cranked bobbin winder.

right: 164. Leclerc electric bobbin winder.

below right: 165. Leclerc stretcher, or temple. A stretcher helps to maintain consistent width of a web.

bottom right: 166. Leclerc warping frame.

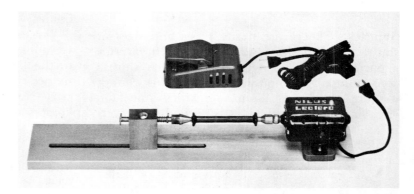

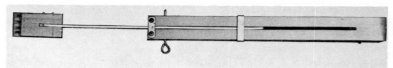

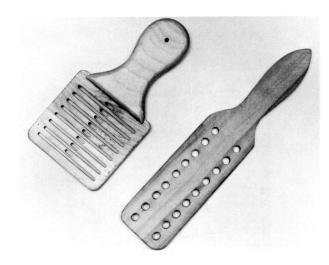

They are employed by experienced weavers to warp a number of yarns simultaneously.

Tension Box A tension box (Fig. 170) is required for sectional warping (see p. 121), in order to impart uniform tension to all the yarns as they are wound onto the loom.

above left: 167. Leclerc vertical warping reel.

below left: 168. Pendleton horizontal warping reel.

above: 169. Two versions of the warping paddle, used for measuring more than three yarns at once on the warping frame or reel.

below: 170. Leclerc tension box. A tension box is essential for maintaining uniform tension in sectional warping.

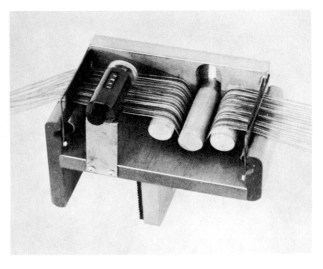

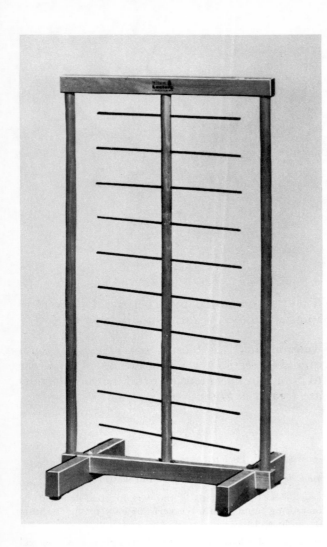

Spool Rack Also called a *warping creel,* the spool rack (Fig. 171) holds the spools or cones of warp yarn during the measuring process. It is essential for sectional warping (see p. 121).

Sleying Hook A sleying hook or *reed hook* (Fig. 172) is needed to thread the warp yarns through the heddle eyes and the dents of the reed. There are two types available. The common reed hook is a long, flat strip of metal notched at one end. This tool is satisfactory for threading both the heddles and the reed. The Swedish reed hook, on the other hand, is an **S**-shaped piece of metal or plastic. Too wide to thread the heddles, the latter instrument is more efficient for threading the reed, since it has no sharp hook that might split the yarns. If a Swedish reed hook is used for the dents, a fine crochet hook will serve to thread the heddles.

Swift An *umbrella swift* or a *squirrel cage reel* (Figs. 173, 174) holds a skein of yarn while it is wound onto spools or shuttles. These devices are also practical for winding skeins from balls of yarn in preparation for dyeing.

left: 171. Leclerc spool rack or warping creel.

below left: 172. A sleying hook or reed hook is needed to draw warp yarns through the heddles and the dents in the reed. The S-shape variety can be used only for the reed.

below: 173. Swedish umbrella swift, for winding skeins.

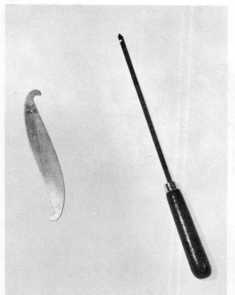

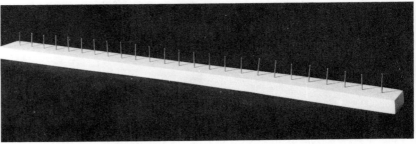

above: 174. Swedish squirrel cage reel, intended for holding skeins of yarn.

top right: 175. Lease sticks serve to maintain the cross.

above right: 176. A spreader divides the warp into inch units.

Lease Sticks   A pair of lease sticks (Fig. 175), made of smooth wood or strips of fiberboard, are placed in the warp yarn immediately after it has been wound to maintain the cross (see p. 110).

Spreader   One can easily construct a spreader (Fig. 176)—also known as a *warping comb* or *raddle*—from available materials. It functions to spread the warp yarns into 1-inch units all across the loom until the warp has been evenly spaced at its full width. A 1-inch by 2-inch strip of pine slightly longer than the loom is wide can be prepared for this purpose by driving a series of finishing nails into the broader surface of the wood at 1-inch intervals.

Miscellaneous Tools

A variety of small implements, not exclusive to weaving, may prove handy from time to time.

1. A knitting needle is useful with some of the finger weaves.
2. A crochet hook, besides helping to thread the heddles, is essential for some finger weaves. The size of the hook would, in the latter case, be determined by the coarseness of the yarns involved. For heddle threading, of course, the crochet hook must be small enough to pass through the eye.
3. Scissors are indispensible and should be kept at hand always. They must be sharp and *never* used for cutting paper.
4. Straight pins are often required to repair broken warp yarns.
5. A yarn needle with a long eye ($\frac{1}{2}$ inch) performs a number of small chores.

Preparation for Weaving 8

One of the pleasant things about weaving is that there are few things that are always right and few things that are always wrong; it is largely a matter of what is convenient for the individual and produces the desired result.

Anonymous

Before weaving can begin, several decisions must be made and a number of preliminary steps carried out. Although there is ample opportunity for variations in pattern once the project is actually on the loom, certain design aspects are necessarily determined in advance and, once established, cannot be changed for that particular web. Such preordained factors include the maximum size of the finished cloth, and therefore the length and width of the warp; the composition of the warp yarns; and the sequence in which the warp yarns are threaded through the heddles and the reed.

When they plan an experimental project, skilled weavers often break some or all of the rules involved in preparing the loom. However, for the average web, employing more-or-less conventional yarns, the following steps are undertaken in sequence:

1. Choose the warp and weft yarns.
2. Calculate the length and width of the warp.
3. Calculate the total quantity of yarn.
4. Wrap the guide string on the warping frame.
5. Warp the required yardage.
6. Secure the cross and choke ties.
7. Chain the warp.
8. Insert the lease sticks in the cross.
9. Spread the warp.
10. Wind the warp.
11. Thread the heddles.
12. Sley the reed.
13. Tie the warp ends at the front of the loom.
14. Check the loom for errors.
15. Prepare the tie-up (floor looms only).
16. Adjust the loom.
17. Fill the shuttle and/or wind the bobbins.
18. Weave the web.

YARN CALCULATIONS

Choosing the Warp and Weft Yarns

The classic web consists of a linen warp and a woolen weft. Through the centuries these two materials have been chosen by weavers all over the world, and the reasons are sound. Linen yarns, which are relatively inelastic, will maintain their proper tension on the loom; their great strength enables them to withstand the wear and tear of constant beating. Woolen yarns, on the other hand, possess neither of these qualities to any marked degree, but strength and rigidity are not needed in the weft. Rather, the superior dyeability of wool makes it ideal for the pattern-carrying element.

The contemporary handweaver need not be hampered by such considerations. Many new yarns, particularly the synthetics, have desirable properties that render them suitable for warp or weft or both. For example, a nylon yarn may be extremely fine yet have more than adequate strength for the warp. Furthermore, a variety of finishes—some applied by the manufacturer, some by the weaver—can be introduced to enhance or change the properties of a yarn. An experienced weaver can successfully use yarn that would cause a beginner trouble.

A warp yarn must be sturdy enough to withstand the tension imposed by the loom and the repeated movement of the reed. However, sturdiness is not synonymous with bulk. Heavy or bulky yarns usually lack strength, because they are slackly twisted. A warp yarn must be twisted more firmly than a weft, in order to hold its shape when stretched. Ply yarns are most often chosen for the warp, and novelty ply yarns can often be used successfully if they are interspersed with more durable fine, smooth yarns. A warp yarn that is particularly hairy may create problems for the novice, for the loose fibers will cause the mass of warps to mat together, and they will not separate readily to open a shed.

Certain fragile yarns can be fortified by *sizing,* in order to render them suitable for the warp. A solution of linseed gluten is boiled to a thick consistency, and the seeds are strained. After the mixture has cooled, skeins of yarn—tied loosely in several places to prevent tangling—are dipped. The excess sizing is pressed out, and the skeins are hung to dry. Before the yarn is completely dry, it should be wound on spools to push the fibers into a compact strand. This procedure also helps to control an excessively hairy yarn.

An alternate sizing mixture can be prepared from 6 quarts of water, $5\frac{1}{4}$ ounces of flour, and $1\frac{3}{4}$ ounces of paraffin. The flour and water are boiled and then removed from the heat; the paraffin is added, and the whole mixture is beaten until it cools. This recipe is adequate for about $4\frac{1}{2}$ pounds of linen yarn. One can either dip the yarn, as with the linseed sizing, or paint the solution directly onto the warps on the loom. If the latter method is used, about twelve hours must be allowed for drying before weaving.

Weft yarn can be practically any size, either single or ply; it can have any degree of twist. Even uncombed, unspun fibers can be laid into a shed and held in place, provided the web is not intended for a garment and is not to be laundered often. Twisted yarns have a tendency to add firmness to the finished cloth.

Calculating the Length and Width of the Warp

Several factors operate to make the finished product considerably smaller in both dimensions than the warp as it is set up on the loom. These factors include:

1. *Loom waste,* the additional warp length necessary for tying on to the cloth beam and for extending through the reed and heddles at the end of the web (the *thrums*). The normal allowance is about $\frac{3}{4}$ yard, or 27 inches. This factor makes it impractical to plan a finished warp length of less than a yard and a half, since the *percentage* of waste is disproportionately high. For example, if one adds a $\frac{3}{4}$-yard waste allowance to a $1\frac{1}{2}$-yard web, the waste is $33\frac{1}{3}$ percent. But if the same allowance is added to a 10-yard warp, the rate of waste drops to less than 7 percent. Some projects, such as wall hangings, can be designed to incorporate the waste as a fringe.

2. *Warp takeup,* the extra amount of warp length necessary to go over and under the weft yarns (Fig. 177). An allowance of 10 percent beyond

177. Warp takeup is the extra warp length consumed as the yarns pass over and under the weft in weaving. A similar yarn allowance is required for the weft as it travels over and under the warp.

the desired length of the web is usually sufficient. However, if either set of yarns is especially heavy, a greater allowance for takeup may be required.

3. *Shrinkage* of the fabric when the loom tension is released, as well as in finishing procedures—steaming, washing, or whatever. Both types of shrinkage are affected by the composition of the fibers involved. The only truly reliable way to predict the amount of shrinkage a fabric will undergo is to weave a small sample from the same yarns and then subject the sample to all the usual finishing procedures, taking careful measurements at each stage. Failing this, an allowance of 10 percent extra warp length should be ample.

Fabric shrinkage can be controlled in a number of ways. A flat, smooth yarn is usually more stable than an irregular or novelty yarn. When yarns of different composition are combined to make a warp, the rate of shrinkage may be uneven. Thus, for example, if rayon and cotton yarns are to be used for a warp, they should be distributed fairly evenly, for a concentration of rayon yarns at one point may cause that area of the web to draw in. Some weavers capitalize on this quality of varying shrinkage to create irregular or crepe effects in parts of the fabric.

4. *Draw-in* or *pull-in* of the web as it is woven. The finished width of the fabric will almost always be slightly narrower than the sleyed width at the reed. An allowance of 5 to 10 percent is usually adequate. However, if the weft is extremely rigid, no allowance for draw-in is necessary.

5. *Hems,* if any, to be added on all sides of the finished web.

The clearest way to demonstrate warp calculations is to give an example. Let us assume that a fabric measuring 10 yards in length and 36 inches in width is to be woven. The *length* of the warp would be calculated in the following way:

length of finished web	10	yards
allowance for warp take-up (10%)	1	yard
allowance for shrinkage (10%)	1	yard
allowance for loom waste (¾ yard)	¾	yard
	$12\frac{3}{4}$	yards

Each warp yarn, therefore, will measure $12\frac{3}{4}$ yards.

The *width* of the warp, as it is set up on the loom, is determined in similar fashion:

width of finished web	36 inches
allowance for draw-in (10%)	3.6 inches
allowance for shrinkage (10%)	3.6 inches
	43.2 inches

Thus, the warp will be about 43 inches wide at the reed. If either the ends or the selvedges are to be hemmed, an extra measure must be allowed for turning.

Once the width of the warp has been established, it is necessary to determine the *number of warp yarns* that will be required. This quantity depends on two factors: (1) the size of the yarn; and (2) the *sett* or density of the planned fabric. A tightly woven web composed of rather fine yarns will, of course, require a great many more warps than an openwork fabric woven from heavy yarns.

If a reasonably firm web is desired, a simple method for calculating the number of warps is to wrap the warp yarn around a small object, such as a pencil or ruler (Fig. 178). The yarns must be laid as close together as possible without overlapping. By counting the number of yarns in an inch of space and dividing by two, one can

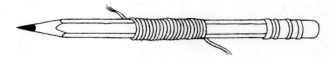

above: 178. One method of calculating the sett, or warp yarns per inch on the loom, is to wrap the yarn closely around a pencil or other small object and then divide the number of yarns per inch by two.

establish the required number of warp yarns per inch and thus, by projection, the total number of warps.

Another system for calculating the number of warps is based upon the size of the reed. If, for example, a number-10 reed is to be used, and a single warp yarn is to be threaded through each dent in the reed, there would be ten warp yarns per inch. Therefore, a web that is 43 inches wide at the reed would require a total of 430 warps ($43 \times 10 = 430$).

Calculating the Total Quantity of Warp and Weft

The total quantity of warp yarn needed can now be determined by simple arithmetic. One merely multiplies the number of warp yarns by the length of each warp. In the example given above, there are 430 warps, each $12\frac{3}{4}$ yards long, so the total amount of warp yarn needed is $5482\frac{1}{2}$ yards ($430 \times 12.75 = 5482.5$).

The total quantity of weft yarn must also be calculated in advance to ensure that there is a sufficient amount of the right colors, textures, and weights on hand to complete the project. If the weave is to be *balanced*—that is, the same number of weft yarns per inch as warp yarns per inch—and if the weft and warp yarns are the same size, then the total quantity of weft yarn equals the total quantity of warp yarn.

For an unbalanced weave or one employing yarns of different sizes, a calculation similar to that for the warp is required. The weaver must first determine the length of each weft yarn, which is equal to the width of the fabric at the reed, plus an allowance of about 10 percent for *weft take-up*—the extra length required for the weft to go over and under the warp. If the warp is 43 inches wide, each weft yarn must be 47.3 inches long ($43 + 4.3 = 47.3$). This figure is multiplied by the approximate number of weft shots the fabric will require. The latter can either be estimated or worked out precisely in a small sample. Let us say there are five weft yarns per inch (180 weft yarns per yard) and the web is to be 12 yards long on the loom. The total number of weft shots will then be 2160 ($180 \times 12 = 2160$). The quantity of weft yarn required will be 102,168 inches or 2838 yards ($2160 \times 47.3 = 102,168$).

The calculation of warp and weft yarns will be simplified for future projects if a precise record, listing all pertinent information, is kept for each web that is woven. With experience, and by evaluating previous webs, the weaver will often be able to estimate the yarn requirement with sufficient accuracy for most projects. A sample Yarn Calculation Form is provided in Appendix B to guide the weaver.

WINDING THE WARP

Warping is a simple enough task, but much of the success of the finished web depends upon the care taken in measuring the warp yarns. In essence, one has only to establish a constant distance—such as the distance between two chairs or around a table top—and wind the yarn around and around until the proper number of warp yarns have been measured. Early weavers wound their yarns around rows of sticks driven into the ground at fixed intervals. Modern warping equipment is not necessarily any more precise than this system, but it eliminates a good deal of walking.

A warping device has two functions: (1) it aids in holding the yarns taut, so that each warp is exactly the same length; and (2) it permits the establishment of the *cross,* the point at which the yarns intersect from opposite directions to maintain their proper sequence throughout the loom-dressing operation. The most common warping aids are the frame and the reel (Figs. 166–168). The latter is more expensive, but it will measure very long warps—greater than 12 yards—which the frame usually cannot. The warping reel can have either a vertical or a horizontal drum to accept the yarn. Since the reel rotates, the operator stands in one spot to manipulate the drum and the yarns. The warping frame can be either a solid board or a four-sided frame with pegs protruding from it. The pegs must be set into the frame securely enough to prevent their turning inward from the tension of the yarns, for if this occurs, the last warps will be somewhat shorter than the first.

Wrapping the Guide String

Warping Reel   The guide string should be of stout cord in a color that contrasts with the warp yarn. It is cut slightly longer than each warp yarn will be, so that it can be knotted at both ends. The string is first tied to the top peg of the reel, and then, as the operator rotates the reel to the left, the string is carried down diagonally to the bottom series of pegs. There should be just enough string to reach the last peg on the bottom. If this is not the case, the angle of descent will have to be adjusted, for the distance from the top to the last bottom peg must equal exactly

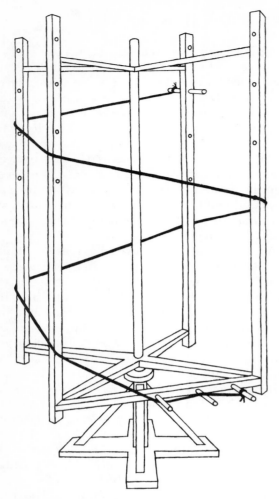

179–180. *The first step in measuring the warp before weaving is to affix a guide string, which establishes a path for the yarn to follow as it is wound on the reel or frame, so that the correct length can be measured.*

left: 179. On the warping reel, the guide string is tied to the uppermost peg and carried down diagonally to the bottom of the reel. The angle of descent is adjusted until the string is exactly the desired length of one warp yarn.

below: 180. On the warping frame, the guide string is initially tied to whichever peg is at a proper distance from the last cross peg to achieve one warp length. The distance between pegs is generally 1 yard.

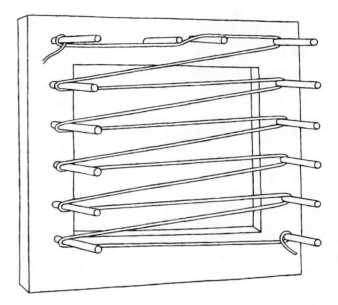

the length of one warp (Fig. 179). When the angle is correct, the guide string is passed *under* the first bottom peg, *over* the center one, and then is tied to the last peg. The guide string must be pushed into the reel so it will not interfere with the yarn.

Warping Frame The procedure for measuring the guide string on a warping frame differs only slightly from that used with the reel. Instead of choosing the *angle* necessary to achieve one warp length in a single circuit, one chooses the *number of pegs* that will be involved (Fig. 180). The pegs on a warping frame are a specified distance apart, often 1 yard. In Figure 180 the guide string is set up to traverse the entire frame, a distance of 11 yards in this case. Should the desired warp be shorter than 11 yards, the operator would begin the guide string on one of the

middle pegs. (The frame in Figure 180 cannot accommodate a warp longer than 11 yards, so a warping reel would be required.)

If more convenient for the weaver, a frame can be set up so that the cross is at the bottom; in this event, the route of the guide string is reversed at the cross.

Warping the Yarn

The warping begins at the end opposite the cross. If, for example, a warping reel is used, and the cross is at the bottom, the yarn is tied to the uppermost peg. Following the route of the guide string, the yarn is brought down to the bottom pegs (Fig. 179); it is run *under* the first peg and *over* the second, then is carried *under* and around the final peg. On the return trip the yarn passes *under* the center and left pegs and continues back to the top of the reel. At this point two complete warp yarns have been measured.

If a warping frame is employed, the yarn is started at whichever peg is at the proper distance from the last cross peg. In Figure 181 the entire frame capacity of 11 yards is to be measured, so warping begins on the peg at bottom right. Again following the guide string, the yarn is zig-zagged across the frame until it reaches the top. It passes around peg A, *over* peg B, *under* peg C, and *under* and around peg D. On the return trip it moves *over* peg C, *under* peg B, and *over* and around peg A, continuing downward to the starting point.

The yarns should never be wound on top of one another but must be laid as close together as possible on the pegs (Fig. 182). It is most important that a smooth, even tension be maintained throughout the winding, so that all warps will be exactly the same length.

If possible, the entire warp should be wound on the same day, because atmospheric conditions may affect the tension. For instance, rayon yarn stretches on damp days, so yarns warped when the humidity is high will be shorter than those measured on a dry day. Wool yarns should not remain stretched on the warping frame or reel any longer than is necessary, for continued tension may impair their elasticity.

When the warp is composed of more than one color or kind of yarn, the new yarn is attached at the original starting peg. It can be tied either to the peg or to the cut-off original yarn. If the first yarn is to be reintroduced later, it is temporarily wrapped around an unused peg to maintain the tension, then unwrapped when it is needed. Should the warp consist of an *uneven* number of yarns, the final warp is cut at the cross end of the frame, and an allowance is left for tying to the loom.

Dressing the loom is easier when the center of the warp has been marked. Therefore, when half the total number of warp yarns have been wound, a cord should be tied around all the warps on the reel or frame. This tie is usually made near the cross and is left in place when the yarn is removed from the frame.

Some weavers like to divide the warp into inch widths as the measuring progresses. Let us say the sett is to be ten warp yarns per inch. When ten yarns have been wound onto the frame or

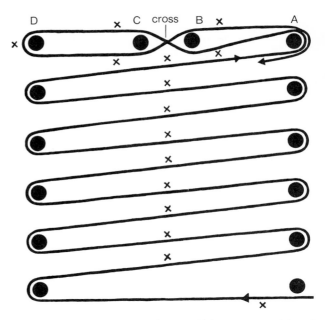

181–182. *The cross is the point at which warp yarns intersect from opposite directions as they are measured. It maintains the sequence of yarns throughout the loom-dressing operation.*

above: 181. To establish the cross on the warping frame, one passes the yarn around peg A, over peg B, under peg C, under and around peg D, over peg C, under peg B, and over and around peg A. The directions can be reversed if a cross is made at the bottom of the frame. A similar procedure is followed on the warping reel.

below: 182. The warp has been properly wound when every other yarn is crossed and when each yarn has been placed next to the previous one, with no overlapping.

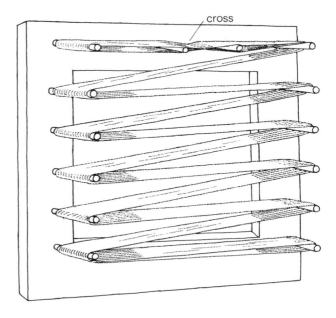

reel (five round trips), a contrasting cord, about a yard long, is draped over the yarns at the bottom and crossed underneath. After another group of ten yarns is wound, the counting cord is crossed again, and so on. When all the warp is measured, the counting cord is tied, and the excess is cut off. If the yarn is not divided during the warping process, it can be counted while dressing the loom.

When an unusually large number of warp yarns is required, the warp will have to be measured in bouts of approximately a hundred yarns to facilitate handling and to prevent the yarns from falling off the pegs. An even number of bouts will automatically indicate the center.

If the warp yarns are consistent in color, texture, and size, the experienced winder can measure from as many as three yarn sources at the same time, thus cutting the warping time to one-third. The yarn is fed from the spools in such a way that each strand passes between two fingers. Therefore, every point at the cross will have three yarns over and three under. Groups of four or more yarns are wound with a paddle.

Paddle Warping In some cases it is desirable to measure yarn from a number of sources simultaneously. This is true when a warp is composed of four or more kinds or colors of yarn in consecutive order. Ordinarily, such a pattern would require that each yarn be cut and tied independently. The warping paddle eliminates this problem.

The warping paddle is an oblong tool made of wood, metal, or plastic, with a handle and about twenty numbered holes. The odd-numbered holes are on the left, the even on the right. To use the paddle, one must first establish the sequence in which the yarns are to be placed on the loom, in a repeat of up to twenty yarns. Next, the spools containing the odd-numbered yarns are arranged on one side of a spool rack, and those holding the even-numbered yarns on the other. The yarns are then threaded through the paddle in order (Fig. 183), yarn number 1 through hole number 1, and so on. The ends are tied together, and the knot is slipped over the starting peg on the frame or reel. The paddle is held between the thumb and forefinger, and the yarn is allowed to run between the ring finger and the little finger.

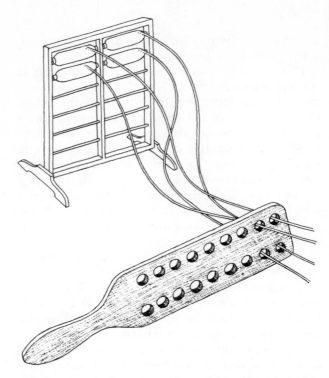

183–188. Paddle warping is a process by which one can measure up to twenty yarns simultaneously on a warping frame or reel, making full provision for the cross. It is particularly efficient when the warp consists of a sequence of yarns.

above: 183. To begin paddle warping, one arranges the spools of yarn in correct order on the spool rack, then threads them through the paddle in the same sequence.

Warping proceeds as usual until the cross is reached. At the first cross peg the paddle is tipped so that the even-numbered yarns go *over* the peg, while the odd-numbered yarns are run *under* it (Fig. 184). At the second peg, the odd-numbered yarns are lifted by hand to go over the peg, while the even yarns run underneath (Fig. 185), thus establishing the cross. All yarns pass over and around the third peg (Fig. 186). On the return trip, the wrist is turned to the right, so that the odd-numbered yarns are uppermost. At the middle peg the number of yarns in the paddle governs the procedure (Fig. 187). Winding an *even* number of yarns, one allows the odd-numbered yarns to float over the peg, with the even-numbered yarns beneath. However, if the number of yarns in the paddle is *uneven*, the even-numbered yarns are lifted over the peg by hand, while the odd-numbered yarns move below. The reverse applies at the third peg (Fig. 188).

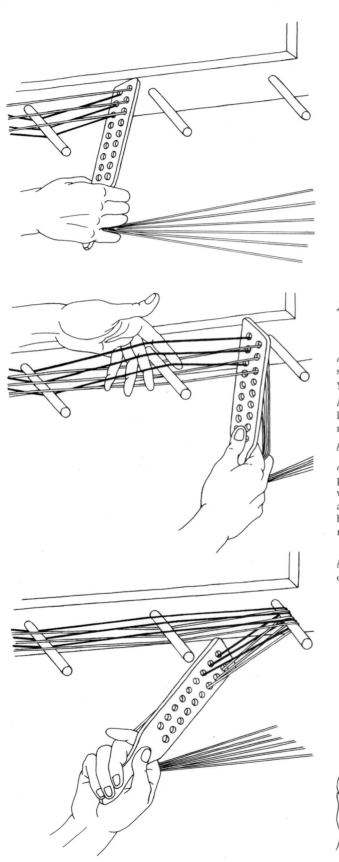

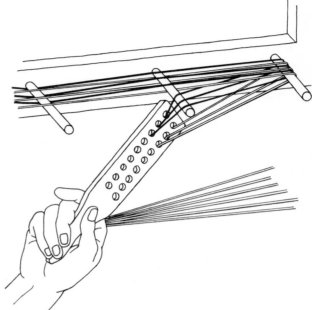

above left: 184. At the first cross peg, the paddle is tipped, so the even-numbered yarns float over, the odd-numbered yarns under.

left: 185. At the middle peg, the odd-numbered yarns are lifted by hand to pass over the peg, while the even-numbered yarns move beneath.

below left: 186. All yarns pass around the third peg.

above: 187. On the return trip, the number of yarns in the paddle governs the procedure at the middle peg. If one is winding an *even* number of yarns, the odd-numbered yarns are allowed to float over the peg, the even-numbered ones beneath. If the number of yarns is *uneven*, the even-numbered yarns are lifted over the peg.

below: 188. The procedure at the final cross peg is the reverse of that followed at the center peg.

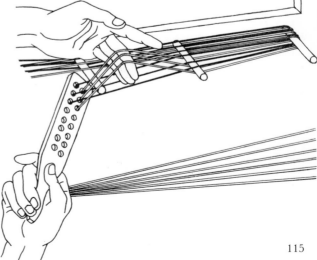

If desired, a second cross can be made at the opposite end of the frame or reel, between the last two pegs. This permits the weaver to see at a glance how many units have been wound, and it also aids in dressing the loom. The second cross is made with the entire group of yarns.

Securing the Ties

When the entire warp—or one complete bout of warp yarns—has been measured, a series of ties must be fastened in order to hold the yarns in proper sequence for removal to the loom (Figs. 189, 190). The most important of these are the *lease ties* or *cross ties*, which should be made with contrasting cord so they can be found easily. The cross ties must maintain the cross until the lease sticks are inserted (see p. 117). Therefore, the tie must be secure, but it need not wrap tightly around the yarns.

In addition to the cross ties, a series of *choke ties* must be fastened around the yarn to hold the strands in the same relative position. These ties must be wrapped very tightly around the yarn. The first choke tie is made at the loop on the final cross peg—the point at which one warp ends and another begins; a second is placed about a yard from the cross, and the others are spaced at intervals of roughly 1 yard. The last tie is made close to the starting peg.

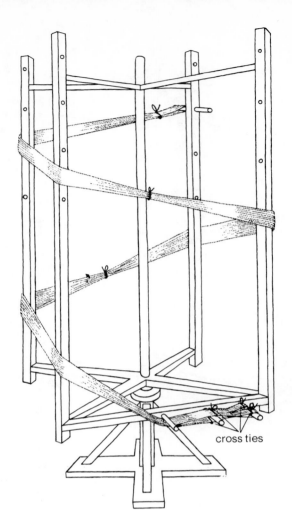

cross ties

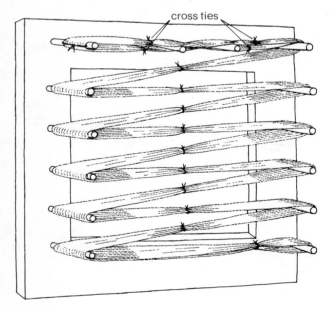

cross ties

left: 189. The arrangement of choke ties and cross ties on a warping frame.

above: 190. The arrangement of choke ties and cross ties on a warping reel.

Chaining the Warp

As the yarn is removed from the reel or warping frame, tension must be maintained to prevent the strands from tangling. The revolving reel must, therefore, be braced with the knee or shoulder. The yarn is grasped firmly at the point of the last choke tie and cut as close as possible to the starting peg (at the opposite end from the cross). Beginning at the starting peg, the warp is looped upon itself in the manner of crocheting (Fig. 191) until the entire warp is chained. The warp is now ready for the loom.

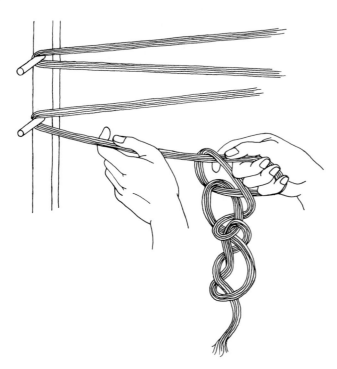

above: 191. As the yarn is removed from the warping frame or reel, it is looped upon itself in the manner of crocheting, a process called chaining.

192–194. *The term "dressing the loom" is applied to all the preparatory stages involved in setting up the warp for weaving.*

below right: 192. The spreader is tied securely to the castle, and the lease sticks are inserted at either side of the cross. A loose tie connects the two lease sticks, while another affixes them to the castle at the back of the loom.

DRESSING THE LOOM

There are almost as many ways of dressing a loom as there are weavers. A procedure that is convenient for one individual may prove awkward for another. The method described on the following pages is certainly not *the* correct way to dress a loom, but if adhered to carefully it will result in a warp that is properly distributed and held under consistent tension. These are always the two most important considerations in dressing a loom.

The first step is to remove, if possible, the beater frame from the loom, so that it is out of the way temporarily. Next, the spreader is placed on the castle, with the nails facing up and the center nail precisely in the middle of the loom (Fig. 192). The spreader is tied securely to the

castle. The chained warp is now draped carefully over the castle, with the looped end near the cross hanging toward the back of the loom and the cut ends toward the front. If the yarn has been measured in bouts, the bouts must be arranged on the loom in their proper order to maintain the sequence of the warp.

Inserting the Lease Sticks

The two lease sticks are inserted at either side of the cross, as illustrated in Figure 192. The sticks are then tied together, allowing approximately an inch of space between them, and one of the sticks is tied to the back of the loom from the castle. Next, the warp stick or metal rod is inserted through the loop at the end of the warp and secured to the back beam. The cross ties can now be removed.

If the lease sticks have been properly inserted, every warp yarn should be under one stick and over the other. However, it is not uncommon, especially with beginning weavers, to find a yarn or two that floats free of the lease sticks—in other words, a yarn that moves under both sticks or over both. This means, of course, that the cross was not correctly made for that particular circuit on the warping frame. When a free yarn is discovered, an attempt should be made to locate the position in which it belongs, especially if there is a color or texture sequence in the warp. After the spot has been found, a cord is tied loosely around the delinquent yarn and the lease

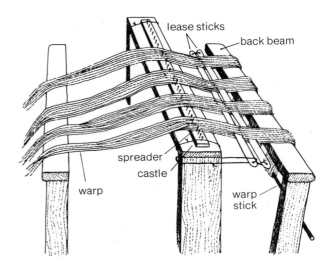

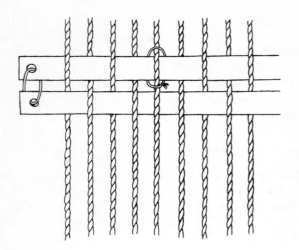

if the warp is to be 36 inches wide, the eighteenth space to the left of the center nail would be the starting point. The first inch group of yarns is laid in this space. If a counting cord has been used, the weaver merely inserts the first group separated by the cord. If not, he must count the yarns individually, choosing first a yarn from one side of the cross, then one from the other side, and alternating in this manner until all the yarns have been counted. When the yarn is spaced evenly across the spreader, a cord is wrapped figure-**8** fashion around the tops of the nails to prevent the yarns from slipping off and becoming tangled.

stick (Fig. 193), allowing the yarn to flow unhampered but harnessing it to a specific location in the warp.

Spreading the Warp

A sufficient amount of warp must be unchained to reach over and beyond the castle, so that the yarns can be distributed in the spreader. An inch of warp is to be placed between each pair of nails on the spreader (Fig. 194); that is, if the warp is to be sleyed at ten ends per inch, ten yarns will be laid in each space. The weaver stands at the back of the loom facing the spreader and works from left to right. The point at which the spreading begins should be marked in some way, with a pencil or a piece of tape. For example,

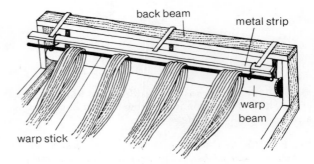

above left: 193. A yarn that floats free of both lease sticks can be controlled with a loop of cord.

below left: 194. The warp yarn is centered on the loom and distributed in inch widths across the spreader.

above: 195. Table looms often have a metal strip attached to the warp beam. A rod or stick passed through the loop in the warp yarns can be overcast to this strip.

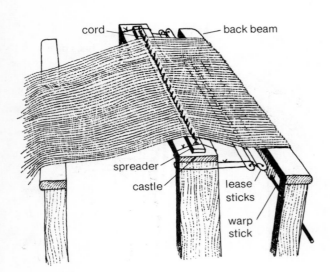

The looped end of the yarn must now be attached to the warp beam, and the method of attachment depends upon how the loom is equipped. Many table looms have a metal strip that serves as a warp stick (Fig. 195). This is brought up over the back beam toward the center of the loom and affixed at both ends to the warp stick that was passed through the looped ends of the yarn. The yarns are now distributed horizontally on the warp stick just as they occur in the spreader. When the yarns have been spread evenly, they should run in straight parallel lines from the spreader through the lease sticks to warp rod. The latter is now overcast to the metal strip with a double length of carpet warp or other heavy yarn.

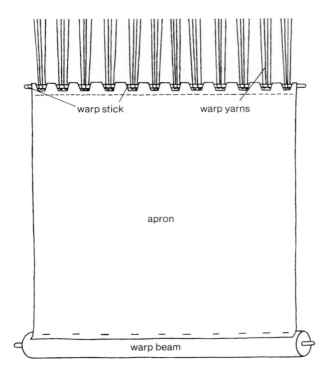

warp stick   warp yarns

apron

warp beam

left: 196. Most floor looms have a metal warp stick joined either by cords or by a canvas apron to the warp beam. The warp yarns are distributed evenly between the openings in the apron.

below left: 197. The lark's-head knot serves many purposes in weaving.

below: 198. When no warp stick is provided, small bouts of warp yarn can be tied to the beam cords.

a small bout of warps to each cord. For example, if the cords appear at intervals of 2 inches, and the warp is set at ten ends per inch, twenty warps would be tied to each cord. The cords are looped around the ends of the warp yarns—which have been gathered in an overhand knot—and tied securely with a lark's-head knot.

Winding the Warp

Several considerations must be borne in mind as the yarn is wound onto the warp beam, a process often called *beaming*. Excessive handling should be avoided, for it will not only soil the yarns but may tangle them and make them fuzzy. The warp must be wound onto the beam at precisely the width to be sleyed at the reed. Most important, the tension of all the yarns must be consistent, so that none will sag in relation to the others.

To maintain the tension, a padding of some kind is usually inserted between the layers of yarn on the warp beam. Such padding may consist of pieces of wrapping paper or corrugated

The floor loom is usually equipped with a metal warp stick attached to the warp beam either by cords or by a canvas apron (Fig. 196). As with the table loom, the warp stick is carried over the back beam toward the center of the loom. The warps must now be distributed evenly between the cords or the openings in the apron. The cords or openings in the apron occur at regular intervals of 2, 3, or 4 inches, so the number of warps in each space can easily be calculated from the sett. When the loom has cords, they are attached to the warp stick with a *lark's-head knot* (Fig. 197).

Some looms have no warp stick at all, but only cords affixed at regular intervals to the warp beam (Fig. 198). In this case, it is possible to tie

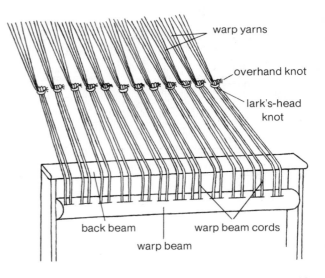

warp yarns

overhand knot

lark's-head knot

back beam   warp beam cords

warp beam

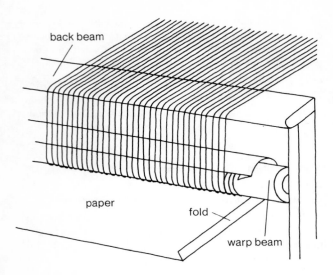

back beam

paper

fold

warp beam

199–201. *Beaming is the process of winding the warp onto the warp beam.*

above: 199. As the warp is beamed, a padding should be inserted between the layers of yarn to prevent bunching and to maintain an even tension.

below: 200. The beaming operation on a floor loom is facilitated if one has an assistant to hold the yarns and regulate warp tension while the crank is turned.

paper (Fig. 199). When paper is used, it is cut to the width of the warp beam. A 1-inch fold at each of the outer edges will prevent the yarn from slipping off the paper. The paper is inserted at the point where the yarn meets the warp beam; as the yarn is wound around the beam, it holds the paper in position. Flat wooden sticks can be substituted for paper, in which case they are placed against the warp beam and, again, held in place by the yarn. The sticks are spaced fairly close together for the first revolution of the warp beam, but after that one or two sticks per layer should be sufficient.

Winding the warp is much easier if one has an assistant to hold the yarns (Fig. 200). This is especially true if the warp is very long or wide, or if it is composed of wool yarns or very fine yarns. The holder should have some knowledge of weaving, so he will understand the importance of maintaining a constant tension. He is also in a position to deal with any problems that may arise at the front of the loom, while the winder concentrates on the back of the loom.

It is fairly easy for anyone but the novice to wind a table loom without assistance. The winder stands to one side of the loom, holding the yarn in one hand and turning the crank with the other. At any time the unwound yarn can be laid down so that both hands are free to deal with whatever difficulties may present themselves. However, with a floor loom, the winder may find it impossible to station himself in a convenient position to hold the warps under tension and at the same time reach the winding apparatus. Some weavers solve this problem by inserting a series of smooth, narrow lath sticks or dowels in the warp at the front of the loom in positions comparable to those occupied by the lease sticks (Fig. 201). These rods help to equalize the tension of the warps as they move through the loom. They should be sanded and waxed to make them slide more easily through the yarn.

As the winding proceeds, the choke ties are removed and the warp is unchained at the point where it reaches the beast beam. The lease sticks serve as general combs, and the spreader functions as a distributor, controlling the position of each warp in relation to the mass of warps. Tangles can be avoided by shaking the yarn or slapping it against the breast beam. When 8 to 10 inches of warp hang down over the breast beam,

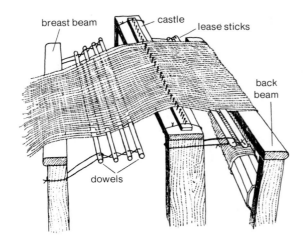

above: 201. When no holder is available, the winder can equalize tension in the warp by inserting a series of dowels at the front of the loom.

winding is complete. The spreader can now be removed and the yarn dropped down between the castle and the lease sticks.

Sectional Warping

Sectional warping is a process by which the warp yarns are wound directly from spools onto the warp beam of the loom. Most of the steps described above—measuring the yarn on a warping frame or reel, chaining the warp, inserting lease sticks, spreading the yarn—are bypassed. Special equipment is required for this method: a pegged or sectional warp beam, a spool rack, and usually a tension box. Sectional warping is feasible only when rather long warps are required.

A sectional warp beam is divided, by means of pegs, into 2-inch segments. It is generally designed to hold 1 yard of warp yarn per revolution (although this does not take into consideration the pileup of yarns on the beam). In order to wind directly onto the beam one must have on hand a sufficient number of spools of the warp yarn to fill one section of the beam. For example, if the warp is set at twenty ends per inch, a total of forty spools would be required. The spools are arranged on a rack in the order in which they are to appear in the warp and then threaded through a tension guide in the same sequence. The tension guide, thus, takes the place of the lease sticks and spreader.

The yarns emerging from the tension guide are attached to the warp beam, and then the beam is rotated until the proper length of yarn has been wound (Fig. 202). It is essential that the

202–203. *Sectional warping is a process by which warp yarns are wound from a spool rack directly onto the warp beam of the loom, thus bypassing the warping frame. A sectional warp beam and a tension box are required for this operation.*

below: 202. Warp yarns are fed from a spool rack through the tension box and attached to the warp beam in the order in which they will appear in the web. The entire warp length is wound on one section of the beam at a time.

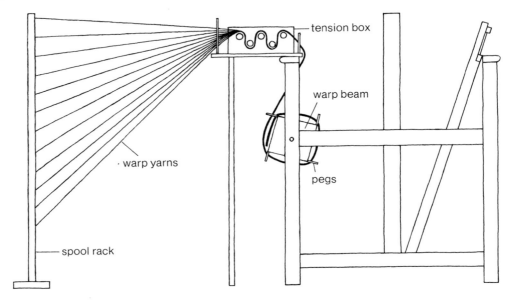

beam be turned always in the same direction and that the number of revolutions be counted carefully to ensure that all the warps are the same length. Some looms are equipped with an automatic counter to record the number of turns.

When the correct length of warp has been wound onto the beam, a strip of masking tape is fixed tightly across the yarns, and the ends are

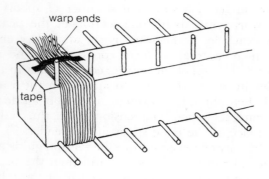

cut directly behind the tape (Fig. 203). The winder then proceeds to the next section, and so on across the beam. Before threading the heddles the tape is removed, and the yarns—held in sequence—are brought over the back beam toward the center of the loom.

Threading the Heddles

In preparation for threading the heddles, the breast beam should, if possible, be removed to permit the weaver to sit as close as possible to the harnesses. A low stool can be placed over the treadles so that the heddles are more or less at eye level. The beater frame is still off the loom, and the warp ends are hanging down between the castle and the lease sticks. The lease sticks remain in position, tied to the castle, so that the yarns can be taken in exact sequence. (If the warps were measured two at a time on the warping frame, resulting in two yarns over and two yarns under the cross, it does not matter which of the two is taken first, as long as excessive twisting is avoided.)

The first step in the threading operation is to ascertain that there are a sufficient number of heddles on each harness. Although it is not impossible to add a heddle or two at a later point,

such additions are much easier before threading commences. Metal heddles are correctly positioned if they nest inside each other when pushed together tightly on the frame. Instructions for making a string heddle appear on page 91.

The number of heddles required for a particular web is determined by the sett of the warp and the pattern to be woven. A pattern is normally broken down into units, which are repeated across the loom until all the warps have been accounted for. Figure 204 illustrates one unit of design for the *honeycomb* pattern, a twelve-warp unit requiring three heddles on each frame of a four-harness loom. If there were to be twenty units of design across the web (making a total of 240 warp yarns), each harness would require sixty heddles. Similar calculations would be made for different patterns. It is a good idea to record the proper number of heddles for each harness on a piece of masking tape and affix it to the harness for future reference.

Weavers differ on the order in which the heddles should be threaded. Some begin at the left, some at the right, and still others prefer to start at the middle and work to both sides alternately. Beginning at the left is certainly a logical method, since the pattern is then read from left

above left: 203. After one section has been wound, a strip of tape is fixed across the yarns, and the ends are cut behind the tape. The winder then proceeds to the next section and so on across the beam.

204–209. *In threading the heddles and sleying the reed, the warp yarns are taken one at a time in the order in which they occur at the lease sticks.*

below: 204. The honeycomb pattern is based on a unit of twelve warp yarns and requires three heddles on each frame of a fourharness loom.

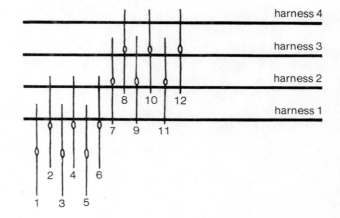

to right. However, any system that is convenient for the weaver and results in the correct threading order can be considered viable. The following directions are intended for right-handed people; left-handed weavers should reverse them.

The entire mass of heddles is first pushed to the extreme right side of the frame. Next, the heddles required for one unit of the design are separated from the rest (in the case of the honeycomb pattern the number would be twelve—three on each frame). The first four yarns at the left of the warp are then selected from the lease sticks and threaded through the fingers of the left hand (Fig. 205). A sley hook or small crochet hook is used to draw yarn number 4 through heddle number 4, yarn number 3 through heddle number 3, and so forth. When one complete unit of the design has been threaded, the ends are tied in a *slip knot* (Fig. 206) and allowed to hang down in front of the heddles. This process is repeated for each unit until all the warps have been threaded. It is advisable to check frequently for threading errors, for they are much easier to correct at this point.

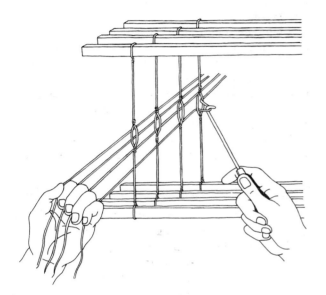

above: 205. Four yarns at a time are separated from the mass of warp to pass through the fingers and be drawn, one by one, through the heddles with a crochet hook or a small sley hook.

below: 206. After one complete unit of the pattern has been threaded through the appropriate heddles, the yarn ends are tied in a slip knot to prevent them from falling out of the heddles and becoming tangled.

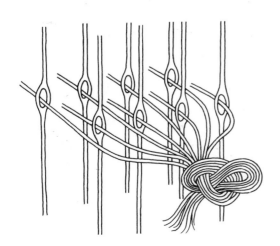

Sleying the Reed

The reed can be threaded either in position in the beater frame or flat on its side, supported at either end by a lengthwise rod (a *lary stick*) lashed to the back beam and breast beam (Fig. 207). If the former method is used, the beater is returned to the loom; in the latter case, the breast beam is restored. The middle of the reed

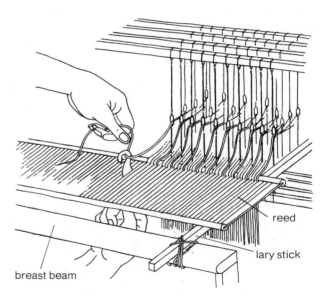

above: 207. The reed is placed flat on two sticks tied between the breast beam and the back beam. The process of drawing warp yarns through the dents in the reed is called *sleying*; it can also be accomplished with the reed in position.

should be marked so that, when all the yarns are sleyed, the warp will be centered on the loom, thus ensuring balanced beating.

As with the heddles, the order of threading is a question of individual preference—right to left, left to right, or center to ends. Right-handed people often find it more comfortable to begin at the right-hand end. In any case, the yarns must be taken in precisely the same sequence as they occur in the heddles in order to avoid breakage. The yarns are drawn through the dents with a sley hook. It is wise to tie each unit once again in a slip knot to prevent the sleyed yarns from falling out of the reed.

The number of warp yarns to be threaded through each dent is determined by several factors: the weight of the warp yarn; the planned density of the fabric to be woven; the material chosen for the weft; the size of the reed; and the design of the fabric. Although it is a common practice to thread one or two yarns through each dent evenly across the loom, many other variations are possible.

The openings in the reed must, of course, be large enough to allow the yarns to flow freely. Therefore, the weight of the warp yarn tends to limit the fineness of the reed. Moreover, it is generally easier to sley two or three yarns per dent in a relatively coarse reed than to attempt threading a reed finer than fifteen dents per inch. Twenty- and thirty-dent reeds *are* sometimes useful, but they require skillful manipulation.

A ridged or shadowed effect can be obtained by grouping warps unevenly in the dents accord-ing to a preordained sequence (Fig. 208). For example, one might sley two or three warps per dent for a space of five dents, then a single yarn per dent for the next fifteen dents, and so on across the loom. Openwork fabrics may call for skipped dents, again in a prescribed order. When bulky natural materials—such as cattails, branches, or corn husks—are chosen for the weft, occasional dents are skipped. By experimenting with different groupings, one can obtain a wide variety of effects.

When the reed has been sleyed, the lease sticks are detached from the castle and tied loosely to the back beam. They remain in this position throughout the weaving operation. If the reed was sleyed in a horizontal position, resting on lary sticks, the beater frame is now returned to the loom, the reed is set into it, and the lary sticks are removed. If it was sleyed vertically, in the beater frame, the breast beam is restored.

Tying the Warp Ends at the Front of the Loom

The last step in the loom-dressing operation consists of tying the cut ends of the warp to the cloth beam. The cloth stick, which is attached by cords or an apron to the cloth beam, is first brought up and over the breast beam. Beginning at the center, an even-numbered group of yarns (usually six or eight) is brought forward, smoothed, and then carried over and around the cloth stick. The group is divided behind the cloth stick, and the two sections are carried around and tied in a half knot (Fig. 209). The same

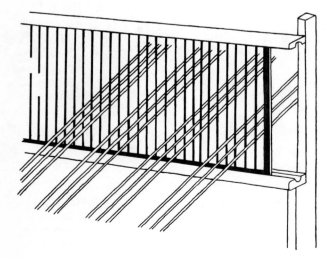

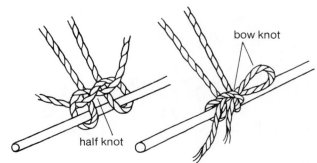

left: 208. A ridged or shadowed web can be produced by grouping warp yarns unevenly in the reed.

below: 209. The warp yarns are tied to the cloth stick in two steps—first a half knot, then a bow knot.

procedure is followed with a group of yarns at either edge of the warp, after which groups alternately left and right of the center are tied on until all the warps are attached to the cloth stick. The entire warp is now tested with the side of the hand to make sure the tension is even throughout. If the warp yarns are tied tighter in the center of the loom than at the sides, the resulting web will form an arc, with the high part of the curve at the center. Conversely, if the tension is greater near the selvedges, the fabric will curve upward at the edges. When the tension is perfect, all the ties are completed with a bow knot.

Checking the Loom for Errors

Even the most meticulous weaver will occasionally make a threading error. Common mistakes are:

1. a missed heddle
2. a missed yarn
3. crossed threads
4. too many yarns in one dent
5. a missed dent

If one heddle has been skipped during the threading process, the omission should be corrected before weaving begins. This is relatively easy when the warp is uniform. A new yarn, the entire length of the warp, is set in and threaded through the heddle and the appropriate dent, then tied in with the proper group of yarns on the cloth stick. The long end is wound around a spool or similar object and weighted at the back of the loom. A warp composed of different yarns would necessitate rethreading the heddles from the point of the error to the edge or removing one entire unit of the pattern. The latter method would, of course, narrow the web.

When a yarn has been skipped in threading the heddles, it will not respond to any of the treadles. This situation can sometimes be corrected by removing the yarn altogether. However, if there is a definite threading pattern, a string or corrective heddle (Fig. 146) may have to be inserted.

Yarns that are crossed between the lease sticks and the heddles or between the heddles and the reed must be rethreaded, for they will prevent a clean opening of the shed and will probably break. The group of yarns containing the errant ones is untied from the cloth stick, the yarns are rethreaded properly, and then the entire group is once more attached to the cloth stick in the usual manner.

If, in sleying the reed, a dent has been skipped or too many yarns have been drawn through a particular dent, the reed must be resleyed from the point of error to the nearest edge.

AN ALTERNATE METHOD FOR DRESSING THE LOOM

Some weavers prefer to reverse the process described above and dress the loom from front to back. In this system the yarn is warped so that the cut ends occur near the cross. The lease sticks are inserted in the cross and tied in front of the beater (Fig. 210), so that the chained warp hangs down over the breast beam. The reed is threaded first, taking the yarns one at a time in order as they occur at the cross. Next, the heddles are threaded from the back of the loom. Finally, the ends are attached to the warp beam, and the entire warp is wound onto the beam.

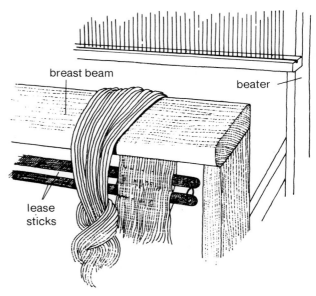

210–211. Some weavers prefer to dress the loom from front to back. In this system, the reed is sleyed first, then the heddles are threaded before the warp is attached to the warp beam.

above: 210. When the loom is dressed in this manner, the lease sticks are tied between the beater and the breast beam.

This method of dressing the loom does not require a second person to hold the warp yarns during winding. Instead, a series of dowels or sticks are inserted in the yarn at the front of the loom (Fig. 211), and these dowels comb the yarn and maintain the proper tension during the beaming process. If a floor loom is used, the treadles are tied up before winding (see below). The winder hand-holds the yarn under sufficient tension to open a shed and then treadles (or depresses the levers for) harnesses 1-3 and 2-4 alternately. Each time the shed is changed, a dowel is inserted, until there are six or more. The dowels are then laced together and tied between the breast beam and the castle. (Holes drilled in the ends of the dowels facilitate the lacing.) If desired, dowels can also be inserted between the castle and the back beam.

When all the yarn has been wound onto the warp beam, the ends are tied to the cloth stick.

THE TIE-UP

The harnesses on a table loom are raised by a series of levers or keys on the right side of the loom or on the castle. Each lever is connected permanently to a single harness, and the weaver can depress one or more levers to create a shed.

Once raised, the harnesses remain in position until the shed is changed. Thus, no tie-up is necessary. The instructions given below apply to the floor loom only.

Preparing the Tie-up

The four-harness foot-powered loom is equipped with six or more treadles connected by lamms to the harnesses. The floor loom differs from the table loom in that the connections are not permanent but can be varied to serve the needs of a particular weaving pattern. Therefore, the treadles must be tied to the lamms for each web (Fig. 212). Although this further complicates the loom preparation, it affords the weaver a distinct advantage. Once the tie-up is complete, any desired shed can generally be produced by depressing only one treadle, whereas the same shed might require manipulation of two or three levers on the table loom.

Most weavers establish a permanent numbering system for the harnesses, lamms, and treadles. It does not matter what order is used, as long as one is consistent. On a four-harness loom it is common to number the harnesses and the lamms 1 through 4 from front to back, and the treadles 1 through 6 from left to right.

above: 211. In order to maintain uniform warp tension during beaming, a series of dowels are inserted in alternate plain-weave sheds at the front of the loom.

212–214. *The tie-up is the process of making connections between the harnesses and the treadles on a floor loom.*

below: 212. As a rule, there are six treadles on a four-harness loom. In this case, the center ones are tied for plain weave.

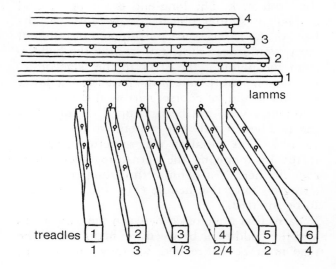

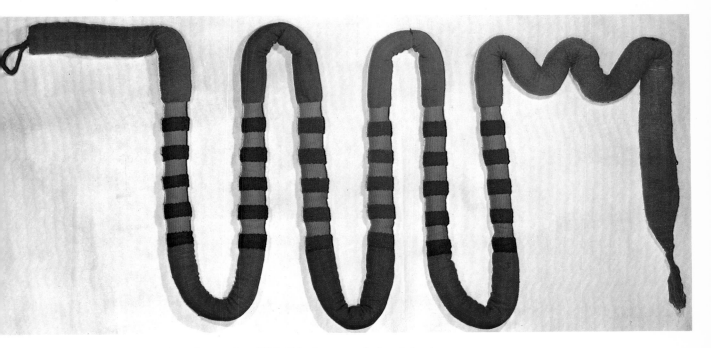

Plate 13. JEAN STAMSTA. *Serpentine*. 1971. Tubular weave in hand-dyed wool and synthetics, 4 x 7'. Courtesy Museum of Contemporary Crafts, New York.

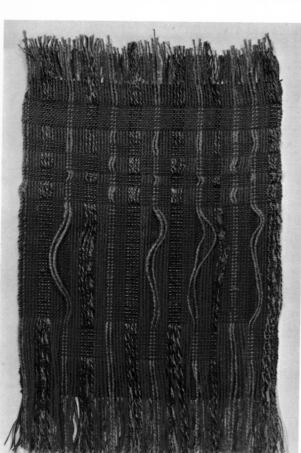

left: Plate 14. Continuous warp brocade, face.

left: Plate 15. Continuous warp brocade, reverse side.

above: Plate 16. Continuous weft brocade.

On a four-harness loom it is possible to connect as many as three harnesses to the same treadle (four harnesses attached to the same treadle would raise all the yarns, so there would be no shed). In Figure 212 treadle 1 raises harness 1, treadle 2 raises harness 3, treadle 3 raises harnesses 1 and 3, treadle 4 raises harnesses 2 and 4, treadle 5 raises harness 2, and treadle 6 raises harness 4. Thus, six different sheds can be created by depressing one treadle at a time. Very complicated weaves sometimes require that two treadles be depressed simultaneously.

The harnesses on a floor loom remain in the raised position only as long as the treadle is depressed. When the foot is removed from the treadle, the harnesses drop and the shed is closed. For this reason, a treadling sequence that alternates the left and right foot is the most efficient and provides for the steadiest rhythm. As a rule, the treadles to the left of center (1 through 3) are depressed with the left foot, and those to the right of center (4 through 6) are operated with the right foot. A convenient treadling order might be from the outsides to the center (treadle 1, 6, 2, 5, 3, 4), from the center to the ends (treadle 3, 4, 2, 5, 1, 6), or from left to right (treadle 1, 4, 2, 5, 3, 6). The tie-up should be formulated so that the sequence of sheds required by the pattern can be obtained from such a treadling order.

Plain weave or *tabby* (Fig. 235) requires only two treadles; harnesses 1 and 3 are attached to one treadle and 2 and 4 to another. When plain weave forms a significant part of a web, it is normally set up on the innermost treadles, as demonstrated in Figure 212.

The method of attaching the lamms to the harnesses and the treadles to the lamms depends upon how the loom is equipped. Some looms have permanent metal connectors that are merely hooked in place. Others have cords with snap-locks on each end. When neither is provided, the cords must be tied individually. One cord is slipped through the hole in the lamm and tied in a half knot (Fig. 213). The treadle cord is doubled, and the cut ends are tied in an overhand knot, while the looped end is passed through the hole in the treadle. The looped end is then folded over to form a lark's-head knot, and the knotted end of the lamm cord is passed through this lark's head. When the treadle is

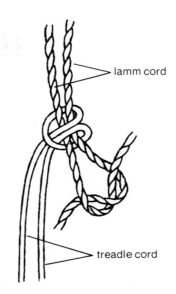

above: 213. When metal connectors are not provided for a particular loom, the tie-up connections must be made with individually knotted cords. A lark's-head knot from the treadle cord is looped over a half knot from the lamm cord.

depressed, the half knot in the lamm cord will be pulled taut against the lark's-head knot in the treadle cord. The height of the lamm can be adjusted by tightening or loosening the half knot where it joins the lark's head.

THE WEAVING PROCESS

Adjusting the Loom

Before weaving can begin, certain minor adjustments must be made to ensure smooth operation of the loom. The first step is to ascertain that the harnesses, lamms, and treadles are in their proper positions. The harnesses must all hang at exactly the same height. The lamms should be roughly parallel to the floor, and the ends connected to the treadles must all be at the same distance from the floor. The treadles should be adjusted to a height that is comfortable for the weaver.

Tying groups of warp yarns to the cloth stick tends to bunch them together. Before the web is started the yarns should be spread, so they run in parallel lines from stick to reed. The easiest way to do this is to treadle for plain weave (harnesses 1-3 and 2-4 alternately) and insert strips of coarse material—paper, rags, or heavy

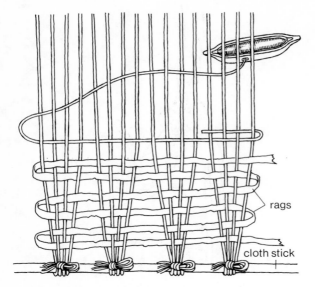

rags

cloth stick

above: 214. Before weaving commences, the warp yarns should be spread evenly across the loom by inserting a few shots of coarse material in alternate sheds.

carpet warp—into the resulting sheds (Fig. 214). Three or four shots are usually sufficient to correct the alignment of the warps.

Filling the Shuttle

A stick shuttle—used for certain weaves or for unusually heavy weft yarns—must be filled manually. However, a boat or throw shuttle con-

taining a bobbin is best filled with a hand-powered or electric bobbin winder (Fig. 215). Bobbin quills made of plastic, wood, or cardboard can be purchased, but a homemade quill of sturdy wrapping paper will be satisfactory (Fig. 216). The paper should be cut a bit shorter than the bobbin well in the shuttle and about 3 inches wide. It is wound into a fine cylinder—just large enough to fit over the bobbin winder—and secured from top to bottom with transparent tape.

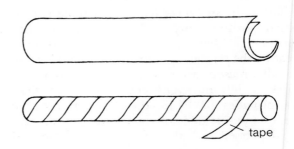

tape

below left: 215. The bobbin is filled with a hand-cranked winder.

above: 216. A bobbin quill can be made by rolling a small piece of paper into a tube and securing it with tape.

below: 217. The bobbin should be filled first at the two ends and then in the center.

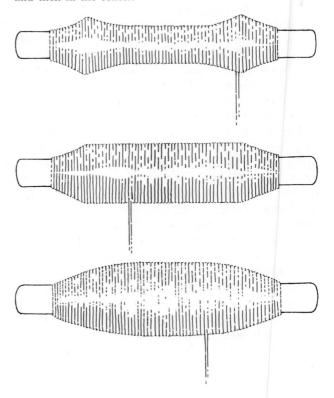

A properly wound bobbin is firm and even. Whether an electric or a hand-cranked bobbin winder is employed, one hand must be kept free to guide the yarn onto the quill, thus maintaining a uniform tension. Winding begins by making a small mound of yarn at one end of the quill, then guiding the yarn to the other end to make another small mound. The middle section of the quill is filled in last (Fig. 217).

Weaving the Web

In essence, the weaving operation consists of four steps:

1. *Shedding,* the depression of a treadle or lever to open a shed.
2. *Picking,* or throwing the shuttle containing weft yarn through the open shed.
3. *Beating,* or packing the weft yarn against the finished portion of the web.
4. *Taking up and letting off,* the process of winding the warp forward onto the cloth beam as each section of the web is completed.

The Shedding Sequence   It is customary to record the sequence of sheds (and therefore of treadles or levers) required by a particular web on a piece of tape or paper and to affix it to the loom. For very complicated weaves it may be desirable to assign a code letter to a certain portion of the treadling sequence. For example, "A" might mean "treadle 1-6-3-4." This shorthand method of notation takes the burden off the weaver's memory.

Throwing the Shuttle   As the shuttle is thrown, a sufficient amount of yarn is automatically unwound from the bobbin to make the complete trip across the web. If thrown by the left hand, the shuttle is caught by the right, and vice versa. The weft yarn is then pulled snugly against the selvedge at the opposite side, but not so tightly that it will cause the web to draw in. The new weft yarn is set in at an angle to the packed filler (Fig. 218) to compensate for the weft takeup that occurs when the yarn is beat in.

Beating   The appearance of the finished web is greatly affected by the force of the beating and the point at which the beater is pulled forward.

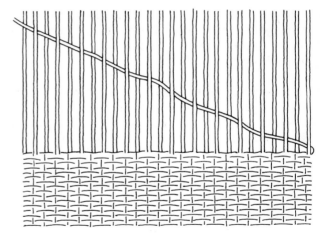

above: 218. Each new weft shot is set at an angle to the finished web to compensate for weft takeup. This prevents excessive draw-in of the fabric.

Most often, the weft is beat in before the shed is changed or just as the shed is being changed. When the warp yarns tend to cling together (as some woolen yarns do), it may be necessary to change the shed before beating, to encourage the creation of a clean shed for the next shot. Very heavy fabrics, such as rugs, are often subjected to a double beating, once before and once after the shed is changed.

The force of beating depends entirely upon the fabric under construction. Heavy fabrics require a firm beating, while delicate or openwork webs are not really "beat" at all. Rather, the new weft yarn is placed gently in position. With practice, one acquires a "feel" for the correct amount of force to be applied. The beater should always be grasped in the center to ensure even packing. Uniform beating results in weft yarns that are perpendicular to the warp and are evenly distributed throughout the web.

Taking Up and Letting Off   When the shed becomes so small that it is difficult to throw the shuttle easily, the warp must be rolled forward onto the cloth beam. This is done by releasing the ratchet on the warp beam. Thus, the processes of *taking up* finished cloth onto the cloth beam and *letting off* additional warp from the warp beam are accomplished simultaneously. Each time the warp is moved, the overall tension must be adjusted. Only a small amount of warp is rolled forward at any one time, for if the edge of the web is too close to the breast beam or to the reed, the angle of beating will not be uniform all across the fabric.

Changing the Weft Yarns　A new weft yarn is begun when a different color or type of yarn is to be introduced or, in the case of a uniform web, when the supply of yarn on the bobbin has become depleted. In either event, the change occurs at the selvedge.

When a new color is to be started in the web, a short tail of yarn from the first color is left dangling at the selvedge (Fig. 219). This tail is wrapped once around the outside warp, then placed back in the *same* shed before the beater is pulled forward. The tail is carried across the web for a distance of a few warps and brought up between the warps. After a few shots of the new color have been inserted and beat in, the protruding tail of the first yarn is cut off cleanly. The same procedure is followed with a tail of the new yarn, preferably at the opposite selvedge.

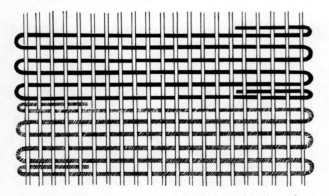

above: 219. When a new weft color is introduced, a short tail of yarn from the previous color is left at the selvedge. This tail is wrapped once around the outside warp, then placed back in the same shed before beating.

The method for changing shuttles in a uniform weft is similar, except that the tail of yarn remaining from the previous shuttle is inserted in the *next* shed, rather than the same one. Occasionally, when the shuttle empties in the middle of its passage across the web, the old and new weft yarns can be overlapped inconspicuously at this point. Such a procedure is possible only with

certain yarns; with others, the overlap would be obvious; the break must come at the selvedge.

Hemming the Start of the Web　In most cases the ends of the web are finished after the entire project has been woven (see Chap. 12). However, it is sometimes desirable to hem the starting edge of the web before it disappears onto the cloth beam, so that it will not unravel when the fabric is removed from the loom. At the outset of the weaving, a 3-yard length of weft yarn is allowed to dangle from the first shed. After about an inch of the web has been woven, the extra length of yarn is threaded through a needle, and the edge of the fabric is hemstitched (Fig. 317).

Maintaining an Even Selvedge　A uniform selvedge forms a straight line parallel to all the warps. It exhibits neither loops of weft yarn nor tightly drawn areas. Only practice will enable the weaver to attain this goal. If the weft yarns are pulled too tightly at the edges, the web will draw in and narrow. This in turn will change the angle of the outside warps at the reed, creating excess friction and possible breakage. Insufficient tension of the warp yarns or inadequate beating may also cause the selvedges to pull inward. When an especially firm selvedge is desired, two or more warp ends should be threaded through a single dent at the edges of the fabric.

It is important to remember that *all* weft yarns must be interlocked with the warps at the selvedges. When weaving alternately with two shuttles, the yarn from one shuttle is always *over* the outside warp, and the yarn from the second shuttle is always *under* the outside warp (Fig. 220). This system of alternate shuttles is sometimes helpful even when the weft is uniform.

below: 220. All weft yarns must be interlocked with the outside warp yarns at the selvedge. Sometimes it is easier to do this by weaving alternately with two shuttles.

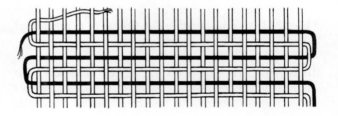

Some weaves, particularly certain twills (see p. 141), have a tendency to leave warp yarns floating at the selvedges. Using two shuttles—in this case containing the same yarn—and interlocking them at the edges may solve the problem.

One method of keeping the selvedges even—especially with troublesome weaves—is to add an extra "guide" thread at either edge of the warp. The guide yarns are threaded through the reed but not through the heddles, so they remain in the middle of the shed. Each weft shot enters the shed *over* the guide yarn and emerges *under* the guide yarn at the other side. Thus, the guide yarns are woven into the fabric, but they play no role in the pattern.

The Pick Count   The number of weft yarns per inch in a woven fabric is referred to as the *pick count*. A *balanced weave* (Fig. 221) has the same number of weft yarns per inch as warp yarns per inch. Two factors create this balance: The warp and weft yarns are of uniform size, and the beating is adjusted to allow for the required number

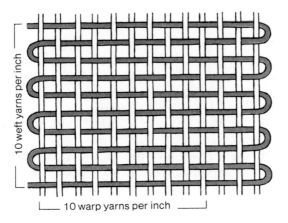

above: 221. A balanced weave has the same number of weft yarns per inch as warp yarns per inch.

of weft yarns per inch. An *unbalanced weave* (Fig. 222), conversely, displays an *un*equal distribution of warp and weft yarns. A web in which the warp yarns predominate is called a *warp-face* fabric; when the weft yarns dominate the surface of the cloth or completely obscure the warp, as in tapestry and certain other pattern weaves, the fabric is referred to as *weft-faced.*

below: 222. An unbalanced weave displays an unequal distribution of warp and weft yarns.

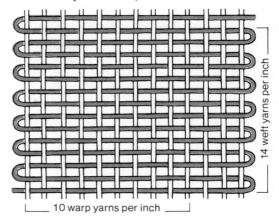

Protecting the Fabric on the Loom   When weaving is interrupted, it is a good practice to release the tension on the warp yarns. This is essential with wool or other elastic fibers that might stretch under prolonged stress. Some materials, including wool and linen, are best woven in a relatively damp room. If the atmosphere is very dry, a pan of water placed under the warp beam or a damp cloth over the beam itself will help to keep the warp moist. No finished yarn should ever be exposed to strong sunlight.

A delicate web may require that paper be wound in on the cloth beam as on the warp beam. If the fabric is very light in color, sheets of plastic rolled between the layers of the web will help to prevent soiling. A knit fabric sewn over the cloth beam like a sleeve will keep the woven fabric from slipping on its first revolution.

Measuring the Web   As the fabric is woven, an accurate measure of its length should be kept. One method is to cut a measuring string the exact length of the proposed web and place it over the warp at the center. The end of the string is tied to the last row of coarse material that was woven in to spread the warp from the cloth stick. The measuring string is then wound onto the cloth beam with the fabric, and when the end of the string is reached, the web should be the proper length. This system, however, is not advisable when many yards of fabric are to be woven, for the string would create a ridge on the cloth beam. Instead, the length is marked by looping a short piece of contrasting yarn over the selvedge warp at the completion of each yard.

Correcting a Broken Warp

If a warp yarn should break during the weaving process, or if a knot appears in one of the warps, the yarn can be spliced. A piece of leftover warp yarn about 24 inches long is cut from the spool. The broken yarn is pulled out of the reed and the heddle to the back of the loom, and the new length of yarn is substituted in the appropriate dent and heddle (Fig. 223). Next, the broken warp and the new warp are tied together in a bow knot at the back of the loom near the lease sticks.

A common pin is inserted about 2 inches into the finished web, then the new warp is pulled to the same tension as the rest of the warp and wound figure-8 fashion around the pin. Weaving proceeds until the broken warp end at the back of the loom reaches a point at which it is long enough to extend into the web. When this occurs, a second pin is inserted into the web, again about

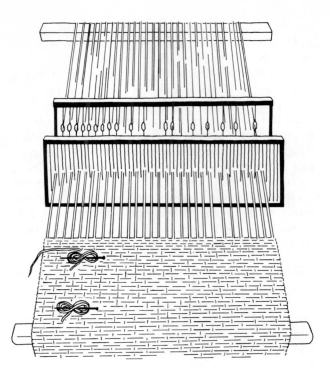

above: 224. Weaving proceeds until the broken end of yarn will reach into the web, at which time it is restored to its position.

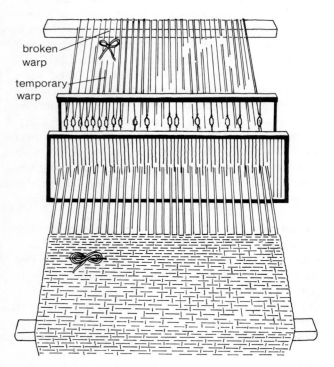

broken warp

temporary warp

223–224. *It is possible to splice a broken warp yarn on the loom by temporarily introducing a length of leftover yarn.*

above: 223. The broken warp yarn is pulled out of the reed and heddle, and a new length of yarn is substituted. The two ends are tied together at the back of the loom.

2 inches from the edge. The new yarn is removed from the heddle and reed, and the broken end is restored to its position and wound around the second pin (Fig. 224). After the fabric is completed, the loose ends are worked into the web.

Removing a Portion of the Web

It is possible to remove a portion of the web from the loom without retying the warp ends. A series of woven items, such as a set of place mats, or a great length of yardage may not fit all at once on the cloth beam. When this occurs, the first unit or length of material is completed, allowing a sufficient amount of warp at the end to finish the project (a fringe, for example). Next, a weft of scrap yarn is woven in for a distance of about 3 inches and hemstitched or taped in place (Fig. 225). On the next shed a dowel or flat stick wider than the web is inserted, followed by another 2 inches of scrap yarn. The second unit of the web can now be started. When the dowel reaches the breast beam, it is temporarily attached to the beam to maintain the warp tension (Fig. 226).

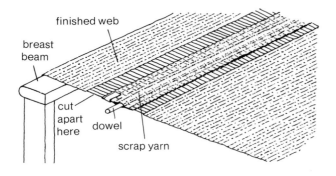

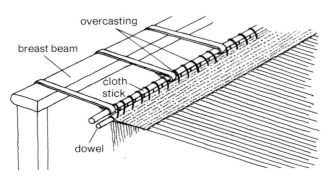

left: 225. To remove a portion of the web from the loom, one weaves in a few inches of scrap yarn, then a dowel, then more scrap yarn.

below left: 226. When the dowel reaches the breast beam, it is overcast to the cloth stick.

The warps are cut between the finished web and the scrap yarn, and the cloth beam is rolled backward to remove the first unit. Finally, the cloth stick is brought up and overcast firmly to the dowel, the dowel is untied from the breast beam, and weaving proceeds as usual.

Removing the Fabric from the Loom   Weaving is complete when the desired length of fabric has been woven or when the warp can no longer move forward. A sufficient length of warp ends will remain to prevent the fabric from raveling, but if desired the end of the web can be hemstitched while still on the loom (Fig. 317). Then the warp ends are cut near the heddles, the cloth beam is rolled back, and the fabric is removed.

Drafting

It is amazing to see what complicated reporting is often resorted to, instead of transcribing the threading construction into the code of draft writing.

Anni Albers, On Weaving[1]

Drafting is a system of notation used to represent graphically the appearance and mechanics of a weave. A complete draft illustrates the intersections of warp and weft for a particular weave, as well as the threading, tie-up, and treadling sequence necessary to produce the weave.

Drafting has often been compared to musical notation, and in some ways the analogy is accurate. However, unlike the symbols used in music, the shorthand of drafting is not universal. Many different drafting systems are or have been used in different countries and at different times. The method described below is both simple and quite common, especially in the United States. Once it is understood, the weaver should not find it too difficult to translate other drafting systems he may encounter.

One occasionally hears of great singers or even musicians who cannot read music. Similarly, many experienced weavers can neither read nor write drafts, preferring to design on the loom. It is certainly possible to pursue a career in weaving without ever resorting to paper and pencil. On the other hand, drafting does have several advantages. A concise draft will show at a glance what might otherwise require pages and pages of explanation. Few serious weavers rely on copying another person's drafts, but it is often helpful to be able to analyze another's work in order to find ideas for one's own. This is particularly true when studying ancient weaves. Furthermore, drafting enables the weaver to record his own results for future experimentation. By designing on paper one can get a fair idea of how a weave will look even before the warp yarn has been unwound from the spools.

Drafts are written on squared graph paper, available from any stationery store.

THE THREADING DRAFT

The order in which the warp yarns are threaded through the heddles is referred to as the *draw*. Figure 227 illustrates the draft notation for a *straight draw* on a four-harness loom, a threading

227–229. *A threading draft is read from bottom to top as the harnesses occur from front to back.*

left: 227. A straight draw for the four-harness loom.

arrangement based on a unit of four warps repeated across the loom. In this draw warp 1 is threaded through a heddle on harness 1, warp 2 through a heddle on harness 2, and so forth. After the first four warps are threaded, one unit or *repeat* has been completed, and the pattern begins again with harness 1. The threading draft is read from bottom to top as the harnesses occur from front to back on the loom. Therefore, the bottom row of squares represents harness 1, and the top row represents harness 4. An eight-harness loom would, of course, require eight vertical rows of squares.

A *pointed draw* is illustrated in Figure 228. In this draw the harnesses are taken in the following sequence: 1, 2, 3, 4, 3, 2 for one repeat of the pattern. A more complicated threading draft is shown in Figure 229.

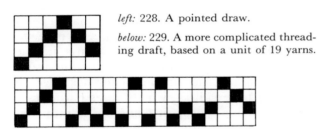

left: 228. A pointed draw.

below: 229. A more complicated threading draft, based on a unit of 19 yarns.

THE TIE-UP DRAFT

The tie-up draft is read from left to right for the treadles and from bottom to top for the harnesses. In other words, each vertical row of squares represents the four harnesses, and each horizontal row indicates the six treadles typical on a four-harness loom. In Figure 230 harnesses

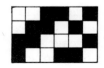

230. A tie-up draft is read from left to right for the treadles and from bottom to top for the harnesses.

1 and 2 have been tied to treadle 1, harnesses 2 and 3 to treadle 2, harnesses 3 and 4 to treadle 3, harnesses 1 and 4 to treadle 4, harnesses 1 and 3 to treadle 5, and harnesses 2 and 4 to treadle 6. The two treadles on the far right (5 and 6) are therefore set up for plain weave, since depressing them alternately will raise first harnesses 1 and 3 and then harnesses 2 and 4. If a table loom is used, the tie-up draft is not necessary, but the weaver must take into account the harnesses that are to be raised for a particular shed. For example, if the first shed in a pattern calls for treadle 1 to be depressed, the weaver must manipulate levers to raise harnesses 1 and 2.

THE TREADLING DRAFT

The treadling draft is read from top to bottom. In Figure 231 the sequence of treadles for the first repeat in the weft is as follows: 1, 2, 3, 4, 3, 2, 1, 5, 6. Again, the use of a table loom requires a certain amount of interpretation. The corresponding manipulation of *levers* would be: 1-2, 2-3, 3-4, 1-4, 3-4, 2-3, 1-2, 1-3, 2-4.

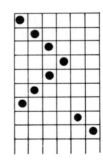

231. The treadling draft is read from top to bottom. When more than one symbol appears in the draft, two or more kinds of weft yarn are indicated.

Sometimes the instructions for a weave will specify the treadling order merely by a sequence of numbers, rather than a graphic representation. A series of numbers separated by *commas* usually indicates *treadles,* while a series separated by *hyphens* stands for either the *levers* on a table loom or the harnesses to be raised.

THE WEAVE DRAFT

The weave draft shows what the weave will look like. Two conventions are generally adhered to in preparing such a draft. First, the *vertical* rows of squares represent *warp* yarns, and the *horizontal*

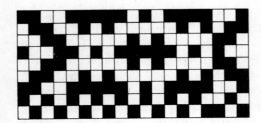

above: 232. The weave draft is a graphic representation of the appearance of a weave. Vertical rows of squares represent warp yarns, and horizontal rows signify weft yarns.

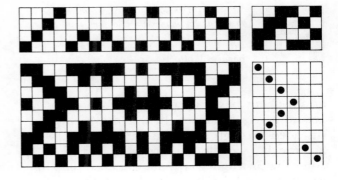

above: 233. A comprehensive draft includes the threading, tie-up, treadling, and weave drafts for a praticular weave.

rows signify *weft* yarns. Second, the *dark* squares indicate a point of intersection at which the *warp* yarn is above the weft yarn, while the *unshaded* squares are areas in which the *weft* yarn is above the warp.

The weave draft is read from top to bottom, actually the reverse of the way the fabric appears on the loom. As a rule, two or three repeats of the pattern in each direction are necessary to form an overall impression of the weave. However, if a very complicated weave is involved, one and one-half repeats across the warp may be sufficient to establish the pattern. Figure 232 illustrates the weave that results from the threading, tie-up, and treadling drafts represented in Figures 229 to 231.

Designers often employ a shortened version of the weave draft, called a *profile draft,* when they plan experimental projects. Profile drafts are discussed in Chapter 20.

THE COMPREHENSIVE DRAFT

By pulling all the foregoing elements together, one creates a comprehensive draft. Therefore, Figure 233 is the comprehensive draft of the weave represented in Figure 232 and achieved by following Figures 229 to 231. On just a few square inches of paper the weaver notes the appearance of the weave and all the mechanics required to produce it.

DERIVING THE WEAVE DRAFT

In experimenting with a new weave it is often desirable to draft the pattern on paper before attempting it on the loom, especially when great quantities of yarn are involved. Once a draw, a

tie-up, and a treadling sequence have been established, the weave draft can easily be sketched. This method of designing on paper is also useful when one intends to change or vary the pattern. By holding two elements constant (for example, the threading and the tie-up) and varying the third (the treadling sequence), the weaver can see immediately how the pattern will be affected by such changes.

Figure 234 illustrates one and one-half repeats of a pattern weave called *honeysuckle.* In order to plot the weave draft, one first draws in the threading, tie-up, and treadling drafts on graph paper. The first shed in the honeysuckle weave is created by treadle 1, which raises harnesses 1 and 2. Starting on the first line of the proposed weave draft, a square is blacked in at each point where either harness 1 or harness 2 is raised. From the threading draft we can see that warp 1 is threaded in harness 1 and warp 2 is threaded in harness 2. Since the shed requires these two harnesses to be raised, thus placing the warp over the weft, the first two squares on line 1 of the weave draft are darkened. Warp 3 is on harness 3, which is not affected by the first shed, so the third square on the top line is left unshaded. This procedure is followed across the line until one and one-half repeats of the pattern have been sketched in.

The second shed is plotted in a similar manner on line 2 of the weave draft. This shed calls for treadle 2 to be depressed, which raises harnesses 2 and 3. Therefore, on line 2 of the weave draft each point where either harness 2 or harness 3 is raised will be blacked in. When a sufficient number of sheds have been plotted—in this case 24—the pattern should become clear.

In the following chapters some of the more common weaves are discussed and illustrated by written drafts, occasionally supplemented by photographs of sample webs. However, it is important to remember that drafts, because they are diagrammatic, present an idealized picture of a weave. The choice of yarns and colors has a considerable effect on the fabric's appearance.

below: 234. The comprehensive draft for a rather complicated pattern, the honeysuckle weave.

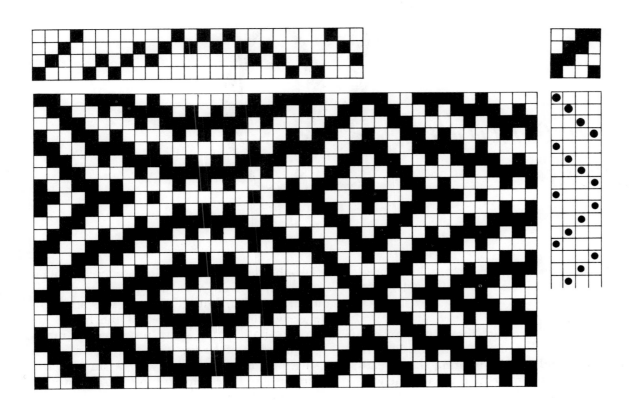

Loom-controlled Weaves

Fair weft and fitting woof weave a web that bideth proof.
Motto of the Canterbury Weavers

Loom-controlled weaves are those that are created by the interaction of the harnesses. Pattern variations are produced by altering the threading, tie-up, and treadling sequences, and the weft yarn is always carried from selvedge to selvedge. There are three basic weave categories: plain weave or tabby, twill weave, and satin weave. Modifications of these three fundamental structures are called *derivative weaves*.

THE BASIC WEAVES

Plain Weave (Tabby)

Plain weave is characterized by a regular interlacing of warp and weft yarns in a 1/1 order. That is, each weft moves alternately over and under adjacent warps, and the sequence is reversed for alternate wefts. When the warp is all one color and the weft all another, plain weave produces a checkerboard effect.

Two harnesses are sufficient to create plain weave, but it is often set up on four to provide a more even distribution of yarns. It is a reversible weave, for the two faces of the fabric are identical. Basic plain weave produces the maximum number of *binding points*—areas in which a single weft is interlaced with a single warp. Therefore, it is the firmest, most durable weave. The comprehensive draft for basic plain weave is illustrated in Figure 235.

235–243. *A basic weave is one not derived from any other weave. The three basic weave categories are plain, twill, and satin.*

235. Plain weave.

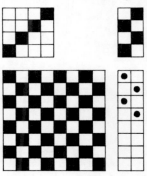

140

Plain weave was undoubtedly the first construction mastered by prehistoric man. Throughout history most fabrics have been woven in plain weave, with color or textural variations providing the major interest. Even today, despite the multiplicity of weaves that are possible on modern looms, plain weave comprises a very large portion of all woven fabrics.

The two major derivatives of plain weave are *basket weave* and *rep weaves*.

Basket Weave A basket weave consists of two or more warp yarns interlaced with two or more weft yarns. For example, a 2/2 basket weave has two warp yarns interlaced as a unit with a unit of two weft yarns. In the warp this effect is produced either by raising two adjacent harnesses simultaneously or by threading two warp yarns through each heddle. The double weft can be created in several ways. Two shuttles can be passed through the same shed, with a beat after each shot; a shuttle containing two bobbins can be thrown through the open shed; a bobbin wound from two spools simultaneously can be

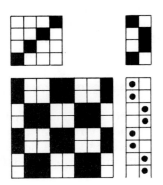

236. A 2/2 basket weave.

used; a single shuttle can be passed twice through the same shed, with the weft yarn wrapped around the outermost warp before the return trip. The comprehensive draft for a 2/2 basket weave is shown in Figure 236.

Rep Weaves A rep weave is produced by extending the basic plain weave *either* vertically or horizontally. In effect, it is an unequal basket weave. A *warp-face rep* is one in which each warp yarn moves over two or more weft yarns. This is called a *float*. Conversely, in a *weft-face rep* each weft yarn floats over two or more warp yarns,

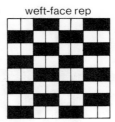 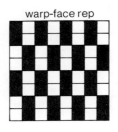

weft-face rep   warp-face rep

above: 237. Weft- and warp-face reps. Rep weaves are derived from plain weave.

and the interlacing is reversed for each successive shot. Figure 237 shows the drafts for two reps.

Twill Weaves

In a twill weave the binding points of warp and weft are staggered to create a pronounced diagonal line. Since the binding points occur less frequently than in plain weave, the fabric is softer and more supple. Unless the twill is balanced—with two warps interlacing over two weft yarns in a diagonal progression—the two faces of the fabric will be the reverse of one another. Twill weaves can be produced with three harnesses, but they are usually set up on four or more.

Straight Twills A straight twill exhibits an unbroken diagonal line. When the diagonal rises from left to right, it is referred to as a *right-hand twill;* a *left-hand twill* rises from right to left. On a four-harness loom the most common straight twills are the 2/2, the 1/3, and the 3/1.

A 2/2 twill is a balanced weave: two warp yarns interlace over two weft yarns (Fig. 238).

238–242. *Twill weaves are characterized by pronounced diagonal lines in the fabric.*

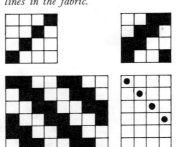

238. A 2/2 straight twill weave.

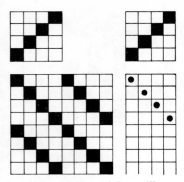

239. A 1/3 straight twill.

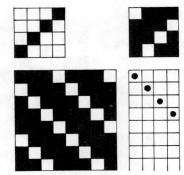

240. A 3/1 straight twill.

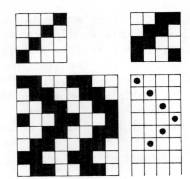

241. A 2/2 reverse twill.

In a 1/3 twill the weft floats over three warps and goes under one, while the warp passes under three wefts and over one (Fig. 239). This creates a weft-face fabric. The warp-face 3/1 twill requires each weft to pass over one warp and under three (Fig. 240).

Reverse Twill A reverse twill creates a zig-zag effect. To produce it, the treadling sequence is altered, so that the diagonal switches back and forth from left to right (Fig. 241).

Herringbone Twill A herringbone or chevron twill also produces a zig-zag, but the progression is horizontal rather than vertical. Unlike the straight and reverse twills, the herringbone is threaded on a pointed draw (Fig. 242).

Satin Weaves

Satin weaves are characterized by long floats on the surface of the fabric (Fig. 243). Because the

binding points are never in contact with one another, the diagonal line typical of twills is fragmented. The fabric is very soft and pliable, and the long floats—in either warp or weft—shimmer with reflected light. At least five harnesses, and sometimes ten or fifteen, are required to produce satin weaves.

LOOM-CONTROLLED WEAVES: A SAMPLER

The sampler is planned to demonstrate the wide variety of patterns that can be obtained from a single threading of the loom, merely by changing the tie-up and treadling sequences, as well as the color and texture of the weft yarns. Properly labeled, the sampler can serve as an excellent reference for future work.

Samplers are variously called *gamps, rags,* or *blankets.* Whatever the name, virtually all weavers resort to sampling in order to test a new design or to see the effect different textures and

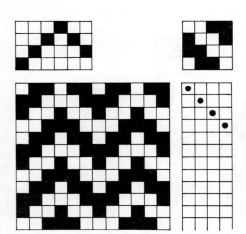

left: 242. A herringbone twill.

below: 243. Satin weaves exhibit long floats on the fabric.

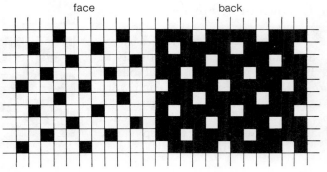

face   back

colors will have on a standard pattern. Many weavers can design more realistically in fabric than on paper. In fact, special looms capable of producing an 8-inch-wide web are manufactured specifically for testing purposes. As a rule, an 8-inch width is sufficient to produce at least two repeats of a pattern, thereby giving a representative sample of the design.

The sampler described on the following pages is planned for a four-harness loom with—in the case of a floor loom—six treadles. The threading pattern is not uniform all across the warp, but even a novice weaver should have no difficulty following the directions. At various points in the course of the sampler the tie-up must be changed. Two colors are included in the warp, and fine or textured yarns are occasionally introduced in the weft to demonstrate the interaction of color, weight, texture, and pattern. The choice of colors is left to the weaver. Contrasting colors will show the development of the pattern most clearly, but black should be avoided by the beginner, for the yarns are difficult to see when threading the heddles.

Specifications for the Sampler

Length of finished web:	8 yards
Length of each warp yarn:	10 yards
Number of warp yarns:	color A: 130
	color B: 124
	total 254
Amount of warp yarn:	color A: 1300 yards
	color B: 1240 yards
	total 2540 yards
Weft yarn:	8/4 carpet warp in two colors
	soft rug yarn in one color
	fine yarn in one color

Amount of weft yarn:	color A: 3 spools
	color B: 3 spools
	rug yarn: 1 spool
	fine yarn: 1 spool
	8 spools
Number of heddles required:	harness 1: 66
	harness 2: 61
	harness 3: 61
	harness 4: 66
Width of finished sampler:	about 15 inches
Width at reed:	17 inches
Size of reed:	No. 15

Warping Instructions

The yarns should be warped in the following sequence on the warping frame or reel:

    32 yarns color A
    28 yarns color B
    36 yarns color A
    32 yarns alternating colors A and B
    30 yarns color B
    28 yarns color A
    36 yarns alternating colors A and B
    32 yarns color B
    254

Threading Instructions

Seven different threading patterns are used across the warp: twill (straight draw), goose eye (pointed draw), rosepath III, cord velveret, broken twill, bird's eye, and wheat. The complete threading draft is given in Figure 244. Each draw is to be repeated the specified number of times before proceeding to the next one. It should be noted that the entire warp contains eight pat-

below: 244. The threading draft for the sampler is divided into eight pattern blocks. Each draw should be repeated the specified number of times before proceeding to the next.

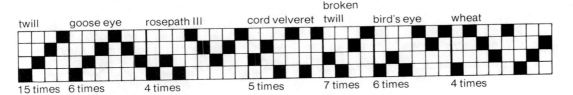

twill   goose eye   rosepath III   cord velveret   broken twill   bird's eye   wheat

15 times   6 times   4 times   5 times   7 times   6 times   4 times

tern *blocks*, and except for the first two, which are threaded in a straight draw, the threading changes each time the yarn color changes.

Sleying Instructions

A single yarn is to be drawn through each dent in a number-15 reed. Therefore, the warp will be 17 inches wide at the reed, with the last inch short one yarn (15 × 17 = 255). In order to center the warp in the loom, the weaver must divide the excess length of the reed by two. For example, if the reed is 20 inches wide, sleying would begin $1\frac{1}{2}$ inches from the right edge of the reed.

Tie-up Instructions

The major portion of the sampler can be accomplished with the so-called *standard tie-up* (Fig. 245): the first four treadles are tied for twill (1-2, 2-3, 3-4, 1-4) and the remaining two for plain weave (1-3, 2-4). It will become obvious to the weaver that this is an extremely flexible arrangement. Further instructions for changing the tie-up are given in the section of the sampler devoted to variations.

Weaving Instructions

The directions given in each of the numbered paragraphs below should be followed for a weav-

left: 245. In the standard tie-up, four treadles are tied for twill, two for tabby.

below: 246. Draft for the plain-weave and basket-weave portions of the sampler.

ing distance of approximately 2 inches to allow for development of the pattern. It is very important to realize that the weave described may appear *only* in the pattern blocks where *both* threading and treadling conform to the needs of that particular weave. For example, even though a tie-up and treadling sequence may specify straight twill, the twill weave will be evident only in the portions of the sampler that are threaded for straight twill—the first two blocks.

A. Plain weave (Fig. 246):

1. Treadle 1-3, 2-4; weft yarn in color A. The weave appears in all parts of the sampler except blocks 5, 6, and 8.
2. Treadle 1-3, 2-4; weft yarn in color B.
3. Treadle 1-3, 2-4; weft yarn alternates colors A and B (two shuttles).
4. Treadle 1-3, 2-4; fine weft yarn.
5. Treadle 1-3, 2-4; textured rug yarn in weft.

B. Basket weave (Fig. 246):

6. Treadle 1-2, 1-2, 3-4, 3-4; weft yarn in color B. The 2/2 basket weave appears only in blocks 1, 2, and 6; block 5, which is threaded for cord velveret, develops a warp-face rep. Figure 247 illustrates the completed portion of the sampler.

C. Twills (Figs. 248, 249):

7. Straight twill—treadle 1-2, 2-3, 3-4, 1-4; weft yarn in color A. The straight twill weave develops only in blocks 1 and 2. Blocks 3, 4, and 7 exhibit the herringbone or chevron twill.

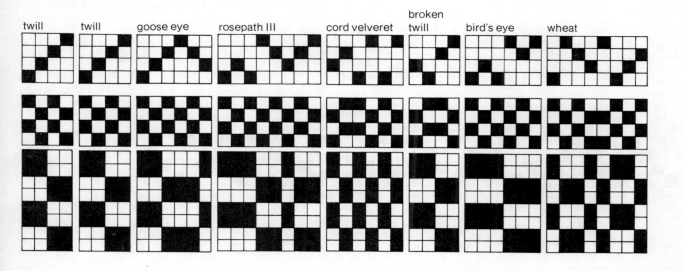

right: 247. The plain-weave and basket-weave portions of the sampler, as they appear in fabric.

below right: 248. The twill portion of the sampler, as it appears in fabric.

8. Straight twill—treadle 1-2, 2-3, 3-4, 1-4; weft yarn in color B. Since the warp and weft are each a single color in block 1, the fabric is striped diagonally.
9. Straight twill—treadle 1-2, 2-3, 3-4, 1-4; weft yarn alternates colors A and B (two shuttles).
10. Reverse twill—treadle 1-2, 2-3, 3-4, 1-4, 3-4, 2-3; weft yarn in color A. The reverse twill is evident only in blocks 1 and 2; a symmetrical diamond-shape pattern is created in blocks 3, 4, and 7.
11. Reverse twill—treadle 1-2, 2-3, 3-4, 1-4, 3-4, 2-3; weft yarn in color B.
12. Reverse twill—treadle 1-2, 2-3, 3-4, 1-4, 3-4, 2-3; weft yarn alternates colors A and B (two shuttles).

D. Twill alternated with plain weave:

13. Straight twill and plain weave—treadle 1-2, 1-3, 2-3, 2-4, 3-4, 1-3, 1-4, 2-4; weft yarn in color A. The pattern is seen only in blocks 1 and 2.
14. Reverse twill and plain weave—treadle 1-2, 1-3, 2-3, 2-4, 3-4, 1-3, 1-4, 2-4, 3-4, 1-3, 2-3, 2-4; weft yarn in color B. The pattern develops only in blocks 1 and 2. Figure 248 illustrates the twill portion of the sampler in fabric.

The weaves in the central portion of the sampler are *tromp as writ,* or treadled in the order in which they are threaded. The term derives from a Colonial expression meaning "tramp as written." Several of the threading patterns have already been treadled. A straight twill treadling (1-2, 2-3, 3-4, 1-4) is the tromp as writ for the twill threading 1-2-3-4. In each case the harness that is threaded *plus* the adjacent harness that is next in order must be raised to create a balanced weave. For example, when the harnesses are threaded 1, 2, 1, 4, 3, 4 (bird's eye), the treadling sequence is 1-*2,* 2-*3,* 1-*2,* 4-*1,* 3-*4,* 4-*1.*

twill   goose eye   rosepath III   cord velveret

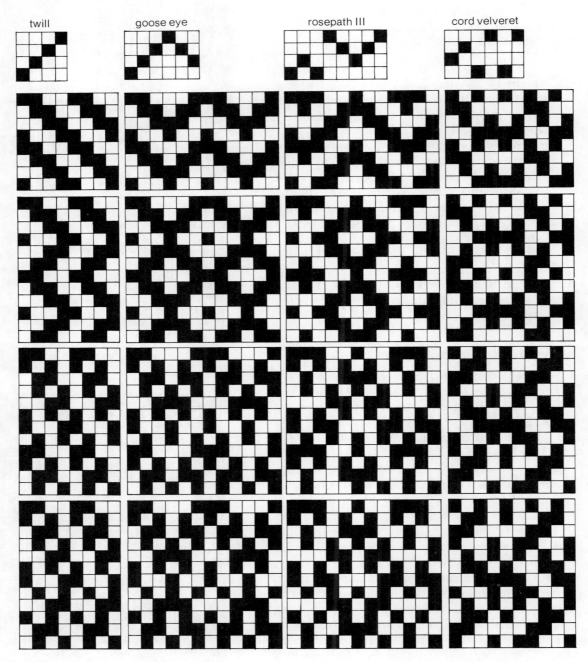

249. Draft of the twill portion of the sampler.

broken twill   bird's eye   wheat

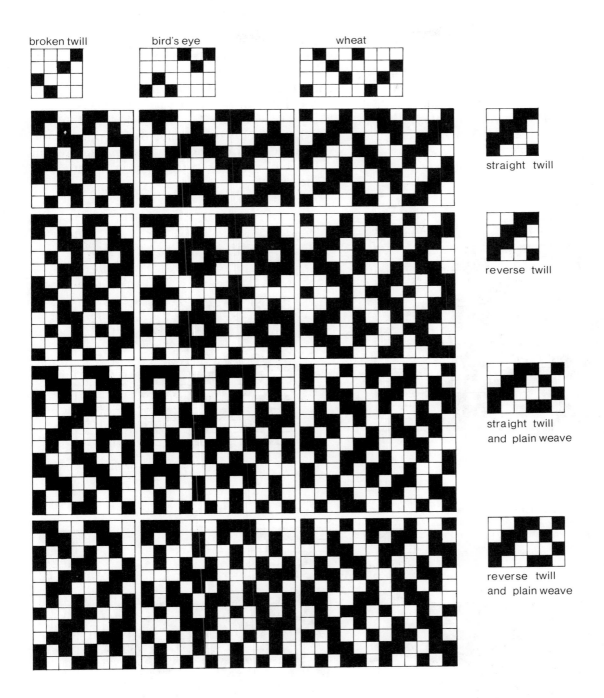

straight twill

reverse twill

straight twill
and plain weave

reverse twill
and plain weave

E. Tromp as writ:

15. Rosepath III (Fig. 250)—treadle 1-2, 2-3, 1-2, 1-4, 3-4, 2-3, 3-4, 1-4; weft yarn in color A. The resultant pattern is similar to that produced when the same threading is treadled for reverse twill (see Fig. 249).
16. Rosepath III—treadle 1-2, 2-3, 1-2, 1-4, 3-4, 2-3, 3-4, 1-4; weft yarn in color B.
17. Cord velveret (Fig. 251)—treadle 2-3, 3-4, 1-2, 1-4, 1-2, 1-4; weft yarn in color A.
18. Cord velveret—treadle 2-3, 3-4, 1-2, 1-4, 1-2, 1-4; weft yarn in color B.
19. Broken twill (Fig. 252)—treadle 2-3, 1-2, 3-4, 1-4; weft yarn in color A.
20. Broken twill—treadle 2-3, 1-2, 3-4, 1-4; weft yarn in color B.
21. Bird's eye (Fig. 253)—treadle 1-2, 2-3, 1-2, 1-4, 3-4, 1-4; weft yarn in color A.
22. Bird's eye—treadle 1-2, 2-3, 1-2, 1-4, 3-4, 1-4; weft yarn in color B.
23. Wheat (Fig. 254)—treadle 1-2, 1-4, 3-4, 2-3, 1-4, 1-2, 2-3, 3-4; weft yarn in color A.
24. Wheat—treadle 1-2, 1-4, 3-4, 2-3, 1-4, 1-2, 2-3, 3-4; weft yarn in color B. The photograph reproduced in Figure 255 is an example in fabric of the various tromp as writ sections of the sampler.

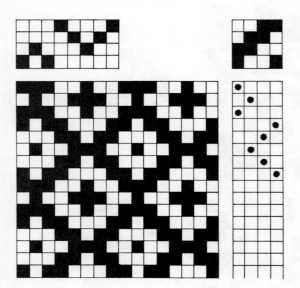

250. Draft for rosepath III.

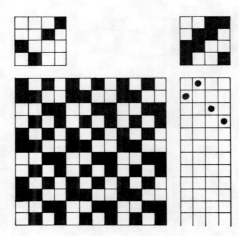

252. Draft for broken twill.

251. Draft for cord velveret.

253. Draft for bird's eye.

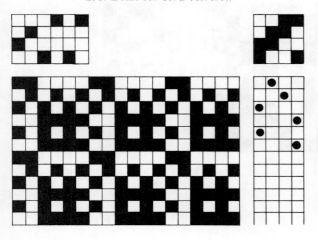

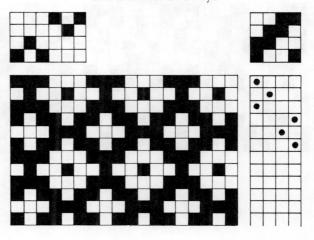

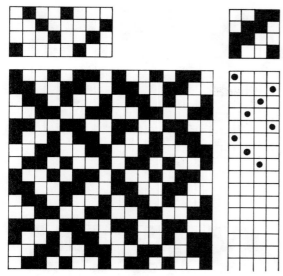

254. Draft for wheat.

below: 255. The tromp-as-writ section of the sampler, as it appears in fabric.

The remaining portion of the sampler is devoted to a series of treadling variations that produce a wide range of patterns. New tie-up instructions are given where necessary, and all the tie-up and treadling drafts are illustrated in Figure 256. Where color variation is important to the development of a weave, this is indicated in the treadling draft by an **x** for a shot of color A and a ● for a shot of color B. In cases where part of a treadling sequence is repeated, it is customary to abbreviate the series as $(1, 2, 3, 4)_3$ rather than listing each combination individually as 1, 2, 3, 4, 1, 2, 3, 4, 1, 2, 3, 4.

below and following page: 256. Draft of the sampler variations, steps 25 through 40.

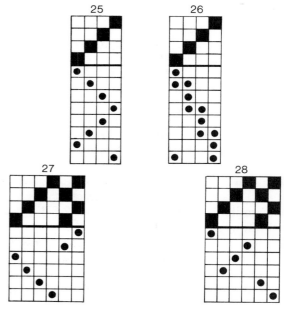

25. Tie-up: 1, 2, 3, 4
    Treadle: $(1, 2, 3, 4)_3$ $(3, 2, 1, 4)_3$
    Weft yarn: color A
26. Tie-up: 1, 2, 3, 4 (depress two treadles where necessary)
    Treadle: 1, 1-2, 2, 2-3, 3, 3-4, 4, 1-4
    Weft yarn: color B
27. Tie-up: 1, 2, 3, 4, 1-3, 2-4
    Treadle: 2-4, 1-3, 1, 2, 3, 4
    Weft yarn: color B
28. Tie-up: 1, 2, 3, 4, 1-3, 2-4
    Treadle: 1, 4, 3, 2, 1-3, 2-4
    Weft yarn: color A

29. Tie-up: 1, 2, 3, 4, 1-3, 2-4 (depress two
               treadles where necessary)
    Treadle: 1-2-3, 2, 2-3-4, 3, 1-3-4, 4, 1-2-4,
               1
    Weft yarn: color B
30. Tie-up: 1-2, 2-3, 3-4, 1-4, 1-3, 2-4 (stand-
               ard)
    Treadle: 1-2, 1-3, 1-4, 2-3, 2-4, 1-2, 3-4, 1-3,
               2-3, 1-4, 2-4, 3-4
    Weft yarn: color A
31. Tie-up: 1-2, 2-3, 3-4, 1-4, 1-3, 2-4 (stand-
               ard)
    Treadle: 2-3, 1-2, 2-3, 3-4, 1-4, 3-4
    Weft yarn: color B
32. Tie-up: 1-2, 2-3, 3-4, 1-4, 1-3, 2-4 (stand-
               ard)
    Treadle: 1-2, 3-4, 2-3, 1-4
    Weft yarn: color A
33. Tie-up: 1-2, 2-3, 3-4, 1-4, 1-3, 2-4 (stand-
               ard)
    Treadle: 2-3, 3-4, 1-2, 2-3, 1-4, 1-2, 3-4, 1-4
    Weft yarn: color B
34. Tie-up: 1-2, 2-3, 3-4, 1-4, 1-3, 2-4 (stand-
               ard)
    Treadle: 1-2, 1-3, 1-2, 2-4, 1-2, 1-3, 2-3, 2-4,
               2-3, 1-3, 2-3, 2-4, 3-4, 1-3, 3-4, 2-4,
               3-4, 1-3, 1-4, 2-4, 1-4, 1-3, 1-4, 2-4
    Weft yarn: alternates colors A and B as indi-
               cated (Fig. 256)
35. Tie-up: 1, 2, 3, 4, 1-3, 2-4 (depress two
               treadles where necessary)
    Treadle: 1, 1-2, 1-2-3, 4, 3-4, 2-3-4
    Weft yarn: color B.
36. Tie-up: 1, 2, 3, 4, 1-3, 2-4 (depress two
               treadles where necessary)
    Treadle: 1-2-3, 1-3, 1-2-3, 2-4, 4, 1-3, 4, 2-4
    Weft yarn: alternates colors A and B as indi-
               cated (Fig. 256)
37. Tie-up: 1-2, 2-3, 3-4, 1-4, 1-3, 2-4 (stand-
               ard)
    Treadle: 1-2, 2-3, 3-4, 2-3, 3-4, 1-4, 3-4, 1-4
    Weft yarn: color B
38. Tie-up: 1-2, 2-3, 3-4, 1-4, 1-3, 2-4 (stand-
               ard)
    Treadle: 1-2, 1-3, 2-4, 2-3, 1-3, 2-4, 3-4, 1-3,
               2-4, 1-4, 1-3, 2-4
    Weft yarn: color A
39. Tie-up: 1-2, 2-3, 3-4, 1-4, 1-3, 2-4 (stand-
               ard)
    Treadle: 1-2, 2-3, 3-4, 1-4
    Weft yarn: colors A and B (Fig. 256)

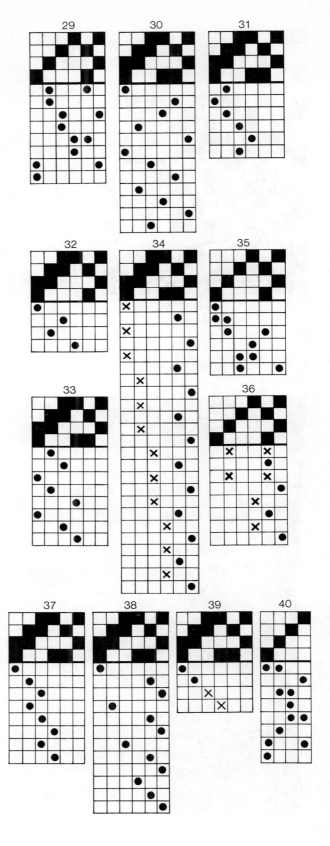

40. Tie-up: 1, 2, 3, 4 (depress two treadles where necessary)
    Treadle: 1-2, 4, 2-3, 3, 3-4, 2, 1-4, 1
    Weft yarn: color B

Finishing Instructions

If any usable warp remains on the loom after all forty strips have been completed, the reader can introduce treadling combinations of his own. The sampler can be finished with a few shots of plain weave, as illustrated in Figure 257, and then hemstitched (Fig. 317) to prevent raveling. After the sampler is cut from the loom, it should be labeled to indicate each threading and treadling combination that was used. Labels should be applied in each block along the bottom of the sampler to show the threading arrangement and in each block along one selvedge to indicate the treadling sequence. Iron-on tape is a convenient method for attaching the labels. The weaver thus has an accurate record of 320 different designs.

The variety in pattern that can be produced merely through the interaction of the harnesses is infinite. After completing the sampler described above, the weaver may wish to experiment with other basic combinations. For example, color can be introduced into both warp and weft in any pattern desired (including random ones) to produce stripes, plaids, and multicolor effects. Textured yarns can influence the development of a weave, as can variations in the sett at the reed. There are hundreds of standard threading arrangements, and the weaver might attempt another sampler substituting eight different drafts for those used previously. Several of the more common drafts are illustrated in Appendix A. However, when combining drafts it is important to consider the effect produced at the juncture of two threadings. In some cases modifications must be made to create a smooth transition. Finally, several different treadling sequences can be applied to the drafts in the sampler and those illustrated in Appendix A. No weaver could ever exhaust the possibilities in simple loom-controlled weaves.

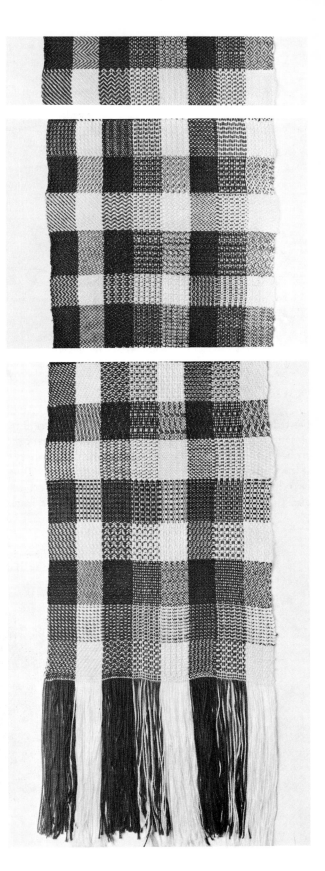

right: 257. The sampler variations, as they appear in fabric. This completes the sampler.

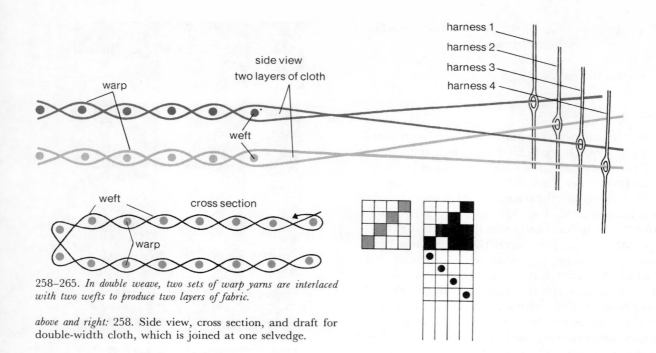

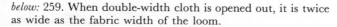

258–265. *In double weave, two sets of warp yarns are interlaced with two wefts to produce two layers of fabric.*

above and right: 258. Side view, cross section, and draft for double-width cloth, which is joined at one selvedge.

DOUBLE WEAVES

Double weave is a technique in which two sets of warps are interlaced with two sets of wefts to create two distinct layers of cloth simultaneously. It is therefore a *four*-element construction. The two layers of fabric are physically attached at one point or at several points. At least four har-nesses are required for double cloth, and an eight-harness loom is capable of producing four separate layers of cloth.

The loom is generally threaded on a straight draw for double cloth. Harnesses 1 and 2 weave the upper layer of cloth, while harnesses 3 and 4 weave the lower layer (or vice versa). However, because the top web must be held out of the way

below: 259. When double-width cloth is opened out, it is twice as wide as the fabric width of the loom.

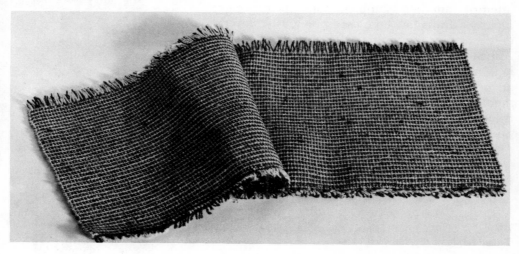

while the bottom web is being woven, the treadling sequence might be 1, 2, 1-2-3, 1-2-4 (Fig. 258). In other words, when the third treadle is depressed (or when levers 1, 2, and 3 are manipulated), the fabric woven on harnesses 1 and 2 is lifted out of the way while at the same time a shed is created between harnesses 3 and 4. Because double cloth requires much treadling of one harness against three, it is difficult to weave on a counterbalance loom.

The sett for double weaves must be rather dense, in order to provide two relatively firm fabrics. Twice as many yarns must be sleyed through each dent as would be required for a single fabric of the same weight.

Double-width Cloth

By employing the double-weave system one can produce a web twice as wide as the loom would normally accommodate. The fabric is woven in such a way that the two layers are joined at one edge and open at the other, so that when it is cut from the loom and opened out, it is twice the weaving width of the loom (Fig. 259). The warp consists of an uneven number of yarns, in order to prevent two warps at the joined edge from being woven alike. The threading, tie-up, and treadling sequences for double-width cloth are those provided in the draft portion of Figure 258.

Tubular Double Weave

Tubular double weave (Pl. 13, p. 127) produces a fabric that is joined at *both* edges to create a cylinder of cloth (Fig. 260). It differs from the double-width cloth only in the treadling sequence (Fig. 261). The treadling for double-width cloth allows first two weft shots for the top layer, then two weft shots for the bottom; in tubular double weave the weft shots alternate between top and bottom.

below: 261. Cross section and draft for tubular double weave.

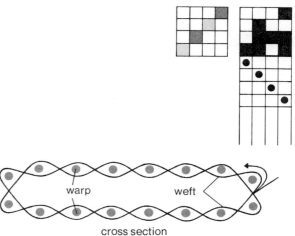

260. Tubular double weave produces a fabric that is joined at both selvedges to create a cylinder of cloth.

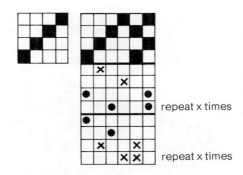

above: 262. A stuffed tubular weave is one in which a padding material is inserted between the layers of fabric during the weaving process. Often, the treadling sequence is reversed from time to time to create sections or pockets of fabric, which are stuffed individually.

above right: 263. Draft for reversing tubular double weave.

The fabric illustrated in Figure 262 was created by reversing the treadling sequence for tubular double weave at planned intervals and by stuffing a padding material between the layers of cloth. The treadling sequence for the top and bottom sections of the fabric is 1, 1-2-3, 2, 1-2-4; the center section is treadled 3, 1-3-4, 4, 2-3-4

(Fig. 263). This reversal of treadling causes the two layers of fabric to come together and then separate again.

Reversed Double Weave

Figure 264 shows a double fabric that is *not* joined at either edge but that is joined across the warp at a point near the center. Two colors have been used in the weft, and the treadling order has been switched at the point of juncture to create a double cloth that reverses upon itself. The draft for this type of web is illustrated in Figure 265. An x represents a weft shot of light-colored yarn, a ● a shot of dark-colored yarn.

left: 264. A double weave can be reversed, so that the two layers of fabric interpenetrate and exchange positions.

above: 265. Draft for reversed double weave.

In addition to the combinations described above, there are a great many pattern double weaves that can be created on a four-harness loom. These are actually finger weaves and are discussed in Chapter 11.

BROCADE

Brocade is a *three*-element construction: in addition to the usual warp and weft, there is a third or decorative element in the web. A brocade effect can be introduced in either the warp or the weft. It can be either *continuous*—running from selvedge to selvedge or from one end of the warp to the other—or *discontinuous*. Discontinuous brocade is described in Chapter 11.

Brocades are most often added to a plain-weave ground. The plain weave exists independently of the decorative element (Fig. 266), so that if all the brocading yarns were to be pulled out, the plain-weave structure would remain intact. Brocades are often referred to as *overshot* patterns. Traditionally, the ground is uniform and rather neutral in color, while the brocade yarn is heavier, softer, and more elaborate. The fabric is usually woven face down.

Warp Brocade

A warp brocade can be woven on only three harnesses. Harnesses 1 and 2 would be threaded for plain weave across the loom, while harness 3 would carry the brocade yarn at each point where it is needed. If desired, a second brocading element could be added on the fourth harness. However, every brocade yarn must have a base yarn on both sides of it to maintain the plain-weave structure. Plates 14 and 15 (p. 128) illustrate a simple warp brocade fabric. The draft is given in Figure 267.

Weft Brocade

To create a weft brocade, the heddles are threaded for plain weave, always alternating between an odd-numbered harness and an even-numbered harness. The base weft yarns are shot through alternating sheds, and the brocade yarn, carried on a separate shuttle, is introduced wherever desired but independent of the plain-weave ground. There must be a plain-weave yarn on

both sides of every brocade yarn. The fabric reproduced in Plate 16 (p. 128) is a simple continuous weft brocade. The draft for this weave is given in Figure 268.

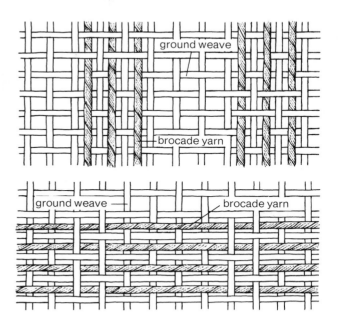

above: 266. In brocade, the ground weave exists independently of the brocading element. The brocade yarn can be introduced in either the warp or the weft.

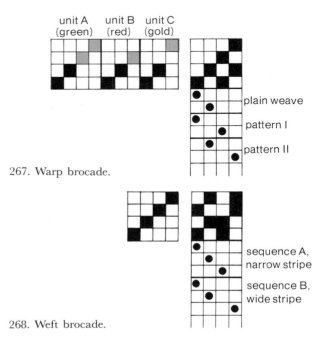

267. Warp brocade.

268. Weft brocade.

Weaver-controlled Weaves

Weaver-controlled weaves are created through
the direct intervention of the weaver. They are
often called finger weaves, because at various
times the shed or a portion of the shed is opened
with the fingers or with some implement—a
needle, crochet hook, or *pickup stick*. Weaver-
controlled weaves differ from those constructed
entirely through the interaction of the harnesses
in several respects: either the warp or the weft
or both may depart from their strict vertical and
horizontal alignments; the weft yarn may appear
only in certain portions of the web, rather than
being carried from selvedge to selvedge; packing
with a beater is often unnecessary or undesirable.

Most finger weaves are based on plain weave.
They frequently require short amounts of weft
yarn, so a *butterfly shuttle* is more practical than
the cumbersome boat shuttle. A butterfly shuttle
can be made by wrapping the yarn figure-**8** fashion around the fingers (Fig. 269). A loop made

from the starting end of the yarn and wrapped
snugly around the cross serves to hold the shape.

LACE WEAVES

Lace weaves comprise one of the largest groups
of weaver-controlled weaves. They have in common an open, "lacy" effect and a distortion from
the parallel of warp or weft yarns. The most
common forms of lace weave are leno, Mexican
lace, Spanish lace, Brook's Bouquet, and Danish
medallion.

Leno

Leno is a form of *gauze weave*—that is, a weave
in which the warp yarns are made to cross each
other at certain points. In preparation for leno,
the loom is threaded for plain weave on two or
four harnesses. A pickup stick that is longer than
the web is wide will facilitate crossing the yarns.
The stick should also be wider than it is thick,
so that when it is placed on end a shed is opened
(Fig. 270).

The simplest form of leno is the 1/1 or *single
cross,* in which two adjacent warp yarns are

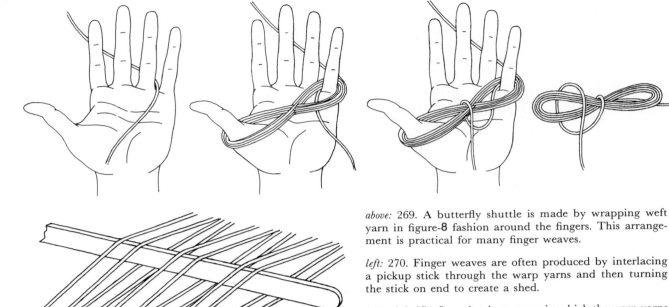

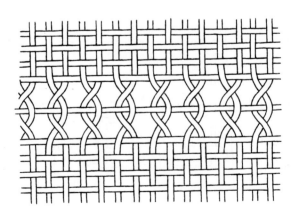

above: 269. A butterfly shuttle is made by wrapping weft yarn in figure-8 fashion around the fingers. This arrangement is practical for many finger weaves.

left: 270. Finger weaves are often produced by interlacing a pickup stick through the warp yarns and then turning the stick on end to create a shed.

below left: 271. Leno is a lace weave in which the warp yarns are crossed at certain points. The simplest form is 1/1 leno.

below right: 272. A 2/2 leno weave.

crossed upon each other. After a few rows of plain weave have been woven, and the shuttle is at the right selvedge, the shed is changed so that the outermost warp yarn at the right is down. The pickup stick is placed on top of the second warp yarn (which is up), and the first warp is crossed under the second and placed on top of the stick to the left of the second warp. The pickup stick then proceeds slightly to the left so that it rests on the fourth warp yarn, and the third warp is crossed behind the fourth and placed on the stick. This procedure is continued across the web. With practice, one can accomplish the crossings by manipulation of the stick alone, without actually lifting the yarns by hand. Left-handed weavers may find it more convenient to reverse the directions and work from left to right. When all the lower yarns are on the pickup stick, the stick is turned on end, and the weft yarn is passed through the resultant shed (Fig. 271). The stick is removed carefully, and the shed is changed. On the return trip, no yarns are crossed, but a cross effect is produced as the yarns untwist themselves.

A double or 2/2 leno (Fig. 272) works on the same principle. Starting at the right, the stick is placed over the second and fourth warp yarns (which are up), and the first and third warps are

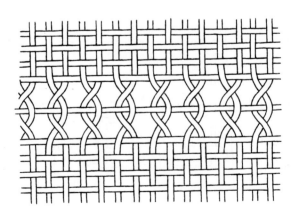

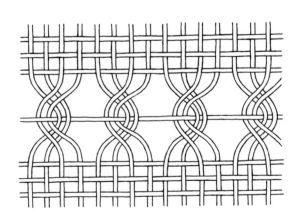

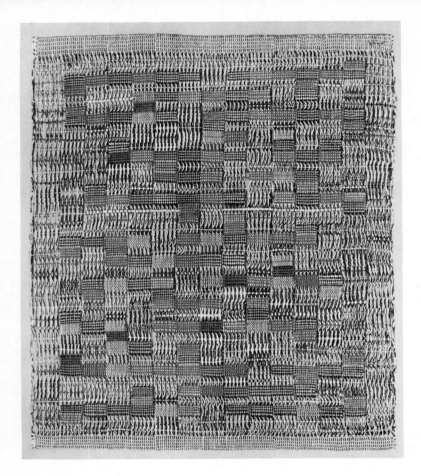

273. ANNI ALBERS. *Tikal*. 1958. Pictorial weaving of cotton in leno and plain weave, 35½ × 29½″. From *Objects: USA,* Johnson Wax Collection of Contemporary Crafts, Racine, Wis.

crossed behind and placed on the stick to the left of the second and fourth yarns. Various other arrangements are possible: three bottom warps crossed on three top warps, one top warp crossed on two bottom warps, and so forth. Several leno combinations are explored in the sampler (pp. 160–165). The "pictorial weaving" by Anni Albers reproduced in Figure 273 is an excellent example of leno alternated with plain weave.

Mexican Lace

The Mexican lace variation of leno causes the warp yarns to cross three times, with the weft inserted in the middle cross (Fig. 274). The pickup stick is manipulated so that all the even-numbered warp yarns are on the stick. Like the leno weave, Mexican lace can be worked with either a single (1/1) or a double (2/2) cross.

274. In Mexican lace the warp yarns are crossed three times, with the weft inserted in the middle cross.

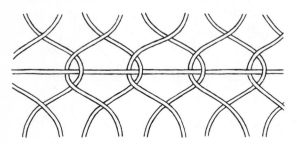

275. To create Spanish lace, one divides the warp into sections and weaves each unit individually with a butterfly shuttle. An attractive pattern results when the units are drawn together with spaces between.

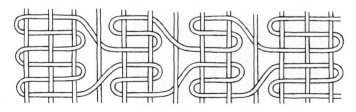

Spanish Lace

To weave Spanish lace one divides the warp into units and interlaces each unit individually, moving from right to left or left to right across the warp. For purposes of demonstration, the warp yarns in Figure 275 have been divided into groups of three, but in practice, on the loom, each group would probably consist of six to ten yarns. The weft is inserted at the right selvedge, with the 1-3 shed open. It traverses one unit of warp yarns, and then the shed is changed to 2-4 and the weft returns to the selvedge. The shed is again changed to 1-3, and the weft is passed to the extent of the warp unit once more. With the 1-3 shed still open, the weft yarn is then carried down diagonally to the level of the first weft shot but on the second group of yarns, and makes the same S-curve on that unit. The weft can be beat—or actually eased—into position only with the fingers or the edge of the shuttle; the beater is never used. When the weft yarn reaches the left selvedge, a total of three new weft shots—in sections—have been added to the web.

Spanish lace is most effective when the grouped units of warp yarn are drawn together slightly to leave an open slit between them. It is particularly attractive when the weft yarn is heavier than the warp or when it is of a contrasting color. Variety of pattern is achieved by altering the size of the warp units, by staggering the number of weft shots in each unit, or by interspersing areas of Spanish lace with solid plain weave. An adjacent section of plain weave may require extra weft shots to keep the rows even.

Danish Medallion

The Danish medallion is an unusual weave in that the weft yarn departs from its horizontal orientation to make a vertical or diagonal loop on the surface of the fabric (Fig. 276). This loop of yarn is the medallion. It is usually woven with a yarn that contrasts in weight, color, texture, or a combination of these with the warp yarn and ground weft, although a purely textured effect can be produced with identical yarn.

The medallion yarn is passed through the normal plain-weave shed, followed by several shots of ground weft (Fig. 277). Then, the medallion yarn is entered in the next shed, passing through

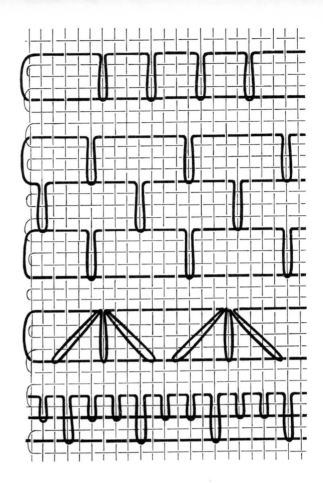

a predetermined number of warps before it is brought to the surface of the fabric. A crochet hook is used to catch a loop of the yarn just below the previous medallion weft yarn and at the same horizontal point where the shuttle emerged from the shed. The loop is enlarged to permit the shuttle to pass through it. To finish

above: 276. Variations of Danish medallion are produced by altering the length, direction, or spacing of the medallion loops.

below: 277. In Danish medallion, the weft yarn departs from its horizontal orientation to make a vertical or diagonal loop on the surface of the fabric.

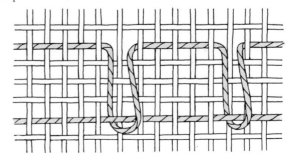

the medallion, the shuttle is replaced in the shed at the same spot and continues across the web until another medallion is required.

By altering the vertical distance between rows of medallion yarn and the horizontal distance between medallions, one can create a wide range of patterns. The weaver can also produce flowerets, radiating rays, and other designs by catching several loops at the same spot and reentering the yarn at different points in the shed. Several variations of Danish medallion are demonstrated in the sampler.

Brook's Bouquet

Brook's Bouquet, sometimes called *back stitch,* is a form of warp wrapping made on an open shed. As indicated in Figure 278, the weft yarn passes under a group of warps, wraps around them completely, and then proceeds to the next group. The warp yarn between groups, because it is at the bottom of the shed, is not affected and appears as a single vertical line between the units of Brook's Bouquet. As the weft is twisted around the warps, it should be held tightly enough to draw the warp yarns together, but not so tightly that the weft cannot be beat into position or that two units of warp pull together. Variation in pattern is created by staggering the units of warp to be enclosed or by alternating with sections of plain weave.

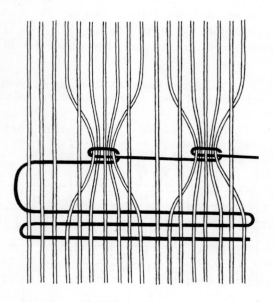

LACE WEAVES: A SAMPLER

The sampler cannot possibly explore all the myriad combinations of the various lace weaves. However, the several examples of each will provide the weaver with a key to developing patterns of his own design. The sampler was planned for four harnesses; however, since all the lace weaves described are based on plain weave, it could easily be duplicated on two harnesses.

Specifications for the Sampler

Length of finished sampler:	2½ yards
Length of each warp yarn:	3 yards
Warp yarn:	10/1 linen *weft*
Number of warp yarns:	208
Amount of warp yarn:	624 yards (one 4-ounce spool)
Weft yarn:	10/1 linen weft linen bouclé in a contrasting color
Amount of weft yarn:	ground weft: 1 spool bouclé: 1 spool
Number of heddles required:	52 on each of four harnesses
Width of finished sampler:	about 10 inches
Width at reed:	10½ inches
Size of reed:	No. 10

Threading, Sleying, and Tie-up Instructions

The warp is threaded in a straight draw (1, 2, 3, 4) throughout. Two yarns are sleyed through each dent in a number-10 reed. The tie-up is 1-3, 2-4 for the entire sampler.

Weaving Instructions

A dividing band of plain weave at least one inch wide should be woven after each of the pattern areas described below. The 10/1 linen weft yarn is used for the first thirteen steps.

left: 278. Brook's Bouquet is a form of warp wrapping in which the weft yarn passes completely around several warp yarns to draw them together.

Plate 17. Chief pattern blanket, Navajo. 1890—95. Wool. Millicent A. Rogers Memorial Museum, Inc., Taos, N.M.

Plate 18. HELENA BARYNINA HERNMARCK with her tapestry *Little Richard*. 1969.
Wool, 8 x 7′. Present whereabouts unknown.

279–283. *The lace-weave sampler on this and the following pages has been turned upside down to be read logically from top to bottom as the instructions are given.*

right: 279. Leno section of the sampler. *Top to bottom:* 2/2 leno alternated with plain weave; 3/3 leno alternated with plain weave; allover 1/1 leno; a staggered pattern of 2/2 leno; a pattern of 3/3 leno alternated with untwisted areas; a block pattern of 2/2 leno; a shaped area of 2/2 leno surrounded by plain weave.

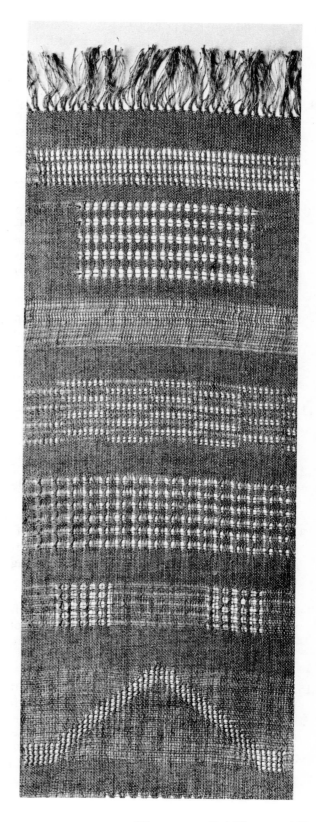

1. Three rows of 2/2 leno (Fig. 279) alternated with three rows of plain weave. A border of plain weave is allowed at each selvedge for a distance of ten warp yarns. Extra weft shots must be made occasionally in the border areas to keep the selvedge firm.

2. A central pattern consisting of five rows of 3/3 leno alternated with seven rows of plain weave. The 2-inch-wide border at each selvedge requires occasional extra weft shots to keep the rows even.

3. Eight rows of 1/1 leno from selvedge to selvedge. A weft shot of ordinary plain weave follows each row of leno.

4. A staggered pattern of 2/2 leno, created by twisting 32 warp yarns and leaving the next group of 32 untwisted. On adjacent rows the twisted areas are alternated. Three shots of regular plain weave separate each pair of leno rows.

5. A 3/3 leno, with six warp yarns left free after each twisted group. Five shots of plain weave follow each row of leno.

6. Block patterns of 2/2 leno separated by plain weave. A single free yarn is left between each pair of leno twists, and the rows are separated by three shots of plain weave.

7. A shaped area of 2/2 leno surrounded by plain weave. At the top of the arrowhead the number of twists per row gradually increases from one to seven; on each of the arms four double twists are made in each row, staggered diagonally as the shape progresses downward and outward.

8. Brook's Bouquet (Fig. 280) wrapped around four warp yarns on an open shed, with five plain-weave weft shots after each row of Brook's Bouquet.

9. Brook's Bouquet wrapped around four warp yarns on an open shed, followed by three plain-weave weft shots. The wrapped warps are staggered in each succeeding row by taking two warp yarns each from adjacent groups in the previous row and wrapping them together.

10. Brook's Bouquet wrapped around three warp yarns on an open shed, alternating both vertically and horizontally with plain weave. In the first three wrapped rows, three warp yarns from the top of the shed are left unwrapped between wrapped groups, and each row is followed by three shots of ground weft. In the next three rows of Brook's Bouquet, the warp yarns that are unwrapped in the first three rows are wrapped, and the alternate groups are left free. The last three rows repeat the first arrangement.

11. A block design in Brook's Bouquet wrapped around four warp yarns on an open shed. Areas of plain weave separate the blocks.

12. Spanish lace (Fig. 281) woven on units of sixteen warp yarns. Three weft shots are made on each unit before moving to the next.

13. Spanish lace woven on warp units that alternate between twelve and 24 yarns. Seven weft shots are made on each unit before proceeding to the next.

14. Spanish lace woven with a contrasting weft yarn (linen bouclé) on irregular warp units of eight and sixteen yarns. Seven weft shots are made on each unit.

15. Spanish lace woven with contrasting weft yarn on warp units of eight yarns. Five weft shots are made through two units at a time, and the units are staggered from row to row. For example, in the first row units 1 and 2, 3 and 4, etc. are woven together. In the second row the weft passes through units 2 and 3, 4 and 5, and so forth.

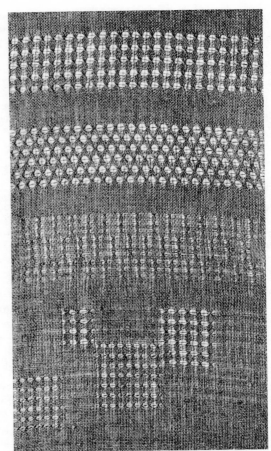

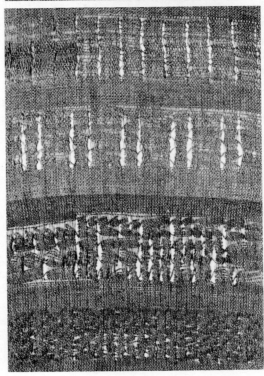

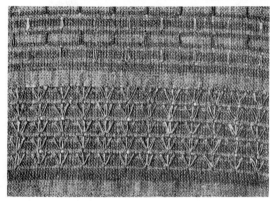

opposite above: 280. Brook's Bouquet portion of the sampler. *Top to bottom:* Brook's Bouquet alternating horizontally with plain weave; staggered units of Brook's Bouquet; Brook's Bouquet alternating vertically and horizontally with plain weave; a block design in Brook's Bouquet, separated by areas of plain weave.

opposite below: 281. Spanish lace portion of the sampler. *Top to bottom:* Spanish lace on uniform sections of the warp; alternate large and small areas of Spanish lace; Spanish lace on irregular warp units; Spanish lace on staggered units of eight warp yarns.

16. Regular units of Danish medallion (Fig. 282) woven with contrasting bouclé yarn. Four shots of 10/1 linen ground weft separate the looped medallion yarns, and there are sixteen warp yarns between loops. Three ground-weft shots follow each row of medallions.

17. Staggered loops of Danish medallion, with the looped yarn alternating between 10/1 linen weft and bouclé. Groups of 24 warp yarns separate the loops, and each loop passes over eight ground-weft shots.

18. A crow's-foot pattern in Danish medallion. For each crow's foot three loops are drawn up in different places, but the shuttle is replaced in the shed at the same point. There are fourteen warp yarns between the points where the shuttle emerges from the shed, and each loop is made over ten weft shots.

19. Five rows of 1/1 Mexican lace (Fig. 283) separated by five shots of plain weave. The weft yarn for steps 19 and 20 is uniformly the 10/1 linen.

20. A pattern of 2/2 Mexican lace, with two plain-weave shots between the twisted rows.

WARP WRAPPING

Warp wrapping is, in a sense, an extension of the lace weaves. The weft yarn wraps around several warps to draw them together, thus producing an open, lacy effect. In ancient Peru warp wrapping was accomplished on the backstrap loom, using a needle or small shuttle to constrict the warp yarns or occasionally the weft. The result was rather like embroidery.

above: 282. Danish medallion section of the sampler. *Top to bottom:* regular units of Danish medallion; staggered Danish medallion; crow's-foot pattern.

below: 283. Mexican lace portion of the sampler. *Top to bottom:* 1/1 Mexican lace; 2/2 Mexican lace.

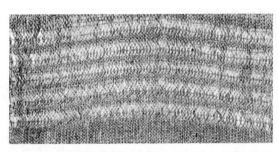

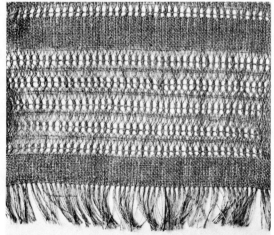

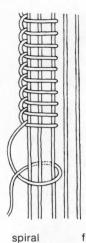

left: 284. Lockstitch can be used for warp wrapping.

below: 285–288. Spiral, figure-8, and vertical twined warp wrapping.

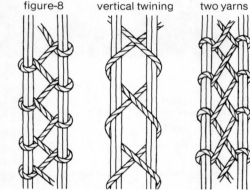

spiral   figure-8   vertical twining   two yarns

Several techniques can be employed for wrapping and gathering the warp. Among the most common is the Greek soumak (Fig. 344) which, when pulled taut, produces a diagonal pattern on the surface of the fabric. Another method is the *lockstitch* (Fig. 284), which resembles Danish medallion. A small shuttle carrying the pattern weft forms a loop around a selected number of warp yarns and then is passed through that loop to hold the stitch. Other warp-wrapping patterns include the spiral, the figure-**8**, and the vertical twining technique (Figs. 285–288).

PATTERN DOUBLE WEAVE

Pattern double weaves differ from the loom-controlled variety described in Chapter 10 (pp. 152–155) in that the two layers of fabric interpenetrate and exchange positions at certain points. The pattern is created either by carrying the weft yarn across only part of the web at a time or by lifting selected warp yarns by hand wherever the design is required.

A very simple form of pattern double weave is illustrated in Figure 289. Each layer of fabric has an identical warp and weft, but the two layers cross and exchange positions at the center

289–294. *Like the loom-controlled form of double weave, pattern double weave is produced from two sets of warp yarns and two sets of weft. However, a pattern is created either by passing the weft yarn across only part of the web or by lifting selected warp yarns by hand.*

left: 289. Two shuttles—one for each side of the web—are employed to create a double cloth in which the two layers exchange positions vertically at the center of the web.

of the warp. This is accomplished by carrying the shuttle from the center of the web to one selvedge and then back again to the center. An alternate shuttle weaves from the center to the opposite selvedge and back. The heddles are threaded in a straight draw with the warp yarns alternating between the two colors (Fig. 290).

The stylized pattern in Figure 291 was created with the aid of a pickup stick or knitting needle. This double fabric is reversible: the design appears in light yarn set against a dark ground on one side, in dark yarn against a light ground on the other. In order to do this, the pickup stick forces the pattern warps from the bottom layer of fabric into the top layer, and the pattern warps from the top layer into the bottom. As the weave draft shows (Fig. 292), there are six steps involved. The weaver first treadles 2-4 and, with the shed open, places the pickup stick under all the warp yarns that are to carry the pattern (Fig. 293). Then, with the pickup stick in position, the shed is changed. The weaver treadles first 1 and then 3, making each time a weft shot with the same color yarn as is threaded in harness 1. The fourth step requires treadling 1-3 and lifting all the background yarns onto the pickup stick—that is, all the yarns not picked up for step 1. Then, 2 and 4 are treadled in turn, and the other weft yarn, color B, is inserted. When the pattern

pick up pattern yarns

pick up background yarns

below: 290. Draft for the fabric illustrated in Figure 289.

above right: 291. A pattern can be created with the aid of a pickup stick, which forces the warp yarns from one layer of fabric into the other wherever the pattern is required.

center right: 292. Draft for the patterned fabric (Fig. 291).

below right: 293. The pickup stick is threaded under all the yarns that are to carry the pattern.

	weave from center to left edge
	weave from left edge to center
	weave from center to right edge
	weave from right edge to center
	weave from center to right edge
	weave from right edge to center
	weave from center to left edge
	weave from left edge to center

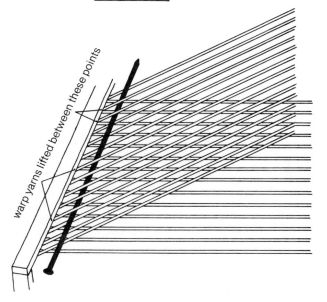

warp yarns lifted between these points

could be removed, leaving the basic fabric intact. In nearly all cases the extra yarn is in the weft.

Laid-in yarns, by definition, are discontinuous; that is, they do not run from selvedge to selvedge but appear only in certain portions of the web. The weaver usually works with the face or "right" side of the fabric down, checking his progress whenever necessary in a hand mirror. In this way the ends of the laid-in yarns can be disposed of easily—either tied off at the end of a pattern area or carried over to the next pattern area as a float on the reverse side. The decorative yarns are wrapped in butterfly shuttles (Fig. 269) for ease of handling.

Discontinuous Brocade

A discontinuous brocade is the free-weaving equivalent of the loom-controlled brocades described in Chapter 10 (see p. 155). Such a brocade technique affords the weaver the greatest possible latitude in creating designs, patterns, and randomly decorated fabrics.

The simplest method of laying in a brocade yarn is to add it to the plain-weave shed (Fig.

area increases or decreases—for example, to create a diagonal line, the change should affect two adjacent warp yarns in each row, in order to permit a smooth transition.

Figure 294 illustrates a slightly more complicated version of the reversible pattern weave. In this case, the pattern reverses itself both from front to back and from top to bottom, because the weave draft has been altered halfway through the web. At the point of juncture, the treadling is adjusted as for reversed double weave (Fig. 265). There are literally infinite variations possible with pattern double weave.

LAID-IN WEAVE

The laid-in weaves, also known as *inlay* or *inlaid*, comprise a large and somewhat amorphous group of weaving patterns characterized by additional and usually decorative yarns superimposed on a plain-weave or other simple background. The extra yarns can add color, texture, pattern, or all three, but the tabby ground exists independently. Theoretically, the laid-in yarns

above left: 294. A double cloth can be reversed in two directions: from front to back and from top to bottom. This fabric was created by combining the techniques in Figures 265 and 292.

295–299. *Laid-in weaves are characterized by additional, usually decorative, yarns superimposed on an independent ground weave. They are by nature discontinuous.*

below: 295. A discontinuous brocade yarn is most often placed in the plain-weave shed beside the ground-weave yarn.

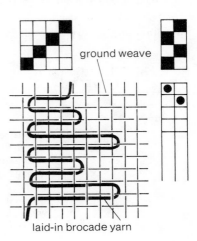

ground weave

laid-in brocade yarn

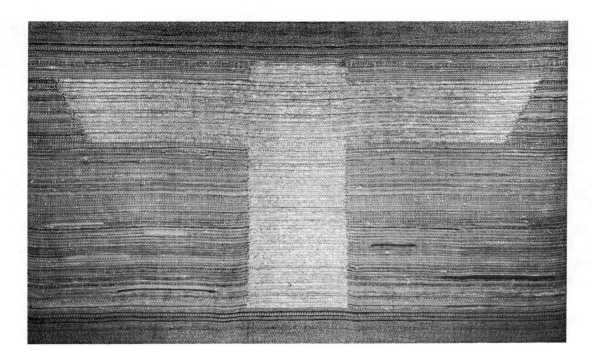

above: 296. ANNI ALBERS. *La Luz I.* 1945. Linen and metal gimp satine weave with discontinuous brocade, $18\frac{3}{4} \times 31\frac{1}{4}''$. Collection Richard Lippold, Locust Valley, N.Y.

below: 297. Dukagång is a version of laid-in brocade in which the decorative yarn floats over three consecutive warp yarns. Nordiska Museet, Stockholm.

295. The loom is threaded in a straight draw and tied up for a 1-3 and 2-4 treadling. Each time the brocade yarn is required, it is placed in the plain-weave shed alongside the regular weft yarn. When the pattern area is completed, the brocade yarn can be tied off and cut or, if it is to appear again, carried across the back of the fabric (which is up) to the next pattern area.

Of course, it is not essential for the brocaded fabric to be based on plain weave. Twills and other weaves can form the background of a brocade, with the additional yarn laid into some or all of the sheds. In any event, the brocade yarn is generally softer and more decorative than the ground-weave yarns. Following the tradition of opulent Renaissance and Baroque brocades, the pattern yarn is often a metallic (Fig. 296).

Dukagång

One variation of the laid-in brocade is Swedish dukagång, in which the decorative yarn floats over three consecutive warp yarns and is tied down by the fourth (Fig. 297). This technique

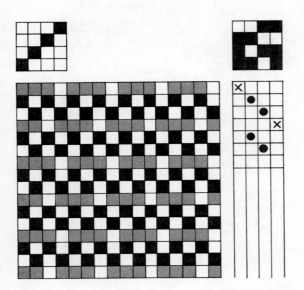

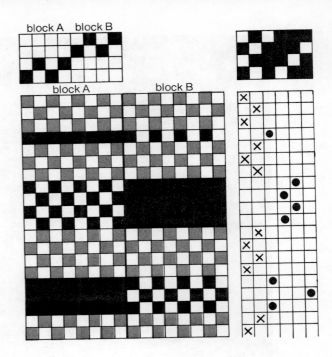

298–299. Drafts for dukagång (*left*) and mock double cloth.

permits greater visibility of the brocade yarn on the surface and produces the "straight little paths in the cloth" from which dukagång takes its name.

As the sample draft (Fig. 298) illustrates, the decorative yarn is not placed in the same shed as the tabby weft. Rather, a separate shed is created for the pattern yarn, followed by one or two shots of plain weave. The fabric is always woven face down. There can be as many as four different dukagang sheds (1-2-3, 2-3-4, 1-3-4, and 1-2-4) or only one. In the sample draft there are two pattern sheds. If the decorative yarn is much heavier than the plain-weave yarn, extra weft shots may be necessary from time to time to fill in the background areas of the fabric and keep the rows even.

Mock Double Cloth

Unlike a true double weave, which has two sets of warp and weft, mock double cloth is a *three*-element construction, with two separate wefts but only one warp. The fabric resembles both brocade and tapestry, in that the pattern yarns appear on the surface of the fabric only in certain areas and float on the reverse side when not needed. As a rule, the plain-weave ground is woven in one color, the pattern blocks in another, usually contrasting, color.

A sample draft for mock double cloth (Fig. 299) shows the web divided into two pattern blocks. Block A is threaded 1,2,1,2; the draw for block B is 3,4,3,4. Whenever the pattern weft is not engaged, it floats on the reverse side of the fabric. As for dukagång, there are four possible pattern treadlings: 1-2-3, 1-2-4, 1-3-4, and 2-3-4. However, the pattern weave can be alternated with tabby in any sequence desired.

TAPESTRY

A tapestry is a weft-face plain-weave fabric in which pattern areas are built up by free-weaving techniques. The design is often, though by no means always, pictorial. There are many traditional styles of tapestry weaving, each deriving its name from the region or group in which it originated. In some cases the names imply a characteristic pattern or design, in others a particular weaving technique. Often, both elements combine to form an identifiable style. The modern tapestry weaver borrows methods and ideas from many sources, both contemporary and historical, in order to achieve his expressive purpose. With the possible exception of the long-established tapestry manufactures and some tradition-bound folk craftsmen, few weavers would insist today that a tapestry must rigidly follow prescribed rules to be "correct." Indeed, the 20th-century weaver is blessed with an enormous wealth of precedent from which to draw his inspiration.

Materials

Two considerations are paramount in choosing the most appropriate materials for a tapestry. First, the warp must be strong enough to resist breakage under tension, to endure a considerable amount of handling during the weaving process, and to lend body to the tapestry. For this reason, linen has traditionally been chosen for a tapestry warp, although some cotton and synthetic yarns are suitable for certain projects. The second variable is proportion, the relative weight of warp and weft yarns. Since it is nearly always required that the weft completely cover the warp, the weft yarn should be a bit larger than the warp and

below: 300. A tapestry loom is a vertical frame with only two harnesses. Tapestries woven on such a loom are called *haute lisse. Basse-lisse* tapestries come from the horizontal loom.

below right: 301. A tapestry fork replaces the beater and reed.

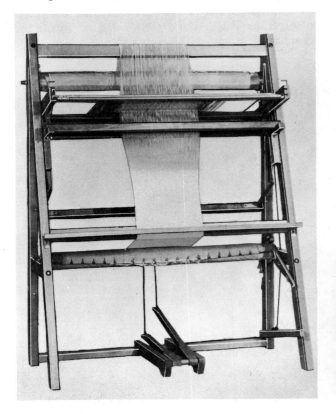

must be soft enough to pack around the warp yarns. Wool yarns are soft and pliable; they accept color easily, which is a decided advantage in the pattern-carrying element. The vast majority of all tapestries are woven in wool.

Equipment

Tapestries are generally divided into two groups, depending upon the type of equipment on which they are woven. *Basse-lisse* or low-warp tapestries are woven on a standard horizontal loom with two or four harnesses—the same type of loom used for other kinds of flat weaving. *Haute-lisse* or high-warp tapestries are woven on the vertical two-harness tapestry loom (Fig. 300) or on an upright frame loom (Figs. 391, 392). Because the structure is always plain weave, only two harnesses or shedding devices are required. For very small or simple projects, the weaver could even dispense with harnesses and heddles altogether and interlace with the fingers. The weaving proceeds a bit faster on the horizontal loom, but, since tapestries are invariably woven with the face or "right" side *away* from the weaver, one can check one's progress only by slipping a mirror under the web. With a vertical loom, the weaver merely walks around to the other side.

An ordinary beater cannot be used for most tapestries. Instead, the weft yarns are laid into place with the fingers, a comb, or a tapestry fork (Fig. 301), a heavy tool that eliminates the need for vigorous packing. If a reed is used, the warp yarns should be sleyed rather far apart, between six and twelve yarns per inch, depending upon the weight of the yarn. In the absence of a reed, the warp yarns are set up on the loom in the same density. This relatively broad spacing permits the warp to be covered by the weft.

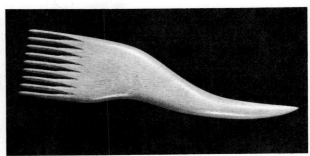

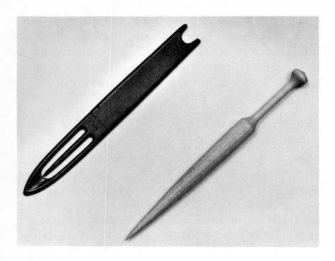

The weft yarns can be wound in small butterfly shuttles or on pointed tapestry bobbins (Fig. 302). A 4-inch length of $\frac{1}{4}$-inch dowel, tapered to a long, dull point at one end, makes an excellent bobbin.

The Cartoon

The tapestry cartoon is the preliminary drawing used as a guide by the weaver. Many great masters have prepared the designs for tapestry, and their sketches survive as oil paintings (Figs. 101, 102, 109, 110). However, the more usual medium is watercolor. Most often the cartoon is drawn to the actual size of the proposed tapestry, but in some styles it is drawn to scale for enlargement on the loom. Either way, the drawing is done in *reverse*, a mirror image of the tapestry to be woven. The cartoon is placed under the warp on a horizontal loom or behind it on a vertical loom. The weaver also works in reverse, from the wrong side of the fabric. Major outlines and pattern areas can be transferred directly to the warp yarns by marking them with a felt-tipped pen (Fig. 303). The ink will not rub off during the weaving, and it will be obscured by the weft in the finished tapestry.

Weaving Techniques

In tapestry weaving a single weft yarn seldom, if ever, travels the entire distance from selvedge to selvedge. Rather, the weft yarns are built up in pattern areas, with each color moving back

and forth in its designated segment of the warp. For very intricate designs a single color of weft yarn might cover only one warp, before disappearing on the back of the tapestry. There are two basic methods of accomplishing this buildup of pattern. The weaver can work in regular horizontal rows, changing colors whenever the design requires it, or he can weave a whole pattern area in one color, working vertically, and then go back to fill in adjacent areas. However, an overhanging shape cannot be woven until the background area has been completed.

The warp yarns should be held under firm tension, to prevent the web from buckling or drawing in at the edges. A heading of plain weave, twining, or chaining (Figs. 338, 340), woven before the tapestry itself is begun, will help to maintain the horizontal dimension of the fabric. The heading can be removed after the tapestry is cut from the loom. While the weaving is in progress, short lengths of cord or twine can be looped through the tapestry and tied to the loom (Fig. 391). This system, too, will help prevent the edges from curling and drawing in. The cords should be set about 2 to 4 inches apart.

Some practice is necessary to acquire the knack of entering the weft yarn. The yarn should be bubbled, so that it will pack around the warp neatly, but there should be no obvious loops, either in the web or at the selvedges. Some forms of tapestry weaving employ a technique called *eccentric weft,* in which the weft yarns depart from the true horizontal and move in arcs or at acute angles to the warp. This method is helpful in fitting wedges or lozenges of color into a background area.

A distinguishing feature of tapestries is the presence or absence of *slits,* vertical openings in the web that are created at the point of juncture between two pattern segments. Because the weft yarns move independently within specified areas, vertical lines in the design will always cause slits, unless measures are taken to avoid them. The simplest way to prevent slits in a design composed of many verticals is to turn the entire tapestry on its side and weave horizontally. Thus, the verticals become horizontals, interlocked with the warp, and no slits occur. If the vertical lines are adjusted so that the weft yarn advances either to the right or to the left one warp at a time (Fig. 304), slits will not develop.

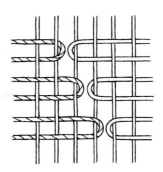

304–306. *Slits are vertical openings in a tapestry fabric created at the point of juncture between two pattern elements. Some tapestries exploit the presence of slits, but when they are not desirable, various measures can be taken to prevent their occurrence.*

above: 304. If vertical lines in the pattern are adjusted so that the weft yarn advances either to the right or to the left one warp at a time, slits will not develop.

below: 305. Gobelin overcasting is a method for closing slits by means of a stitch that runs parallel to the weft.

Historically, there have been three basic methods of dealing with slits. Some medieval tapestries exploited them to create a shadowed effect in the fabric. In this event, the slits were simply left open, and their scale was adjusted to the size of the tapestry. The Polish *kilim* also incorporates unsewn slits. In other tapestry styles the slits are sewn closed after the tapestry is finished. A buttonhole stitch worked on the reverse side of the fabric will not be conspicuous if the two sides of the opening are butted together properly, with no overlapping. In French Gobelin tapestries the slits are sewn on the face in an overcast stitch parallel to the weft (Fig. 305). No attempt is made to conceal the stitch.

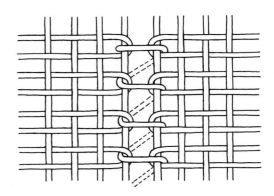

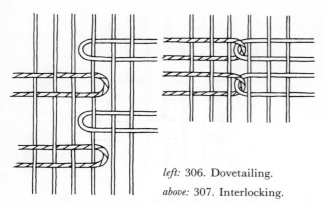

left: 306. Dovetailing.

above: 307. Interlocking.

306–307. *Weft yarns can be wrapped around a common warp or around each other to avoid slits.*

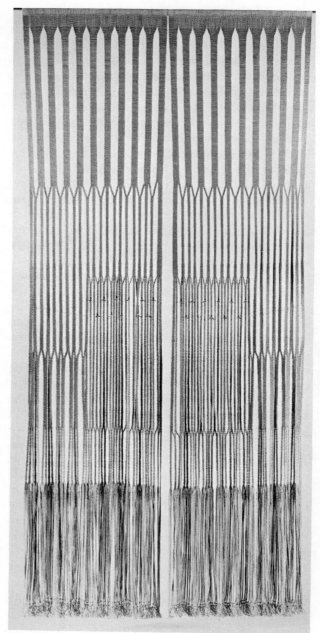

The third method dispenses with the slits altogether. The weft yarns are wrapped around a common warp—a system called *dovetailing*—or around each other (Figs. 306, 307). The latter method of weft interlocking is employed in Scandinavian *rölakan* weaving.

Some tapestries, such as Navajo rugs (P1.17, p. 161), are reversible, with the two sides equally finished in appearance. This is accomplished by wrapping the weft ends around a warp yarn at the perimeter of the design area and passing the weft back into the shed. More commonly, the ends of the weft yarn are simply tied off and allowed to hang free on the reverse of the tapestry, so there is only one presentable surface.

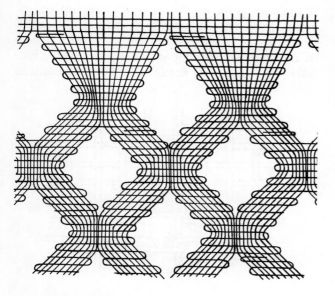

308–309. *Slit tapestry is a technique in which the warp is divided into sections, each of which is handled independently.*

left: 308. In slit tapestry, the warp yarns are drawn together to produce slits in the web.

above: 309. LENORE TAWNEY. *Ark Curtain.* 1965. Slit tapestry and rep weave in natural linen, 10 × 4½′. Congregation Solel, Highland Park, Ill.

Slit Tapestry

Slit tapestry, often called *woven slit openwork,* is a technique in which the warp is divided into sections, each of which is handled independently. The warp yarns are drawn together to produce long slits in the web (Fig. 308). Different effects can be created by regrouping the warp yarns from time to time, so that staggered slits develop. This was the method employed by Lenore Tawney in *Ark Curtain* (Fig. 309), a delicate, linear wall hanging.

Contemporary Tapestry Weaving

During the past two decades a number of serious artists have attempted to translate the tradition-steeped principles of tapestry weaving into an idiom relevant to the 20th century. As a result, the art of tapestry has enjoyed an exciting renaissance. Much of this new popularity is traceable to the work of Jean Lurçat, a painter and designer who is credited with reviving the old Aubusson manufactury. The titles of Lurçat's major tapestries—*Liberty, Man, The Apocalypse*—evoke the grandeur of their 17th- and 18th-century ancestors, but the forms are bold, fresh, and inventive (Fig. 310). Most of Lurcat's tapestries are conceived on an architectural scale.

All three of the great 17th-century French tapestry works—Aubusson, Gobelins, and Beauvais—are still in operation. It is interesting to compare a tapestry woven at Gobelins under the patronage of the Sun King (Pl. 9, p. 60)

below: 310. JEAN LURÇAT. *The Apocalypse.* 1947–48. Tapestry, 15′ × 39′8″. Church at Assy, France.

left: 311. Serge Poliakoff, design; executed by Gobelins. *Formes.* 1970. Tapestry, 15'3" × 12'4". Mobilier National, Paris; courtesy International Biennial of Tapestries, Lausanne, 1971.

opposite right: 312. Graham Sutherland. *The Eagle: Emblem of St. John,* detail from *Christ in Glory.* 1958–62. Tapestry, overall height c. 23 yards. Courtesy Pallas Gallery Ltd., London.

opposite far right: 313. Klára Cságoly. *Vollkommenheit.* 1970. Tapestry, 8'5" × 6'4". Collection Hungarian Ministry of Culture; courtesy International Biennial of Tapestries, Lausanne, 1971.

with one created at that manufactury just three hundred years later (Fig. 311). The extreme simplification of form and total abandonment of representational imagery in the recent work echo the trends of Minimal Art, just as *The Life of the King* mirrored the Baroque style of painting in 17th-century France.

Tapestry has always been used to embellish church architecture, and religious symbolism has traditionally been considered one of the few kinds of subject matter sufficiently elevated for grand-scale tapestry weaving. The huge altar hanging in Conventry Cathedral, designed by the British painter Graham Sutherland, continues this tradition, but in a manner thoroughly conversant with contemporary art. The tapestry, which is claimed to be the largest in the world, is dominated by a central figure of Christ, flanked by the four gospel symbols (Fig. 312), a striking reinterpretation of a centuries-old iconographical theme.

The interplay of texture and the projection of three-dimensional form have been among the main preoccupations of the modern weaver. Klára Cságoly's *Vollkommenheit* (Fig. 313) explores the subtle contrasts of texture produced by varying the tapestry technique. While Cságoly's overall form is a simple oval in a rectangle, the inner complexities of texture and pattern carry the viewer's eye in an ever-changing progression.

In recent years many weavers have been commissioned to execute large-scale tapestries for secular as well as sacred environments—offices, terminals, and other public buildings (Fig. 314). Even three-dimensional effects can be achieved by manipulating flat-woven fabrics. Herman Scholten weaves each of his tapestry components individually, then loops and interlaces various

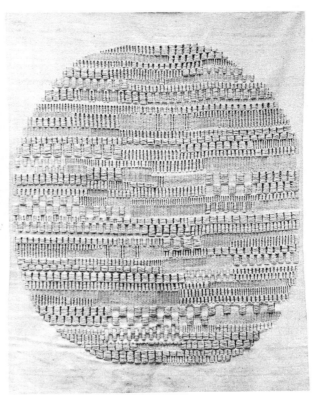

below: 314. WILHELMINA FRUYTIER. Tapestry. 1972. Heavy rope, c. 8 × 31′. Collection European Research Center, SKF, Jutphaas, Holland.

above: 315. HERMAN SCHOLTEN. *Light and Water.* 1969. Tapestry, 5'9" × 11'8". Courtesy Ruth Kaufmann Gallery, New York.

316. DORIAN ZACHAI. *Lady Performing.* 1971. Tapestry of wool, rayon, feathers, silk, metallic lace, and Dacron stuffing; height 4'6". Courtesy the artist.

parts to build imposing tapestry "assemblages" (Fig. 315). Scholten's major interest lies in the interplay of light and shade, plane against plane. His wall hangings are never static, but appear to be constantly shifting and intertwining.

The modern tapestry weaver has by no means disavowed pictorial representation; he has merely restated it in terms of a developing culture. Dorian Zachai was trained in classical tapestry methods, but her work has evolved into a free expression that would have been incomprehensible to a weaver of a hundred or even fifty years ago. Her *Lady Performing* (Fig. 316) incorporates many kinds of yarn, feathers, lace, and stuffed areas to produce an effect of sculpture in the round. Like the shaped canvases of recent painting, Zachai's works have their contours dictated by form, rather than by the arbitrary conventions of square and rectangle.

The work of Helena Barynina Hernmarck provides a link between tapestry weaving of the past and that of the present. Her large-scale wall tapestries are identical in concept to those of three and four hundred years ago. Hernmarck's weaving methods are traditional, her craftsmanship meticulous. Furthermore, just as the subject matter of 17th-century tapestries mirrored the preoccupations of that era—allegory, mythology, religion—so too Hernmarck's work reflects the interests of our own—news events, sports heroes, and rock stars (Pl. 18, p. 162). Large photographic blowups, reproduced dot for dot, serve as her cartoons. Hernmarck's guiding principle is the same as that implicit in art throughout history—from the earliest cave paintings through modern Pop Art: "I can engage people more easily when they are able to understand what they are seeing."[1]

Finishing Procedures 12

Cloth that cometh fro the wevying is nought
   comly to were
Tyl it is fulled under fote, or in fullying strokes
Wasshen wel with water and with tasles crached,
Y-touked and y-teynted, and under tailloures hand.
                        Piers Plowman, *B. XV 444*

The weaver's task is not quite complete when the woven fabric is cut from the loom. In almost all cases a variety of finishing procedures must be applied to the web, and these can be divided into two general categories. *Edge finishes* prevent the fabric from raveling and sometimes provide a decorative border. *Functional finishes* affect the web itself: they clean it, shrink it, and change or enhance the appearance of the fibers. The typical woven project may be subjected to either or both types of finishes.

EDGE FINISHES

The type of finish that must be applied to the edges of a fabric depends upon the nature of the woven article. Yardage, which is to be cut for dressmaking, needs no edge finishing whatever. A knotted fringe may or may not be effective on

a wall hanging. Each project must be analyzed to see which finish would best serve its needs.

Stitching

Hemstitching, overcasting, cross-stitching, and blanket stitching are all devices to prevent the ends of a woven fabric from raveling. Hemstitching (Fig. 317) is best done while the fabric is still on the loom. If necessary, both ends of the web

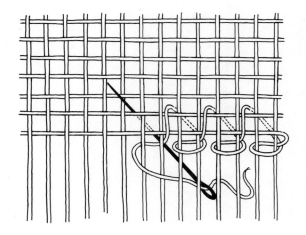

can be hemstitched—the first end after a few inches have been woven but before the fabric is rolled forward onto the cloth beam, the other end at the completion of the project.

Hemstitching is done on a closed shed. The following directions are intended for right-handed people and should be reversed if one is left-handed. A needle threaded with weft yarn is passed up through the fabric at the edge, two warps in from the selvedge. The yarn is then carried around the outermost two warp yarns and behind the fabric and brought up through the fabric at a point two warps from the selvedge

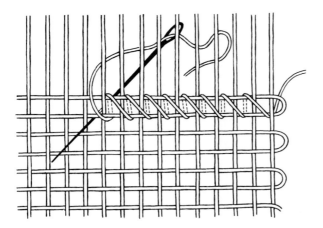

317–320. *Various stitching techniques can be employed to prevent the ends of a woven fabric from raveling.*

opposite: 317. Hemstitching.

above: 318. Overcasting.

below: 319. Cross-stitching.

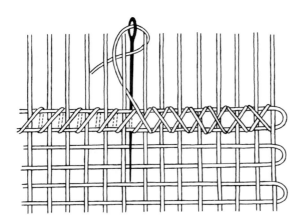

and two wefts from the edge. This procedure is followed until all the yarns are caught.

Overcasting, cross-stitching, and blanket stitching can be accomplished either on or off the loom. The overcast stitch is illustrated in Figure 318. Cross-stitching (Fig. 319) requires a second trip across the web after the overcast is

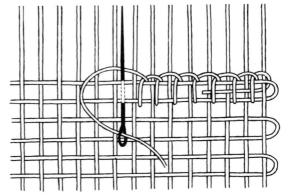

above: 320. Blanket stitching.

below: 321. A rolled hem.

complete. The blanket stitch (Fig. 320) gives a more finished appearance to the fabric.

Hemming

A hem is often the best edge finish for a place mat or similar project. When the fabric is very delicate, the hem can be rolled and held in place with tiny stitches (Fig. 321). Otherwise, an ordinary skirt hem about 1 inch wide, plus $\frac{1}{4}$ inch

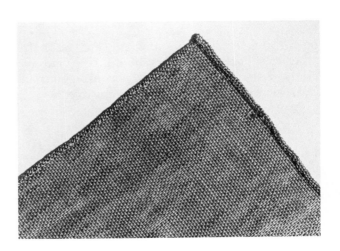

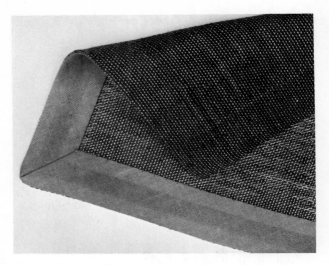

across the fabric to hold the weft in place. Then, the warps are turned back and stitched in position on the reverse side of the fabric. The raw edge is covered with bias seam binding (Fig. 323) or with a facing (Fig. 324). In some cases it is desirable to cover the entire back with a lining.

Knotted and Braided Fringe

A plain knotted fringe is one of the easiest edge finishes to make. As illustrated in Figure 325, the warp ends are grouped and tied in a half knot. Care must be taken to ensure that the fringe is

top left: 322. A skirt hem.

above: 323. Binding the raw edge of a fabric.

top right: 324. Facing the reverse side of a fabric.

for turning, is usually sufficient (Fig. 322). In either case the hemming should be done by hand, so that the stitches are inconspicuous. If warp yarn is used, they will be invisible.

Binding

A fabric that is to be seen from one side only—such as a tapestry or wall hanging—can be finished with seam binding on the reverse side. When the web is cut from the loom, an excess warp length of 4 or 5 inches is left on both ends. The warp ends are knotted together at intervals

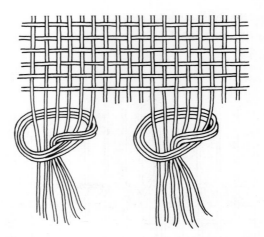

325–329. *A knotted fringe is a suitable edge finish for many woven projects.*

above: 325. Simple knotted fringe.

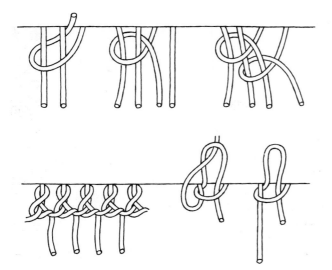

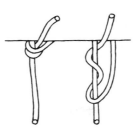

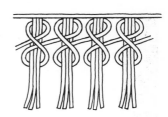

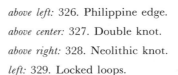

above left: 326. Philippine edge.

above center: 327. Double knot.

above right: 328. Neolithic knot.

left: 329. Locked loops.

straight and the ends parallel to one another. The warp yarn for such a fringe must have a rather tight twist, or the ends will become frayed. Single-ply yarns are not sufficiently durable for a fringe, particularly when the woven article is to be subjected to wear or handling.

Figures 326 through 329 illustrate several more complicated knotting techniques often used to finish rugs, shawls, and similar items. The *Philippine edge* (Fig. 326) is both practical and decorative, for it holds the weft yarns in position and at the same time creates an attractive border. The warp ends must be at least 7 or 8 inches long, and even longer if a wide border is to be worked. The Philippine edge is knotted from left to right; if desired, the fabric can be turned and the edge worked in the opposite direction, continuing back and forth for several rows. The *double knot* and the *neolithic knot* (Figs. 327, 328) both provide a firmer edge than the half knot. A system of *locked loops* (Fig. 329), worked from right to left across the edge, provides a decorative transition between the fabric and the fringe.

Macramé was originally developed as an edging technique, and it is often used today to finish woven projects. In Figure 330 the warp ends have

330. Rows of horizontal clove hitches—a macramé knot—can serve to finish the raw edge of a woven fabric.

above: 331. A decorative border of diagonal clove hitches.

been knotted in rows of clove hitches (see p. 225), with and without a fringe. When a fringe is not wanted, the warp ends are worked back into the fabric with a crochet hook and cut short on the reverse side. The wide border in Figure 331 was also made with clove hitches, in this case diagonal rows that create a diamond pattern.

A simple braided fringe becomes an important design element in the wall hanging reproduced in Figure 332. Such a finish might also be effective on a garment, for it is much more durable than a knotted fringe.

Woven Fringe

A fringe can be woven on one or both ends of a fabric while it is on the loom (Fig. 333). The warp is divided into groups, and each group is woven as a unit with a butterfly shuttle (Fig. 269). After the web is cut from the loom, the warp ends must still be knotted or finished in some other way to prevent raveling.

It is also possible to weave a decorative fringe along the *selvedge* of a fabric. The weaving space on the loom must be wide enough to accommodate the web itself, plus the proposed fringe length on both sides. Either a cut or an uncut (looped) fringe can be woven, but in both cases a group of temporary warps must be set into the loom at the outer edge of the fringe.

To weave a cut fringe three or four warps are tied between the breast beam and the back beam at the point where the fringe is to end. These warps are passed through a single dent in the reed. As the weaving progresses, the weft yarn is carried out to the edge of the fringe on some shots but only to the selvedge of the fabric on others. In Figure 334 a series of four weft shots has been carried to the end of the fringe, followed by two shots to the selvedge. When it is time to roll the fabric forward onto the cloth beam, the fringe is cut at the ends and allowed to hang free. The temporary warps remain stationary throughout the weaving process.

The procedure for making a looped fringe is similar, except that the temporary warp yarns are continuous, moving from warp beam to cloth beam with the rest of the warp. The temporary warps are threaded through a dent in the reed but not through the heddles. They are removed after the fabric is cut from the loom.

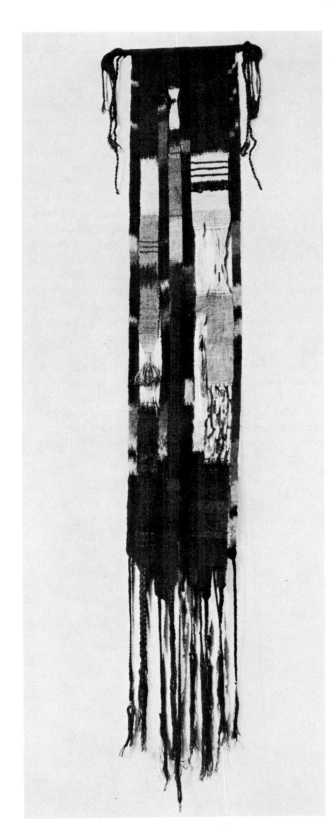

left: 332. Dorothy L. Meredith. Ikat hanging, 1968. Linen, 6'9" × 1'3". From *Objects: USA,* Johnson Wax Collection of Contemporary Crafts, Racine, Wis.

above: 333. A woven fringe can be added to the ends of a fabric by weaving each segment individually as for slit tapestry. Here the warp ends have also been braided.

below: 334. A woven fringe can also be added to the selvedge of a fabric, by carrying some weft shots to the extent of the fringe—marked by a temporary warp yarn—and the remainder only to the edge of the fabric.

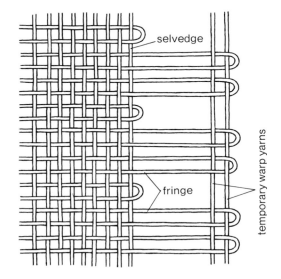

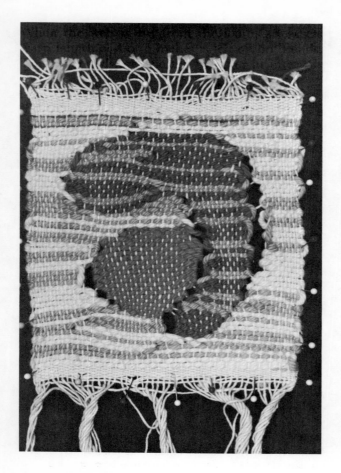

ing the weaving process, but it also binds the yarns together, improves the *hand* or feel of the fibers, and preshrinks the fabric.

Special consideration must be given to woolen fabrics that have been spun and woven *in the grease*—that is, without prior scouring to remove surface oil from the sheep's wool. (Weaving in the grease is common with certain tweed yarns.) The fabric must be soaked for about an hour in lukewarm water to which a few drops of ammonia have been added. Next, the fabric is washed in warm water with a thick solution of one part detergent to two parts soap, and then rinsed thoroughly. The washing and rinsing may have to be repeated two or three times to remove all the oil. Finally, the fabric is squeezed gently, blotted with a towel, and rolled on a large blanket-covered tube for drying. It should be left for at least 24 hours, then rerolled from the opposite direction on another tube. This procedure is repeated until the fabric is completely dry. A gentle brushing or *napping* will expose the fibers, soften the fabric, and increase the warmth of a woolen garment.

FUNCTIONAL FINISHES

Cleaning

Most fabrics must be either washed or dry cleaned after they are taken from the loom, the choice depending upon the fiber composition of the yarns involved. Such cleaning not only removes any soil that may have accumulated dur-

Blocking

Certain items, such as tapestries or wall hangings, require blocking to make them conform to the proper shape. The fabric is tacked all around at short intervals to a solid flat surface (Fig. 335). It is then moistened with warm water and allowed to dry slowly away from sunlight and excess heat.

part three
OTHER CONSTRUCTION METHODS

13 *Pile Weaves*

Pile weaves are, by definition, those that display a raised surface, thrusting the normally flat, planar weave into a third dimension. There are two forms of pile weaves, comparable to the bas-relief and haut-relief of sculpture. *Low-pile weaves,* such as those produced by chaining, twining, or soumak, present only a slightly elevated surface. Many people do not consider them to be pile weaves at all, but merely a thick, closely woven fabric. Most low-pile weaves are two-element constructions: the weft yarn serves for both the ground and the pile effect. By contrast, *high-pile weaves* are generally composed of three elements—a warp and weft ground, plus an extra series of yarns running weftwise to form the pile. The pile may vary from a fraction of an inch to several inches or even feet in length. High-pile weaves can be made from a continuous yarn, leaving loops on the surface of the fabric

(*uncut pile*), or from short lengths of yarn knotted individually on the stretched warps (*cut pile*). Looped piles can also be severed to produce a cut pile. Long cut piles are often referred to as *shag* weaves.

The common trait of the techniques described in this chapter is that they were originally, or are most frequently, applied to the manufacture of rugs. However, the pile weaves have broken free of any such restraint and are today included in a wide variety of forms—sculpture, wall hangings, upholstery fabric, garments, and other kinds of textiles. Only in the 20th century have rugs become a luxury. Prior to the advent of central heating, rugs were stark necessity, providing both warmth and insulation. They served on floors and in doorways, on beds, as sleigh and carriage blankets—anywhere the heavy fur-like structure was needed to keep out the cold.

As noted in Chapter 1, the earliest surviving rug was found in a Scythian grave in Siberia (Fig. 6). With that sole exception, only fragmentary carpets predating the 13th century still exist, although pile weaves were used in many other types of fabrics (Fig. 63). Most of the techniques

used for creating rugs originated and reached their highest level of development in the East. One easily free-associates the terms "Oriental" and "Persian" when carpets are brought to mind. Indeed, Persian carpets are among the finest ever produced anywhere in the world (Fig. 336). So lush were the Oriental carpets of the 15th and 16th centuries, that painters such as Hans Holbein often used them as "props" (Fig. 337). A certain style of carpet woven in Asia Minor is to this day known as the "Holbein carpet."

above: 336. *The Ardebil Carpet,* medallion Tabriz rug from the shrine of Sheik Safī at Ardebil, Iran. 1539–40. Wool pile and silk, 17′6″ × 34′6″. Victoria & Albert Museum, London.

left: 337. HANS HOLBEIN THE YOUNGER. *Portrait of George Gisze of Danzig.* 1532. Panel, 37¾ × 33″. Staatliche Museen, West Berlin.

Fabric knotting in the rya technique has been an important folk craft in Scandinavia since the 13th century. However, only in recent decades, when large quantities of rya-knotted fabrics began to be exported, has the process been applied to rugs. The weaver who had spent weeks or months painstakingly tying thousands and thousands of knots would not have dreamed of putting his creation on the floor to be trampled upon. Instead, rya fabrics assumed a place of honor in Scandinavian households and comprised the most important part of a bride's dowry.

Most of the techniques explained in this chapter can be carried out on a simple frame loom, such as any of those illustrated in Chapter 14. However, the work moves faster and larger fabrics can be produced on a conventional four-harness loom.

LOW-PILE WEAVES

Chaining

Chaining is a two-element construction based on plain weave, in which the weft yarn is looped around groups of warp yarns to form a surface

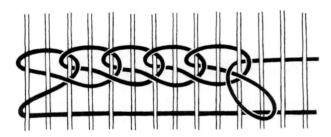

pile. As illustrated in Figure 338, the weft yarn is first passed completely through the shed, leaving a small loop at the selvedge. The shuttle is laid down, and the loop at the opposite selvedge is carried across the web for a distance of two warps (in this case from left to right), at which point a second weft loop is drawn up through the first one. The second loop is in turn carried over for a distance of two warps, and a third weft loop is drawn through it at that point. This procedure continues until the opposite selvedge is reached. Then, the shuttle is drawn through the last loop to prevent the chain from unraveling.

The pattern of chaining can follow any direction required by a particular project. The chain can move from left to right or right to left; it can be carried from selvedge to selvedge or appear only in certain portions of the web, in which case it functions as a laid-in design (see p. 168). Two yarns of different colors are sometimes placed in the same shed and chained back and forth alternately, so that adjacent loops vary in color. Whatever the design, each row of chaining should be surrounded by a row or two of plain weave on each side to provide a firm ground for the fabric. Chaining tends to cover neighboring rows of flat weave, and even three consecutive rows of plain weave will usually be hidden by the pile. The sample fabric reproduced in Figure 339 was woven in two colors with a chaining design that is almost entirely laid-in. Chaining is often used as a spacing device on simple looms, replacing the reed that normally maintains the horizontal dimension of a fabric.

below left: 338. In chaining, the weft yarn is looped around groups of warp yarns to form a low surface pile.

below: 339. A pattern of overall chaining.

Twining

Twining is a two-element construction in which two or more weft yarns are twisted around one another as they move across the warp. Solid rows of twining nearly always produce a weft-face fabric, for the weft completely obscures the warp.

The simplest form of twining is done with two strands, actually one continuous weft yarn doubled over the outermost warp at one selvedge

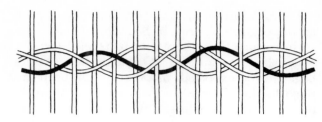

341. Three-strand twining.

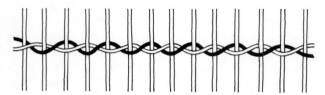

340. Two-strand twining.

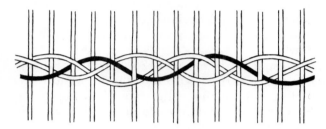

342. Braided-weft twining.

(Fig. 340). The entire weft yarn should be about eight times as long as the distance to be covered. With the center of the yarn looped around the first warp yarn, the ends are drawn to the face of the fabric between the first and second warp yarns, twisted around one another, then passed around the second warp yarn. If desired, the double weft can cross two or more warps before being twisted. The twists should always be made in the same direction for a single row. When alternate rows are twisted in opposite directions, a chevron pattern develops. Regrouping the warp yarns for subsequent rows will produce a lattice effect.

Three-strand twining is a bit more complicated. As illustrated in Figure 341, each of the three weft yarns moves over and under two warps, but the weft yarns are staggered so that they interlock. A variation of this technique consists of braiding three weft strands over the warps, just as one would braid hair (Fig. 342). The Chilkat Indians employed three-strand twining for their famous blankets (Fig. 26).

Occasionally, twining is adapted to produce a higher pile, by leaving loops on the surface of the fabric (Fig. 343). This is accomplished with the aid of a gauge of some sort, a wooden dowel or knitting needle, for example. Each time one of the weft yarns appears on the face, it is slipped on the gauge before being twisted.

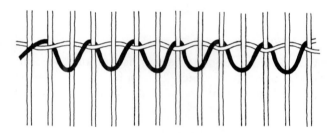

343. Looped twining.

Twining is often done on the vertical warp-weighted loom (Fig. 149) or its cousin, the Ojibway Indian loom (Fig. 393). It is not necessary that the warps be held under tension as for conventional weaving.

The contemporary handweaver has adapted twining to a variety of purposes. It is used as a trim, to outline pattern areas, and to hold back flat weaving around sections of exposed warp. The solidly twined fabric is thick and quite durable, so it has an obvious application for rugs and mats. Like chaining, a row or two of twining can serve as a spacing element for simple looms.

Soumak

Soumak is the technique that was originally used for making rugs in Caucasia. It is done by wrapping the weft yarn around a warp or a group

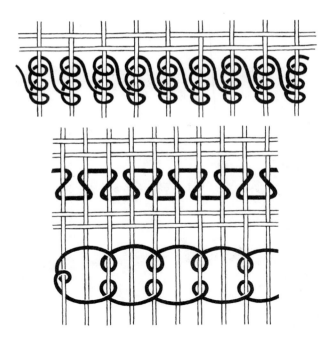

above: 344–346. Soumak is a low-pile weave done by wrapping weft yarn around a warp or group of warps. The Greek soumak (*top*) is the most elaborate of the patterns.

below: 347. A pattern of overall soumak.

of warps according to any of several patterns (Figs. 344–346). The most ornate is the *Greek soumak,* in which the weft yarn is wrapped three or more times around a single warp yarn before proceeding to the next warp. Closely packed rows of soumak, therefore, conceal the warp altogether to produce a weft-face fabric. The weft yarn is easiest to work with if it is wound in a butterfly shuttle (Fig. 269). Soumak can be worked on either an open or a closed shed. If the shed is open, only the top layer of warp yarns is wrapped. When rows of soumak are alternated with plain weave, a ribbed effect develops.

The soumak fabric illustrated in Figure 347 was woven by passing the weft yarn over four warps and back under two. Any other combination of warps could be substituted, depending upon the weight of the yarn and the desired effect. When the soumak is worked alternately from left to right and right to left, a herringbone pattern is created; when all the rows are wrapped in the same direction, a twill results. To change colors, one simply carries the first yarn to the underside of the fabric and draws the new color through in the same place. The two ends can be worked into the web vertically in such a way that they are invisible.

Generally, care must be taken with soumak to avoid distorting the vertical alignment of the warps, especially with long overshots of five or six warp yarns. However, one can also take advantage of this tendency for the warps to bunch together and create an openwork fabric. A lattice effect is produced by staggering the warps to be wrapped in various rows.

HIGH-PILE WEAVES

Looping

Looping is a three-element construction. The warp and weft ground exists independently of the pile yarn, which can be inserted wherever it is needed. Usually, though not always, the pile yarn is heavier than the plain-weave yarns.

Looping is begun in the same manner as chaining. The pile weft yarn is inserted in a shed, and loops are drawn to the surface between two warp yarns. In order to maintain a consistent size in the loops, each is slipped over a gauge—a knitting needle, a wooden dowel, or any similar

Pile Weaves   193

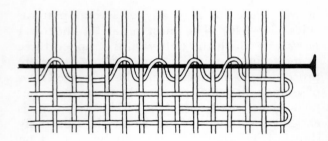

left: 348. Looping is a three-element construction in which a weftwise yarn passes over a gauge to form a surface pile.

object (Fig. 348). The diameter of the gauge determines the height of the loops. After all the loops needed for a particular row have been made, the pile yarn is beat into place, and a shot or two of flat plain weave is made with the regular binder weft. When the warp is very dense, a loop can be drawn through every second or third space between the warps.

Maria Chojnacka-Gontarska's tapestry hanging reproduced in Figure 349 exhibits a loop pile only in selected areas (Fig. 350), with the loops gradually decreasing from left to right until they vanish altogether. The result is a sensitive diminution of both texture and tonal value. Loops can also be used to emphasize figural or pattern areas, a fact well known and delightfully exploited by the Copts (Fig. 63).

below: 349. MARIA CHOJNACKA-GONTARSKA. *Le Son.* 1970. Flax, 7'4" × 10'8". Courtesy International Biennial of Tapestries, Lausanne, 1971.

above: 350. Detail showing the looped and plain sections of *Le Son* (Fig. 349).

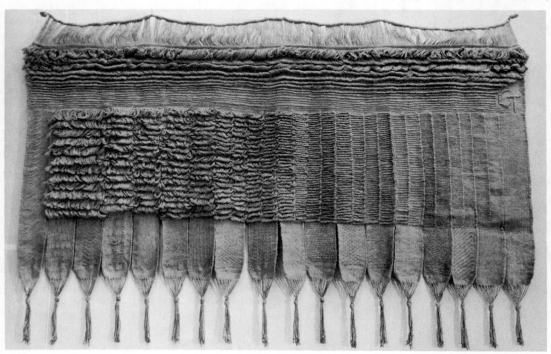

Plate 19. OILI MAKI. *Missa Monserata.*
Wool rya, 6' x 4'6". Courtesy the artist.

Plate 20. ANNE HORNBY. Flossa rug. 1964. Wool on linen warp, 3′5″ x 4′10″. Courtesy the artist.

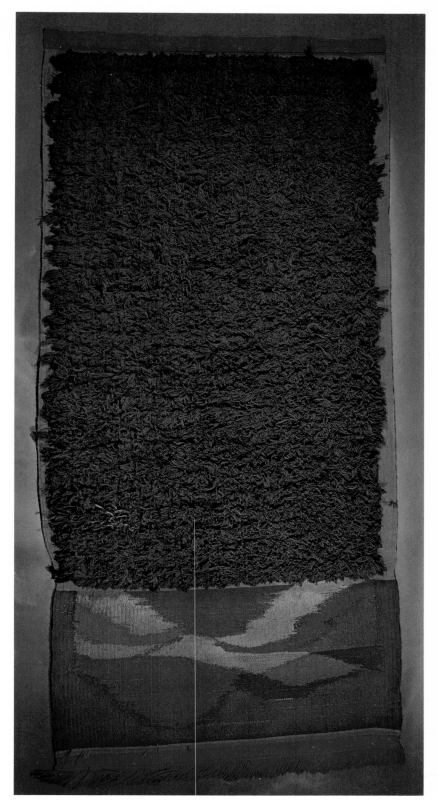

Plate 22. SHEILA HICKS. *Barber's Pole*. 1964–65. Wool and silk pile shot through backing with a mechanical pistol; 11'3" x 3'8". Private collection, Germany.

above: 351. An overall looped fabric. The checkerboard effect is produced by inserting two pile yarns into each shed and drawing loops only from the color that is needed for that part of the pattern.

The fabric illustrated in Figure 351 is looped over its entire surface in two colors. The checkerboard effect is produced by inserting two pile yarns—one in each color—into the shed simultaneously and drawing loops only from the color that is needed on the surface. The other yarn is absorbed into the plain-weave ground and covered by the looped pile.

Rug Knots

Three distinct knots have been identified in classical rug weaving. The *Ghiordes knot* or *Turkish knot* formed the basis of Turkish rugs and is identical to the Scandinavian rya or flossa knot. Similarly, the *Sehna* or *Persian knot* was employed for making rugs in Persia. The *Spanish knot* is quite rare compared to the other two. While all three knots are still used widely in rug weaving, they

have been adopted by contemporary craftsmen for purposes far removed from floor coverings.

Each of the knots can be made with a continuous weft yarn wound in a butterfly shuttle. The pile is formed by the loops of yarn between each pair of knots, and the loops can be cut or left as they are. However, it is a more common practice to tie short lengths of yarn individually around the stretched warps. The height of the pile thus measures half the length of each yarn, minus the small amount needed for wrapping around the warps.

The weaver has more design freedom in rug knotting than in any other fiber-construction process. The act of tying individual strands of fiber is comparable only to painting, and one's palette consists of all the colors and textures of yarn available. Since the warp and ground weft are invisible and the pile weft is discontinuous, any color can be placed at any point.

The Ghiordes knot is made by placing a length of yarn over two warps and wrapping it around the warp yarns, drawing the ends through the

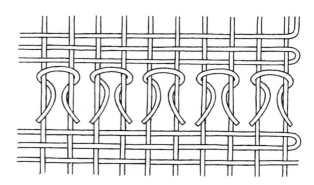

352. Individual Ghiordes knots.

center space (Fig. 352). The knot is then pulled taut against the previous weft shot and, when the row is complete, beat into place. Each row of Ghiordes knots is followed by a few shots of the binder weft. The warp for a knotted rug is set no denser than eight to ten ends per inch in order to allow room for the knotting. All the knots are tied on a closed shed. One obtains different effects by varying the length of the knotting yarns and the width of the flat-weave strips between the knotted rows. If the pile yarns are relatively short and the knotted rows are close together, the pile will stand straight, whereas rows of long pile yarns set farther apart will cause the pile to sprawl. In classical rug weaving all the pile ends were trimmed evenly to achieve a flat surface. As many as two hundred knots were tied per square inch. However, many contemporary weavers prefer the informal appearance of random-length pile yarns, which produce an undulating face on the knotted fabric.

The continuous Ghiordes knot is made with a gauge much like that used for looping. The pile weft yarn can be threaded through a needle (Fig. 353) or wound in a butterfly shuttle (Fig. 269). If a cut pile is desired, the loops between each pair of knots are slashed with a knife or razor blade before the gauge is removed. Special Swedish gauges with a cutting groove along one edge facilitate the slashing (Fig. 364).

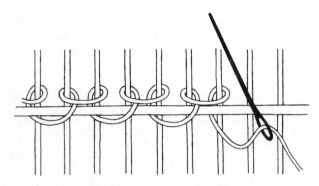

353. Continuous Ghiordes knots.

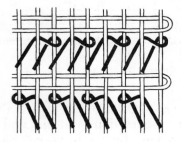

354. Sehna knot.

The Sehna knot is also tied over two adjacent warp yarns. In this case, the pile weft yarn passes under one warp and over and around the other, so that a pile end emerges between each pair of warps (Fig. 354). The knots can be tied so that the pile slants either to the right or to the left, which is a definite design advantage. By tying

each knot with two or more yarns simultaneously, one can introduce a variety of colors to build a pattern. Sehna knots can also be made with a continuous yarn looped over a gauge.

Figure 355 shows a sample fabric knotted entirely with Sehna knots, each knot made with two individual yarns. The pile rows have been spread to demonstrate the half inch or so of flat weaving between them. Ordinarily, the pile covers the plain-weave ground completely, and the latter is never visible.

top: 355. A pile fabric made with Sehna knots. Although several shots of plain weave are inserted after each row of pile knots, the ground weave is completely obscured unless the pile is spread.

below: 356. Spanish knots.

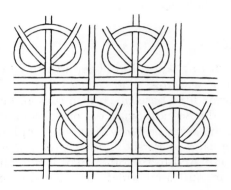

The Spanish knot (Fig. 356) is actually a simple twisting of the pile weft around a single warp yarn. Generally, the knot is made around every other warp, working alternately in rows. Spanish knots have a greater tendency than the other two to slip out before they can be locked into place with a few ground weft shots, so the knot is usually easier to make with a single continuous yarn looped over a gauge.

One typically thinks of pile in terms of rugs, with a soft raised surface perhaps an inch or two high. Polish weaver Wojciech Sadley has stretched this concept drastically in *Sleepless Night* (Fig. 357), a wool and linen tapestry into which pile yarns several feet long have been knotted. The result is a biomorphic mass of free-floating yarns that makes one long to reach out and stroke the fiber, while at the same time being repelled by its brooding presence. One can readily see the endless possibilities for pile knotting, once the stereotype has been abandoned.

Rya and Flossa

The rya or flossa knot is identical to the Ghiordes knot used in Turkish rug weaving (Fig. 352). The only difference is that rya knots generally are made with coarser yarn, and from two to six strands are handled as one in making a single knot, whereas in Turkish rugs each pile yarn is

357. WOJCIECH SADLEY. *Sleepless Night.* 1966. Wool and linen tapestry with knotted pile, 9'10⅛" × 6'6¾". Courtesy the artist.

knotted individually. Rya, which in Finland is called *ryijy,* is for all practical purposes the same as flossa. However, when a distinction is made, the rya fabric is considered to have a longer pile (greater than $1\frac{1}{8}$ inch) and more widely spaced knots. In this book the two terms are used interchangeably.

Much tradition governs the rya technique in Scandinavia, particularly in Finland, where any variation on the centuries-old methods and materials is considered by some second only to desecration of the national flag. Wool or goat-hair yarns must be used for the ground, and only wool for the pile. The pile ends are all trimmed to exactly the same height. Formerly, the yarns were colored with natural dyestuffs—leaves, spruce cones, wild rosemary, and various tree barks. The older patterns are generally pictorial, often containing religious symbols. In recent years many rya weavers—even in Scandinavia—have begun to challenge such arbitrary restrictions and experiment with variations in pattern, pile length, and materials. Among the more common designs in modern Scandinavian rya are subtle gradations or explosions of color (Pl. 19, p. 195).

Figures 358–362 illustrate several versions of the rya knot, the first of which is most common. The best materials for conventional rug weaving are an 8/3 or 8/5 linen rug warp and wool rug yarn or wool and goat or cow hair for the ground weft. Swedish long-staple wool rya yarns can be used for the knotting pile. It is rather difficult to estimate the amount of yarn one will need, because the length of the pile, the number of yarns

knotted together, the weight of the yarn, and the distance between knotted rows all influence the quantity. Perhaps the easiest method of calculating the total yarn requirement for a given project is to knot a small sample in the same yarns, keeping track of the amount of each color consumed, and multiply that quantity by the number of times the finished rug size will exceed the sample.

The alternative to making a sample involves a fair amount of mathematics. For example, if a 3-by-5 rug has 308 warp yarns, and the rug is to be knotted according to the pattern shown in Figure 358, there will be 150 knots in each row, with four unknotted warp yarns at each selvedge. Allowing three individual yarns for each knot brings the total to 450 pile yarns per row. Since approximately eighty rows (with weft ground between) are required to make the 5-foot length, the total number of pile yarns will be about 36,000. Swedish rya yarn is sold in skeins of $3\frac{1}{2}$ to 4 ounces, each containing roughly 126 yards of yarn. If each pile yarn is 4 inches long, and there are 36,000 yarns altogether, the rug would require 4,000 yards of yarn, or 32 skeins. The warp and weft ground are calculated in the same manner as for flat weaving (see pp. 109–111).

Most rya weavers work from full-scale cartoons prepared in advance and tacked in sections to the loom under the warp. The cartoon need not be in color; tonal gradations can be employed to indicate the different shades of yarn. A less cumbersome—but also less accurate—method involves drawing a small cartoon scaled down for enlargement on the loom.

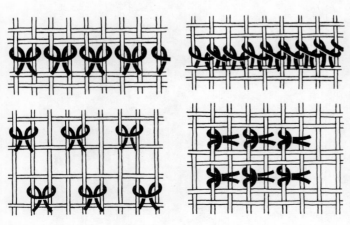

358–362. Rya is a Scandinavian pile-weaving technique based upon versions of the Ghiordes knot. In recent years it has become associated with rugs. The yarn involved is most often wool, knotted in several short strands at a time over warps stretched on the loom. Several versions of the Ghiordes knot used in rya weaving are illustrated here, of which the first (*top left*) is the most common.

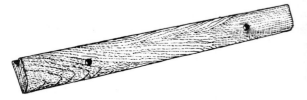

above: 364. Continuous Ghiordes knots can be looped around a Swedish rya stick, which provides a slot for cutting the loops after each row is finished.

The loom is threaded as for conventional weaving (Fig. 363) using any of the standard drafts—twill, rosepath, bird's-eye, etc. (see Appendix A). The tie-up should be planned to produce the most compact and simplest ground, perhaps 1-2 and 3-4. In order to prevent excessive narrowing of the web, a stretcher is sometimes left in place on the loom during the entire weaving process.

As a rule, no knots are tied on the outside four yarns at each selvedge. Extra filler yarns will occasionally have to be inserted in these narrow bands to take up the space not occupied by the pile yarn and keep the rows consistent. The beating should be quite firm, for a loosely woven rya rug will not wear well.

If a single continuous pile yarn is to be knotted, the weaver can wind the pile loops around a Swedish rya stick (Fig. 364), which provides a slot for cutting the loops before the gauge is removed. However, if a perfectly even pile length is not desirable, the loops can easily be measured around the fingers.

The wool and linen rug in Plate 20 (p. 196) is an excellent example of freely conceived design in rya. The rather long pile tends to blur outlines and causes pattern areas to flow into one

another. The technique of rya knotting is handled somewhat differently in Ruben Eshkanian's *Haystack* (Pl. 21, p. 197). Nearly all the pile yarns are of uniform color, forming a solid block to offset the brightly colored tapestry panel below and around the border. The surprising juxtaposition of color and texture in this wall hanging is made all the more effective because one's eye is unwittingly drawn again and again to the few tiny pile yarns of vivid color in the lower left corner of the rya section. The placement of these yarns is a masterfully subtle use of emphasis in design.

Corduroy

In terms of handweaving, corduroy is not a ribbed cotton material but a relatively fast method of creating a shag fabric. The corduroy rug was invented by the English weaver Alastair Morton, and Peter Collingwood has improved upon Morton's idea. In essence, the corduroy method is a flat weave with long weft floats on the surface of the fabric, and the floats are cut to form the pile. The pile is, therefore, half the length of the weft float, provided the float is cut precisely in the center.

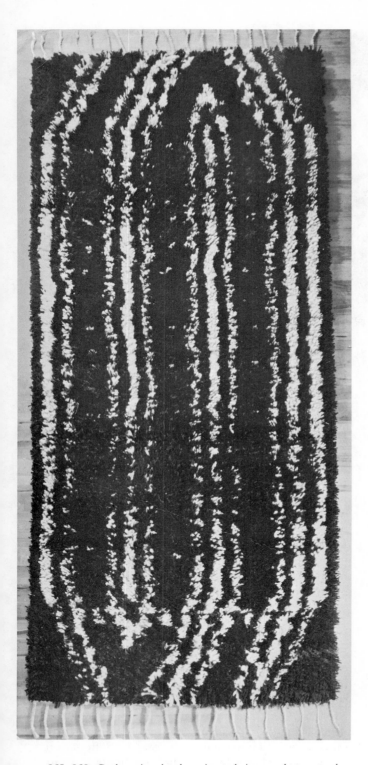

left: 365. Peter Collingwood. Corduroy rug. c. 1965. Wool on linen warp, 7 × 3′. Courtesy of the artist.

A corduroy rug (Fig. 365) requires more yarn than a rya rug of comparable size, for the pile yarn is also absorbed into the ground fabric. Furthermore, the design possibilities are as limited as those in any flat-weave textile. One cannot "paint" with fiber. However, the execution of the textile is four times faster than rya knotting. There are two basic drafts for a rug of this type, the *single corduroy* and the *double corduroy*. The latter produces a denser pile and is usually preferred. Like all the other pile techniques described in this chapter, the corduroy weave need not be confined to rugs but can be applied to a wide variety of shag fabrics.

The draft for a single corduroy rug appears in Figure 366. In order that the two edges of the fabric will be symmetrical—with either floats or ground weave—the warp should be planned for a half repeat of the threading unit at the right selvedge. The warp is sleyed at about five ends per inch, and it is wise to double sley the warp yarns at the two points in the draft where the transition is from 1 to 4 and from 3 to 2 (Fig. 366). The × on the treadling draft indicates a shot of ground weft, the · a shot of pile weft. Four, six, or even more pile yarns are set into the same shed simultaneously, so the pile yarn can be finer than the ground yarn.

Figure 367 illustrates the draft for a double corduroy, which is just a bit more complicated. Either a whole or a half repeat can be ended at the right selvedge, because, as the double corduroy diagram in Figure 368 shows, there are nearly always two floats per shot in each repeat of the threading draft.

After 4 or 5 inches of web have been woven and a ground-weave shot inserted to bind the pile, the weft floats in that portion should be cut with a knife or a razor blade. A doubled loop of wire (Fig. 369) will help to lift the pile floats for cutting and prevent accidental slashing of the ground weave. When it is necessary to start a new pile yarn in the center of the web, the ends can be planned to fall in the middle of a float, so they become a precut segment of the pile. The sett at the reed and the density of the weft regulate the closeness of the resulting pile. For exam-

365–369. *Corduroy is a handweaving technique used to create shag or long-pile fabrics on the loom. Although it consumes more yarn than rya knotting, it is four times faster, because the pile and the ground are woven simultaneously.*

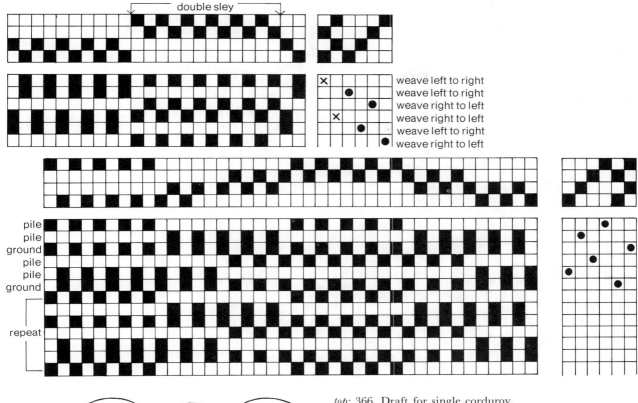

double sley

	weave left to right
×	weave left to right
●	weave right to left
×	weave right to left
●	weave left to right
●	weave right to left

pile
pile
ground
pile
pile
ground

repeat

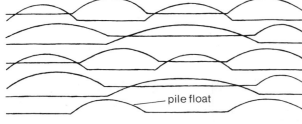

pile float

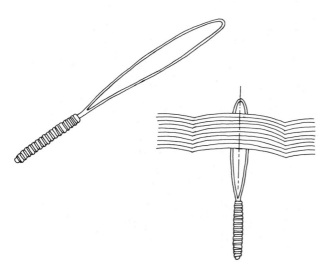

top: 366. Draft for single corduroy.

above: 367. Draft for double corduroy.

left: 368. Diagram of double corduroy.

below left: 369. A simple wire loop aids in lifting the floats to cut the corduroy pile.

ple, if the warp is set at six ends per inch and six individual yarns are inserted in each pile shed, a fairly heavy shag will result.

Hooking

In the strictest sense, hooking is not a weave at all. The process, which in industry is called *tufting,* consists of forcing loops of yarn with a needle through a previously woven backing. The backing material may be burlap, two-ply monk's cloth, Duraback, or Warpcloth. However, hooking was originally done on fabrics handwoven in the home, and many contemporary weavers utilize hooking to embellish their woven forms.

Hooking developed as a handcraft in the United States during the 18th century. A "bedd rugg" hand-hooked by Hannah Johnson in 1796

370. Hannah Johnson, New London County, Conn. Bed rug. 1796. Wool hooked through a tabby wool foundation, 7'10" × 8'2". Art Institute of Chicago (gift of Needlework and Textile Guild).

(Fig. 370) is astonishing in the intricacy and delightful counterpoint of its stylized floral forms. It is interesting to contrast Hannah's rug with one hooked in the United States more than a century and a half later. Bruce Duderstadt's rug (Fig. 371) features rows of circular forms moving in a diagonal progression that seems to suggest the wheels in an enormous machine passing against one another—a phenomenon quite unknown in the pastoral era when Hannah Johnson sat at her hooking frame. The result has a dynamic quality that pushes outside the contours of the rug.

A frame of some kind is essential for hooking, in order to hold the backing material rigid while the loops are hooked through. Figure 372 illustrates a square frame that can easily be constructed from four pieces of high-grade pine attached at the corners in a half-lap joint and secured with glue and wood screws. The frame need not be as large as the project to be hooked, for a portion of the backing can be tacked to the frame at one time, then adjusted as the hooking

below: 371. Bruce Duderstadt. Hooked rug. 1972. Wool on cotton backing, 4' square. Courtesy the artist.

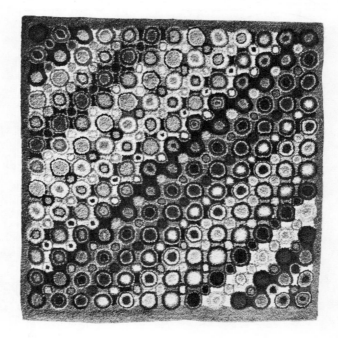

in each section is completed. The backing material for a given project should be 6 inches longer in each dimension than the planned size of the hooked fabric, to allow a margin for attachment to the frame and for hems. The backing is stapled to the frame or tacked firmly all around with carpet tacks. Alternatively, one can attach a triple thickness of firm fabric permanently to the frame and then overcast the backing material to this fabric.

The design for the hooked project is drawn in reverse on the wrong side of the backing before it is mounted on the frame. All hooking is done from the wrong side, following the sketched outlines.

Wool rug yarn is the best material for a hooked pile. Although cotton yarn can be hooked, it is not nearly as durable as wool, so it is hardly worth the expenditure of time and energy required for hooking a rug. About half a pound of yarn should be adequate for each square foot of fabric.

The only tool needed for hooking is, in fact, a hook. A short-handled crochet hook will work, but the standard hooking tool (Fig. 373) is much more efficient, since it provides a gauge to control the length of the loops. The yarn is threaded through the hook, which is then pushed into the backing material from the reverse side to the limit set by the gauge (Fig. 374). As the hook is withdrawn, a loop forms on the face of the fabric. One normally works in rows, covering the portion of the design that requires a particular color.

After the hooking has been completed, the back of the rug must be painted with latex—available from rug suppliers or mail-order houses—to prevent the loops from pulling out. One first paints a narrow strip all around the rug in the area that will be covered by the hem. Next, the corners of the rug are mitered (Fig. 375) and the rug hemmed all around with strong carpet thread. Then, the entire back of the rug can be painted. About a quart of latex will cover 12 square feet of rug.

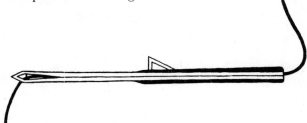

above: 373. The standard hooking tool provides a gauge to control the length of the loops.

below: 374. The pattern to be hooked is drawn in reverse on the wrong side of the backing. The hook is pushed through, and as it is withdrawn, a loop forms of the face of the fabric.

bottom: 375. After the hooking is completed, the corners of the fabric are mitered and the back painted with latex.

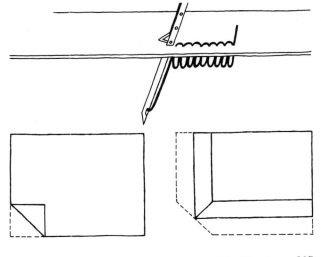

above: 372. A hooking frame is a vertical wooden support to which the backing material is tacked before work begins.

376. *Bird's Nest.* 1967. Tufted paper yarn on polypropylene nonwoven material around quilted center, diameter 4'6". Elenhank Designers for Regal Rugs, North Vernon, Ind.

Many craftsmen and even manufacturers have recently begun to experiment with techniques related to hooking. *Bird's Nest* (Fig. 376) is a novelty rug created by hooking paper yarn through a nonwoven polypropylene backing. This is an excellent example of an old process adapted to modern materials. A wall hanging by Sheila Hicks, though composed of classic yarns, is even more innovative in its utilization of industrial-age methods. *Barber's Pole* (Pl. 22, p. 198) is a voluptuous cascade of yarns literally shot through the backing with a mechanical pistol, a technique Hicks inaugurated in 1963 at the Arterior Company workshop in Germany. Hicks' work typifies a willingness among contemporary craftsmen to avail themselves of all the resources at hand, no matter how unconventional, in order to achieve the effect they seek.

14 *Simple Looms*

Of all materials I choose wool. Of all equipment I choose the simplest. For a place to work I choose the sun.
Sheila Hicks in Craft Horizons, *1963*

Many professional handweavers use simple looms to supplement or even replace the conventional loom. The overriding advantage is cost, for a simple loom can be constructed for a tiny fraction of the amount required to buy a commercial four-harness loom. If one is a purist, a backstrap loom can even be assembled from sticks and twigs, just as primitive tribes have done for centuries. Only the shed sword and beater need be shaped and refined to any extent; the other components can simply be cut to the proper length.

In addition to the financial aspect, simple looms offer further advantages, both practical and aesthetic. Frame and backstrap looms are lightweight and highly portable; they can be stored in a very small space. Most attractive to some contemporary weavers is the fact that simple looms permit a much more intimate contact between the craftsman and his materials. For this reason many novice weavers prefer to learn the process of interweaving warp and weft on a simple loom, before having to master the mechanics of a complex table or floor loom.

Weaving progresses at a rather slow rate on simple looms. However, the range of fabrics that can be constructed is really limited only by the ingenuity and patience of the weaver. A great many of the textiles illustrated in Chapters 3 and 4, notably those from pre-Columbian America, were created on simple looms, and their quality has seldom been equaled in any other time or part of the world.

THE BACKSTRAP LOOM

A simple backstrap loom has almost all the functioning parts of a modern commercially produced loom, albeit in crude form. The framework consists of a warp stick and a cloth stick, the former attached to a tree or some other stationary object, the latter joined to a backstrap

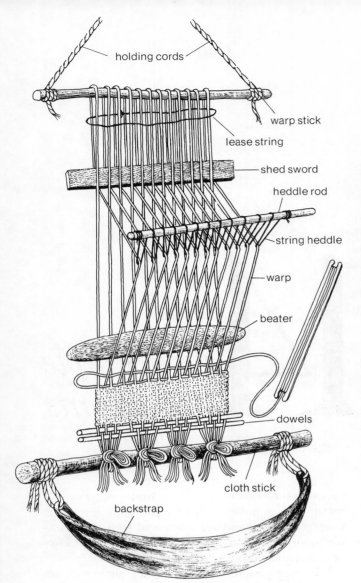

holding cords

warp stick

lease string

shed sword

heddle rod

string heddle

warp

beater

dowels

cloth stick

backstrap

377–383. *A backstrap loom is a simple weaving device in which the warp yarns are stretched taut between a tree or other stationary object and the body of the weaver.*

left: 377. The fully assembled backstrap loom.

above: 378. John Young Bear, Fox Tribe, Tama, Iowa. Slot-and-eye heddle. Before 1920. Carved black walnut, $13\frac{1}{2} \times 9\frac{1}{8}''$. Great Lakes Indian Museum, Cross Village, Mich. (Chandler-Pohrt Collection).

passed around the weaver's waist (Fig. 377). Often, there is also a cloth roll, adjacent to the cloth stick, around which the finished web is wrapped as weaving progresses.

The shedding device may take any of several forms. Figure 378 illustrates a wooden slot-and-eye heddle, used by the Indians in the Great Lakes region of North America. With this ingenious tool, half the warp yarns were passed through the slots, and the other half—the alternate warp yarns—were threaded through the eyes (Fig. 379). When the heddle was lifted, all the warps in the eyes were raised to create a shed. When it was pushed down, the alternate warps moved to the top of each slot to produce the

opposite shed for plain weave. A complicated weave would require that the warp yarns be lifted individually.

A more common shedding system relies upon a shed roll or *sword* and a heddle rod (Fig. 380). The sword is threaded alternately over and under the warp yarns; when turned on end, it produces the first shed for plain weave. All the yarns that lie under the sword are attached by string heddles (or by one continuous string heddle) to the heddle rod, which when lifted raises the alternate yarns for the second shed.

The beating mechanism is equally simple. On the Indian version of the backstrap loom the slot-and-eye heddle also serves as a beater. If the sword and heddle rod system is employed, an extra stick is inserted in the warp for beating.

Construction of a Backstrap Loom

The backstrap loom can be as wide or as narrow as one can handle with ease. For the beginner, a width greater than about 22 inches would be awkward, so all the components of the loom described below have been adjusted to that size. The materials for the backstrap loom include:

> four 22-inch lengths of 1-inch dowel
> one 22-inch length of ¾-inch dowel
> two wooden slats, each 22 inches long and 1½ inches wide
> one wooden slat, 22 inches long, shaped to a smooth point at both ends for the beater (Fig. 377)
> one ball of stout twine
> one ball of linen cord for the string heddle
> one length of cord or tape about 4 feet long for the backstrap

If the weaver desires, he can construct a rigid slot-and-eye heddle similar to that illustrated in Figure 379. This would obviate the necessity for the linen cord, the pointed beater, the ¾-inch dowel, and one of the wooden slats.

For the most part, the backstrap loom is constructed as the loom is dressed. It cannot be fully assembled until the warp is in position.

Preparation for Weaving

The warp yarns can be measured on a warping frame or reel as for conventional weaving. If neither is available, the warp can be wound around the backs of two chairs held at a fixed distance apart, or around two stakes driven into the ground. In any event, some provision should be allowed for making the cross (see pp. 111–114). For the first project—until the weaver is accustomed to the mechanics of the loom—the warp should be no longer than about 3 yards.

After the entire warp has been measured, it is cut from the warping frame at the end opposite the cross. The looped end near the cross is slipped over one of the 1-inch dowels, which will serve as the warp stick. Next, a length of twine is attached securely to each end of the dowel and then tied to a tree, a doorknob, or whatever support the weaver intends. Another length of twine is cut slightly longer than double the width of the warp. This is inserted in the cross to take the place of lease sticks. The cross ties can now be removed and the warp spread on the stick.

The next step depends upon which type of shedding arrangement is to be used. If the weaver prefers a slot-and-eye heddle, the heddle must be threaded before the warp is attached to the cloth stick. In order to center the warp in the heddle, the weaver must divide the total number of warp yarns by two, and find the center of the heddle. He then counts from center

below: 379. Operation of the slot-and-eye heddle.

right: 380. The shed sword and heddle rod.

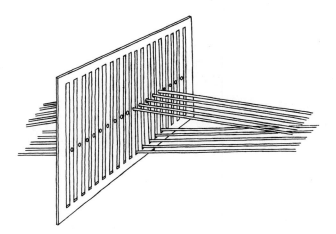

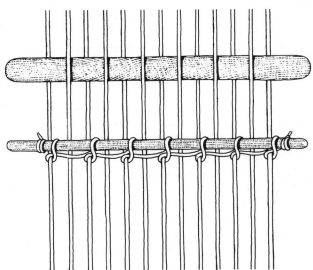

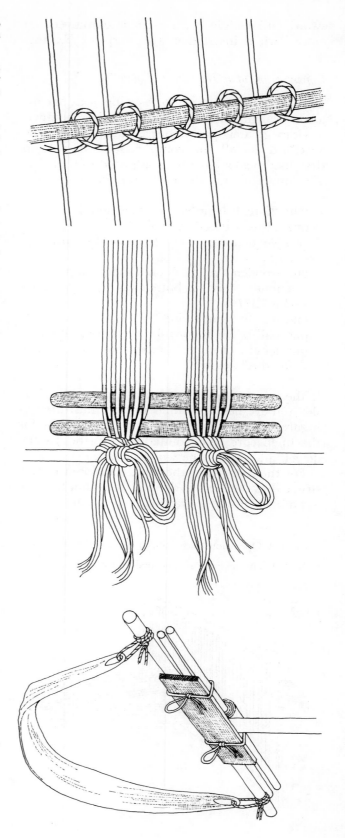

right: 381. A length of cord is looped over the heddle rod, catching all the yarns not engaged by the shed sword. When pulled taut, the heddle rod opens plain-weave shed.

center right: 382. To begin weaving on the backstrap loom, one inserts two dowels in alternate plain-weave sheds near the cloth stick. These dowels help to spread the warp yarns and also serve as a cloth roll as weaving progresses.

bottom right: 383. When a length of fabric has been woven, the backstrap is removed from the waist and the dowels are rolled forward and secured by lashing a slat beneath them. Then the strap is replaced, and weaving resumes.

to left the number of slots plus eyes to equal one half of the warp. This point is marked on the heddle. The heddle can be clasped between the knees or propped between two heavy objects for threading. Working from left to right, the weaver draws the warp yarns alternately through a slot and an eye, taking the yarns first from one side of the cross and then from the other. When all the yarns have been threaded, the ends are tied in a slip knot to prevent them from falling out of the heddle.

The backstrap is tied to one end of another 1-inch dowel, which will serve as the cloth stick. The strap is then passed around the weaver's waist in such a way that the cloth stick will be held at a comfortable distance from the body, and fastened to the other end of the dowel. The cut ends of the warp are attached to the cloth stick in the same manner as for conventional loom weaving (Fig. 209).

If the sword and heddle rod arrangement is to be employed, the two sheds for plain weave must now be made. For this operation the warp is held under tension by pressing back slightly on the backstrap. The first shed is created either by lifting gently on the lease cord and passing one of the wooden slats—the shed sword—through the opening, or by threading the sword alternately over and under the warp yarns. If desired, a length of cord can be passed across the warp and tied to each end of the sword, to hold it in position.

The second shed is produced with the first shed open, so the sword must be turned on end. The ball of linen cord is placed in a container—a heavy bowl or cooking pot, for example—to the right of the warp, and the end is threaded across the warp in such a way that it is passed *under* all the warp yarns that are below the sword and *over* all the yarns that are on the sword. The cord should then be tied to one end of the ¾-inch dowel—the heddle rod. To begin forming the string heddle (Fig. 381), the weaver reaches through the warp and grasps the cord to the right of the first warp yarn that is *under* the sword. The cord is pulled through the warp and twisted clockwise in one complete turn to form a loop. This process is repeated to the right of each warp yarn that is under the sword. When all the alternate warp yarns have been affixed to the heddle rod, the cord is cut and tied to the other end of the rod. The heddle rod should be pulled up firmly a few times to equalize the loops. The loom is now ready for weaving.

A boat or throw shuttle is usually too heavy for weaving on a backstrap loom, but a flat stick shuttle will work very well. Alternatively, one could simply wind the weft yarn around a stick bobbin. For free weaving, a series of butterfly shuttles should be made (Fig. 269).

The Weaving Process

To begin weaving, the first shed is opened, and one of the remaining 1-inch dowels is inserted in the shed. The other dowel is placed in the second or opposite shed (Fig. 382). Besides helping to spread the warp yarns on the cloth stick, these two dowels will serve as a cloth roll. Once the dowels are in position, the weft yarn can be introduced. Each weft shot should be beat into position with either the slot-and-eye heddle or the beater stick. A certain amount of practice is required to master the rhythm of backstrap weaving. Minute shifts of body weight will affect the tension of the warp, so an effort must be made to keep the tension consistent.

When the weaving has progressed to a point at which it is no longer comfortable to reach forward and throw the weft, the web must be rolled onto the cloth stick. The backstrap is removed from the waist, and the three wooden dowels are rolled forward. They are secured by lashing the remaining wooden slat to the underside (Fig. 383). Then, the backstrap can be replaced, and weaving proceeds.

Virtually any weave can be constructed on a backstrap loom, although anything more complicated than plain weave would, of course, necessitate the warp yarns being lifted by hand.

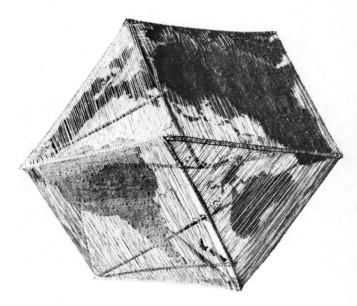

384–387. *A permanent frame loom is an integral part of the woven article that is created upon it. The fabric is actually woven on the structure to which it will remain attached, so the loom is not reusable.*

above: 384. Nana Nissen. *Vector Equilibri Um.* 1969. Wool yarn over a bamboo frame held together with wire, diameter 31¼″. Courtesy Den Permanente, Copenhagen.

The Indians of Latin America have developed astonishing dexterity with the backstrap loom, creating intricately patterned cloth several yards long and often a yard wide.

PERMANENT FRAME LOOMS

A frame loom is permanent when it becomes an integral part of the woven article created upon it. In this sense, the frame used for sprang (Fig. 421) could be considered a permanent loom, since it cannot be removed without collapsing the sprang-work. Many weavers have experimented with self-contained looms to achieve three-dimensional effects. The permanent loom illustrated in Figure 384 was constructed from lengths of bamboo tied together with wire.

Obviously, the permanent loom should reflect the character of the proposed weaving. Four sticks lashed together might be the basis of a rough-textured wall hanging woven from heavy natural yarns. On the other hand, a more "formal" work could be woven on a frame of beautifully grained wood or polished metal. The

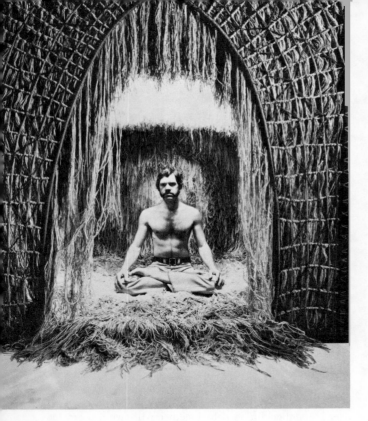

the upper and lower ends of the web will help to stabilize the horizontal dimension of the fabric. Any lightweight shuttle or even a tapestry bobbin or needle can be employed to hold the weft yarn.

Because frame looms seldom provide for a shedding device, they lend themselves particularly well to finger weaves. The major problem lies in the fact that there is no way to adjust the warp tension. Therefore, a closely woven web is difficult to achieve, for the warp takeup will gradually tighten the yarns until it is almost impossible to open a shed. In extreme cases, the dowels will bow in from the tension in the warp. For this reason, projects woven on frame looms tend to be linear in character, with spaced pattern areas and sections of exposed warp or openwork (Fig. 387).

left: 385. TED HALLMAN. Woven meditation environment. 1970. Acrilan carpet fibers on steel frame; cube, more than 6′ in all dimensions. Courtesy the artist.

below: 386. A simple frame loom.

frame can be of any size or shape required by the particular project (Fig. 385).

If the frame loom is made of wood, two principles govern the size of individual members. The frame must be strong enough to support the yarns and it should relate in terms of scale to the yarn one intends to use. The wooden structure should not overpower the woven fabric, unless, of course, the weaving is intended to remain subsidiary to the framework.

A simple frame loom can be constructed from four lengths of 1 by 2 inch lath attached in a rabbet or half-lap joint at the corners and secured with glue and countersunk wood screws (Fig. 386). Before the frame is assembled, a hole must be drilled near each end of the uprights to accept a half-inch dowel. The dowels are set at a sufficient distance from the horizontal bars to allow for manipulating the yarns during warping.

A continuous warp yarn is wrapped around and around the dowels in figure-8 fashion to within about 2 inches of the uprights (Fig. 386). If the warp were carried too close to the uprights, it would be difficult to insert the weft yarn. A few rows of chaining or twining (see p. 191) at

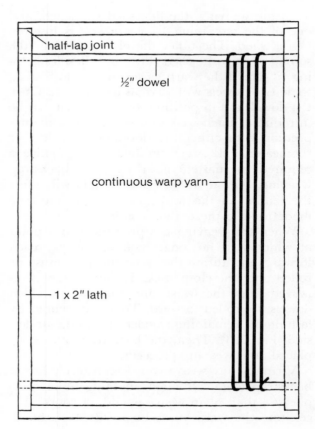

387. FRANCES SCHROEDER. *Mandala*, weaving on permanent metal hoop loom. The warp for this project was threaded through yarn covering the ring. From *Needleweaving: Easy As Embroidery,* by Esther Warner Dendel. Philadelphia: Countryside Press, 1972.

REUSABLE FRAME LOOMS

As the name implies, many frame looms can be used over and over again, for the fabric is cut from the loom in the normal manner after weaving. Some looms of this type can be purchased either readymade or in kit form from weaving-supply houses, but they are simple enough to construct, and the problems of delicate balance and smooth operation do not arise, as they do when one attempts to build a complex loom.

I-form Looms

Among the simplest of frame looms is the I-form (Fig. 388). The materials needed are:

one pine board, 1 inch by 5 inches by 30 inches
two pine boards, 1 inch by 3 inches by 16 inches
four wooden blocks, 1 inch by 3 inches by 5 inches
eight 2½-inch wood screws
102 rustless 1-inch finishing nails
white glue

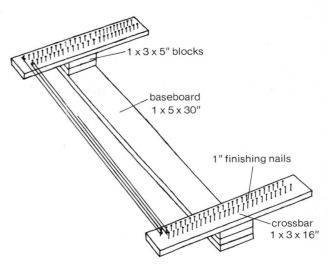

388. The I-form loom.

One assembles the I-form loom as in Figure 388, with the two crossbars centered on the long baseboard and two wood blocks between them at each end. The parts are glued together and left in a wood clamp overnight. When the glue is dry, four holes (about 2 inches deep) are drilled from the underside into each end of the baseboard, and a wood screw is countersunk in each hole so that the head of the screw is even with or just below the surface of the wood. The final step consists of driving 51 finishing nails in two rows into each of the crossbars. The nails are driven at an angle to counteract the tension of the warp yarns. Each nail projects from the wood about ½ inch.

The I-form is warped with a continuous yarn that zig-zags back and forth across the loom. For a denser warp the yarn can be returned in a second trip to the starting point. As with the permanent frame loom, there is no provision for adjusting the warp tension to compensate for yarn takeup, so the loom is more adaptable to loose finger weaves. If desired, a shed sword and heddle rod similar to those used with the back-strap loom (Fig. 380) can be employed, but for most free weaving it is simple enough to pick up the yarns manually. A few rows of twining or chaining (see p. 191) at each end of the web will help to spread the warp yarns evenly across the loom. The flat stick shuttle or a series of butterfly shuttles (Fig. 269) are best for holding the various colors of weft yarn.

Simple Looms   215

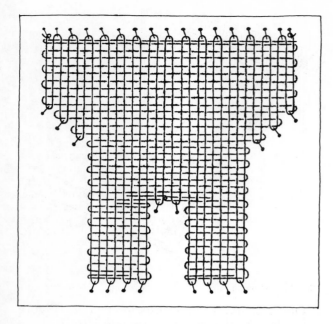

The Indians of ancient Peru undoubtedly utilized a principle similar to that of the I-form loom in constructing shaped garments with a selvedge all around (Fig. 389). By driving nails in a flat surface at each point where the fabric changes direction, one can weave a textile in almost any shape and with a finished edge around the entire border.

Square Frame Looms

There are probably thousands of designs for square frame looms, some much more flexible than others. The following section describes three basic designs, of which the first is really a variation on the I-form loom. The other two offer the unique feature of a warp-tension control.

Fixed-warp Loom   The square loom with a fixed warp is quite similar to the permanent frame loom (Fig. 386). It is fashioned from two uprights sandwiched between a pair of horizontal crossbars at each end (Fig. 390). For extra support, a small wood block is nailed between each pair of crossbars at the center. The materials needed for a rather small version of such a loom include:

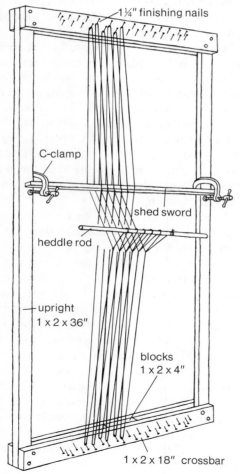

1¼" finishing nails

C-clamp

shed sword

heddle rod

upright
1 x 2 x 36"

blocks
1 x 2 x 4"

1 x 2 x 18" crossbar

two wooden slats, each 1 inch by 2 inches by 36 inches, for the uprights
four wooden slats, each 1 inch by 2 inches by 18 inches, for the crossbars
two wooden blocks, each 1 inch by 2 inches by 4 inches
white glue and wood screws or finishing nails
64 1¼-inch rustless finishing nails

The loom is assembled as in Figure 390, following the procedure outlined for the I-form loom. The finishing nails are placed in two rows—32 nails in each crossbar—and driven at an angle to support the warp tension. They should be set about two per inch except at the edges, where a denser concentration of nails will provide a firm selvedge.

Warping and weaving procedures are the same as those for the I-form loom. The only difference in the square loom is that the selvedges cannot be brought too close to the uprights, or it will be difficult to enter the weft. A shed sword and heddle rod can be constructed and attached to the uprights with C-clamps (available from any hardware store).

Short-web Tapestry Loom   The loom described below is most often used for weaving tapestries, but its principles could be applied to almost any small web. The framework of the loom is identical to that of the fixed-warp loom; however, provision is made for adjusting the warp tension when the yarns draw in during weaving (Fig. 391). The extra materials needed to allow for tension control on the short-web tapestry loom are:

> two wooden slats, each 1 inch by 2 inches by 16 inches, to serve as the tensioners
> one ball of linen cord
> about twenty small flat sticks—popsicle sticks or tongue depressors

The yarn is warped over the two tension slats. It can be either a continuous warp, wound over and over the two slats, or individual warps, doubled over one slat and tied to the other. Then, the tensioners are attached to the uprights with linen cords set at 2-inch intervals. Small twist sticks—such as popsicle sticks—are inserted in the cords and tightened. As the weaving progresses and the weft yarns take up some of the warp length, the twist sticks are gradually unwound at both ends.

Weaving proceeds in the same manner as on the fixed-warp loom, with, if desired, a sword and heddle rod clamped to the uprights. One special precaution should be taken when creating a tapestry or other closely woven fabric. Short lengths of linen cord should be looped around the selvedges and tied—one on each side—to the uprights to stabilize the horizontal dimension of the fabric.

Long-web Tapestry Loom   The only advantage of this loom over the one previously described

is that it can accommodate a web almost twice as long as the frame. The yarn is warped over the two tensioner boards in the same manner as for the short-web loom. However, instead of attaching the tensioners to the framework of the loom, one joins them to each other, by means of cords, at the back of the loom. The warp yarn thus travels up and over the top crossbar, down the entire front of the loom, under the bottom crossbar and up to the starting point.

391–392. *The tapestry frame loom allows for adjustments in the warp tension as the yarns draw in during the weaving process. A series of small flat sticks—such as tongue depressors or popsicle sticks—are twisted and untwisted between the tensioner bars to regulate the warp length.*

below: 391. Short-web tapestry loom, showing holding cords at both sides to maintain the horizontal width of the fabric.

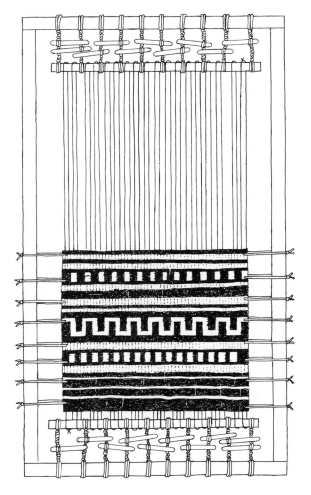

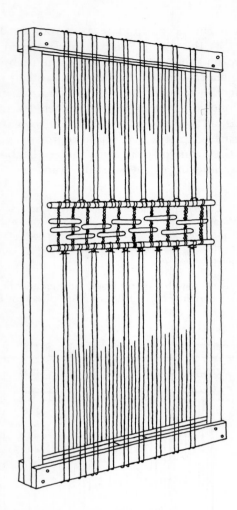

The Ojibway loom consists of two sturdy upright dowels supporting a horizontal crossbar (Fig. 393). A heavy nonelastic cord is wound four or five times around the uprights about half an inch below the crossbar and tied securely. Nails, thumbtacks, or wooden dowels can be added to hold the leader cord in position. All the warp yarns are doubled over the leader cord in a lark's-head knot (Fig. 197) and allowed to hang free. The loom is used primarily for chaining and twining (see pp. 191–192).

Inkle Looms

The inkle loom is the most complex of the frame looms described in this chapter. It can weave a fairly long web, there is a built-in shedding mechanism, and a tension adjustment is provided. However, the *width* of the web is restricted to about 4 inches, and inkle-woven fabrics are usually even narrower. Therefore, the loom is used primarily for weaving decorative bands—belts, headbands, guitar straps, shoulder straps, dog leashes, and trimming bands for garments. Sometimes strips of inkle-woven fabric are sewn together to make a larger, striped textile. In many respects inkle weaving is similar to card

left: 392. Long-web tapestry loom, back view.

below: 393. The Ojibway loom is similar to a warp-weighted loom. It is used primarily for chaining and twining.

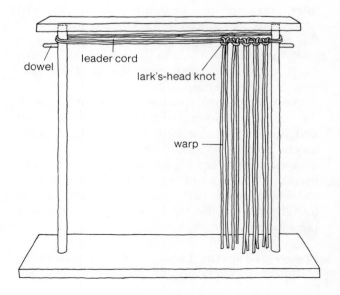

Nails can be driven into the crossbars, as on the fixed warp loom, but in this case they serve only as a general comb and as a spreader for the warp yarns.

As the weaving progresses, the web can be turned around the loom (Fig. 392), so the working space is always in the same position. To turn the yarn and web, the twist sticks must be unwound and the cords holding the tensioners slackened temporarily.

The Ojibway Loom

The loom used by the Ojibway Indians is nothing more than a warp-weighted loom without the weights (Fig. 149). The weavers of this tribe, native to the Great Lakes region of North America, employed such a loom for making tightly woven bags of rushes and twine.

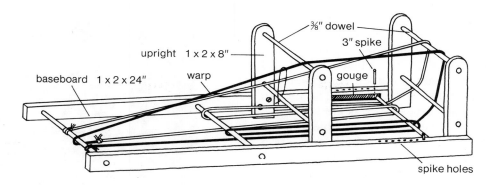

Labels on figure: ³⁄₈" dowel · upright 1 x 2 x 8" · 3" spike · baseboard 1 x 2 x 24" · warp · gouge · spike holes

above: 394. The inkle loom is ideal for weaving long, narrow decorative bands. The product of such a loom is generally a warp-face plain-weave fabric.

weaving (see pp. 241–244), except that on the inkle loom there is a limit to the length of the web, whereas a card-woven fabric could theoretically be infinite in length. Mary Atwater is credited with introducing the inkle loom to the United States. It had long been popular in Scandinavia and in England, where it served for weaving garters and braces.

The loom can be fabricated from high-grade pine, but maple, walnut, or oak will give longer service and provide a more attractive finish. Above all, the framework must be sturdy enough to support yarns under tension. A medium-size inkle loom can be constructed with the following materials:

> two wooden boards, each 1 inch by 2 inches by 24 inches
> four wooden boards, each 1 inch by 2 inches by 8 inches
> seven 9-inch lengths of ³⁄₈-inch dowel
> two 3-inch spikes
> eight ¹⁄₂-inch wood screws
> white glue
> up to sixty 8-inch lengths of linen cord

The fully assembled loom is illustrated in Figure 394. The four 8-inch boards that serve as the uprights are rounded on one end, and two holes are drilled in each to accept the ³⁄₈-inch dowels. The long boards are also drilled with two dowel holes apiece, in the positions indicated in Figure 394. Eight narrow holes—just large enough to accommodate the spikes—are drilled

into the 1-inch edge of each baseboard, and the inside face of the wood is gouged out to half the depth of the board in an area ³⁄₈ inch wide and 4¹⁄₂ to 5 inches long around the spike holes. The tensioning dowel that is inserted at this point must be cut slightly shorter than the others, so that it will slide smoothly in the cutout area. The uprights are attached to the baseboards in a half-lap joint, with glue and two wood screws at each juncture.

One continuous yarn is used for the warp, and warping is accomplished directly on the loom. To begin warping, the spikes are placed in the holes that are closest to the back of the loom. As weaving proceeds and the warp takeup increases tension in the yarns, the spikes are gradually moved forward. String heddles sufficient to accommodate one-half the warp yarns are tied to the heddle rod dowel. The heddles must be of exactly equal length when tied and must be long enough to catch the yarns coming over the top dowel.

The warping pattern is shown in Figure 394. Each time a yarn passes over the top dowel at the center of the loom, it must be threaded through a heddle. The string heddles, therefore, project through the lower section of the warp. When a new color is introduced into the warp, it should be tied to the end of the preceding color at the starting point. The final end is tied in an overhand knot to the starting end of the first warp yarn. The tension should be held constant for each circuit of the loom, for it is difficult to adjust after warping is complete.

Inkle looms provide for two sheds. When the yarn is in its normal position, as warped, the first shed is automatically open. To broaden the shed and allow for insertion of the weft, one pushes down the lower layer of yarns by hand. The opposite shed is created by lifting the lower yarns and pushing down those in the heddles.

Whenever the weaving space becomes too small, the entire web can be pulled forward and rolled around the loom. A flat stick shuttle is the best tool for holding the weft yarn, while an ordinary comb can serve as the beater.

Although finger weaving is possible on the inkle loom, the product of the loom is most often a warp-face plain weave (Fig. 395). Because there is no reed, the warp yarns tend to bunch together, all but obscuring the weft yarn. Pattern is achieved by varying the color of the warp. In order for the weft yarn to be as inconspicuous as possible, it should be of the same color as the two edges of the warp.

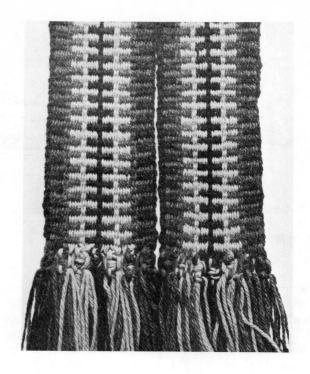

right: 395. SHIRLEY MAREIN. Scarf. 1970. Mexican wool, woven on the inkle loom in a traditional American Indian pattern; width 5″. Courtesy of the artist.

15 *Nonloom Techniques*

There was the greatest freedom when there was hardly any kind of mechanization. When you just manipulated the yarns with your fingers, you could do everything; with every step toward mechanization, however, something has been lost.

Anni Albers in Craft Horizons, *1965*

It is common to classify yarn-interlacement methods according to the number of strands involved and their orientation. All fiber construction techniques—except matting and felting—can therefore be categorized as either single strand or multiple strand. The major yarn-interlacement systems are grouped as follows:

I. Multiple strands

knotting
macramé
sprang
plaiting
braiding
bobbin lace
twining
hooking
weaving

The first category is further subdivided into techniques based on one set of yarns oriented in the same direction—such as macramé and sprang—and those employing two or more sets of yarns, usually perpendicular to one another—including twining and weaving.

II. Continuous single strand

crocheting
tatting
netting
knitting
needle lace
coiling

This chapter explores a number of constructions that require no loom, though in a few cases a simple frame or support is necessary. Nonloom techniques are especially appealing to those who cannot or do not wish to invest in a loom, as well as to those who find loom weaving restrictive. Many nonloom constructions can be effectively combined with conventional loom weaving in wall hangings, sculpture, accessories, and similar projects.

MACRAMÉ

Macramé is a multiple-strand construction employing one set of yarns oriented vertically. The technique has long since broken free of its original application to fringes and decorative borders; today it is used for entire garments, wall hangings, sculpture, jewelry, and many other items. Because the knotted structure is extremely strong, it is even suitable for furniture. Two simple knots—the square knot and the clove hitch—are basic to macramé. The great variety of pattern that is possible derives from the endless ways in which the knots can be combined (Fig. 396).

Materials

Any nonelastic cord or yarn that will hold a knot can be used for macramé (Fig. 397). Jute, linen, and cotton are the most popular fibers, but many other materials can be adapted for specific projects. Wool yarns—especially knitting yarns—are usually too stretchy for knotting, and excessively hairy yarns will tend to obscure the knots. Nylon cord or twine is usable, but in many cases the ends will have to be melted to prevent the knots from untying. Soft cotton yarns are easier to handle if they are dipped in a starch solution before knotting. The starch can be washed out after the project is completed. Seine cord, packing twine, upholsterer's cord, surveyor's chalk line, and rug yarn are all excellent knotting materials. Many of the major yarn suppliers have recently introduced special lines of yarn recommended for macramé.

Equipment

Sharp scissors and a support of some kind are all the equipment needed for macramé. The support may be removed after knotting is complete or it may be incorporated into the finished article as part of the design. The type of support depends, of course, on the nature of the project to be undertaken. Wall hangings, for example, are often knotted on a rigid dowel or metal rod, which becomes a permanent part of the structure. Very large pieces can be knotted on a framework suspended from the ceiling, or on an easel. Tubular knottings originate from any circular support—an embroidery hoop, a lampshade frame, or a length of wire shaped into a circle. When a small or delicate item is planned, most knotters prefer to work on a board or a foam cushion. In this case T-pins (Fig. 398) are used to hold the knotting in position.

Measuring the Cords

It is often difficult to estimate the correct length of cord or yarn that will be required for a given

left: 396. VIRGINIA HARVEY. Wall hanging. 1968. Black-brown upholsterer's linen in square knots and clove hitches, 19½ × 10″. From *Objects: USA,* Johnson Wax Collection of Contemporary Crafts, Racine, Wis.

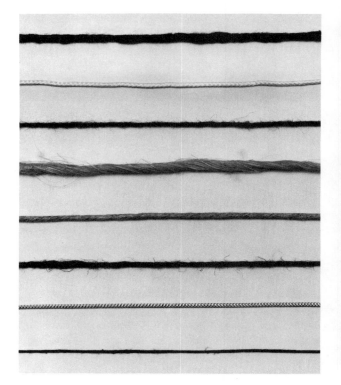

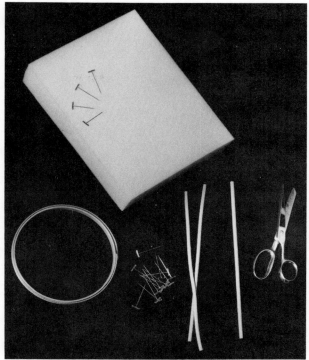

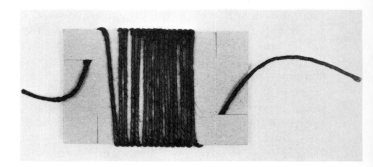

above: 397. Any sturdy, nonelastic cord or yarn can be used for macramé. *Top to bottom:* wool rug yarn, nylon Venetian blind cord, Hagarn wool, sisal, packing twine, 2-ply jute, metallic cord, upholsterer's twine.

above right: 398. The equipment required for various macramé projects may include a foam support cushion, an embroidery hoop, T-pins, dowels, and scissors.

right: 399. For ease of handling, the long macramé cords can be wrapped around small pieces of cardboard with slits to catch the ends. They can also be wound into bunches on the hand and secured with rubber bands.

project. Different knots consume yarn at varying rates, but in general a length of cord that is three to five times the projected length of the finished piece should be adequate. Since the cords are doubled over the support, each cord must be twice the working length—that is, six to ten times the finished length. In an emergency an extra length of cord can be added as the knotting progresses, but the splice is usually difficult to conceal.

The total number of cords in a macramé project is usually divisible by four, since so many of the knots are based on that unit. Most knotted pieces require cords several yards long. For ease

of handling, the yarns can be wrapped around a small piece of cardboard with a slit to catch the ends (Fig. 399), or wound into bunches on the hand and secured with rubber bands. As more yarn is needed, it is pulled free.

The Basic Knots

The Half Knot The half knot or *half square knot* is made on a unit of four cords. The two outside cords perform the actual knot, while the inner two are merely *foundation cords* upon which the knot is built. The foundation cords must be held rigid while the knot is being tied. To make a half

above: 400. The half knot.

right: 401. A sinnet of half knots spirals automatically.

left: 403. A flat sinnet of repeated square knots.

below: 404. A pattern of square knots on alternating cords.

knot (Fig. 400) one passes cord 4 in front of the foundation cords, then brings cord 1 over cord 4, behind the foundation cords, and through the loop formed by cord 4. If the half knot is repeated over and over on the same four yarns, the result will be a *sinnet* that spirals automatically as the knotting progresses (Fig. 401). From time to time the work will have to be turned as cords 1 and 4 exchange positions.

The Square Knot   The square knot is a continuation of the half knot. After a half knot has been tied, cord 1, which is now at the right, is passed behind the foundation cords, and cord 4 is carried behind cord 1, in front of the foundation cords, and through the loop formed by cord 1

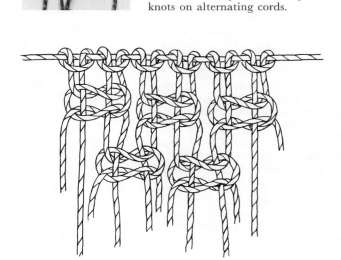

402. The square knot.

(Fig. 402). Cords 1 and 4 are then back in their original positions. The foundation cords are held rigid throughout. If a series of square knots is tied on the same four cords, the result is a *flat sinnet* (Fig. 403). Square knots can also be tied on alternating groups of yarns to produce an allover lacy effect (Fig. 404).

The Clove Hitch   The clove hitch or *double half hitch* is an extremely versatile knot. It can be tied horizontally, vertically, diagonally, or in almost any direction to produce a wide range of effects.

The *horizontal* clove hitch is illustrated in Figure 405. The first cord at the left becomes the foundation cord; it is drawn in front of all the other cords and held under tension in a straight horizontal line. (If this tension is relaxed, the knot will not tie properly.) The second cord is lifted up and around the foundation cord, then passed through the space between the two cords and pulled taut. This procedure is repeated with cord 2 before continuing to cord 3. Each clove hitch thus consists of *two* loops over the foundation cord with the same knotting cord. When all the cords have been knotted over the foundation cord, it can be turned back and the process repeated from right to left. Cord 1 is thereby returned to its original position.

Rows of horizontal clove hitches are often used to separate pattern areas, because they provide a firm structure to maintain the width of the knotting. They are also excellent for finishing the edges of a handwoven fabric (Fig. 330).

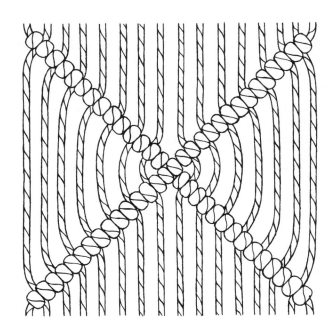

407. An **X** motif in diagonal clove hitches.

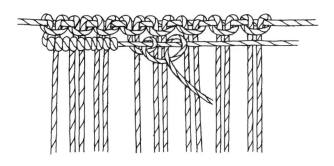

above: 405. The horizontal clove hitch.

below: 406. The diagonal clove hitch is shown proceeding from both sides toward the center.

The *diagonal* clove hitch is made in exactly the same manner. The only difference is that the foundation cord is held at an angle, so that the row of clove hitches proceeds downward gradually (Fig. 406). An **X** pattern can be developed by starting a foundation cord from each side of the knotting, with the two cords descending toward the center (Fig. 407). When they meet, the foundation cords are knotted over one another before proceeding toward the opposite edges.

The *vertical* clove hitch (Fig. 408) is made by knotting the cord at far left over each of the remaining cords. Therefore, cord 1 becomes the knotting cord, and all the others serve in turn

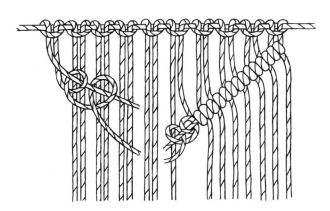

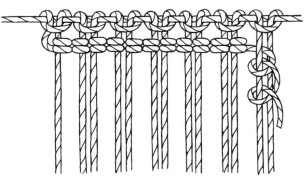

408. The vertical clove hitch.

as foundation cords. When a row of vertical clove hitches is knotted, only the knotting cord appears on the surface. The other cords are completely hidden.

To make a vertical clove hitch cord 1 (at left) is passed behind and around cord 2 and emerges between the two cords. This process is repeated for the second half of the clove hitch. The knotting cord then moves to cord 3, and so on across the row. If desired, the knotting cord can be turned back and a second row made from right to left. The vertical clove hitch consumes yarn very rapidly, so the knotting cord must be considerably longer than all the others.

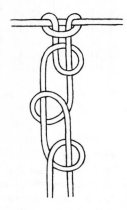

409. A chain of half clove hitches is produced by alternating the knotting cord from side to side.

A *chain* of half hitches (half clove hitches) is produced by alternating the knotting cord from side to side. In Figure 409 the first knot is made with cord 1, the second with cord 2, and the third with cord 1. A heavier chain will result if several yarns are grouped and knotted as a unit.

In addition to the two basic knots, there are special knots that may be encountered from time to time. The *Josephine knot* (Fig. 410) consists of two interlocked loops and resembles a pretzel. It can be tied with two single yarns or with two groups of yarns each considered as a unit. The knot can be pulled taut, but it is usually more attractive if a bit of slack is left in the yarns. The *overhand knot* is a simple loop with the end of the yarn passed through it (Fig. 411). It can be tied with one yarn or with a group of yarns handled as a unit. The *lark's-head knot* (Fig. 197) is frequently used to attach the cords to a support.

above left: 410. The Josephine knot can be tied with two single yarns or with two groups of yarn handled as a unit.

above right: 411. The overhand knot.

A Macramé Sampler

The sampler is planned to demonstrate several combinations of the basic knots and to show some of the ways in which color can be controlled. All the knots described above appear in the sampler, but the square knot and clove hitch predominate.

Specifications for the Sampler   The sampler illustrated in Figure 412 was knotted from two-ply jute yarn. If desired, a different yarn or twine can be substituted, but the size and shape of the knots may be altered.

Yarn:	2-ply jute in two colors
Number of yarns:	12 yarns color A 6 yarns color B (each doubled on the support to make a total of 36 cords)
Length of yarns:	17 yarns each 6 yards long 1 yarn (color A) 10 yards long
Support:	two 7-inch lengths of $\frac{1}{4}$-inch wooden dowel
Length of sampler:	19 inches, plus fringe
Width of sampler:	$5\frac{1}{2}$ inches

Knotting Instructions   The dowel that supports the knotting can be suspended from any fixed object or attached to a wall or door.

412. The macramé sampler was worked primarily in square knots and clove hitches. Three Josephine knots appear at lower center, and the overhand knot is employed for attaching the second dowel.

1. All the yarns are doubled and attached to one of the dowels with a lark's-head knot. The first yarn at left is much longer than the rest because it will serve as the foundation cord for horizontal clove hitches and the knotting cord for vertical clove hitches. It is mounted on the dowel in such a way that cord 1 (at far left) is 7 yards long and cord 2 is 3 yards long, like all the others.

2. Two rows of horizontal clove hitches, from left to right and right to left.

3. Seven rows of alternating single square knots. In the first row the square knot is made with cords 1 through 4, 5 through 8, etc. In row two the knot is made on cords 3 through 6, 7 through 10, etc. Cords 1, 2, 35, and 36 are left unknotted. Row three repeats row one, row four repeats row two, and so on, with the seventh row knotted like row one.

4. Two rows of horizontal clove hitches, from left to right and right to left.

5. Nine flat sinnets of square knots, each containing fifteen knots. Four of the sinnets are crossed in order to transpose the colors.

6. Two rows of horizontal clove hitches, from left to right and right to left.

7. The X motif in diagonal clove hitches. One foundation cord is started from each edge and knotted toward the center. Where they intersect, the two foundation cords are knotted over one another before continuing to the opposite edges. Cords 1 and 36 thereby exchange positions, and the long cord is at the right.

8. Two rows of horizontal clove hitches, from *right* to *left* and left to right.

9. Two rows of *vertical* clove hitches, from right to left and left to right. Only the foundation cord appears on the surface, so color B is completely obscured.

10. Two rows of horizontal clove hitches, from right to left and left to right.

11. *Left to right:* a chain of half hitches knotted on four cords, each pair considered as a unit; a spiral sinnet of half knots; two crossed spiral sinnets of half knots; a series of three Josephine knots tied on four cords, each pair considered as a unit; two crossed spiral sinnets of half knots; a spiral sinnet of half knots; a chain of half hitches knotted on four cords.

12. Two rows of horizontal clove hitches, from right to left and left to right.

13. Three rows of triple alternating square knots. Each group of four cords is tied in three square knots before alternating the rows.
14. Two rows of horizontal clove hitches, from right to left and left to right.
15. Each cord is tied in an overhand knot, and the second dowel is slipped through the loop before tightening.
16. Two rows of horizontal clove hitches, from right to left and left to right.
17. A double chevron pattern in square knots—nine rows.

Row one: all cords in groups of four, beginning with cord 1.
Row two: cords 3–6, 11–14, 23–26, 31–34
Row three: cords 5–8, 13–16, 21–24, 29–32
Row four: cords 7–10, 15–18, 19–22, 27–30
Row five: cords 9–12, 17–20, 25–28
Row six: cords 11–14, 23–26
Row seven: cords 13–16, 21–24
Row eight: cords 15–18, 19–22
Row nine: cords 17–20

18. The fringe is cut off evenly.

Finishing a Macramé Project

Like the sampler, many macramé pieces are terminated by a fringe. When this is not appropriate, the cut ends can be worked back into the fabric with a crochet hook and trimmed cleanly on the reverse side. Cord ends drawn back onto a fabric of clove hitches are almost invisible. For extra durability one can stitch across the fabric with a sewing machine or by hand.

The final knots in a macramé project can be secured by painting the reverse side with a transparent glue or clear nail polish. Nylon cords are often subjected to heat so the fibers will melt together and prevent raveling of the knots.

below left: 413. HESI BODLAENDER. Macramé necklace. 1970. Seine twine with silver beads knotted in; length 27″. Courtesy the artist.

below right: 414. FRANÇOISE GROSSEN. *Contact,* detail. 1971. Knotted construction of white cotton piping cord, 10 × 22′ overall. Courtesy the artist.

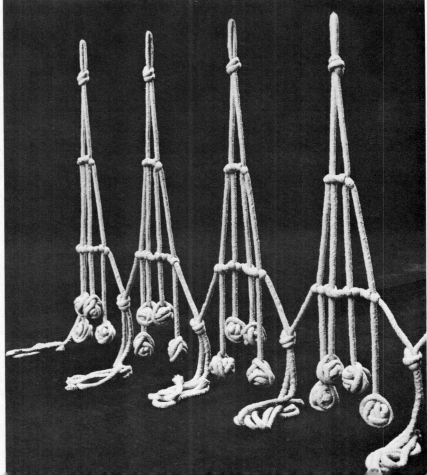

Designing for Macramé

The necklace in Figure 413 and the sculptural construction in Figure 414 are both examples of macramé—the first a delicate network of knots on very fine cord, the second a heavy rope tied in only a few places. These two illustrations will serve to indicate the vast range of potential projects for macramé. Because the possibilities for knotting are so extensive (Pl. 23, p. 231), no single set of design principles can be applied.

A flat or three-dimensional hanging may be a virtuoso display of knot combinations (Fig. 415) or a cascade of unknotted yarns emerging from or combined with knotted areas (Fig. 416).

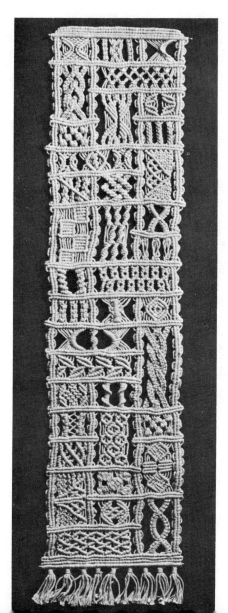

left: 415. JOAN MICHAELS PAQUE. Macramé hanging. 1971. Polished cotton, 36 × 12″. Las Vegas Art Museum, Nev.

above: 416. CLAIRE ZEISLER. *Red Madagascar.* 1971. Raffia and jute, knotted and wrapped; height 7′8″. Courtesy Ruth Kaufmann Gallery, New York.

above: 417. AURELIA MUNOZ. *Tres Personnages.* 1970–71. Sisal, height 5′7″. Courtesy International Biennial of Tapestries, Lausanne, 1971.

above right: 418. Detail of *Personnages* (Fig. 417).

right: 419. JOANNE ASHER THOMPSON. Hanging chair. 1971. Macramé knots in cotton cord; height 7′4″, diameter 2′.

Freestanding works (Fig. 417) are necessarily based on a very closely knotted structure (Fig. 418), while furniture—such as hammocks, benches, and chairs (Fig. 419)—need not be closely tied, provided the cords are strong enough.

Some knotters can design realistically on paper, plotting in advance the areas of concentrated, closely knotted work and the simple lines and planes. Squared graph paper is useful for this purpose, because the grid provides a scale for the overall project. Designers who work this way often invent a code to suggest the various knots; for example, an *x* might represent a square knot, an *o* a vertical clove hitch. Other people find it impossible to visualize a knotted project in terms of marks on paper and prefer to design in yarn. In any case, the knots selected for a given project should be tested on the specific yarn or cord to be used.

Plate 23. NEDA AL-HILALI with her environmental hanging *Nar*. 1971. Knotted yarns, 16 x 12 x 12′. Courtesy the artist.

Plate 24. Lillian Elliott. *Tribal Cloth.* 1966. Mohair and wool card-woven strips sewn together, ikat and tie-dye printed; 10 x 6'. Collection Robert Cranford, San Francisco.

above: 420. MICHI OUCHI. *Blue and Purple.* 1970. Wool and linen weaving with macramé and braided fringe, 5′5″ × 2′6″. Courtesy the artist.

The knotted structure can be combined with other techniques—weaving, knitting, rya, braiding (Fig. 420); it can incorporate a wide variety of nonfibrous materials—ceramic or wooden shapes, feathers, beads, or plastic. There is virtually no limit to the possibilities for macramé.

SPRANG

Like macramé, sprang is composed of one set of yarns—a group of stretched, parallel warps supported, in this case, at all four sides. The lacy structure is created by twisting the warps around one another in a planned fashion and then securing the twists. The mechanics of sprang are much like those of a gauze weave, except that no weft

is inserted. Without some stretching or beating, the visible sprang network would disappear.

Materials

Sprang can be worked with any elastic yarn or cord—linen, cotton, jute, nylon, or wool rug yarn. As with macramé, an extremely fuzzy yarn will tend to hide the structure, so a clean-surfaced yarn is preferable.

Equipment

A square frame of wood or metal is the best support for sprang. Alternatively, the sprangwork can be suspended between two wooden dowels, with vertical rods at either side to maintain the crosswise stretch. In either case, the horizontal crossbar at bottom must be movable, so that it can be raised as the sprang contracts. This can be managed by weighting the movable dowel sufficiently to hold the warps under tension. The weights should not be so heavy that they prevent the dowel from moving upward. Figure 421 illustrates a wooden frame that could be constructed easily. The top and vertical portions are fixed,

below: 421. A simple rectangular frame for sprang. The lower crossbar is movable so it can be adjusted.

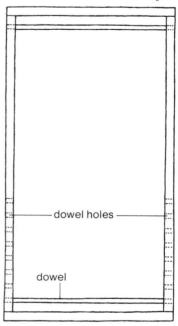

— dowel holes —

dowel

and holes have been drilled at several intervals along the uprights so that the bottom dowel can be raised gradually.

In addition to the frame, three flat sticks or dowels no longer than the frame is wide are required for making the twists.

Mounting the Yarns

There are several methods for stretching the warps between the horizontal supports at top and bottom. The warps can be doubled and attached to the top crossbar with a lark's-head knot (Fig. 197), then secured to the lower cross-bar. Some people prefer to use one continuous yarn for the warp, wrapping it around and around the two crossbars in figure-**8** fashion (Fig. 422). This system eliminates the need for knots or a fringe at the bottom, and both ends of the sprangwork present a finished appearance.

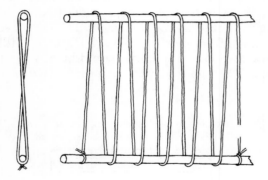

422. One continuous yarn is wrapped around the frame.

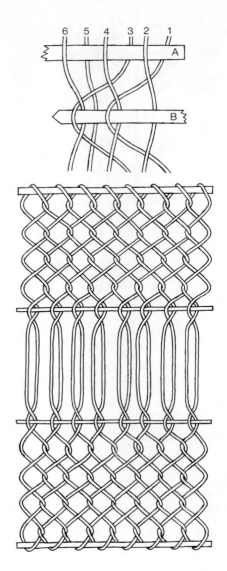

Procedure for Sprang

The simplest form of sprang is the 1/1 mesh, accomplished in the following manner. Beginning at the right, one of the sticks (stick A) is threaded through the warp as for plain weave, with the warp at far right *under* the stick (Fig. 423). A second stick (stick B) is placed on the warp below stick A. Yarn 1 (at far right) is looped *under* yarn 2, *over* yarn 3, and *under* yarn 4, then is placed on the stick. Yarn 3 is passed *under* yarn 4, *over* yarn 5, *under* yarn 6, and placed on the stick. This process is repeated across the row, with the right hand manipulating the stick and the left hand drawing the loops. If the warp

consists of an even number of yarns, the complete threading of one row will leave two yarns under the stick at right and two yarns over the stick at left.

When the first row has been threaded all across, stick A is removed, and stick B is pushed up to the top of the sprang. A third stick (stick C) is inserted into the same shed as B and pushed *down*, which forces an identical system of twists to the bottom of the sprang (Fig. 424). This dual direction explains the symmetrical nature of sprang. The meshwork grows from the top and bottom edges to meet in the center.

The second row is threaded in a similar manner to the first, except that the two yarns at right

opposite above: 423. Step one for the 1/1 mesh.

opposite below: 424. Sprang is always symmetrical. After the first row of twists has been made and pushed to the top of the sprangwork, an identical set is forced to the bottom.

below: 425. Step two for the 1/1 mesh.

bottom: 426. Each row of twists must be attached to the vertical supports at either side to maintain the shape of the sprangwork. At the center, the final twists are looped upon one another to prevent unraveling. One can also leave a dowel or other support in position.

must be accounted for. Stick *A* is placed on the warp at right, and the outside yarn (now yarn 2) is looped over yarn 4 and under yarn 1, then is placed on the stick (Fig. 425). After this step, the row proceeds as usual. Stick *B* is removed, and stick *A* is pushed upward; then stick *C* can be removed, placed in the same shed as *A*, and pushed down again. At this point one unit of the 1/1 mesh has been completed, and it is necessary to secure the twists. The two outermost yarns at top and bottom must be affixed to the vertical supports with a short length of wire or yarn (Fig. 426). After each repeat of the twist, the four outside yarns are again tied to the uprights. When the sprang is complete, these temporary ties can be replaced with a single continuous yarn at each side or with some other binder.

Where the twists developing from each end meet at the center, they must be fastened to prevent the structure from untwisting (Fig. 427).

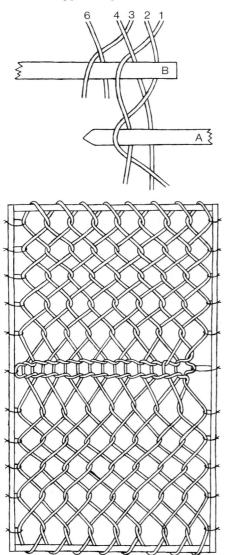

right: 427. PETER COLLINGWOOD. Sprang hanging. 1963. White linen, c. 36 × 10″. Collection Ted Hallman, Berkeley, Calif.

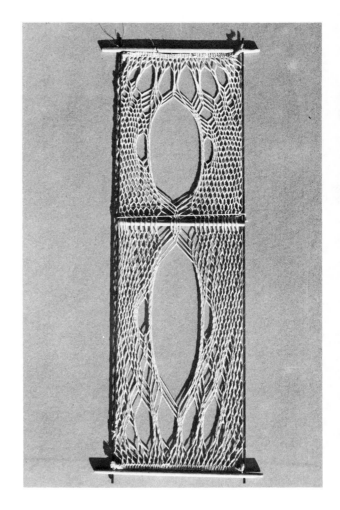

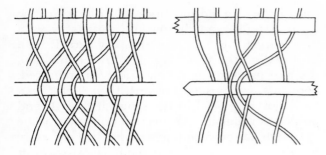

above left: 428. The 2/2 mesh.

above right: 429. Openings in the sprang are created by leaving certain yarns untwisted for a few rows.

below: 430. HELLA SKOWRONSKI. *Sprang No. 6.* 1968. Dark gold silk, 20 × 12″. Courtesy the artist.

The easiest method is to loop each yarn through the adjacent one, as illustrated in Figure 426. The final loop is tied to the vertical support. If the overall design warrants it, a center dowel can be left in position and secured to the uprights.

Variety of design in sprang can be achieved in several ways. The basic 1/1 mesh can be expanded into a 2/2, a 2/1, a 3/3, or any other combination. Figure 428 illustrates the manipulation for a 2/2 mesh, in which two adjacent yarns are twisted around two others. Another possibility is the creation of *openings,* points at which the yarns are left uncrossed. This technique has been exploited very effectively in the wall hanging reproduced in Figure 427.

Figure 429 illustrates the first step in making an opening. It corresponds to Figure 423, except that yarns 3 and 6 are left uncrossed. In the next row the two sides of the opening are treated as separate pieces of sprang and twisted accordingly. When a very small opening is desired, row three is twisted in the usual manner, with yarn 3 crossing yarn 6. However, the yarns can be left uncrossed for any *even* number of rows, and the opening will gap wider and wider.

Sprang fabric is highly elastic in all directions. Each yarn interacts with every other yarn, so the overall design cannot be perceived until the sprangwork is complete. At present the technique is applied most often to wall hangings (Fig. 430), but contemporary artist-craftsmen have only begun to explore its potential.

NETTING

A net is an openwork fabric constructed from a single continuous strand knotted repeatedly over a gauge. In certain variations of the netting technique the twine or yarn is merely looped upon itself, a process known as *knotless netting.* However, the knotted version is more common, and the directions that follow apply to knotted nets.

A wide variety of materials can be used for netting. As with macramé and sprang, relatively nonelastic yarn with a minimum of surface texture will best display the netted structure. Only two pieces of equipment are required: a stick shuttle or netting shuttle and a netting gauge—a dowel or flat strip of wood slightly broader than the filled shuttle (Fig. 431). The width of the gauge determines the size of the open spaces.

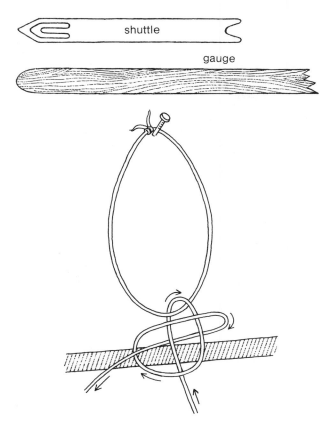

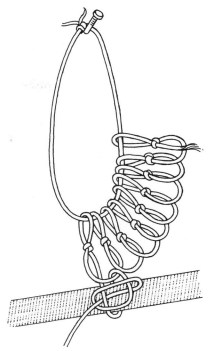

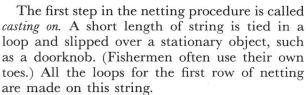

above left: 431. A netting shuttle and gauge.

left: 432. Casting on for a net.

above: 433. Netting the second and subsequent rows.

The first step in the netting procedure is called *casting on.* A short length of string is tied in a loop and slipped over a stationary object, such as a doorknob. (Fishermen often use their own toes.) All the loops for the first row of netting are made on this string.

The gauge is grasped in the left hand, and the free end of yarn from the shuttle is held firmly against the gauge (Fig. 432). The shuttle moves up through the holding loop, from back to front, and down again to the gauge, where the yarn is held in position. To complete the knot, the shuttle describes a sweeping clockwise curve and is drawn through the curve from back to front and right to left. The second knot is begun by passing the yarn around the gauge, then again through the holding loop. Once each knot has been tightened, there is no danger of its coming undone or losing its shape. After a sufficient number of knots have been made to cover the proposed width of the net, the gauge can be removed. The work is then turned, and netting again proceeds from left to right, but this time the loop of yarn between each pair of knots in

the first row serves as a holding cord (Fig. 433). The procedure for making a circular net is only slightly different. The first knot in the second row is hooked onto the first knot in the previous row, and work proceeds in a spiral, rather than back and forth.

The netting technique has obvious applications in hammocks, mesh shopping bags, curtains, garments, and similar items. Its lacy structure, alone or in combination with other fiber construction processes, can be adapted to wall hangings and large-scale sculpture.

PLAITING AND BRAIDING

Plaiting and braiding are both simple finger-weaving techniques long used by primitive peoples for making belts, straps, bands, and other narrow fabrics.

Plaiting is done over a dowel, a stick, or some other holding device. A string is tied at each end to the dowel, so it can be attached to a stationary object. The yarn or twine should be cut into lengths at least four times as long as the band

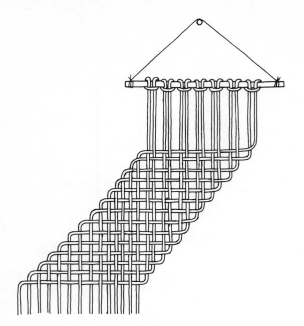

434. Diagonal plaiting.

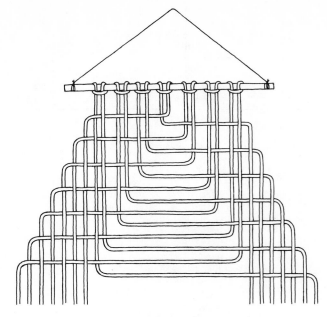

435. Plaiting in a chevron pattern.

is to be, and then each strand is doubled over the supporting rod by means of a lark's-head knot (Fig. 197).

The plaiting is begun by picking up the yarn at the far right and interweaving it through the other yarns in turn as for plain weave (Fig. 434). When the yarn reaches the opposite side, it can be draped over the supporting rod temporarily. Next, the second yarn is woven through the fabric in the same manner, interlacing last with yarn 1, which is brought down and allowed to hang free. A diagonal band develops as the process is repeated, working always from right to left. When the plaiting is finished, the ends can be braided or knotted together. If the band is intended for a belt, the initial loops can be tied to a buckle. One variation on the plaiting technique is the *chevron* pattern, woven as in Figure 435 by starting at the center and working alternately to the two sides.

Three-strand *braiding* is familiar to almost everyone as a method for dressing hair. When the number of strands is increased to four, eight, twelve, or even more, an intricate round braid develops. Four-strand braiding follows the pattern illustrated in Figure 436. Working alternately from left and right, a strand is placed behind the two adjacent strands, carried around, and allowed to hang between them. Three-

below: 436. Four-strand braiding.

right: 437. Twelve-strand braiding.

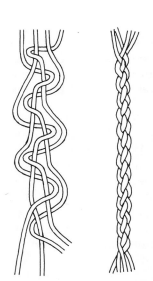

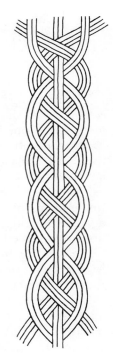

dimensional braids are often woven around a core of yarns (Fig. 437). Any number of strands can be used, but the example demonstrates a twelve-strand braid, actually a braid woven with ten strands around a core of two. When the braid has reached the desired length, the ends can be secured by whipping an extra yarn around them.

SPOOL AND SLOT KNITTING

Spool knitting and slot knitting are both processes in which a single continuous yarn is looped upon itself, by means of a simple loom, to produce fabric. Spool knitting always results in a tubular cloth, while slot knitting usually creates a flat fabric.

Spool knitting derives its name from the fact that an ordinary thread spool, or some variation thereof, serves as the loom. The size of the spool regulates the diameter of the fabric produced. To convert the spool to a loom, one must drive an *un*even number of finishing nails into the top, evenly spaced around the circumference of the spool (Fig. 438). For a larger cylinder of fabric one can substitute a wooden ring into which dowels have been inserted at regular intervals

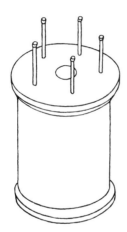

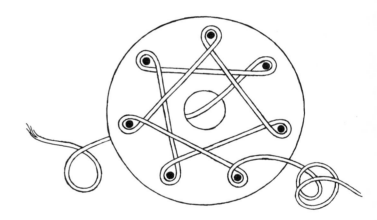

(Fig. 439). By spacing the nails or dowels close together, one produces a finer knit mesh.

Knitting begins by drawing the free end of the yarn through the hole in the center of the spool. Next, the yarn is wrapped around every other nail on the spool until, after two circuits, each nail has a loop of yarn around it (Fig. 440). The spool is then rotated to add a second loop around each nail. The first loop on each nail is then lifted over the second and off the nail with a knitting needle, a crochet hook, or simply with the fingers. Repetition of this process—alternately wrapping the nails and lifting off the lower loop—produces the knit cylinder, which is drawn through the hole in the center of the spool. One knits by wrapping clockwise, purls by

above left: 438. An ordinary thread spool, with finishing nails driven into the top, can be used for spool knitting.

top: 439. A wooden ring with dowels inserted at regular intervals yields a larger tube of fabric.

above: 440. Spool knitting proceeds as the yarn is alternately wrapped around the nails or dowels and lifted off, loop by loop. The fabric emerges at the center of the ring.

wrapping counterclockwise. The completed fabric will not unravel if each loop is drawn through the adjacent one as for chaining (see p. 191), or if the free end of the yarn is passed through all the loops.

Slot knitting is based on exactly the same principle; only the shape of the loom changes. To

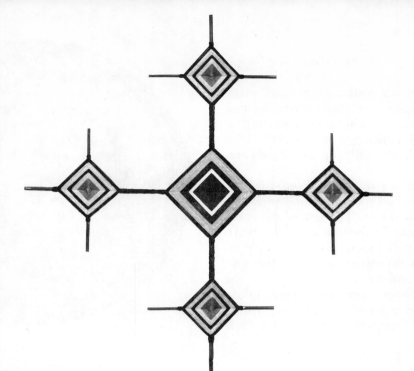

make a slot loom or *knitting rake,* one fastens two boards together so that about half an inch of space is left between them (Fig. 441). A series of 1-inch finishing nails are driven into each board near the slot edge. If there is any danger of the wood splitting, the nails in each board can be staggered in two rows.

The yarn is wound around the nails following the pattern illustrated in Figure 442. When two complete circuits of the loom have been wound, and the yarn is back at the starting point, the lower loop on each nail is lifted over the second

one and off the nail. Alternately wrapping and lifting off the loops results in a flat knit fabric, which is drawn down through the slot. One can knit from the end nails, where the yarn turns, only on every second row. The final loops are finished as for spool knitting.

GOD'S-EYE

The Eye of God is a ritual symbol among the Indians of Latin America. Either alone or in combination with other fiber-construction tech-

below: 441. A slot loom is made from two boards nailed together with a bit of space between them.

bottom: 442. The pattern for winding yarn on a slot loom.

top: 443. Luke Curtis. Multiple God's-eye. Multicolor wool yarns, height 28½″. Courtesy the artist.

below: 444. The pattern of yarn wrapping for God's-eye.

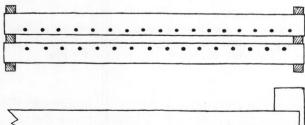

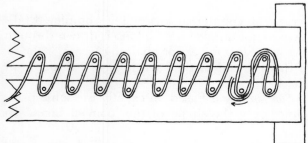

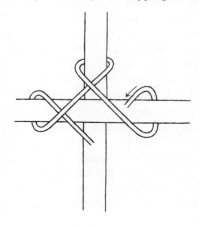

niques, the diamond-shape God's-eye is a striking form (Fig. 443).

The only materials needed for working a God's-eye are smooth sticks or dowels and a supply of yarn in various colors. In Mexico and South America the yarns are always brightly colored—sunny yellows, vivid reds and pinks, clear greens and blues. Three or more colors may be used to suggest the wisdom and light radiating from the central "eye."

To begin the God's-eye, one must hold two sticks together at right angles to form a cross. Following the pattern shown in Figure 444, the yarn is wound repeatedly around the four arms of the cross. Each new yarn is placed next to the previous one, with no overlapping. When the color is to be changed, both loose ends are held by the thumb until they are covered and secured by the buildup of yarn. After the God's-eye is finished, the end of the yarn can be looped over one of the sticks and pulled into a knot. One method of incorporating a God's-eye into a woven form is to place the ornament on the warp and weave the weft around the sticks (Fig. 445).

CARD WEAVING

Card weaving is a two-element construction employing both a warp and a weft. Since ancient times it has been used for making long, narrow bands of fabric. Square ivory tablets with holes at each of the corners were discovered in Egypt long ago, but at first they were thought to have been part of a game. Later, it was ascertained that the cards were used for weaving before the Egyptians developed the warp-weighted loom (Fig. 48). Weaving tablets were also found in the Oseberg Burial Ship in Norway (Fig. 446), in this case wooden cards numbering 52 in all. A half-finished band accompanied the tablets.

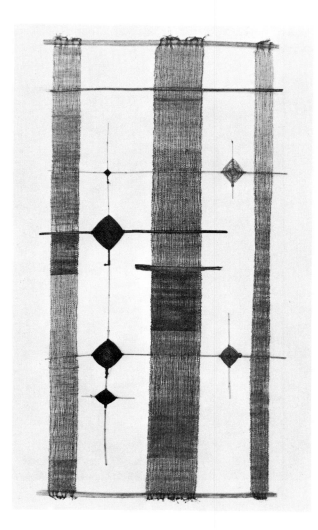

left: 445. ALICE PARROTT. *God's Eye Hanging.* 1958. Maguey strings, wool, cotton, and willow branches in plain-weave and wrapping techniques; 6 × 3′. Collection Nordenfjeldske Kunstindustrimuseum, Trondheim.

446–452. *In card weaving a series of square or other geometrically shaped cards replace the loom.*

below: 446. Weaving tablets, from the Oseberg Burial Ship, Norway, A.D. 830. Wood, 52 tablets in all. University Museum of Antiquities, Oslo.

Card-woven fabric is always warp-faced. The weft is visible only at the selvedges, and if the weft is the same color as the outside warps, it is barely noticeable. Therefore, the pattern in a card-woven band is created by varying the color of the warp yarns.

Any smooth, firm yarn can be used for card weaving—linen, cotton carpet warp, crochet cotton, firmly twisted silk or worsted. Soft materials that pull apart easily should be avoided. The only equipment needed is a series of cards with holes punched in the corners. The cards can be triangular, pentagonal, hexagonal, and so forth, but most often they are square, with a hole punched in each of the four corners. Ordinary playing cards, cut square, are excellent for card weaving. Failing this, the cards can be made from firm, thin cardboard cut 2½ inches square. Holes should be punched at least ⅜ inch from the edge to prevent them from tearing easily. The number of cards determines the width of the proposed fabric. A novice card weaver should not attempt to handle more than twenty, but with experience one can introduce more.

Preparation for Weaving

In card weaving the cards themselves take the place of harnesses and heddles. Warp yarns are threaded through the holes in the cards according to a planned pattern. Then, the cards are stacked together, and, as they are rotated, the warp yarns twist to open a shed.

The warp can be measured on a conventional warping frame or substitute (such as the backs of two chairs held at a fixed distance apart). Warping should follow the color sequence that is planned for a particular project. All the normal warping procedures are adhered to: a cross is made and tied, the warp is chained, and small lease sticks or lease cords are inserted to maintain the cross as an aid in threading the cards (see pp. 111–118).

The pattern for a card-woven band can be drafted on squared graph paper just as for any other kind of weaving, but the method of draft notation is a bit different. In Figure 447 each vertical row of squares represents a single card, and each horizontal row indicates a particular hole in all the cards. It is helpful to number the cards sequentially and to code the holes A, B,

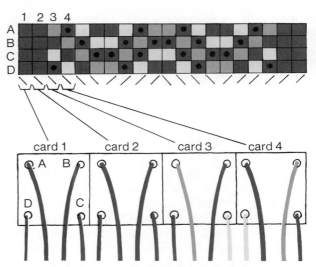

above: 447. A sample draft for card weaving. Each vertical row of squares represents a single card, and each horizontal row indicates a particular hole in all the cards.

below: 448. For card weaving, the warp ends are tied to the back of a chair and pass under the weaver's arm to a fixed support at the other end. Unlike the situation in loom weaving, work proceeds away from the weaver.

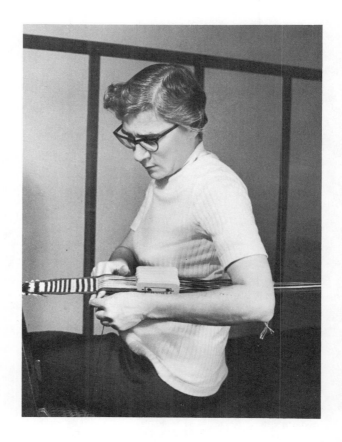

C, D, working clockwise. The design in this draft allows for two repeats of a pointed pattern, plus a selvedge border. The drafted squares have been color coded for four different colors of yarn. This system makes it very easy to follow the sequence of colors when threading the cards. Below the draft is a series of slashes, which indicate the *direction* for threading. For example, the first six cards are threaded from the face of the card to the back, the next four are threaded from back to front, and so on. All the holes on a single card must be threaded in the same direction.

To begin threading, one stacks the cards in order near the lease sticks. Each card is threaded clockwise according to the draft, and the four yarns are knotted together on either the face or the back of the card, depending on the direction of threading. A change in the direction of threading is made at each point of emphasis in the pattern. As each card is threaded and the

below: 449. Strips of card woven fabric can be braided to create a more intricate design. In this illustration, the band is divided into three strips, each of which is woven individually. Then the strips are interchanged before being rejoined and woven as a unit.

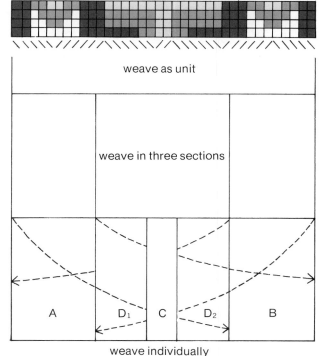

ends knotted, the card is slipped about 8 inches from the knot. The ends should be kept as even as possible. When all the cards have been threaded, they are stacked face up, directly on top of one another, with the corresponding holes (A, B, C, D) in the same positions.

Some card weavers use a frame to hold the two ends of the warp. However, if one end is tied to a stationary object—a doorknob or hook on the wall—and the other is tied to the chair in which the weaver sits, the tension can easily be adjusted when necessary.

The Weaving Process

The most efficient posture for card weaving is illustrated in Figure 448. The warp ends are tied to the back of a chair and pass under the weaver's arm. Weaving proceeds *away from* the weaver, rather than toward him as on the loom.

When the cards are in position, the first shed is automatically open. A small stick shuttle containing the weft yarn is entered in the shed, and the shed is changed by rotating the cards one quarter turn. Pattern is determined by the direction in which the cards are turned. They can be rotated either forward or backward for the entire weaving process, or, if desired, the cards can be turned forward for a set number of times and then back for a certain number of times. When the cards are turned always in the same direction, the warp yarns will gradually become twisted. This situation is rectified by untying the warp ends and combing out the tangles. The weft yarn can be beat into position with the fingers, a comb, or the shuttle.

A surprising variety of designs can be created with simple card weaving. One such variation is illustrated in Figure 449. After a portion of the band has been woven, it is divided into three strips, and each strip is woven as a unit, with the weft yarn carried only to the selvedge of that particular strip. For the third section of the web, the warp yarns are further subdivided, and the center strip is woven in three units. Then, the various strips are braided with sections *A* and *B* exchanging positions, passing over *D* and under *C*. Finally, the entire band is reunited and woven solidly from selvedge to selvedge.

Even double cloth can be woven with cards. The cards are turned on end, so that the points are facing up and down (Fig. 450), thus opening two sheds. The weft is passed first through one shed and then through the other before the cards are turned.

Card weaving is generally associated with belts, straps, and similar narrow fabrics (Fig. 451). More adventurous weavers have experimented with methods of combining the card-woven elements to create hangings and sculptures (Fig. 452). Strips of card-woven cloth can also be sewn together to make striped, patterned fabric or even garments. *Tribal Cloth* (Pl. 24, p. 232) was made from 35 narrow card-woven strips sewn together. All the strips were printed in the ikat technique (see Chap. 18), some before weaving and others after. The fringes are tied in the manner of Hopi wedding sashes.

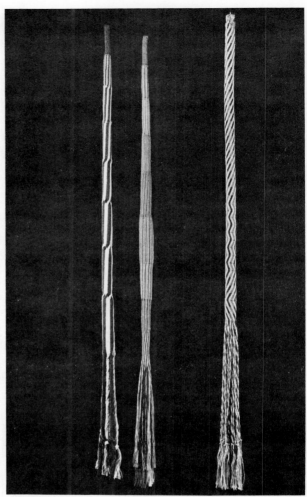

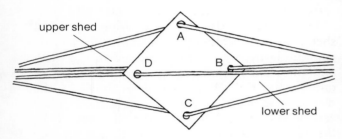

above: 450. Double cloth can be card woven by arranging the cards so that the points face up and down, thus opening two sheds.

below: 451. Card woven belt with macramé ties.

above: 452. KAY SEKIMACHI. *Marugawa V, VI, VII.* 1972. Card-woven tubes, height 7′. Courtesy the artist.

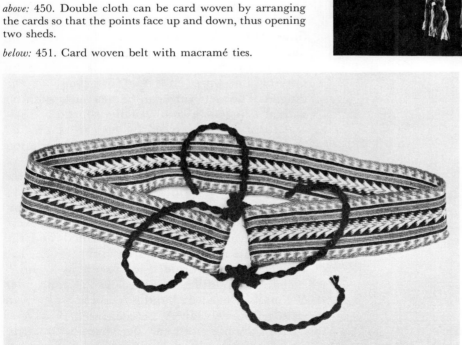

part four
SPINNING AND COLORING

16 *Handspinning*

Anyone dealing with yarns and textiles in any craft sense must ultimately spin in order to have complete design control over his product.
Allen Fannin, Craft Horizons, *February 1971*

Handspinning of yarns offers several advantages to the designer-craftsman, but economy is probably not one of them. The labor involved in fiber preparation as well as in the spinning itself nearly always outweighs whatever saving the craftsman may realize by eschewing commercially spun yarns. Still, handspinning currently enjoys a revival similar to that of all the other crafts. By far the strongest argument for handspun yarns is the opportunity to design a yarn ideally suited to a particular end-use. Certain artists have exploited this potential with works in which the yarn construction becomes a major design element. Susan Weitzman's *Unwoven Tapestry* (Fig. 453) consists of two layers of exposed warp yarns spun with a differential of twist to produce long slubs (see also Fig. 134). Such an effect would be difficult or impossible to create with commercially produced yarns.

The spinning process consists of three basic operations. *Drafting* is the procedure by which

453. Susan Weitzman. *Unwoven Tapestry.* 1969. Handspun wool with a differential of twist in two layers of exposed warp, 4′ square. From *Objects: USA,* Johnson Wax Collection of Contemporary Crafts, Racine, Wis.

247

prepared fibers are compressed and extended into a continuous strand, or yarn. (Yarn drafting bears no relation whatever to the weave draft discussed in Chapter 9, which is a graphic notation of a weave pattern.) The insertion of *twist* encourages cohesion of the spun yarn. The *take-up* motion consists of winding the spun and twisted yarn onto a spindle or spool to produce a *yarn package*.

A HISTORY OF SPINNING

Primitive man probably drew his inspiration for spinning from observing the natural twist of some vegetable fibers. Certain grasses and other cellulosic fibers have a tendency to twist as they dry and are thereby much stronger than in their original state. Man's increasing skill at the craft of weaving led him to seek both longer and more flexible materials, and he soon learned to augment this natural twist and introduce it when it was absent. In its crudest form spinning was accomplished with the hands alone; the fibers were drawn out between the fingers of one hand and rolled between the fingers of the other to insert twist. After a length of yarn had been spun, it was wound onto a stick or a stone to make the yarn package. A variation of this technique consisted of rolling the fibers along the thigh with the palm of one hand while the other hand controlled the drafting. The most important breakthrough in spinning technology came when ancient man discovered that the stick used as a base for the yarn package could be made to rotate, thus inserting twist semiautomatically. With minor refinements this simple device evolved into the *handspindle* (Fig. 454), which is used in virtually identical form by many handspinners today.

The handspindle resembles a top with an unusually long axis (Fig. 460). It consists of two parts: The *spindle* portion or shaft and the *whorl* or weight. In its modern form the spindle is a tapered shaft about 9 inches long with a notch at the top to catch the yarn. The whorl, a disc-shaped object mounted on the shaft, provides sufficient weight to maintain spinning momen-

left: 454. Double spindle with yarn in position, Peru. American Museum of Natural History, New York.

tum. The use of the handspindle in ancient Egypt and the Swiss Lake region has been well documented. In the cave paintings at Beni Hassan (Fig. 48) the figure at far right is manipulating a handspindle (see also Fig. 8). Prehistoric spindle whorls often were simply a stone or a lump of clay. The American Indians carved their whorls from wood, with intricate stylized designs (Fig. 455).

above: 455. Cowichan spindle whorl. Wood, diameter 7½″. National Museum of Natural History, Smithsonian Institution, Washington, D.C.

Because the handspindle was light and portable, it could be picked up whenever the hands were free. In his story of Darius and the Paeonian woman, Herodotus wrote: "She bore a pitcher upon her head and with one arm led a horse while all the way she went she spun flax . . . she came back the same way she had gone, with the pitcher of water on her head and the horse dragging on her arm while she kept twirling her spindle."

The spinners of ancient India were particularly renowned for the quality of their yarns. The famed Dacca muslins—transparent, gauzelike cottons—were woven from yarns so fine that a pound equaled 200 *miles* in length. By comparison, the finest yarn in use today would be less than 4 miles long per pound. One can well imag-

ine the skill required for weaving with such a minute yarn. Dacca muslins were woven in 20-yard lengths each 1 yard wide, a unit that kept two spinners occupied for between ten and thirty days.

Except for minor improvements in the handspindle, the process of spinning underwent little change from earliest times until the Middle Ages (Fig. 456). The spinning wheel was invented in India, though the date is rather uncertain. However, it is much easier to pinpoint the development of the flyer mechanism for spinning. Like almost every other mechanical device, it was first conceived by Leonardo da Vinci in the 15th century.

Leonardo's notebook drawings do not indicate any power source (such as a drive wheel), and it has been suggested that he intended some large external source of power—perhaps a water

below: 456. ISRAHEL VAN MECKENEM THE ELDER. *Woman Spinning and Entertaining a Visitor.* c. 1450. Bibliothèque Nationale, Paris.

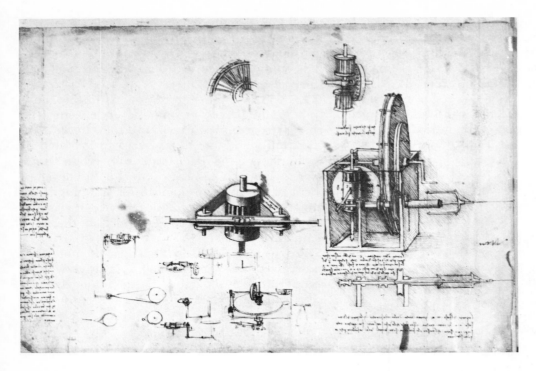

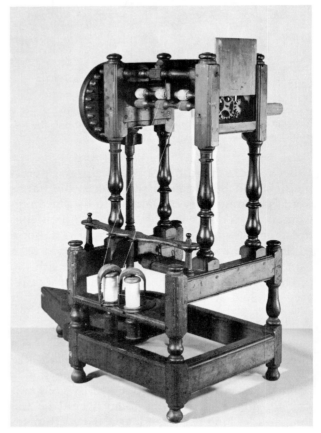

above: 457. LEONARDO DA VINCI. Design for a hand-driven spinning machine with automatic yarn distributor. c. 1490. From *Codex Atlanticus.* Biblioteca Ambrosiana, Milan.

right: 458. RICHARD ARKWRIGHT. Spinning machine. 1769. Science Museum, London (Crown Copyright).

wheel—to operate the spindle (Fig. 457). Apparently, no model was ever constructed from Leonardo's drawings, but in 1530 Johann Jürgen actually built a flyer spinning wheel based on similar principles. Eventually, a foot treadle was added, thus completing the essentials of the flyer wheel still common today.

The Industrial Revolution had an equally devastating effect upon the craft of handspinning as it had on handweaving. In the mid-18th century inventions by James Hargreaves, Richard Arkwright (Fig. 458), and Samuel Crompton vastly increased the rate at which yarns could be produced, with the result that handspinning was no longer viable as a profession. However, the craft never completely died out in rural areas or in isolated regions such as the Southern Highlands of the United States (see p. 75). When the interest of 20th-century craftsmen began to grow, there were still spinners to teach the new generation and spinning wheels to spin upon.

MATERIALS FOR SPINNING

Virtually any fiber can be spun by the hand processes. Wool and flax are most popular among contemporary spinners, but cotton and hair fibers are also used, alone or in blends. In addition, the waste from broken or damaged silk cocoons can be spun into silk yarn, and manmade filament fibers—nylon, rayon, acrylic, and so forth—are often cut for spinning.

Different fibers require different degrees of preparation before spinning can be undertaken. Wool, in particular, demands special handling in the preparation stage. It is possible to buy untreated wool fleece from the Wool Cooperatives in the Middle West and at agricultural fairs, as well as from many national and international suppliers (see Appendix C). Most fibers can be purchased from mills at various stages of readiness for spinning, thus eliminating some of the preliminary steps described below (pp. 255–260).

Natural fibers vary in length, diameter, and inherent *crimp* or waviness, all of which characteristics contribute to their *spinning quality*. Flax fibers are relatively long—from 5 to 20 inches—and have no natural crimp. The fiber is usually made available to handspinners in bundles of short lengths called *ultimates,* which after spinning produce a yarn that is smooth, lustrous, and quite strong. Cotton fibers are much shorter—less than 2 inches—and evenly convoluted.

Wool presents the widest variation in fiber characteristics, depending upon the breed of sheep from which it was taken. The fibers range from very fine to very coarse and between $1\frac{1}{2}$ and 15 inches in length. Different grades of fiber may be found even in the same breed or on the same animal (Fig. 459). A higher percentage of foreign material—dirt, grass, twigs, manure—is found in wool than in any other fiber. Furthermore, the *felting quality* of wool may present special problems to the handspinner. As discussed in Chapter 2 (p. 11), felting occurs in the presence of heat, moisture, and pressure or friction. Should the wool fibers be subjected to some or all of these conditions during the preparation processes, the fibers may interlock. Once felted, they are extremely difficult to separate, so spinning may be impeded or prevented. However, in spite of all these drawbacks, wool is probably the most popular fiber among handspinners.

EQUIPMENT

The equipment needed for handspinning can be divided into two categories: the spinning implements themselves and yarn preparation devices.

Spinning Equipment

The Handspindle   The basic principle of momentum—that a body set in motion will tend to remain in motion (until some force slows it down)—underlies the functioning of the handspindle (Fig. 460). The body in this case is the

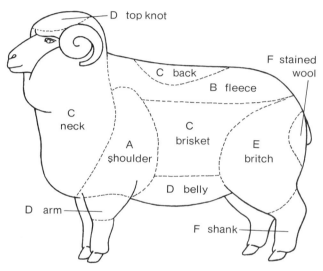

above: 459. Wool fibers can vary in quality even on the same animal. The **A** indicates the highest grade, the **F** the lowest.

below: 460. A handspindle consists of two parts: the long shaft and the weight, usually mounted near the bottom.

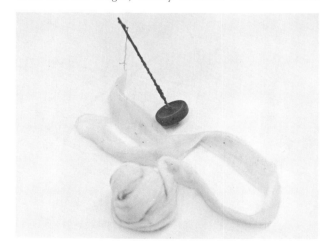

whorl, centered at some point (usually near the bottom) on the spindle shaft. When the spindle is flipped, the whorl helps to maintain the momentum of its rotation, which in turn imparts twist to the yarn. The drafting and twisting motions are simultaneous on the handspindle, but the take-up is a separate operation. After a length of yarn has been spun, the spinner must stop, undo the yarn hitches at the top and base of the spindle, and wind the yarn manually. Then, the hitches are restored, and spinning continues. The construction of yarn on a handspindle is therefore much slower than on either type of spinning wheel. On the other hand, the *quality* of yarn spun on a handspindle can be just as high as that produced on a conventional spinning wheel.

There is enormous variation in the style and weight of handspindles. Essentially, however, any spindle that is properly balanced and of a correct weight for the yarn to be spun—that is, heavy enough to establish a twist but not so

heavy that it will drag on the yarn—is perfectly acceptable, regardless of the design.

below: 461. The high wheel is operated by turning the large drive wheel with one hand, while the other hand draws out the loose fibers to be spun.

above right: 462. A treadle powers the flyer wheel, leaving both of the spinner's hands free for drafting the fibers.

The High Wheel   The high wheel (Fig. 461) is a very simple device. Its framework consists of a *stock*, usually three legs (though sometimes four), a *wheel post*, and a *head post*. The head post supports the *spinning head*, which, as it turns, imparts twist to the spun yarn and builds the yarn package. The spinning head is connected by a *drive band* to the large *drive wheel*, which is turned manually to rotate the spinning head. Because the drive wheel is so much larger in diameter than the spinning head, there is a multiplication of motion between the two. For example, if the drive wheel is 40 inches in diameter and the spinning head only ½ inch, one revolution of the drive wheel will cause the spinning head to turn eighty times.

Some high wheels are fitted with a *multiplying head*, which further increases the multiplication of motion. In this case, the large drive wheel is connected by a band to a smaller wheel mounted on the spinning head, which in turn is connected by a second band to the spindle.

The Flyer Wheel   The flyer wheel (Fig. 462) differs from the high wheel in several respects. It is equipped with a foot treadle to turn the

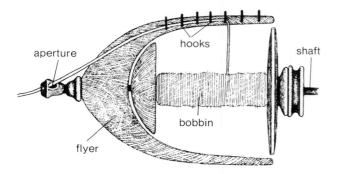

left: 463. The flyer assembly automatically imparts twist to the spun yarn. Buildup of the yarn package is controlled by a series of hooks along the top of the flyer.

above: 464. The card clothing wires are bent at an angle to catch the fibers as they are drawn across the card.

drive wheel, leaving both hands free. In place of the spinning head is the *flyer assembly* (Fig. 463), which includes the flyer itself and the yarn bobbin mounted on the spindle shaft. As the flyer rotates, the spun yarn passes through a small opening at the end of the shaft and emerges from an opening at the side. At this point twist is inserted in the yarn. The yarn then moves onto the flyer itself, where it is held in position by hooks for winding onto the bobbin.

The flyer wheel is in many ways the most efficient handspinning device. Its operation is faster than the high wheel and considerably faster than the handspindle. Unlike the high wheel, it leaves both hands free for drafting; unlike the handspindle, its operation is constant.

Fiber Preparation Equipment

Carding Tools Yarns can be carded either on flat hand cards or on a hand-cranked carding machine. Whichever the case, the actual work is done by the *card clothing,* comprised of a group of wires or spikes driven through a foundation, usually of leather. The wires are bent at an angle (Fig. 464).

Flat hand cards (Fig. 465) are always used in pairs. The card itself consists of a handle and a backing—most often of wood—to which the card clothing is nailed or attached in some other way. As the loose fibers are transferred from one card to the other, the very short fibers and any remaining foreign material are carded out, and the fibers are straightened to some degree. As a rule, three sets of hand cards are required, with card clothing in various degrees of coarseness. The clothing for the first carding would have relatively heavy wires spaced rather far apart, while more densely set fine wires would be used

for the final carding. An intermediate set of cards would complete the equipment. From time to time the card clothing wires must be ground to restore their sharpness.

The hand-cranked card machine (Fig. 466) permits somewhat faster carding. The fibers are

above: 465. Flat hand cards are always used in pairs. As a rule, three sets of cards are required, with card clothing in various degrees of coarseness.

below: 466. A hand-cranked card machine.

above: 467. *Wool Comber.* Engraving from *The Book of Trades,* 1807. Smithsonian Institution, Washington, D.C. Combing prepares the fiber for worsted spinning.

spread on the *feed pan,* and, as the handle is turned, they are caught by the *licker-in roll* and transferred to the *swift* or *main cylinder.* The card clothing is tacked to both of these cylinders. As with the flat hand cards, it is necessary to have either three card machines or three sets of interchangeable cylinders.

Combs Many spinners use dog combs or other long-toothed implements for worsted combing, but old-fashioned worsted combs (Fig. 467) are sometimes available. The latter tool consists of a wooden handle from which protrude several rows of very long metal tines. During the combing process each comb in turn is attached by means of a *pad* to a post or some other fixed object.

PLANNING THE YARN

Ideally, the end-use to which a yarn will be applied should be established before spinning begins, and even before any fiber preparation is attempted. Only in this way can one be sure that a sufficient quantity of yarn of uniform size, texture, blend, and quality will be spun. Therefore, several decisions must be made even before the fiber is purchased.

The choice of a particular fiber or fibers is, of course, the most elementary step in this process. If two or more fibers, colors, or textures are to be blended into the finished yarn, the blending is most often accomplished during the fiber preparation stage.

The second step is to determine the desired weight or count of the finished yarn (see p. 86). It is a good idea to spin a small sample of yarn from the appropriate fiber and to keep the sample at hand during the entire spinning process, especially when large quantities of yarn are to be spun. By referring to the sample from time to time, one can avoid serious deviations from the proper count that might occur when the spinning is done in several sittings. Once the end-use and the yarn count have been determined, one can extrapolate the total quantity of yarn that will be required. If the yarn is to be a ply, with two or more single yarns twisted together (see p. 83), this will also affect the total quantity needed.

The degree of twist to be imparted to the yarn must also be established in advance. This factor is most often expressed in *turns per inch.* Optimum twist is dependent upon many variables, including the nature and length of the fibers, the amount of stress the fiber can undergo, and the end-use. Slackly twisted yarns are often suitable for a weft, as well as for knitting and crocheting. In essence, any process that does not subject a specific portion of the yarn to repeated handling can employ a low-twist yarn. On the other hand, a warp yarn—which will be held under tension and endure constant beating—should be firmly twisted, as should a yarn to be used for macramé.

Even before preparing the fibers, one should decide whether the yarn is to be spun according to the *woolen system* or the *worsted system.* The terms woolen and worsted do not necessarily mean that the fiber involved must be wool. Flax and certain synthetic fibers can be spun by either process. Worsted yarns are composed of relatively long fibers arranged in as highly parallel a configuration as possible. The resultant yarns are rather smooth and have few fibers protruding from the yarn surface. To this end, every step in the fiber preparation and spinning processes is aimed at encouraging this parallel arrangement. The fibers are sorted, picked, and carded in such a way that the shorter fibers are winnowed out, and they are subjected to combing as well as carding. Two-handed drafting helps to ensure the parallel orientation of fibers, so worsted spinning on the high wheel is generally not practicable. A yarn spun according to the woolen system is, by contrast, more textured, with many individual fibers protruding from the yarn mass. The yarn includes both short and long fibers that have not been combed, and two-handed drafting is not necessary. Any parallel orientation of the fibers is accidental.

FIBER PREPARATION

Of the processes described below, only sorting, picking, carding, and formation of the roving are general to all fibers, and even these steps may be omitted occasionally to achieve a particular effect. The remaining processes are required only for a specific fiber (usually wool) or spinning system. The fiber preparation stages have been described in consecutive order; in most cases, several of them can be skipped.

Sorting

Wool fibers purchased in fleece form generally must be sorted for quality, length, and degree of cleanliness before anything else is done. In any fleece there will be portions in which the fibers are longer than in others and sections with finer and coarser fibers. Some parts of the fleece may be so badly stained as to render them useless. The type of sorting that is necessary would depend upon the end-use of the yarn. For example, if the yarn is to be spun according to the worsted system, one would sort for the longer fibers and perhaps save the shorter ones for some other purpose. On the other hand, a high-count yarn to be spun on the woolen system would require sorting for fineness, without much regard to fiber length. Ideally, the sorting should be done on a screen or wire mesh, so that coarse dirt particles and foreign matter can fall through and not recontaminate the wool.

Picking

Most fibers must be picked, a process by which the tight fiber mass is initially opened up. Picking also serves to blend the fibers, distributing irregularities evenly throughout the mass.

Natural fibers that contain dirt and foreign material should be picked over a clean surface, such as a large sheet of paper, so that when the particles drop free of the fiber they can be removed easily. An efficient method of working is to place the pile of unpicked fibers to one side and, as each batch is picked, transfer it to the other side, with the area directly in front of the picker kept free for collecting debris.

Picking begins by separating a handful of fiber from the unpicked mass. With a pulling and teasing motion, the fibers are gradually transferred from one hand to the other (Fig. 468). After each handful has been treated, it should be gently worked back into the mass of picked fibers on the other side. The end result of picking, then, is a blended mass of fibers that are cleaner and less tightly packed than the original mass, *not* a pile of discrete handfuls of fiber.

The degree of force to be applied in picking depends upon the fiber. Firmly packed areas or portions in which dirt has matted the fibers together may need fairly vigorous picking, but at no time should the pulling motion be so violent

below: 468. Picking is a process by which the tight fiber mass is initially opened and cleaned. It is accomplished with a pulling and teasing motion of the hands.

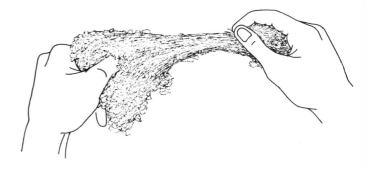

that it will damage or break the fibers. Clean fibers, such as flax, may need only one picking to open up the fiber bundles. However, unusually dirty wools may have to be picked several times, until no more debris falls easily.

Scouring

Wool fibers are most often scoured after picking, though occasionally woolens are carded, combed, spun, and even woven in the grease. Scouring removes the natural oils from the sheep, as well as any dirt that adheres to the fiber after picking.

It is during the scouring operation that the greatest danger of felting exists, since the conditions for felting—heat, moisture, and pressure—are all present. For this reason it is far better to subject the wool to a series of scourings in warm water and with gentle pressure, rather than trying to speed up the process with too-hot water and excessive agitation.

The scouring bath consists of warm water—up to 120°F—in which a commercial wool-scouring solution or mild soap has been completely dissolved. The quantity of water must be sufficient to allow the wool to move about freely. If possible, the scouring vat should be fitted with a false bottom of screening, so that heavy dirt particles will settle to the bottom and not remain mixed with the fiber. The wool is placed in the bath in layers and pressed gently to circulate the scouring solution. From time to time a small sample can be removed from the bath and examined. When it appears that all the oil and dirt have been loosened, the wool is lifted out of the bath and rinsed thoroughly in water of the same temperature as the scouring bath. A spray rinse that is drained out below the fibers will permit the most complete removal of dirt and grease. After rinsing, the fibers are squeezed very gently to extract excess moisture or, if desired, run through the spin cycle of a washing machine. They can be dried in the air or in an automatic dryer that is equipped with a cool cycle. Very long wool fibers that are to be spun according to the worsted system should be air dried to prevent unnecessary tangling.

After drying, the wool fibers are sprayed evenly with an oil specially prepared for this purpose. Oiling lubricates the fibers to facilitate spinning.

Carding

Virtually all fibers are subjected to at least one carding. To a large extent, the success of the spinning depends upon how efficiently the fibers have been carded. Carding opens up the fiber mass to a greater degree than picking. It also partially aligns the fibers and helps to remove those that are too short for spinning. This is accomplished by moving two surfaces of card clothing against each other, either by hand or by machine, in such a way that the fibers are gradually transferred from one to the other.

Hand Carding   The first step in hand carding is to *charge* the first or bottom card with fiber. With the card held in the left hand, as illustrated in Figure 469, a small mass of fiber is stroked across the card clothing so that the fibers are caught by the wires. Stroking continues until the card is fully charged, a condition that depends upon the type of fiber, the degree of entanglement, and several other factors. Actually, one learns only by experience how much fiber a card can hold at one time. Too much fiber on the card would prevent thorough carding, while too little would be wasteful of one's time.

When the bottom card is fully charged, the second or top card is grasped with the right

469–474. *Carding is a fiber-preparation step by which the fiber mass is opened to a greater degree than in the picking. Carding also partially aligns the fibers.*

below: 469. The bottom card is charged with fiber.

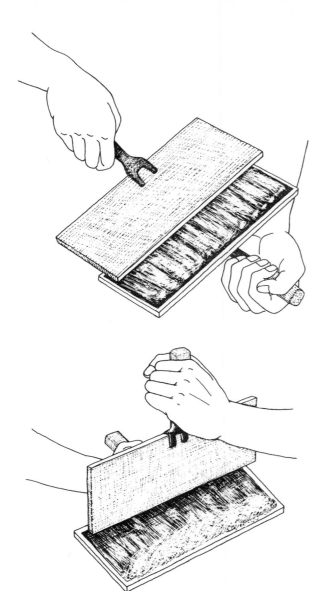

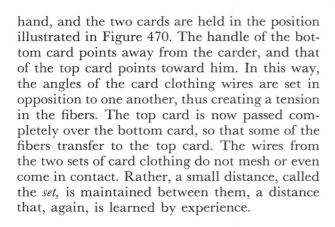

above left: 470. The top card is stroked across the lower one until no more fiber will transfer easily.

left: 471. All the fibers are returned to the lower card, a procedure known as stripping.

above: 472. The lower card is stripped, so that all the fibers are on the top card.

hand, and the two cards are held in the position illustrated in Figure 470. The handle of the bottom card points away from the carder, and that of the top card points toward him. In this way, the angles of the card clothing wires are set in opposition to one another, thus creating a tension in the fibers. The top card is now passed completely over the bottom card, so that some of the fibers transfer to the top card. The wires from the two sets of card clothing do not mesh or even come in contact. Rather, a small distance, called the *set,* is maintained between them, a distance that, again, is learned by experience.

The stroking of top card across bottom continues, without decreasing the set, until no more fiber will transfer easily from the bottom to the top. The cards must then be *stripped*—that is, returned to their former condition of one full card and one empty one. The purpose of stripping is to transfer all the fibers from one card to the other without unduly disturbing the fiber arrangement that has been created by carding. To accomplish this, the top card is twisted in the hand and drawn at an angle across the bottom card (Fig. 471). Unlike the carding motion, stripping requires that the card clothing wires actually interpenetrate. The correct position of the cards for stripping from bottom to top is illustrated in Figure 472. With all the fibers now on the top card, the two cards are exchanged in the hands—the top card becomes the bottom—and carding proceeds.

After each batch of fiber has been carded, it must be *doffed* or released from the cards, again without disturbing the fiber arrangement. The

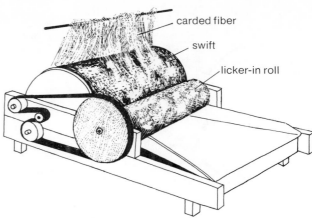

carded fiber

swift

licker-in roll

left: 473. The carded fiber is doffed from both cards.

above: 474. The card machine aligns fibers by gradually transferring them from the small licker-in roll to the large roll, the swift.

cards are held as in Figure 473 and drawn across one another as for stripping, except that in this case the fibers are released from *both* cards and removed. This initial carding is usually followed by two or more cardings with progressively finer card clothing. The product of the carding operation is called a *card sliver*. The fibers are either left in sliver form for combing or rolled into a roving to prepare for spinning.

Machine Carding   The same principles apply to machine carding as to manual carding, except, of course, that the entire operation is faster and more automatic. The machine must first be adjusted to make sure the two cylinders are exactly parallel to one another and to allow for the correct set between them. As with hand carding, determining the proper set for a given fiber is a matter of experience.

To begin carding, the fiber is spread evenly across the length and breadth of the feed pan in such a way that it can be caught by the licker-in roll. As the crank is turned, the fibers are picked up by the licker-in roll and gradually transferred to the swift. The actual carding takes place as the fibers move onto the swift. A small amount of fiber may remain on the licker-in roll, but this can be left until carding is complete. After each batch of fiber has been carded, it must be doffed from the machine without disturbing the fiber alignment. This is accomplished by

passing a narrow metal rod across the swift through an opening in the card clothing and then lifting the rod with both hands to divide the web of fibers (Fig. 474). With the end of the web held in one hand, the crank is turned backwards, and the web is lifted gently from the swift. If necessary, the carding operation can be repeated several times with progressively finer card clothing. When all the fiber has been carded, the webs are either compressed into card slivers for combing or rolled to form a roving.

Combing

Only fibers that are to be spun according to the worsted system are combed after carding. Combing creates a more uniformly parallel arrangement of fibers and helps to remove any short fibers that may remain in the sliver after carding.

One of the two combs must be attached very firmly to a fixed support (Fig. 475). The comb is then charged with fiber in much the same manner as the card was charged, by stroking or sweeping the card sliver across the tines of the comb so that the fibers are gradually caught in the comb. When the first comb is fully charged, the second comb is drawn repeatedly across the fiber mass, picking up more and more fibers as it moves ever closer to the first comb (Fig. 476). The combing is complete when the two combs are actually touching but no more fiber will

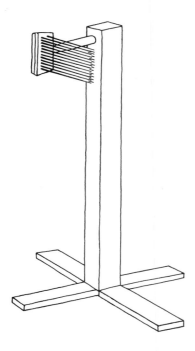

transfer to the second comb. Most of the fiber remaining on the first comb will consist of *noilage*—shorter, tangled, or broken fibers that are not appropriate for worsted spinning. However, the mass of fibers should be examined, and if too many long fibers are mixed in with the noilage, the fibers can be recarded and recombed to separate the longer ones.

More care is required in doffing the fibers from a comb than from a card. The card doffing only *preserves* a fiber arrangement that has already been established during carding. By contrast, the comb doffing actually helps to *create* a more highly parallel orientation of the fibers. Doffing is accomplished with the full comb mounted on the support. One grasps the outermost ends of the fibers in one hand and gradually draws them out in a thick, uniform strand called a *top* (Fig.

475–477. Combing is a process that creates a more uniformly parallel arrangement of fibers and also helps to remove any relatively short fibers that remain after carding. Only fibers that are to be spun according to the worsted system are subjected to combing.

above: 475. One of the two combs is attached by means of a pad to a post or other sturdy support and charged with fiber gradually stroked across it.

below: 476. The second comb is stroked repeatedly across the first, with the two moving ever closer together, until no more fiber will transfer easily.

right: 477. The fibers are drawn from the comb in a thick, uniform strand, called a top.

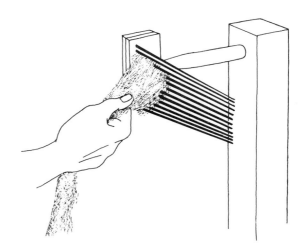

477). Once the top has been completely drawn from the comb, only short fibers should remain.

As a rule, the fibers must be subjected to a second and even a third combing before the fiber arrangement is adequately parallel. The top that is drawn from the final combing should be continuous; in other words, as each batch of fiber is combed, it should be overlapped and pieced with the previous one to form an unbroken top.

Forming the Roving

Depending upon the spinning system involved, the roving is made either from groups of card

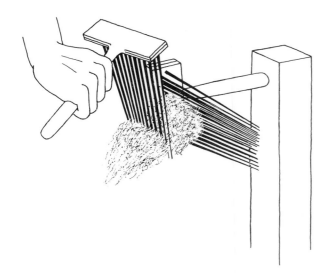

slivers or from a combed top. In either case, the *roving* is a long strand of fibers ready for spinning.

A card roving is formed simply by taking a card sliver and rolling it crosswise with the palms of the hands across the lap or any flat surface (Fig. 478). In rolling, the hands move gradually farther apart, thus compressing and attenuating the fiber mass.

To convert a combed top to a roving, the top is drawn through the hands under tension, as illustrated in Figure 479. The resultant roving is longer and narrower than the top, but the parallel orientation of the fibers has been maintained or even enhanced. If a fine yarn is to be spun, the top should be subjected to two or three drawings to create a very narrow roving.

The fiber preparation is now complete, and spinning can begin.

THE SPINNING PROCESS

Spinning consists of drawing out the prepared roving into an even finer strand—now identifiable as yarn—and simultaneously imparting a twist to the yarn. Figure 480 illustrates graphically the configuration of the fibers at the drafting point. At left is the fiber supply (the roving) and at right the spun yarn. The center portion of the diagram shows the *drafting zone,* the point at which one's fingers regulate the number of fibers that are allowed to pass through to become yarn. Therefore, the number of fibers in the

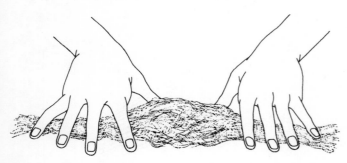

478–479. *The roving is a long, narrow strand of fibers ready for spinning. Depending upon the spinning system employed, the formation of a roving follows either the carding or the combing stage.*

above: 480. The drafting zone is the point at which fibers are drawn out and compressed into yarn. At left is the fiber supply in the form of a roving; at right is the spun yarn.

above: 478. A card roving is formed by rolling the card sliver crosswise over any flat surface.

below: 479. The combed top is drawn through the hands under tension to form a roving.

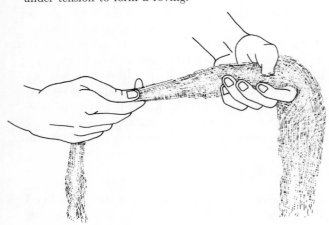

drafting zone at any given time determines the weight of the yarn. Regardless of the spinning implement employed, the twist is actually inserted at a point well beyond the drafting zone, after which it travels back along the yarn toward the fingers.

Spinning always begins by joining, or *piecing-up,* a section of the new fiber supply to a length of spun yarn already attached to the spinning mechanism. In order to achieve as smooth a transition as possible, the end of the yarn should be unraveled slightly, so that loose fibers can be joined to loose fibers. Drafting begins at the point where the yarn is unraveled (Fig. 481). As the fibers move through the hand, there are increasingly fewer fibers from the old yarn and more fibers from the new source, until the splice is complete.

left: 481. The fibers from two separate rovings are unraveled slightly so they can be pieced up or joined smoothly.

below: 482. The most efficient posture of spinning on the foot-powered flyer wheel.

bottom: 483. Drafting takes place between the left and right hands. The right hand also encourages a twisting motion as the yarn moves toward the flyer assembly.

The Flyer Wheel

The best position for spinning on the flyer wheel is illustrated in Figure 482. The right foot operates the treadle, which turns the drive wheel to rotate the flyer mechanism. The yarn is grasped in both hands, with the left hand controlling the drafting and the right hand the insertion of twist. A steady rate of spinning takes practice to coordinate the treadling, drafting, and twisting motions simultaneously.

On the flyer wheel drafting takes place between the left and right hands. The left hand is held in such a way that only as many fibers are allowed to slip between the thumb and forefinger as are required for the weight of yarn to be spun (Fig. 483). The fingers of the right hand create a tension on the drafted fibers, further attenuating them to the desired yarn thickness. Twisting occurs between the right hand and the flyer mechanism. Twist is inserted at the end of the flyer shaft and travels down the spun yarn toward the hands. The right hand serves as a brake, preventing the twist from moving into the drafting zone until the proper number of fibers have been drafted. When the draft is correct, the right hand relaxes its grip and encourages the twist with a rolling motion of the fingers. After the twist has been inserted, the right hand again grasps the yarn as a brake, and new fibers are drafted.

The buildup of yarn on the bobbin is regulated by a series of hooks on the arms of the flyer (Fig. 463). In order to permit an even distribution of yarn on the bobbin, the spinner must occasionally stop the wheel and move the yarn from one hook to the next, working back and forth across the bobbin.

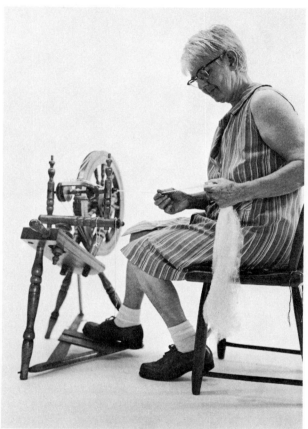

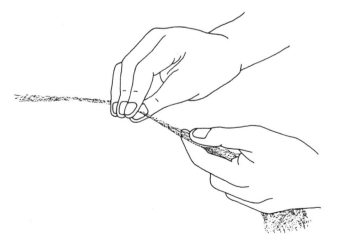

above: 484. When spinning on the high wheel, the left hand moves steadily away from the spindle, while the right hand turns the drive wheel.

right: 485. The spun yarn is coiled along the spindle to its tip. As the spindle turns, the outermost coil is alternately dropped and rewound, thus imparting twist to the yarn. To wind the yarn package, one must unwind the coil.

The High Wheel

Spinning on the high wheel differs in several ways from spinning on the flyer wheel. Only one hand—usually the left—is used for drafting, while the other hand rotates the drive wheel. The drafting hand does not remain stationary, as it does on the flyer wheel, but moves gradually away from the spinning mechanism as a length of yarn is spun. The drafting, twisting, and take-up motions are not simultaneous; rather, spinning must be halted to wind a length of yarn onto the bobbin. In other words, the drafting and twisting are accomplished in one operation and the yarn take-up in another.

The most efficient posture for spinning on the high wheel is illustrated in Figure 484. As the right hand rotates the drive wheel, the left hand drafts the yarn, moving steadily away from the spindle. As with flyer drafting, only as many

fibers as are needed for the correct yarn weight are allowed to slip through the fingers at any given time. The spun yarn is coiled along the spindle to its tip (Fig. 485). When the spindle turns, the outermost coil is alternately dropped and rewound, thus imparting twist to the yarn. In order to maintain an even twist throughout the yarn, the length of yarn spun in each bout and the number of turns of the drive wheel during the spinning of one bout must always be constant. After a length of yarn has been spun, the left hand is held stationary, and the drive wheel is turned to give a final twist to the yarn.

When it is time to wind the yarn, the drive wheel is turned in the opposite direction (*backing off*) to remove the coil from the end of the spindle. Then, with the wheel turning in the original direction, the yarn is wound onto the inside of the spindle, and a new coil is built up to the tip for spinning the next bout of yarn.

The Handspindle

While it is probably not advisable to spin while taking one's horse to the well, the handspindle does offer a great deal of flexibility, because the tool is so simple. The operation of the spindle is shown in Figure 486. The yarn wound around the spindle is hitched at the botton and top of the shaft (Fig. 487). Before drafting begins, the spindle must be flipped to set it in motion. As the yarn is drafted through the fingers of both hands, the revolving spindle imparts twist. In this case, it is the spindle that gradually moves away from the hands, rather than the other way around as on the high wheel. Periodically, the spindle must again be flipped to renew its turning motion. When a length of yarn has been spun, the hitches are removed, the yarn is wound around the shaft, and the hitches are restored to spin the next bout of yarn.

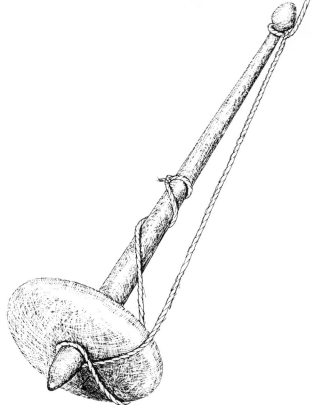

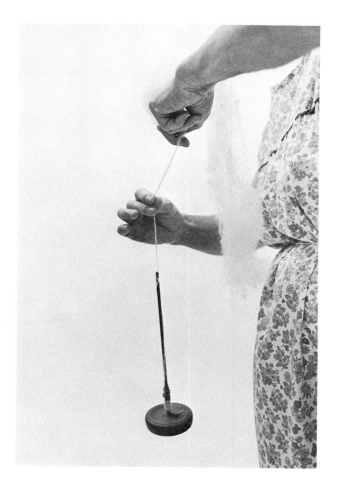

left: 486. Operation of the handspindle.

above: 487. The yarn is hitched at both the top and the bottom of the spindle shaft. In order to wind spun yarn onto the shaft, the hitches must be temporarily undone.

YARN DESIGN

Spinning one's own yarn offers a far greater opportunity for achieving special design effects than would be possible in relying strictly on commercial yarns. The design of a finished yarn can be controlled at several stages during the construction process. First of all, certain design decisions are implied in the choice of a fiber or fibers, the selection of a spinning system, and the degree of fiber preparation that is undertaken—all of which is established even before spinning commences. Further design elements are controlled by the spinning operation itself—the weight of the yarn, the amount of twist, and the presence or absence of slubs or other novelty effects. Finally, the yarn design continues after a single yarn has been spun, for a variety of effects can be achieved by plying two or more yarns together.

The blending of colors, textures, or fibers in a yarn can be accomplished at any point in the construction process. However, the earlier the blending is done, the more thorough a blend will result. For example, when two different colors are to be blended in a yarn—perhaps a dark and a light—the blend might be made in the picking stage, so that by the time the yarn has been spun, the two colors will be so completely integrated as to produce a third color. If the blend is made in the carding or combing stage, it will be somewhat less intimate, and so on. The least well integrated blend is produced by twisting together two single yarns of different colors to form a ply. Such a ply yarn exhibits a striped appearance.

Any of the novelty yarns illustrated in Figure 133 can be created by the hand processes, as well as by machine. Slub and flake yarns (Fig. 488) are usually constructed during spinning. If, for a short distance, more fibers are drafted at a single time than are required for the normal yarn count, a slub will appear at that point. The slub may be just a tiny bump on the surface of the yarn or a long thickened area, as in Figure 453. Flakes are produced by introducing a small quantity of unspun fibers into the drafted yarn and allowing the twist to hold them (Fig. 489).

above: 488. ALLEN and DOROTHY FANNIN. *Stairwell.* Casement fabric of handspun flake yarn blended from very long and very short fibers. From *Objects: USA,* Johnson Wax Collection of Contemporary Crafts, Racine, Wis.

below: 489. Flakes are produced by introducing a small quantity of unspun fibers into the drafted yarn and allowing the twist to hold them in place.

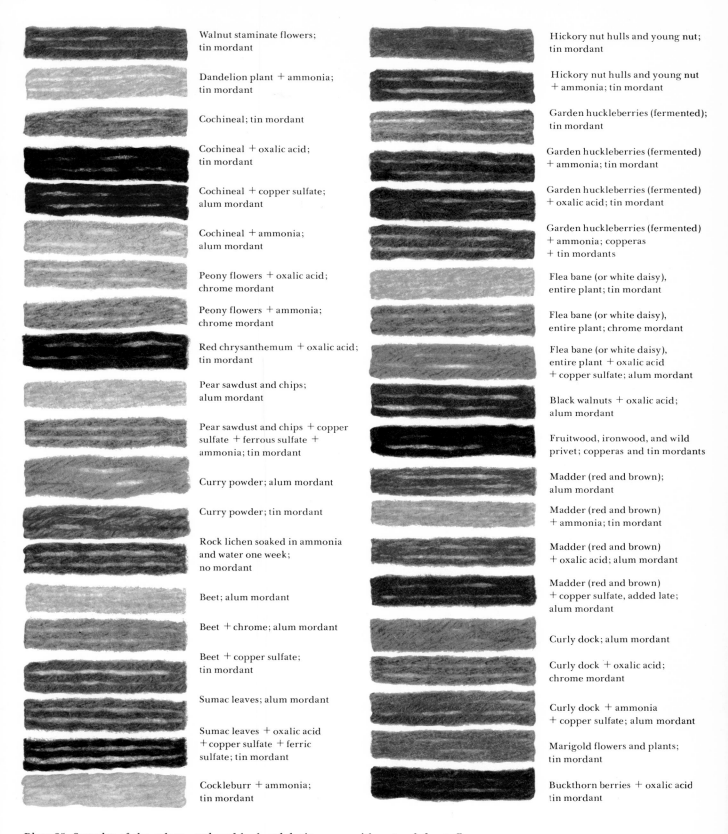

Walnut staminate flowers; tin mordant

Dandelion plant + ammonia; tin mordant

Cochineal; tin mordant

Cochineal + oxalic acid; tin mordant

Cochineal + copper sulfate; alum mordant

Cochineal + ammonia; alum mordant

Peony flowers + oxalic acid; chrome mordant

Peony flowers + ammonia; chrome mordant

Red chrysanthemum + oxalic acid; tin mordant

Pear sawdust and chips; alum mordant

Pear sawdust and chips + copper sulfate + ferrous sulfate + ammonia; tin mordant

Curry powder; alum mordant

Curry powder; tin mordant

Rock lichen soaked in ammonia and water one week; no mordant

Beet; alum mordant

Beet + chrome; alum mordant

Beet + copper sulfate; tin mordant

Sumac leaves; alum mordant

Sumac leaves + oxalic acid + copper sulfate + ferric sulfate; tin mordant

Cockleburr + ammonia; tin mordant

Hickory nut hulls and young nut; tin mordant

Hickory nut hulls and young nut + ammonia; tin mordant

Garden huckleberries (fermented); tin mordant

Garden huckleberries (fermented) + ammonia; tin mordant

Garden huckleberries (fermented) + oxalic acid; tin mordant

Garden huckleberries (fermented) + ammonia; copperas + tin mordants

Flea bane (or white daisy), entire plant; tin mordant

Flea bane (or white daisy), entire plant; chrome mordant

Flea bane (or white daisy), entire plant + oxalic acid + copper sulfate; alum mordant

Black walnuts + oxalic acid; alum mordant

Fruitwood, ironwood, and wild privet; copperas and tin mordants

Madder (red and brown); alum mordant

Madder (red and brown) + ammonia; tin mordant

Madder (red and brown) + oxalic acid; alum mordant

Madder (red and brown) + copper sulfate, added late; alum mordant

Curly dock; alum mordant

Curly dock + oxalic acid; chrome mordant

Curly dock + ammonia + copper sulfate; alum mordant

Marigold flowers and plants; tin mordant

Buckthorn berries + oxalic acid tin mordant

Plate 25. Samples of the colors produced by hand-dyeing yarn with natural dyestuffs.

right: Plate 26. Scarf woven from yarns mordanted separately in alum and in tin, then piece-dyed after weaving in a marigold dye bath. The tin mordant produced the outer dark stripes. The weave is Brook's Bouquet.

below: Plate 27. NORMAN KENNEDY and his assistant dyeing yarn at Colonial Williamsburg, Va.

Either a left-hand twist (**S** twist) or a right-hand twist (**Z** twist) can be imparted to a yarn during spinning (Fig. 490). In plying two single yarns together, the ply may take the opposite direction from the singles twist or it may be made in the same direction. The latter is sometimes referred to as *cabling*. Often, an **S**-twist and a **Z**-twist yarn are twisted together to make a ply. To ply two (or more) yarns together, the yarns are simply attached to the spinning wheel and held under tension while the drive wheel is turned in the proper direction, one way for plying, the other for cabling. One can also ply on a handspindle, but the process is much slower, and it is more difficult to control the rate of twist insertion. Interesting effects can be achieved by holding the yarns under different degrees of tension as they are plied. If one yarn is held under greater tension than the other, the taut yarn will form a core with the slack yarn wrapped around it (Fig. 491).

Throughout this chapter the design of handspun yarn to serve a particular purpose has been stressed. However, the process can also work in reverse. Experimentation with different design effects may actually suggest a certain end-use and open up new creative possibilities for the craftsman working in fiber.

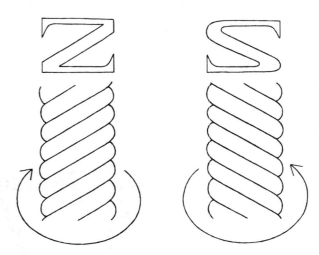

above: 490. Yarns exhibit either a left-hand twist (**S** twist) or a right-hand twist (**Z** twist). The direction of the twist can be controlled during the spinning operation. Often, in plying two yarns together, an **S**-twist and a **Z**-twist yarn are combined, with either a left-hand or a right-hand plying motion.

below: 491. A core yarn is developed by plying together two yarns that are held at unequal tension. The yarn that is held taut forms the core, while the other yarn wraps slackly around it. Various other effects can be achieved by varying the yarn tension during plying.

Yarn Dyeing 17

O might it be, that Readers find delight
  In this Work that to the living is so opportune
  Set apart are Purple, Yellow, and how to brown,
  To color in Wine, and faded shades,
The green, the blues, and scarlets
  And those that carry the emblem of fortune.
  Of velvets, damasks and all styles
  Furnished by Art.
                    Gioanventura Rosetti, The Plictho, *1548*

Many craftsmen have recently begun to express interest in dyeing their own yarns, particularly with natural dyestuffs. The colors obtained from natural materials (Pl. 25, p. 265) are much more subtle—and infinitely more diverse—than those produced commercially with synthetic dyes. When working with natural dyestuffs there is always an element of chance. Two individuals following exactly the same recipe may obtain quite different results, partly because animal and vegetable substances can vary widely according to climate and geographical location. Furthermore, minute changes in storage and handling procedures will often affect the coloring properties of a dye. However, with experience one can achieve a high degree of predictability.

Color can be introduced at various points in the manufacture of a textile. The fleece from a sheep will occasionally be dyed before spinning, and it is sometimes desirable to dye a fabric after it has been woven (Pl. 26, p. 266). But the most common practice is to add color in the yarn stage (Pl. 27, p. 266), and that is the procedure emphasized in this chapter.

A HISTORY OF DYES

Man learned to color his fabrics almost as soon as he learned to make them. Textile remnants discovered in the tombs of Thebes—and dating from about 3500 B.C.—show traces of blue indigo dye. It is believed the Egyptians even experimented with dyeing the live sheep. According to Virgil, a sheep that was fed on madder plant would produce red wool!

In the ancient world the Phoenicians were considered masters of the dyeing trade. It was they who developed the rare purple dyes, made from a mollusk found along the coast near Tyre, that were so prized by royalty. Each gram of the dyestuff required twelve thousand of the little

combine with the dyestuffs to make the colors fast—was important to the development of dyeing techniques. Mordants were used in India by 2000 B.C. and perhaps by an even earlier date in the Far East.

In Europe the art of dyeing was a highly secretive one until the 16th century. Dye methods and recipes were closely guarded, though "care ought always to be taken that a good secret never remain in the hands of one Person alone, lest it should be lost by his leaving the Kingdom or his death."[1] In 1548 Gioanventura Rosetti of Venice published the first complete printed reference book on dyeing, *The Plictho* (Fig. 493). The product of sixteen years of research, Rosetti's book compiled dye recipes from Venice, Genoa, Florence, and other Italian cities, with special emphasis on the famed reds and blacks of Venice. One can only speculate what methods Rosetti might have used in persuading dyers to surrender their secret recipes for publication. In 16th-century Italy a black dye was made in the following manner:

animals, and for centuries only monarchs could afford garments colored with Tyrian purple. The Phoenicians were indefatigable traders; their ships sailed the Mediterranean to Gibraltar and beyond, carrying with them a knowledge of dyeing techniques. Their neighbors to the south, the Hebrews, were also skilled dyers. In ancient Palestine a dyer served an apprenticeship of two and a half years, after which he was entitled to wear a badge of dyed wool behind his ear and to trademark his cloth.

A surprising range of colors was available to the early dyers. Safflower yielded reds and yellows, and indigo was used for blue (Fig. 492). Madder, an important red dye, was known to the Egyptians, the Persians, the Indians, the Greeks, and the Romans. In addition to the rich Tyrian purple, there was also a bluer purple called Byzantium. The saffron plant produced yellow, and a tiny insect found on the Kermes oak made a popular red dye. In the Americas cochineal, obtained from the female of an insect species native to Mexico, provided brilliant red, and logwood bark was used for dark colors. The discovery of *mordants*—chemical substances that

above left: 492. The indigo plant has provided a source of blue dye since the 4th millennium B.C.

below: 493. Woodcut from *The Plictho: Instructions in the art of the dyers . . .* , by GIOANVENTURA ROSETTI, 1548. Universität Bibliothek, Göttingen, West Germany.

494. Walnut hulls, lichens, and oak galls all yield substantive dyes, which do not require the addition of a mordant to make the colors fast.

Measure shells of eggs in quantity and make them boil in clear water until it drops by half. Then you remove the shells, and return the water to the fire. Take filings of iron and grindings from the milling of galls so that these things are 2 ounces, roche alum half ounce, gum arabic, very strong lye, and human urine so that the gum and the water be two ounces. Make it boil till it drops to half and this is a good black dye.

The recipe for dyeing "feathers, bones, tables of wood and handles of knives, and all other things" was also rather specific:

Measure red vinegar very strong as much as you want and put it in a glazed vase and into it much filings of copper and of brass, Roman vitriol, roche alum, verdigris. Put each thing together for several days but first let it boil a little, that is a good boil. You will make a fine tincture of green so strong that never more will it go away.

A green color on skins was produced by combining "apples of the buckthorn of the month of September" with white vinegar or strong wine and roche alum, then allowing the mixture "to boil for the space of saying six paternosters and not more."

The Plictho is subtitled: *Instructions in the art of the dyers which teaches the dyeing of woolen cloths, linens, cottons, and silk by the Great Art as well as by the Common.* This division of dyers into two groups—"those who Dye the greater, and those who Dye the lesser Dyes"—prevailed in Europe well into the 18th century. The great dyes were considered to be Madder-Red, Crimson Violet, Green, Brown Tawney, and Woad and Madder Black, while "blew," red, yellow, and brown were among the lesser colors. In order to qualify as a master dyer of the great dyes one served a four-year apprenticeship, followed by another four years of indenture. It is apparent that air pollution was a problem even in those gentler times, for a text of 1813 cautions: "In the country the scarlet cloth preserves its brightness much longer than in great cities where the urinous and alkaline vapours are more abundant."[2]

Only natural dyes were available until 1856. In that year the English chemist Sir William H. Perkin developed, quite by accident, a synthetic purple dye. Perkin continued his experiments with dyestuffs, and dye chemistry advanced rapidly. By the middle of the 20th century more than fifteen hundred dyes were offered by American manufacturers. However, in spite of the proliferation of chemicals, certain natural materials, such as logwood, are still used in modern dyehouses.

THE DYEING PROCESS

Three major variables affect the ultimate color of a dyed yarn: the nature of the dyestuff, the mordant employed, and the fiber content of the yarn itself. Vegetable dyestuffs are capricious. Two batches of goldenrod, for instance, gathered from the identical spot but at different times, might yield different shades of yellow. The same goldenrod, mordanted with copperas instead of alum, will produce a greenish dye. Woolen and cotton yarns, immersed in the same dyebath, will exhibit different shades of color.

There are two general groups of dye materials. *Substantive dyes* are permanent when heated alone with the fibers. Walnut hulls, lichens, and oak galls are among the few materials in this category (Fig. 494). *Adjective dyes* require the addition of a chemical substance—a mordant—to facilitate absorption of the color and increase its permanence. No dyes are absolutely permanent, except possibly those injected into the solution for a synthetic fiber. However, when properly mordanted, natural dyes can be as long-lasting as their chemical counterparts.

Many yarn distributors offer natural and bleached yarns in wool, cotton, linen, jute, and sisal, as well as in different weights. In general, untreated yarns are stronger than those that have been bleached or stripped of color. A list of the major yarn suppliers appears in Appendix C.

Gathering Natural Materials

In 1710 it was written: "There is scarce one peasant in these four Diocesses that doth not know when Woad is ripe, and when 'tis necessary to gather it."[3] In fact, there is an optimum time of the year for harvesting most vegetable dyestuffs (Fig. 495). Roots, such as bloodroot, perform best

below: 495. With most natural materials, like the birch leaves and goldenrod shown here, there is an optimum time of the year for harvesting.

when they are collected in the autumn. Lichens can be gathered all winter, but they are easiest to find in wet weather. Most above-ground plants yield more color if they are harvested in autumn rather than spring, because of the long exposure to sunlight. Day lily leaves, lily of the valley, and rose shoots in particular need much sun. Barks and tree roots should be collected between February and June, when they have the most sap and therefore a more intense color. Berries and fruits—such as ornamental crab-apples, grapes, sumac, and pokeberries—must be picked when they are fully ripe; those with the least water content make the best dyes. Leaves, blossoms, twigs, stems, and shoots are generally cut at maturity, although in a few cases the young spring plants are good dye sources. Nuts should be collected after they have fallen to the ground.

A large paper bag or grocery sack is the best container for accumulating vegetable materials, because it is porous and allows the plants to breathe. After harvesting, most dyestuffs can be stored for later processing, although there is sometimes a loss or change of color. Twigs, branches, grasses, and leaves can be tied in bunches and hung from the rafters of a garage or dry basement. Lichens, berries, barks, and roots should be dried slowly in the air and then stored in porous containers until they are needed.

above: 496. The equipment needed for dyeing may include: plastic and enamel tubs and kettles, wooden stirring pole, glass jars, scale, plastic funnel, coffee filter disks, plastic measuring bottle, glass stirring rod, measuring spoons, thermometer, rubber gloves.

Nut hulls and shells must be stored—after drying—in paper bags so they will not oxidize. Some flowers can be dried and preserved, but golden-rod and dandelion must be used fresh.

Materials and Equipment for Dyeing

The following equipment is required at various stages of the dye process (Fig. 496):

glass quart measuring container
stainless steel, Pyrex, or enamel pails and kettles (copper and brass are also usable, but aluminum is too porous, and iron will contaminate the dye bath)
plastic measuring spoons
plastic buckets or dishpans
large glass or plastic funnel
candy thermometer
coffee filter disks
airtight glass jars
glass stirring rod
scale for measuring pounds and ounces
rubber or plastic gloves

Most of the chemicals listed below can be obtained in drug stores, but they are less expensive if purchased in bulk from a chemical supply house (see Appendix C).

alum (aluminum potassium sulfate)
chrome (potassium dichromate)
blue vitriol (copper sulfate)
copperas (iron; ferrous sulfate)
tin (stannous chloride)
tannic acid
tartaric acid
Glauber's salts (sodium sulfate)
acetic acid (or vinegar)
sodium benzoate
oxalic acid
ammonia
precipitated chalk
sulphuric acid
litmus paper

Certain natural materials are not indigenous to the United States and must be purchased in powdered form from commercial suppliers. These include cochineal, indigo, and madder.

Only soft, nonmineralized water should be used for scouring, mordanting, and dyeing yarn. Rain water is the cheapest and most readily available form of soft water, but if it is not feasible to collect large quantities of rain water, distilled water or the moisture from a dehumidifier can be substituted. If necessary, tap water can be temporarily softened by adding one of the following:

1 teaspoon of borax per gallon of water
2 tablespoons of vinegar per gallon of water
a 4-percent solution of acetic acid

A mild soap (not detergent), sal soda, and a water softener are needed for scouring the yarns.

Extracting the Dye

The quantities of dyestuff and water needed to make a dye bath depend upon the amount of yarn to be dyed. In general, 1 pound of yarn requires $2\frac{1}{2}$ to 3 gallons of water, plus 1 peck of plant material or 1 pound of nut hulls, wood, or bark. Heavy yarns may require a higher ratio of dye material to water than fine yarns to produce the same color.

Woody materials such as bark, twigs, and roots must be cut into short pieces (1 to 3 inches) or ground with a coarse plate in a food mill. The pieces are soaked for at least 12 and preferably 24 hours, then boiled for 5 or 6 hours. Except for flowers, fruits, and berries, most other natural materials should be soaked for about 12 hours before boiling (Fig. 497). The boiling time varies according to the material, but one can usually see when a dyestuff has yielded all its color.

497. In order to extract the dye, natural materials must be boiled for several hours, until they will release no more color.

Then, the pulp or waste matter is strained out (Fig. 498), and the dye bath is ready.

In some cases the *pH factor* or acidity-alkalinity ratio of the dye bath can affect the color produced or the quality of the dyed yarn. The addition of either ammonia or oxalic acid to the dye bath—as specified for some dyestuffs in the list on pages 280–289—can increase the acidity or alkalinity of the dyebath and cause varied color results. Litmus paper is used to measure the pH factor of the dye bath.

If the dye bath is not to be used immediately, it can be preserved for several months with no loss of strength by adding 1 teaspoon of sodium benzoate per quart of liquid and sealing in an airtight container. Dye baths can also be frozen.

Scouring

Before the yarns are processed they should be wound into skeins for easier handling (Fig. 499). The skeins are tied loosely in at least four places, with the beginning and tag end of the yarn tied together. If one intends to dye an unspun wool fleece, it should be placed in a net or cheesecloth bag—large enough to allow adequate movement—to facilitate lifting in and out of the baths. Automatic washers and dryers should not be used for any step in the yarn-dyeing process.

All natural fiber yarns must be scoured to permit even absorption of the dye. Scouring removes the grease and surface soil from woolen yarns and the wax from vegetable fibers.

Wool   The scouring solution for wool is based on 2 to 3 gallons of water for each pound of yarn. To this is added enough water softener to make the water slippery, 1 to 2 percent sal soda, and a 1 to 3 percent solution of soap. The yarn is immersed and the mixture is heated to a temperature that is comfortable to the hands (110–120°F). It should be held at that temperature for 20 minutes to an hour. Then the yarn is rinsed thoroughly in at least three changes of warm water, and the excess moisture is squeezed out.

Cotton and Linen   Vegetable fibers can stand much higher temperatures than wool. The solution for scouring 1 pound of cotton or linen con-

below: 498. After all color has been extracted from the materials, the waste matter is strained out. The dye bath is then ready for use or storage.

above: 499. Yarns are easier to handle throughout the dyeing process if they are tied loosely into skeins. The beginning and tag end of the yarn are tied together.

sists of 5 parts sal soda, 2 parts soap, and 93 parts water—plus enough water softener to make the water slippery—for a total of 2 to 3 gallons of liquid. The yarn is boiled in this mixture for 1 to 2 hours, then rinsed thoroughly and squeezed to remove excess moisture.

Mordanting

Yarn can be mordanted at various stages of the dyeing process. Sometimes the mordant is added to the dye bath itself, or the yarn is mordanted both before and after dyeing. The most common procedure is to mordant *before* dyeing (*bottom mordanting*), which allows yarns prepared with different mordants to be placed in the same dye bath. One exception to this practice is the copperas (iron) mordant, which is usually added to the dye bath. (By using an iron kettle for the dye bath, one can eliminate the iron mordant. Yarns dyed in this fashion will be darker.)

The mordants most often used with natural dyestuffs are: *alum*, a universal mordant compatible with nearly all dyestuffs and fibers; *tin*, which produces the brightest colors; *chrome*, which tends to brown colors; and *copperas* (iron), a darkening mordant. An excess of alum will make yarns sticky and gummy, while a too-strong concentration of tin will cause brittleness in woolen yarns. Chrome must be stored in a covered container, for it is very sensitive to light.

Wool   The following recipes can be employed to mordant 1 pound (dry weight) of wool yarn with alum, tin, or chrome. Iron mordanting is discussed as part of the dye bath (p. 277). The tartaric acid included in the recipes has no mordanting value but helps to brighten colors.

alum:	4	ounces alum
	1	ounce tartaric acid
	3–4	gallons warm water
tin:	$\frac{1}{2}$	ounce tin
	1	ounce tartaric acid
	3–4	gallons warm water
chrome:	$\frac{1}{2}$	ounce chrome
	1	ounce tartaric acid
	3–4	gallons warm water

Yarn Dyeing   275

After the chemicals (Fig. 500) are completely dissolved in the water, the wet scoured yarn is added, and the solution is heated slowly—over a period of 45 minutes—to the simmering point (200–211°F). Fine wool yarns are simmered for 20 to 25 minutes, while heavy rug yarns are held at the simmering temperature for about 45 minutes. Then the mixture is allowed to cool naturally, the yarn is removed and rinsed, and the excess moisture is squeezed out gently. The dye bath will produce the best results if the mordant is allowed to age for a short time and if the mordanted yarn is added to the dye bath while still wet. Therefore, when the yarn is removed from the mordant solution, it should be wrapped in a bath towel and allowed to stand for at least 24 hours. However, if the yarn must be held for more than two or three days before dyeing, it can be dried and then resoaked in plain water for half an hour to prepare it for the dye bath. Yarn mordanted with chrome must be kept covered before dyeing, for if light penetrates the fibers, they will turn a grayed blue-green, and this will influence the ultimate color.

Cotton and Linen   Vegetable yarns are not susceptible to high temperatures, so they can be boiled safely in mordanting. The following recipes are intended for 1 pound (dry weight) of cotton or linen yarn.

alum:	4	ounces alum
	$\frac{1}{4}$	cup sal soda
	3	gallons warm water
tin:	2	teaspoons tin
	3	gallons warm water
chrome:	1	tablespoon chrome (2 for darker colors)
	3	gallons warm water
tannic acid:	8	tablespoons tannic acid
	3	gallons warm water

The chemicals are dissolved in the water, after which the yarn is added and the solution is brought to a boil (212°F). Fine yarns should be boiled for 1 hour, heavier yarns for 2. The yarn is allowed to remain in the bath for 24 hours and then rinsed. It should be dyed while still wet or remoistened if it is allowed to dry.

Because vegetable fibers are not as easy to dye as wool, some people prefer a more complicated three-stage mordanting process, which predisposes the yarn to better dye absorption.

below: 500. A mordant is a chemical substance that combines with a dyestuff to facilitate its absorption and encourage the development of a permanent color. Here the mordanting chemicals are measured precisely on a gram scale.

501. The yarn is removed from the dyebath after all the color from the solution has been exhausted. If left in the dyebath for cooling, the yarn will be darker in color.

1. Into 3 or 4 gallons of water are dissolved 4 ounces of alum and 1 ounce of washing soda. The yarn is added, and the mixture is boiled for 1 hour. The yarn is left completely covered by the solution for 24 hours and then rinsed.
2. A mixture is made of 1 ounce of tannic acid and 3 to 4 gallons of water. The yarn is immersed and simmered in solution for 1 hour. This second solution is allowed to stand for 24 hours, and the yarn is rinsed again.
3. The yarn is reimmersed in the first bath and left for 12 hours before rinsing. It should be dyed while still wet.

The Dye Bath

The same instructions apply for dyeing both wool and vegetable fibers. In fact, yarns of different fiber content can be put into the same dye bath simultaneously.

The dye bath should be lukewarm when the wet yarn is immersed. If the yarn is to be mordanted with copperas (iron), 1 ounce of copperas and 1 ounce of tartaric acid are dissolved in the dye solution before the yarn is added. The bath is then heated to the simmering point (200–211°F) and maintained at that temperature for ten minutes. Care must be taken to ensure that the yarn remains completely covered by the dye bath. After the solution has simmered for ten minutes, the yarn is removed, and 1 tablespoon of Glauber's salts is dissolved in the dye bath. The Glauber's salts exhaust the color from the dye bath and encourage more uniform dyeing results.

The yarn is then returned to the bath and simmered for approximately thirty minutes, or until the desired color is reached. Colors appear darker when the fibers are wet, so an allowance must be made for lightening as the yarn dries. The yarn can be removed immediately from the hot dye solution (Fig. 501) or permitted to cool naturally in the dye bath, but the latter procedure will tend to darken the colors. If it is necessary to remove the yarn from the dye bath before thirty minutes has elapsed, it should be transferred to clear water of the same temperature containing 2 tablespoons of Glauber's salts and left in that solution for the remainder of the half hour. After removal, the yarn is rinsed three times, the first rinse at the dye bath temperature, the second somewhat cooler, and the third lukewarm. The yarn is then dried slowly away from strong light or heat.

In spite of all precautions, the final color of the yarn after drying is sometimes uneven. This can be corrected by reimmersing the yarn in the dye bath, to which Glauber's salts have been added in an amount equal to 40 percent of the dry weight of the yarn. The new solution is reheated for an additional thirty minutes. This treatment should level the color.

Occasionally it is necessary or desirable to subject a yarn to two subsequent dye baths of different colors, a procedure known as *top dyeing*. For example, greens—which are difficult to obtain from a single dyestuff—are often produced by top dyeing blue on yellow. Top dyeing is also useful when the first dye bath is quite unsuccessful. Only mordanted yarns should be top dyed, for otherwise the first color is likely to bleed. It is preferable that the yarn be dry before a second dye bath is attempted, so that the color can be evaluated accurately. Commercially dyed yarns can be top dyed with natural dyes.

To ensure the best possible color fastness, a yarn can be *top mordanted*—that is, mordanted once again after dyeing. However, unless the same mordant is used both before and after dyeing, the color of the yarn will be affected. Some interesting (though rather unpredictable) results can be obtained by bottom mordanting the yarn with one chemical and top mordanting with another.

Special Dye Procedures

Certain dyestuffs require unusual handling in the dye bath. These include madder and indigo.

Madder   An eccentric property of madder is that it performs better in tap water than in rain or distilled water. A half pound of madder roots should be cut into short pieces ($\frac{1}{4}$ to $\frac{1}{2}$ inch) and covered with 2 gallons of water. The temperature of the water is raised *very slowly*—over a period of an hour—until it is just below the simmering point. Madder roots contain both red and yellow dye substances, and if the water becomes hot too quickly, brown will be released. The water is held at the warm temperature until all the dye has been extracted, after which the waste material is strained out. Then, a third gallon of water is added and the yarn is immersed. The dye bath is held at the simmering point for fifteen to twenty minutes or until the proper color is attained. (If the dye bath is permitted to boil, it will turn black.)

Indigo   The best natural source of blue dye is indigo, which is available commercially in powdered form. Powdered indigo is not soluble in water; it must be dissolved—and the dye extracted—with concentrated sulphuric acid. The recipe for preparing indigo extract consist of:

5   ounces 99-percent strength sulphuric acid
$2\frac{1}{2}$ tablespoons indigo powder
$2\frac{1}{2}$ teaspoons precipitated chalk

Sulphuric acid is an extremely dangerous chemical. Serious (or even lethal) burns may result if the fumes are inhaled or if the acid comes in contact with one's skin. Therefore, the mixture should be prepared outdoors or in a well-ventilated room, and the utmost precaution should be observed in measuring. Only glass implements—containers, measuring beakers,

below: 502. Indigo dye requires special handling, for it can be dissolved only in concentrated sulphuric acid.

opposite: 503. A few of the many natural materials that can be used for making dyes.

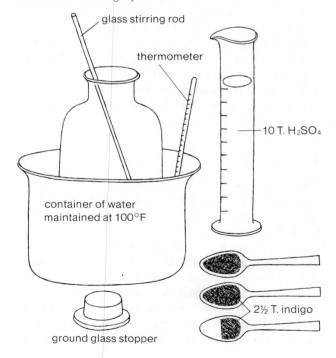

glass stirring rod

thermometer

10 T. H$_2$SO$_4$

container of water maintained at 100°F

2½ T. indigo

ground glass stopper

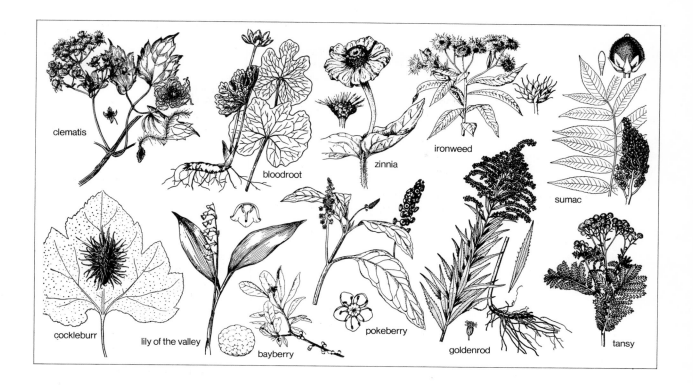

clematis

bloodroot

zinnia

ironweed

sumac

cockleburr

lily of the valley

bayberry

pokeberry

goldenrod

tansy

stirring rods—can be used with sulphuric acid, for the acid would literally consume wood or metal objects.

The required amount of acid is poured slowly into a small glass container (Fig. 502). (Pouring against a glass rod set in the middle of the container will help to prevent spills.) Next, the indigo powder is added a little at a time and stirred very gently with a glass rod. This will cause the acid to become hot. When all the indigo has been added, the temperature should be between 75° and 100°F, and it is held at this point, with occasional stirring, until the acid and indigo are completely combined (about two hours). Then, the container is sealed with a tight-fitting glass stopper and set in a safe place until the mixture has turned blue, which may take up to two weeks. Finally, the precipitating chalk is added a little at a time, and the mixture is allowed to stand for about three days with occasional stirring. When the chalk is completely dissolved, the indigo extract is ready to use.

Indigo dye is potent and is absorbed very quickly into the yarn. A solution of 1 teaspoon of extract in 2½ to 3 gallons of water will dye 1 pound of yarn to a medium blue.

Documenting the Results

When using natural dyes it is most important to keep accurate records so that successful results can be replicated (and unsuccessful ones avoided in the future). A small swatch of yarn from each dye lot should be set aside and labeled with the following information:

dyestuff employed
time and place of collection
mordant and time of mordanting (before or after dyeing or both)
fiber content of yarn
date of dyeing

NATURAL DYESTUFFS

Not all natural materials are suitable for making dyes. Some vivid plants and flowers do not release their color and are therefore useless as dye sources. The following list describes natural dyestuffs that are known to be successful (Fig. 503). However, the list is by no means exhaustive. With experimentation the reader may discover local materials that will produce wonderful dyes.

Material	Mordant(s)	Colors produced	Material	Mordant(s)	Colors produced
acorn nuts and cups	alum	tan	blackberry shoots	copperas	black
	alum with oxalic acid	yellow-tan	black-eyed susan (blossom)	alum	pale grayed yellow
	tin with oxalic acid	yellow-tan		tin	bright yellow
ageratum	alum	light yellow		tin with oxalic acid	light rose
	tin	bright yellow		tin and copperas with oxalic acid	medium brown
alfalfa	tin and copperas	green-gold	bloodroot	no mordant	orange
	alum	cream		alum	orange and rust
	tin	pale yellow		tin	red and pink
alder bark	alum	soft brown	broom, scotch	alum	yellow
apple bark	alum	lemon yellow		chrome	gold
	tin	bright yellow	broomsedge	alum	green-yellow
	chrome	brass		chrome	brass
	alum and copperas with oxalic acid	dark brown	buck brush berries	tin	light yellow
	alum with ammonia	yellow		alum with ammonia	soft yellow
	alum or tin with copper sulfate	old gold		tin with ammonia	yellow
asparagus plant (fall)	tin	yellow	buckthorn bark	alum	golden yellow
aster, wild (white)	alum	yellow	buckthorn berries	alum	lime green
	chrome	gold		tin	orange-brown
aster, cultivated (purple)	tin	soft yellow		alum with ammonia	gold
barberries	alum	yellow-gold to coral		tin with ammonia	bright gold
	tin with copper sulfate	light khaki		alum with oxalic acid	deep rose-tan
barberry stem or root	alum	yellow		tin with oxalic acid	dark brown
	tin	deep yellow	buttercups	alum	yellow
bayberry leaves or berries	alum	gray-green to light yellow	butternut hulls	alum	dull red-orange
	tin	light yellow		tin	dull yellow-orange
	copperas	dark brown		alum with ammonia	pink-beige
beets (entire plant)	alum	tan to red-orange		tin with ammonia	gray-brown
	tin	gold to yellow-orange		alum or tin with oxalic acid	bright orange-brown
	alum with oxalic acid	light red-orange		copperas and alum	medium brown
	tin with copper sulfate	dark yellow-green	calliopsis	chrome	brick red
birch leaves	alum	green-yellow to tan	camomile blossoms (golden marguerites)	alum	buff
	tin	yellow		chrome	gold
	rinsed in weak birch ash lye	red-orange	canna leaves and stems (fall)	alum	yellow-tan
bittersweet berries	alum	light tan		tin	gray-yellow
	tin	bright orange-yellow		alum or tin with ammonia	yellow
	tin with oxalic acid	pink-tan		alum or tin with oxalic acid	grayed red-orange
blackberries	alum with salt	blue-gray	carrion plant (berries and leaves, fall)	alum	yellow-tan
	tin in acid	purple		tin	light yellow
	alum	brown-purple		alum with oxalic acid	light yellow-orange
			carrot tops	alum	light green-yellow
				tin	bright yellow

Material	Mordant(s)	Colors produced	Material	Mordant(s)	Colors produced
carrot tops (cont'd.)	alum or tin with ammonia	bright yellow	cochineal (cont'd.)	chrome with acetic acid	purple
	alum or tin with ammonia (fermented)	blue		oxalic acid	geranium red
				no mordant	rose-pink
catnip (fall)	alum	light yellow	cocklebur	alum	gold
	tin	gray-yellow		tin with ammonia	yellow
	tin with oxalic acid	gray-gold		chrome	brown
cedar roots	alum	purple		tin with oxalic acid	gold
cherry bark	alum	pale rose		copperas	dark green
	tin	peach	coleus (purple)	alum	gray-brown
	alum with oxalic acid	light red-orange		tin	green-brown
	alum with copper sulfate	olive green		alum with ammonia	olive green
cherry wood	alum	tan		alum with oxalic acid	rose
	tin	bright gold		tin with oxalic acid	medium gray-brown
	copperas and alum with oxalic acid	dark brown	coleus (green and pink)	alum and tin	yellow-tan
	alum or tin with oxalic acid	light grayed red-orange		alum with oxalic acid	grayed red-orange
	tin or alum with ammonia	light red-orange		tin with oxalic acid	medium brown
	alum with copper sulfate	olive green	coreopsis (blossoms and leaves)	tin	bright yellow
	alum or tin with copper sulfate and oxalic acid	red-gold		chrome	burnt orange
			coreopsis (stalks)	alum	yellow
chestnut, horse (bark)	alum	brown	crabapple, yellow, ornamental	alum	light yellow
	copperas	warm gray		tin	bright gold
chestnut, horse (leaves and hulls)	chrome	gold		alum with ammonia	dark yellow
choke cherry (root and bark)	no mordant	purple-brown	cranberry	alum	pink
				tin	red-gold
choke cherry (fruit)	alum	red		alum with oxalic acid	pink
chrysanthemum (blossoms, yellow)	tin	yellow		tin with oxalic acid	light red-violet
				alum with ammonia	grayed pink
chrysanthemum (blossoms, red)	alum	medium gray		tin with ammonia	dull gold
	tin	bronze	curry powder	alum	bright gold
	alum with ammonia	light yellow		tin	bright orange
	tin with ammonia	lime green	dahlia (blossoms)	alum	yellow
	alum with oxalic acid	red-violet		chrome	orange
	tin with oxalic acid	deep red-violet	dahlia (leaves, fall)	tin	grayed gold
				alum with oxalic acid	dark tan
clematis (leaves and branches)	alum	yellow		copperas and alum with ammonia	warm gray
cochineal	acids	orange		copperas and tin with ammonia	yellow-brown
	alkalies	crimson violet	dandelion root (U.S.)	alum	yellow-brown
	alum	red	dandelion root (Scotland)	alum	magenta
	tin	orange-red		copperas	dark khaki
	copperas	deep red-violet	dandelion (blossoms)	alum or tin	light yellow
	copper sulfate	red-violet to violet	dock, broad leaved (leaves)	alum	yellow

Material	Mordant(s)	Colors produced	Material	Mordant(s)	Colors produced
dock, broad leaved (root)	alum	dull yellow	indigo (roots or powder)	alum	blue
	chrome	light brown		chrome	green
	copper sulfate	rich brown	indigo, false	alum	blue
fennel plant	alum	bright yellow	iris (blossoms)	alum or tin	yellows, greens, blues
	chrome	gold			
fern, bracken (buds, spring)	alum	lime green		chrome	green
	chrome	olive green	ironweed	alum	tan
fern, bracken (shoots)	alum	creamy yellow	joe-pye weed	alum or chrome	yellow
	copperas	dull green	juniper berries	alum	yellow
fern, bracken (roots)	alum	dark yellow		copper sulfate and ammonia	olive brown
fern, sweet (summer)	alum	pale yellow		copperas	brown
	tin	golden yellow	knotweed	alum	pale yellow
	alum or tin with oxalic acid	light red-orange		tin	yellow
				alum with oxalic acid	pink
geranium (blossoms, scarlet)	tin	pink		tin with oxalic acid	peach
gloxinia (blossoms, red)	alum or tin with oxalic acid	deep pink	lamb's quarter	no mordant or alum	red
	alum	pale pink	larch needles (newly fallen)	alum	brown
	tin	grayed yellow	larkspur (petals)	alum	blue
goldenrod (blossoms)	alum	yellow	larkspur (plant, fall)	alum or tin	grayed tan
grapes, Concord	alum	lavender and purple		alum or tin with oxalic acid	medium brown
grapes, wild	alum	lavender to violet	lichens (Evernia prunastri)	no mordant	plum
hawthorn apples	alum	deep fawn	lichens (green tree)	alum or tin	grayed red-orange
hickory nut hulls	alum	deep red-orange			
	tin	orange		alum or tin with oxalic acid	deep grayed red-orange
	alum or tin with oxalic acid	deep red-orange			
	alum with ammonia	deep brown		copperas and tin with ammonia	medium brown
	tin with ammonia	orange brown	lichens (Parmelia molluscula)	alum	red-tan to light orange
hollyhock (mixed colors)	chrome	orange and rust	lichens (Peltigera)	alum	yellow-tan
hollyhock (red)	alum	pink		chrome	dark rose-tan
	tin	deep red	lichens (Umbilicaria pistilata—soaked in ammonia)	alum	deep red-violet
hop, wild (leaves and flowers)	alum	yellow		tin	red-violet
hop, wild (stalks)	alum	brown-red		no mordant	deep red-violet
hornbean (inner bark)	no mordant	yellow	lichens (Usnea)	alum	buff to green-yellow
horsebrier fruit	alum	violet	lilac (branches and leaves)	alum	medium yellow
	table salt	blue		tin	medium yellow
horsetail stalks	alum	grayed yellow		chrome	warm gray
huckleberries, garden	alum	violet		oxalic acid and alum or tin	buff
	tin	blue			
	alum with ammonia	light blue-green		oxalic acid, copper sulfate, and alum	green gold
	tin with ammonia	deep green			
	alum with oxalic acid	violet		oxalic acid, copper sulfate, and tin	gold
	tin with oxalic acid	deep blue			
	copperas and tin with ammonia	dark green		copper sulfate and alum or tin	olive green

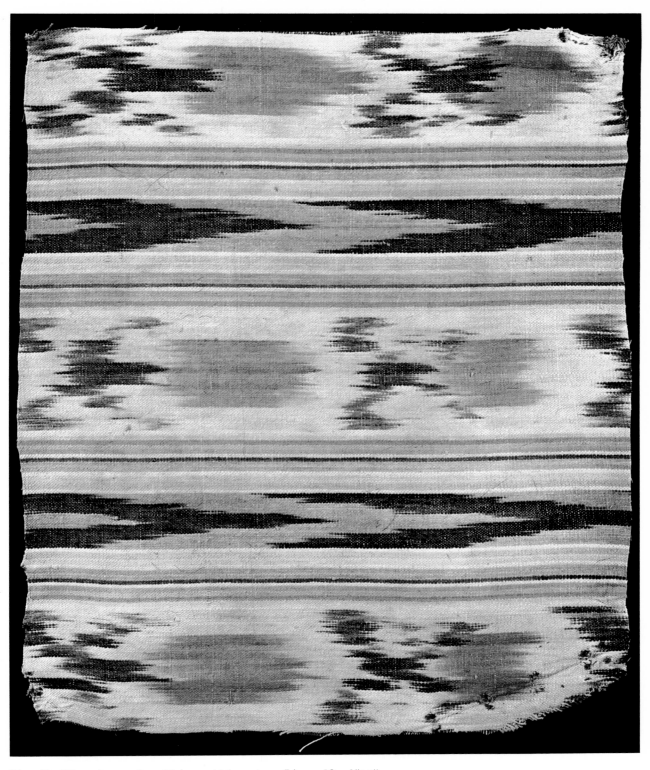

Plate 28. *Tela se lengua* ikat, Majorca. 18th century. Linen, 19 x 15¼".
Montreal Museum of Fine Arts (Arthur Byne Collection).

Plate 29. SUSAN R. THOMPSON. *Blazing Star*. 1970. Warp ikat with overshot weave in horsehair twine and handspun Mexican wool, 7'6" x 3'4". Courtesy the artist.

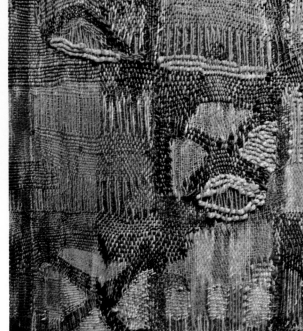

above: Plate 30. KAREN CHANG. Ikat hanging. 1965. Tapestry, gauze, and brocade weaves with embroidery and braided finish; wool warp, wool, silk, and synthetic-fiber weft; 7′6″ x 3′4″. Collection Robert Pfannebecker, Lancaster, Pa.

right: Plates 31, 32. Details of KAREN CHANG's ikat hanging (Pl. 30).

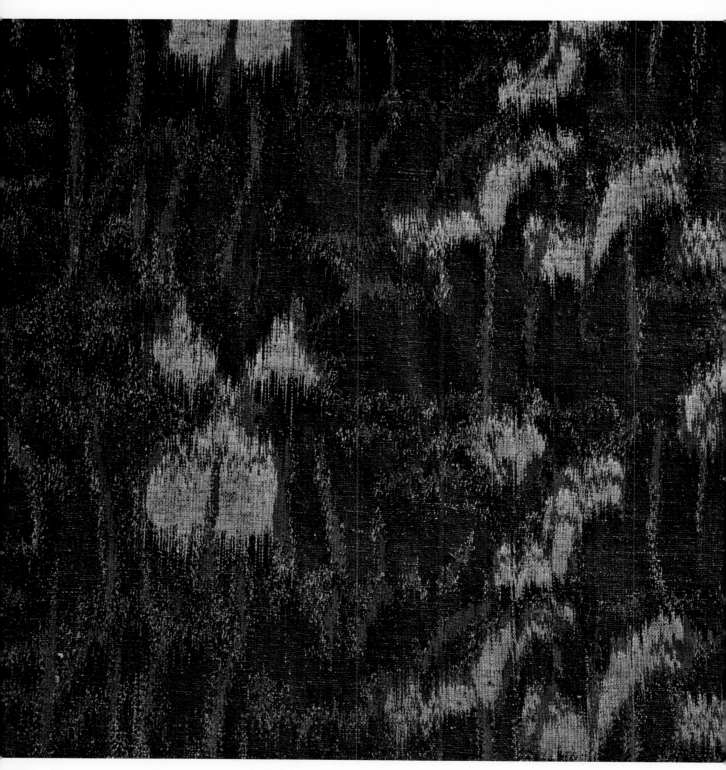

Plate 33. ED ROSSBACH. Fabric detail. 1964. Stenciled linen warp with silk weft, hand-painted background areas. Courtesy the artist.

Material	Mordant(s)	Colors produced
lily of the valley (fall)	alum	peach
	tin	red-orange
	alum with oxalic acid	grayed brown
lily of the valley (spring)	alum	yellow-green
	alum with lime	yellowish green
	alum with ammonia	greenish yellow
liver plant (foliage, fall)	alum or tin	clear lemon yellow
locust seed pods (dark brown)	alum	tan
	tin	bright orange
	alum with ammonia	grayed yellow-orange
	copperas and alum with ammonia	dark gray
	copperas and tin with ammonia	deep bronze
	copperas and alum with oxalic acid	warm light gray
	copperas and tin with oxalic acid	gold
locust seed pods (rust)	alum	pale peach
	tin	clear yellow
	alum with ammonia	grayed yellow
	tin with ammonia	clear yellow-orange
	alum with oxalic acid	pale peach
	tin with oxalic acid	light red-orange
locust (yellow)	alum	yellow
lupines (entire plant)	alum	green-yellow
madder roots	chrome	red-brown
	alum	bright red-orange
	tin	bright orange
	alum with ammonia	light yellow
	tin with ammonia	clear yellow
	alum with oxalic acid	bright rust
	tin with oxalic acid	medium orange
maple bark	alum	pink-tan
	copperas	purple
marigold, bur (sticktights or pitchfork, fall)	alum	yellow
marigold, French (plant and blossoms)	alum	lemon yellow
	tin	bright orange
	alum with ammonia	yellow

Material	Mordant(s)	Colors produced
marigold, French (cont'd.)	tin with ammonia	yellow-orange
	alum with oxalic acid	tan
	tin with oxalic acid	yellow
	alum and copperas	grayed olive
	copperas and tin	orange-brown
marigold, American (plant and blossoms)	alum	yellow
	tin	yellow-green
	chrome	orange
marigold, marsh (blossoms)	alum	yellow
meadow rue (roots)	alum	yellow
mulberry	alum	purple
	oxalic acid	pink
	ammonia	blue
nectarine (leaves, fall)	alum	lemon yellow
	tin	bright yellow-orange
	alum with ammonia	light yellow
	copperas and alum with ammonia	bronze
	copperas and tin with ammonia	orange-brown
nettle (flowers)	alum	dull gold
nettle (entire plant)	alum	yellow
nightshade (berries)	alum	purple
	tin	blue
oak, black (bark)	tin	orange on silk
	alum	yellow
	chrome	gold
oak, black (galls or gallnuts)	no mordant	brown
onion skins (red or yellow)	alum	orange
	chrome	red to brass
	tin	yellow-orange
	tin or alum with oxalic acid	red-orange
	alum with ammonia	gold
	tin with ammonia	green-gold
	copper sulfate	yellow-green
Oregon grape (roots, leaves, and stems)	alum	dull green-yellow
osage orange (bark or wood chips)	alum	strong yellow-green
	tin	yellow
	chrome	gold
oxalis (foliage, fall)	alum	light peach
	tin	grayed red-orange
	alum with ammonia	light yellow

Material	Mordant(s)	Colors produced
oxalis (cont'd.)	tin with ammonia	clear yellow
	alum and copperas with ammonia	olive green
	tin and copperas with ammonia	gold
paprika	alum	tan
parsley, wild (plant minus roots)	alum	gold or green-yellow
pear (sawdust and chips)	alum	peach
	tin	rose
	alum with ammonia	red-orange
	tin with ammonia	dusty rose
	alum or tin with oxalic acid	red-orange
	copperas and alum with ammonia	warm gray
	copperas and tin with ammonia	cool gray
	alum with copper sulfate and ammonia	grayed green
peony (blossoms, red and pink)	alum	yellow
	alum with oxalic acid	red and pink
pine cones (long boiling)	alum	dull brown-yellow
	alum with oxalic acid	rose-tan
plantain (leaves and roots)	alum	green
plum, Damson (fruit)	alum	strong grayed purple
plum, wild (roots)	alum	red-purple
plum, wild (bark)	alum	red
pokeberry	alum	red and pink
	chrome	rust
	tin	bright red
polyporous lucidus (red shelf fungi or lichens)	alum	pale orange
	tin	pale red-orange
	alum or tin with oxalic acid	stronger orange
	copperas and alum with oxalic acid	deep brown
polyporus versicolor (wavy semicircular grown on trees—soaked in ammonia one month)	alum	pale orange
	tin	grayed orange
	alum with oxalic acid	grayed orange
pomegranate skins	alum	yellow
	copperas with ash lye	violet-blue
poplar (leaves)	alum	lime yellow

Material	Mordant(s)	Colors produced
poplar (bark)	alum	rich yellow
	chrome	golden brown
poplar, Lombardy (leaves)	alum	yellow-brown
	chrome	brass
poplar, Lombardy (catkins)	alum with ammonia	yellow-green
poppy, oriental (petals)	alum with oxalic acid	salmon pink
poppy, oriental (stamens only)	alum with oxalic acid	violet
privet (berries)	alum with salt	blue
privet (clippings)	alum	tan
	tin	deep gold
	copper sulfate	green
	copperas and tin with ammonia	golden brown
	chrome	tan to gold
privet, wild (or ironwood—berries)	alum	tan
	tin	dark brown
	alum with ammonia	grayed gold
	tin with ammonia	brass
	alum with oxalic acid	dusty rose
	tin with oxalic acid	dark grayed brown
	copperas and alum	dark grayed green
	copperas and tin	dark grayed brown
purslane, garden	alum	beige
Queen Anne's lace (wild carrot)	alum	pale yellow
	chrome	tan
ragweed (young)	alum	green
	copperas and alum	dark green
rose bush cuttings	alum	tan
	copperas	green to brown-black
rose bush (wild, fall)	alum	gray to brown
rose hips	alum	grayed rose
	tin	gold
rudbeckia (flower heads)	alum	green
	chrome	green-gold
saffron (flowers or powder)	alum	yellow
salvia (plant with blossoms, fall)	alum or tin	pale yellow
	tin with ammonia	grayed gold
	alum or tin with oxalic acid	peach
	copperas and alum with ammonia	cool gray
	copperas and tin with ammonia	grayed gold
	copperas and alum with oxalic acid	grayed dark green

Material	Mordant(s)	Colors produced	Material	Mordant(s)	Colors produced
salvia (cont'd.)	copperas and tin with oxalic acid	grayed gold	thyme foliage (fall)	alum	grayed gold
scabiosa (blossoms)	alum	bright green-yellow		tin	yellow
	tin	yellow-green		alum with ammonia	brass
	alum with ammonia	clear yellow		tin with ammonia	gold
	tin with ammonia	green-yellow		alum with oxalic acid	grayed red-orange
	alum with oxalic acid	dusty rose		tin with oxalic acid	yellow-brown
	tin with oxalic acid	grayed rose		copperas and alum	bronze
	copperas and alum	dark yellow-green		copperas and tin	grayed red-orange
	copperas and tin	grayed gold	tomato plant (before frost)	tin	clear yellow
scabiosa (entire plant)	tin	clear yellow		alum with ammonia	grayed yellow
	alum with ammonia	grayed yellow		tin with ammonia	grayed golden yellow
	tin with ammonia	golden yellow		copperas and alum	cool gray
	copperas and alum with ammonia	grayed olive green		copperas and tin	deep yellow
	copperas and tin with ammonia	yellow-brown	tulip (petals)	alum	beige and yellow
sedge grass	alum	yellow-green to tan		oxalic acid	red
	chrome	gold	tulip tree (leaves)	chrome	gold
	copperas	gray-green	turmeric	alum	yellow
seaweed or dulse (spring)	alum with ammonia	yellow-fawn	wahoo (berries, fall)	alum	pale yellow-orange
	tin with ammonia	red-brown		tin	deep yellow-orange
sheep's sorrel	alum	soft pink		alum with ammonia	golden yellow
	chrome	mushroom pink		tin with ammonia	deep yellow-orange
smartweed	alum	yellow-green		copperas and alum with ammonia	brass
solomon seal (leaves)	alum	green			
spiderwort (blossoms)	alum	blue		copperas and tin with ammonia	golden brown
sumac (leaves and berries)	alum	tan	walnut, black (hulls)	alum	brown and tan
	copper sulfate	green		no mordant	brown
	copperas	gray or gray-brown		copperas	black and gray
sycamore (fruit)	alum	gray-yellow		alum with oxalic acid	red-brown
tansy (flower heads)	alum	green-yellow	willow (leaves)	alum	yellow
	tin	brown	willow (bark)	alum or chrome	gold to orange-red and brown
thistle, Russian (entire young plant)	no mordant, but yarn and plant soak together one week while plant ferments	dull olive green	yarrow	copperas	green

Yarn Printing 18

... that all calicoes of China, Persia or of the East Indias, that are painted, dyed, printed, or stained there, which are, or shall be, imported into this kingdom, shall not be worn, or otherwise used, in Great Britain.

By an Act of Parliament, 1700

Yarn printing is nothing more than a *selective* dyeing of the warp or weft yarns or both before weaving. Color is introduced only in certain predetermined areas to create a pattern. Warp yarns are printed after they have been measured and—depending upon the process to be employed—either before or after they are installed on the loom. Weft printing is somewhat more difficult and less predictable, for it requires estimating the length of each weft yarn.

In order to ensure the best dye receptiveness, natural-fiber yarns should be scoured before measuring. If fast colors are desired, the yarns should also be mordanted (see pp. 275–277).

The most common methods of yarn printing are ikat and silk screen.

IKAT

Ikat is a very old technique that probably originated in Southeast Asia or in India (Fig. 504).

504–514. *Ikat is a technique in which warp or weft yarns or both are printed by resist methods before weaving.*

above: 504. Warp- and double-ikat fabric, India. 20th century. Cotton, dark areas 4¾″ square. Textiles and Clothing Department Collection, Iowa State University, Ames.

above left: 505. Warp-ikat fabric, Peru. 13th–16th century. Cotton. American Museum of Natural History, New York.

above right: 506. Double-ikat kimono fabric, Japan. 19th century. Width 12½″. Metropolitan Museum of Art, New York (Seymour Fund, 1966).

In some geographical regions it may be called *jaspé, chiné, kasuri,* or *kashiri,* but ikat is the most universal term. The process involves dyeing portions of the warp or weft yarns—by a method similar to tie-dye—after they have been measured but before they are set up on the loom. When both the warp and weft are printed, the result is called *double ikat.*

The Spaniards apparently learned ikat from the Moors during the period of the Islamic Empire. A special type of ikat, called *tela se lengua* (cloth of tongue), is associated with Spain (Pl. 28, p. 283). The name derives from the long "tongues" of color that appear on the printed cloth. This effect was produced by dip-dyeing portions of the white linen warp in indigo and interlacing a weft dyed entirely blue. The result was a random streaking of blue and white. One variation of *tela se lengua* involved an all-yellow warp with a weft dyed partially in blue.

Examples of ikat-printed cloth have been found in the Americas, but it is not known whether the technique was carried by the *conquistadores* or had been developed previously by the Indians. The Peruvian fabric in Figure 505 is dated roughly to the time of Pizarro's arrival.

Japanese kasuri or kashiri is usually a double ikat (Fig. 506), and the patterns are produced in a variety of ways. One ingenious method for controlling the weft printing involved weaving a fabric with a very coarse warp. The weft yarns were then dyed, the cloth was unraveled, and the printed weft was used to weave another fabric of the same dimension. Sometimes the yarns were pressed between boards that had been carved with relief designs, so that when the yarn was immersed in the dye bath, only the background received color. The most meticulous control was exercised by hand rubbing color into selected portions of the yarn. Kasuri is still a highly regarded art among Japanese craftsmen.

Yarn Printing   291

natural-fiber yarns must be scoured to remove any trace of grease or soil.

Extreme care must be taken in measuring the warps to make sure they will remain in the same relative positions when threaded on the loom. It is best to warp with one yarn at a time and to make small bouts of 25 to 50 ends each. The length of each warp yarn must, of course, allow for loom waste beyond the pattern area (see p. 109). The cross ties should be loose, so they will not interfere with dye absorption, but one very tight choke tie should be made at the cross end. This knot will prevent the yarns from shifting during the printing, drying, and loom-dressing.

A stretch frame of some sort is recommended for keeping the yarns aligned before and after dyeing. One design for such a frame requires the following materials:

two pieces of $\frac{1}{2}$-inch plywood, each 24 by 26 inches
one piece of $\frac{1}{2}$-inch plywood, 24 inches square
four metal hinges, with screws
two wooden lath strips, each 1 inch by 2 inches by 32 inches

left: 507. Ikat-printed shroud, Dutch East Indies. Late 19th century. Metropolitan Museum of Art, New York (Rogers Fund, 1930).

below: 508. The yarn for warp ikat is easier to handle before and after dyeing if it is stretched on a frame.

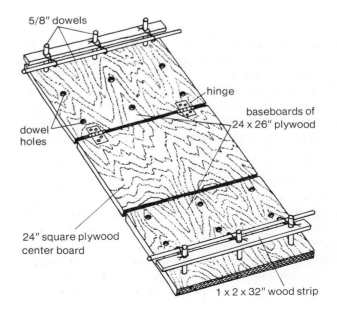

In 20th-century Indonesia ikat is associated with a sacred ritual (Fig. 507), so it is difficult for an outsider to learn the methods practiced in that region. Native Indonesians have been known to err deliberately, rather than disclose a dyeing or weaving secret. Only by trial-and-error experimentation, combined with bits of information gleaned from observation and from the literature, have Western craftsmen been able to duplicate the results.

There is no single procedure for ikat printing. Each craftsman must discover the methods that work best for him. The techniques described on the following pages have been proved successful and can be adapted, when necessary, to the needs of a particular project.

Warp Ikat

The yarns for a warp ikat must be strong, dye receptive, and dimensionally stable. Both natural and man-made fiber yarns are acceptable, but

six 6-inch lengths of ⅝-inch dowel
two 36-inch lengths of ⅝-inch dowel

To construct the frame, nine ⅝-inch holes are drilled in each of the two larger sections of plywood, as in Figure 508. The three sections are then hinged together, allowing a maximum warp length of 76 inches. The two wood laths are each drilled with three holes to correspond to a row of holes in the plywood.

When the warp is removed from the warping frame, *no* cut is made, so there is a loop at each end. One of the longer dowels is slipped through each loop, and the dowel is in turn lashed to a wooden lath strip. The lath is then fitted over three of the small dowels set in the row of holes appropriate for the warp length.

The warp printing may require several stages, depending upon how many colors are to be used. Only one color can be printed at a time, and dyeing proceeds from the darkest to the lightest shade. Ikat is a *resist* technique, which means that certain areas of the ground are prevented from absorbing color, while only the untreated portions are exposed to the dye. A time-honored method for *stopping out* the absorption of color in selected areas is to tie nonporous materials—rubber balloons, rubber bands, plastic strips, pieces of inner tube, and so forth—around the sections that are not to receive a particular color (Fig. 509). A commercial product called Lubasin S has proved quite effective as a resist material. Lubasin S is a clear liquid plastic of syrupy consistency that can be painted on the yarns. The substance hardens when immersed in very hot water (150°F or warmer), but cold soapy water will restore it to its liquid form for easy removal.

The first step in ikat dyeing is to stop out with one or more of the resist materials all the areas that are not to receive the first or darkest color. This procedure is best carried out on the stretcher frame. Sometimes a cut paper cartoon is used to transfer a design to the yarns. Sheets of paper from which the pattern for each color has been cut out are placed in turn on the stretched yarns, and the design is traced in pencil as a guide for applying the resists. The yarn is then dipped in the dye bath, rinsed thoroughly, and stretched on the frame—which is protected with plastic—to dry. For the second dye bath, the resists are removed in the areas meant to be

above: 509. Resists of nonabsorbent material cover sections of the yarn that are not to receive a particular color. In this instance, different-colored balloons serve as a code to indicate which resists should be removed for each dye bath.

printed with the next-lightest color. (If Lubasin S or a similar chemical is used, it will be impossible to remove only a section of the resist. The areas intended for the third, fourth, and fifth dye baths—if any—will have to be repainted.) This process continues until all the colors have been printed and all the resists removed. It is wise to code the resists associated with each dye bath, so that only the correct ones are eliminated at each stage.[1]

When a portion of the yarn is top dyed—that is, when a previously dyed dark section of the warp is exposed to a second or third dye bath—the results are occasionally unpredictable. For example, when the first dye bath is dark blue and a subsequent bath is yellow, the dark blue area of the yarn may assume a greenish cast. It is a good idea to test a small sample of yarn in each dye bath before immersing the entire warp, so that any problems can be compensated for. In some cases it may be necessary to reapply a resist to the portions of the warp that have already been dyed with the darker colors, so that later dye baths will not contaminate them. Prevention of errors is, of course, much easier than correction. However, if the resists should slip, causing two colors to bleed into one another, it is possible to remove the color by soaking the affected portion of the yarn in a commercial color stripper.

Ikat-printed warps are more efficiently beamed from the front to the back of the loom (see pp. 125–126), so that any yarn slippage that may occur can be rectified. The warp yarns are first attached to the cloth beam, then cut and threaded through the reed and heddles. Before

the warp is tied to the warp beam, it should be checked to make sure the design has not shifted. The entire warp is then rolled carefully back onto the warp beam. The weaving pattern should, obviously, be chosen to produce a warp-face fabric, in order to best exploit the design.

The Indians of ancient Peru would occasionally introduce extra *skeleton* or *scaffold* yarns into the warp to enhance the ikat design. This is accomplished in the same manner as the repair of a broken warp (see p. 134 and Figs. 223, 224). The scaffold yarn can either supplement or replace the regular warp yarn in a particular position. It can be threaded through a heddle already in use, through a corrective heddle, or through no heddle at all, in which case it is lifted by hand whenever necessary.

Warp ikat designs are often so striking that they can stand alone, with very little weft interlacement. Such is the case in Figure 510, a wall hanging in which widely spaced weft yarns are twined across the web only to hold the warp in place. The printing itself, rather than any weaving pattern, is the major design element.

Blazing Star (Pl. 29, p. 284) was constructed with an overshot weave to produce a stepped pattern in vivid, fiery colors reminiscent of pre-Columbian weaving. The warp was ikat-printed with dyes made from onion skins, cochineal, and natural indigo, while the weft is of horsehair twine and Mexican wool. The pattern is weaver Susan Thompson's own adaptation of an old overshot weave variously known as "Blazing Star," "Blooming Leaf," and "Bow Knot."

Some of the most brilliant contemporary ikat prints have been created by Hawaiian-born Karen Chang (Pls. 30–32, p. 285), who writes: "The ikat technique . . . eliminates many of the obstacles of weaving and has many of the advantages of both painting and sculpture."

Weft Ikat

The dyeing process for a weft ikat is much the same as that for a warp. However, before stretching the yarns on a frame to tie the resists, one

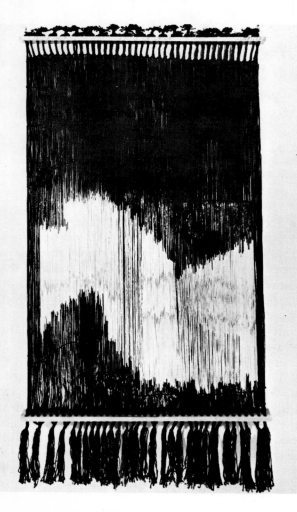

left: 510. CYNTHIA SCHIRA. *Ikat with Walnut.* 1968. Off-loom weft-twined jute, 6′7″ × 3′4″. From *Objects: USA,* Johnson Wax Collection of Contemporary Crafts, Racine, Wis.

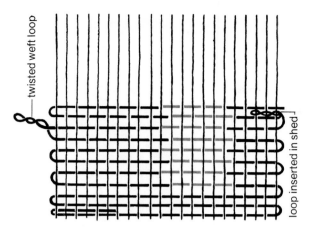

above: 511. To control the pattern in a weft ikat, loops of yarn are often twisted and inserted back into the fabric.

below: 512. Huipile with weft ikat, detail, from Guatemala. Weft-face twill, 44 × 34″ overall. Textiles and Clothing Department Collection, Iowa State University, Ames.

must calculate the length of each weft yarn. This length can be estimated roughly, allowing a percentage for weft take-up (see p. 111), or, for greater accuracy, a small sample can be woven to the same width as the projected fabric and then unraveled slightly to measure the length of each weft shot. Once the distance is known, the weft yarns can be measured on a warping frame and then placed on the stretcher.

The weft yarn for a narrow fabric can be wrapped around a small sheet of Plexiglas and then painted with Lubasin S for the resist. If this system is used, the yarn can be dyed without removing it from the Plexiglas. However, the fact that adjacent wefts are on opposite sides of the Plexiglas makes patterning difficult. Such a procedure might be practical for a double weave.

The weaving process for a weft ikat requires very careful attention, to ensure that the patterned area of the weft falls exactly where it is needed. One must usually sacrifice perfect selvedges in order to arrive at the desired effect. If a very long loop projects beyond the selvedge once the weft is positioned, the loop can be twisted and inserted back into the shed before beating (Fig. 511). This procedure was followed by the Indians and the peoples of Southeast Asia even in their finest ikats. The weave pattern for a weft ikat is, of course, weft faced (Fig. 512).

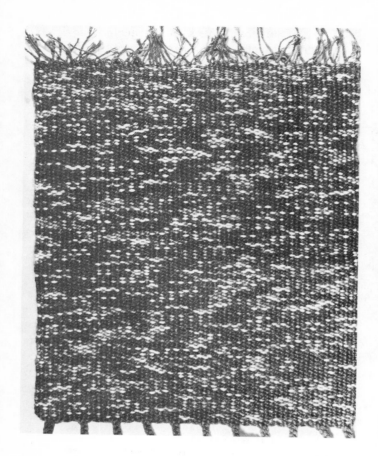

While most ikats are planned for a definite pattern, in some cases the ikat printing is employed to produce a random textured effect (Fig. 513). This device is equally successful when the printing is in the warp.

Double Ikat

The double ikat combines the two techniques described above to produce a pattern in both the warp and the weft (Fig. 514). The utmost care is required to make the design coincide in both sets of yarns.

SILK SCREEN

Silk screen is a form of *stencil printing,* which means that a precut pattern is placed upon the ground to be printed, and one traces around or inside the pattern to transfer the design. For silk-screen printing, a length of silk (or occasionally some other porous material) is stretched

above left: 513. Weft ikat printing can be employed to produce a random textured effect.

above right: 514. MARY EHLERS MATHEWS. Double ikat hanging. 1970. Plain weave in linen, with Lubasin S as a resist; 4′6″ × 2′6″. Courtesy the artist.

tightly in a frame, and all the areas that are *not* to print are stopped out with a substance that closes the pores in the silk. Next, the frame is placed over the printing surface—in this case a warp held under tension—and a dye or textile paint is forced through the screen. The dye penetrates the screen only in the portions that have not been coated, and thus a design is transferred to the warp.

A warp is best printed by the silk-screen process *after* it has been installed on the loom. One should attach the warp yarns to the warp stick individually with a lark's-head knot (Fig. 197) to inhibit slippage of the yarns. The warp yarns are then beamed, threaded and sleyed in the usual manner (see Chap. 8). However, instead of attaching the cut ends of the warp directly to the cloth stick, one should tie them to a supplementary metal or wooden rod, which is, in turn, tied to the cloth stick (Fig. 515). This permits easy removal and reattachment of the warp yarns for printing.

After the loom has been dressed and warp tension adjusted at the cloth stick, the cords joining the supplemental rod to the cloth stick are removed. The yarn is unwound from the warp beam and extended to its full length on a well-padded table or other flat surface at the front of the loom. The warp yarns should be carefully

of boiling water. After all the dyestuff has dissolved, 600 grams of gum tragacanth is added, and the mixture is allowed to cool. Finally, a solution of 50 grams of tartaric acid and 25 grams of water is stirred into the mixture.

The silk screen is placed on the warp (Fig. 516), and paint or dye is forced through the screen with a rubber squeegee. When more than one color is to be printed, the several screens must be *registered* or aligned, so that all the colors printed in a given portion of the warp fall in the proper relation to one another. A simple method of registering the screens is to affix small pieces of tape to the table under the warp and line up

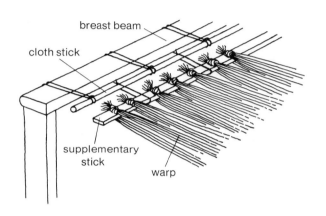

breast beam

cloth stick

supplementary
stick

warp

515–517. Silk screen is a form of stencil printing. A length of silk is stretched tightly in a frame, and all areas that are not to print are stopped out with a substance that closes the pores in the silk. Then, a dye is forced through the screen. A warp should be printed after it has been installed on the loom.

left: 515. A warp that is to be screen printed should be attached to a supplementary cloth stick, which is in turn tied to the cloth stick of the loom. This system permits easy removal and reattachment of the warp yarns.

below: 516. The silk screen is placed on the warp, and paint or dye is forced through it.

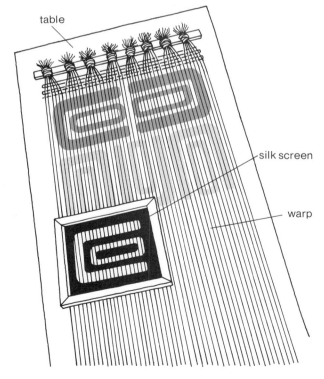

table

silk screen

warp

arranged, so that the horizontal spacing is, as nearly as possible, equal to the sleyed width at the reed. The printing can now begin.

Ready-made silk screens can be purchased in a variety of sizes and with screen meshes of varying density. One screen will be needed for each color included in the planned design. There are several methods used for preparing the stencil, but perhaps the easiest is to paint a nonporous material directly on the silk screen in all the areas that are not to print. A commercial substance called WaterSol is recommended for this purpose. WaterSol solidifies to close the pores in the silk, but it can be removed easily in cold water. An alternate stop-out can be made from equal parts of water and LePage's Original Glue.

Commercially sold textile paint is excellent for making the print. However, an acid dye for wool or silk yarns can be made by dissolving 40 grams of dyestuff and 50 grams of glycerin in 10 ounces

each screen with the tape marks. After the warp has been printed, the paint or dye is allowed to dry completely. If an acid dye has been used, the yarns must be steamed, rinsed, and redried. Then the warp is rolled carefully back onto the warp beam, the supplementary rod is reattached to the cloth stick, and weaving begins.

There is almost always a certain amount of yarn slippage during the beaming and weaving processes, which causes sharp outlines to become blurred. For this reason, large, simple designs are often the most successful. Because the yarns invariably rotate to some extent during weaving, the pattern is nearly as complete on the reverse side as on the face. One can take advantage of this effect in a room divider or other freestanding project.

The wall hanging reproduced in Figure 517 was created by interweaving grasses and fine cotton yarns with a screen-printed warp. A more complex technique was utilized to produce the fabric in Plate 33 (p. 286). The warp is white linen stenciled in red, and the weft is chartreuse silk. Background areas were hand painted with blue dye, which suggests yet another method for coloring individual yarns or small pattern areas. The potential for yarn printing, in terms of the handcraftsman, has barely been explored.

517. SHIRLEY E. HELD. Wall hanging with screen-printed warp. 1961. Native grasses and cotton yarns, 4'1" × 1'3".

part five
DESIGN IN FABRIC CONSTRUCTION

19 Elements and Principles of Design

Design . . . is the organization of materials and processes in the most productive, economic way, in a harmonious balance of all elements necessary for a particular function.

László Moholy-Nagy, Vision in Motion

Throughout this text the word *design* has been used rather freely, often as a synonym for pattern or motif. No attempt has been made to establish a definition for the concept; in fact, it is in some ways more difficult to *explain* design than it is to *do* it. However, before attempting to catalogue the components of design and the principles that govern its implementation, we must clarify our terminology. Therefore, for purposes of this discussion, design is defined as *the ordered arrangement of parts to make a whole.* The *parts,* in this case, are the raw materials of weaving—the fibers, yarns, and miscellaneous objects the weaver has at his disposal. The *whole* is, of course, the finished product—the wall hanging, sculpture, garment, yardage, or whatever. Order*ed* does not necessarily mean order*ly,* for a tangled mass of yarns may in fact be planned and therefore designed (Fig. 520).

It is impossible to make anything without designing it, either consciously or unconsciously, for design implies a series of choices: the choice of one yarn over another, the choice of one color instead of a second, the choice of a particular size or shape. The weaver's concern is not with designing *per se,* but with creating an *effective* design—one that fulfills the requirements of the item to be woven and that simultaneously satisfies the artist's aesthetic goals.

Design is sometimes divided into two categories—*structural* and *decorative.* The first refers to the inner skeleton, the "body" of an object, the second to its surface treatment or embellishment, which can be varied without modifying the structure itself. Yet structural and decorative design are inseparable; neither can exist without the other. One cannot embellish the surface of nothing, nor can one create a structure with no surface, and that surface must have some degree of decorative design, however simple. Weaving exemplifies this bond especially well, for both structural and decorative design are carried by the yarns. If the two kinds of design are to be divided at all, it is only to illustrate their very intimate connection, for effective design results only when decoration expresses structure and structure supports decoration.

A concept related to design is that of *form*, which at one time was considered to be synonymous with shape. However, the form·of an object encompasses not only its external shape but its inner structure, the mode of expression, the interrelationship of parts. To quote László Moholy-Nagy, that most articulate spokesman of the Bauhaus:

> "Form"—in today's terminology—is reserved for "the mode in which a thing exists or manifests itself" [Oxford Dictionary]. Form is the unity of all elements which produce a synthesis in the different realms of expression, in painting, sculpture, architecture, drama, poetry, motion picture as well as in the technological sphere. "It has form" signifies coherence and structure of a genuine intrinsic arrangement which is defined by the specific way in which the elements were employed.
>
> "Shape" generally defines either an elemental figure or a configuration as visually perceived without analyzing its component parts in a set order. . . . The fewer connotations [shapes] have, the more elemental they are.

Central to Moholy-Nagy's reasoning is the dictum that "form follows function"—that a work of art or industry is not successful if it does not fulfill the purpose for which it is intended. Thus, for example, an umbrella that is physically beautiful but does not keep out the rain is not effectively designed; a chair that is so over-decorated that it discourages sitting fails in its function and therefore in its form. In weaving this notion is best understood in terms of functional objects—place mats, bedspreads, garments, and the like. A furry, high-pile place mat might be interesting and amusing and even attractive, but it would certainly cause the dishes to wobble about. Moreover, such considerations are equally relevant to nonutilitarian items. A wall hanging planned for a particular spot is not effective if its design is so striking that it dominates the whole room, unless, of course, the sole purpose of the room is to display that particular wall hanging.

In creating a woven object—or indeed, anything at all—the individual must work with certain visual elements: shape, line, space, texture, light, and color. Actually, such "elements" can be isolated only in theory; in practice they are inextricably bound together. Shape cannot exist without establishing a line, and color is meaningless in the absence of light. Space is delineated by the presence of shapes and lines. Nevertheless, one must identify these elements in order to see their relationships in a work of art.

DESIGN ELEMENTS

Shape

The shape of any object is fairly self-evident. Terms such as round, square, oval, or cubic are more or less universally understood. Certain of the items a weaver will undertake to produce have their shapes predetermined: a place mat is usually rectangular within a limited range of size; a tablecloth must cover the table; a garment conforms generally to the outlines of the body. But what of a sculpture or wall hanging? Will it be two dimensional or three, rigidly geometric or free form? In planning—that is, in designing—the shape of an object the weaver must take into account the limitations of his equipment and his materials.

A loom-constructed web will have its size and shape restricted to some extent by the size and complexity of the loom. A very fine yarn may be unable to support a large sculptural construction. When a weaving contains pictorial elements, its shape can either control or be controlled by those elements. For instance, the narrative scenes of 17th-century tapestries are contained by the traditional square or oblong shape of the fabric (Fig. 109). All action exists within those perimeters. On the other hand, the figure in Dorian Zachai's tapestry (Fig. 316) actually controls the outline of the weaving. In the end, the shape of a woven object is viable if it fulfills the purpose—functional, aesthetic, or both—that object is to serve.

Line

Line is closely related to shape, for the external contours of an object create a line. In basic mathematical terms, a line is an extension of a point. It can move in any direction, be straight, curved, or convoluted. A woven object displays many kinds of lines. When the warp and weft yarns are heavy, contrasting in color, or loosely

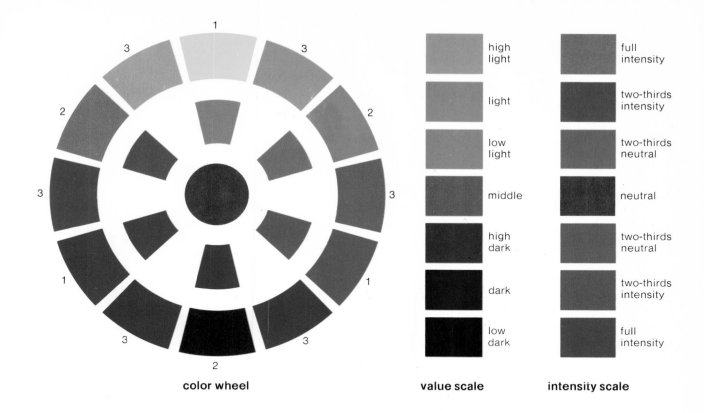

color wheel

	high light
	light
	low light
	middle
	high dark
	dark
	low dark

value scale

	full intensity
	two-thirds intensity
	two-thirds neutral
	neutral
	two-thirds neutral
	two-thirds intensity
	full intensity

intensity scale

Plate 34. The traditional color wheel takes as its primary colors red, yellow, and blue. In this representation, the numeral 1 indicates a primary color, 2 a secondary color, 3 a tertiary color. The value scale shows seven different values for the hue green; the intensity scale demonstrates levels of saturation for orange and blue, approaching neutral gray.

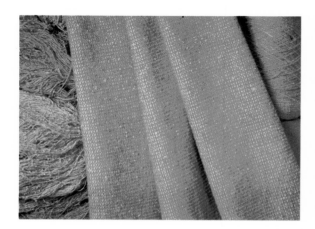

Plate 35. LARSEN DESIGN STUDIO. *Connemara*. Power-loomed wool fabric. Jack Lenor Larsen, New York.

Plate 36. LARSEN DESIGN STUDIO. *Four Courts* Power-loomed casement fabric. Jack Lenor Larsen, New York.

Plate 37. NEDA AL-HILALI. Decoration on vest, detail of back. 1970–72.
Knotted fiber on leather. Courtesy the artist.

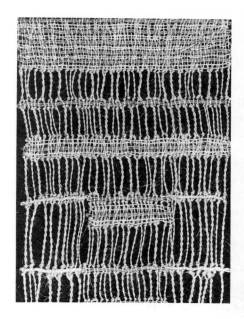

above: 518. SANDOR TOTH. Hanging, detail. 1970. Sisal and hemp in mixed technique, 1′7½″ × 8′1½″ overall. Courtesy the artist.

above: 519. AHZA COHEN. *Arrow in Four Parts.* 1969. Tapestry of wool and rayon on cotton warp, 9′2″ × 8′6″. From *Objects: USA,* Johnson Wax Collection of Contemporary Crafts, Racine, Wis.

woven, they can produce a distinct line (Fig. 518). By comparison, the warp and weft in Ahza Cohen's tapestry (Fig. 519) are so tightly meshed as to be imperceptible except at very close range. Here the strong vertical, horizontal, and diagonal lines are created with contrasting colors. An arrangement of textures or patterns can similarly describe a line within the woven form.

One often speaks of the *quality* of a line, the characteristics implied by such adjectives as broad, narrow, bold, sketchy, crisp, delicate, smooth, and so forth. When the warp and weft yarns describe a line, the yarns themselves establish its quality. A fine carpet warp is very different in appearance from a slub, chenille, or bouclé yarn, yet each produces a single continuous line. Similarly, the lines created by color, texture, or pattern areas can exhibit many different qualities.

Another variable of lines is their *direction*—vertical, horizontal, diagonal. In general, horizontal lines are associated with calmness and repose, vertical lines with force and stability, and

diagonal lines with action, interrupted motion, or anxiety. The viewer can readily perceive a difference of "feeling" between the horizontal bands in Figure 519 and the dynamic upward thrust of the stripes in the upper right corner. Of course, such interpretations are by no means absolute, for the impact of a work is influenced by other factors—color, texture, shape. Line is a very powerful tool, which the designer must learn to control for his own purposes.

Space

Space is the three-dimensional volume in which form occurs. It is also the distance between forms, a condition that changes constantly when form is set in motion. Space is often described as *positive* or *negative,* the positive referring to form

Elements and Principles of Design   305

and the negative to the void between forms. On a flat surface considerations of space involve the relationship of forms to one another and in some cases the impression of three-dimensional space created by means of perspective and other optical devices (Fig. 101). In a free-form sculpture the problem of space becomes somewhat more complex, for the object's space includes not only the relationship of forms and the area between them but the whole environment of the sculpture. When we approach a large sculptured hanging and move around or inside it, we become part of its space and interact with it in ever-changing ways (Fig. 520).

Texture

Texture refers to the surface quality of an object. The most obvious form of texture is *tactile,* the feeling of smooth, rough, grainy, hairy, rippled, or whatever that we experience when we run our hands over a surface. If we were to touch one of Barbara Shawcroft's "interchangeable forms"

(Fig. 521), our fingers would transmit the sensation of "fuzzy" or "hairy" that the artist has contrived with her use of horsehair, mohair, and rough wool yarns. Yet, in a sense, this texture is *visual,* for we know just by looking at a photograph of Shawcroft's forms more or less what they would feel like. An elaborate learning process begun at birth has trained us to recognize by sight alone textures that are essentially tactile. Much of the charm of rya rugs, for example, derives from the impression of warmth and luxuriousness that is created when we see them, even before we touch or walk upon them (Pls. 19, 20, pp. 195–196).

There is another class of textures that are predominantly or entirely visual, exemplified by the Larsen Design Studio's *Galaxy* (Fig. 522). This fabric presents a distinctly grainy, pebbled ap-

below: 520. *Entanglements,* a participatory event of the *Fiber as Medium* symposium, 1971, cosponsored by the University of California, Los Angeles, and the Pasadena Art Museum.

create an impression of warmth, crisp linens and silks a sense of coolness. The designer must be aware of subtle reactions to texture—both visual and tactile—and the way in which it can enhance his work.

pearance, yet the surface is absolutely smooth to the touch. A more sophisticated interpretation of known facts enables us to translate the sensation of touching a handful of grain or pebbles into a purely visual experience. Texture of this sort is usually created through the use of color or pattern. For example, an all-black or all-white surface provides little visual texture, but by placing black on white or white on black in selected areas or in prearranged patterns, one can simulate a wide variety of textures.

Texture is of great importance in weaving, particularly with utilitarian objects. A garment or upholstery fabric that is to come in contact with the body must be pleasing to the touch as well as to the eye, or its function is violated. Psychological response to texture is almost as powerful as to color. Certain textures repel us, others make us long to stroke them; furry piles

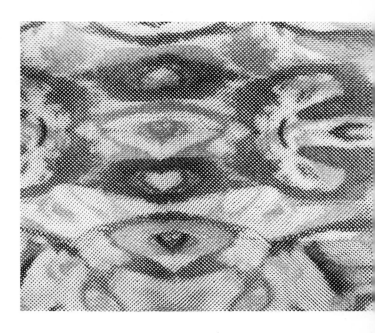

Color is far and away the most complex of the visual elements. Many scientists have taken as their life's-work the investigation of color phenomena. While the modern textile designer has little need for an in-depth study of color theory, some knowledge of the characteristics of colors, and how they interact, will be useful.

In its purest sense, color is the prismatic breakdown of white light into separate hues—red, orange, yellow, green, blue, and violet (Fig. 523). Black is the absence of light and therefore of color. Strictly speaking, black and white are not colors at all, but since they are used as such in everyday life, they can be considered along with the "real" colors.

Color is implicit in everything, for the eye cannot separate an object from its background unless there is some color contrast. This contrast may be of *hue*, of *value*, or of *intensity*, the three color dimensions or qualities that are generally identified by color theorists.

Hue   The pure state of any color is referred to as its *hue*. For example, *red* is the name of a hue, and when we speak of red as a hue we mean a pure red, unmodified and unmixed. A hue is considered *primary* when it cannot be mixed from other colors. Generations of color theorists have disagreed about what the primary hues actually are, although there always seem to be three. To a physicist red, green, and blue are the basic colors, while in pigments the primaries are magenta, yellow, and turquoise—the bases for mixing all other colors. Despite these differences of opinion, color theory can be understood equally well in any of the various systems.

The traditional color wheel (Pl. 34, p. 303) takes as its primary colors red, yellow, and blue. The combination of two primary colors in the proper amounts will create a *secondary* color, such as orange—the product of red and yellow. *Tertiary* or *intermediate* colors derive from the combination of adjacent primary and secondary colors. Red-orange, yellow-green, and blue-violet are examples of tertiary colors. An infinite range of colors can be produced by combining the primary hues in different proportions—1:1, 1:2, 1:3, 1:4, and so on, until the variations are not discernible even to the eye of a trained colorist.

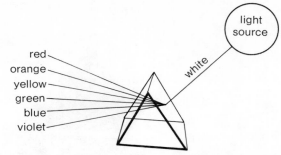

above: 523. Color is the prismatic breakdown of white light into separate hues.

Value   Value is the lightness or darkness of a color. The *normal value* of any hue is the state in which it appears in the prismatic spectrum produced by white light. According to this criterion, yellow is a light color and blue is a dark color. However, any color can exhibit a range of values that deviate from the normal value of the hue. Colors that are lighter than the norm are referred to as *tints;* those that are darker are called *shades.* Pink is a tint—a deviation toward the light end of the spectrum—of red.

Albert Munsell has devised a scale of values that helps to standardize the range of colors and to measure value. On this vertical scale, white is at the top and black at the base. Between the two extremes are seven distinct gradations (Pl. 34, p. 303), referred to as high light, light, low light, middle value, high dark, dark, and low dark. It is possible to establish the normal value of any color in its appropriate position on the value scale. Thus, pure green is the equivalent of low light, while tints or shades of green fall at other points on the scale. Similarly, pure yellow is equal to high light, yellow-green to light, orange to low light, red-orange and blue-green to middle value, red and blue to high dark, red-violet and blue-violet to dark, and violet to low dark. Any variation from these positions constitutes a change of value.

Intensity   The third dimension of color is variously called *intensity, chroma,* or *saturation.* It refers to the relative purity or grayness of a color. A hue can be bright or dull by degrees, depending upon the amount of contamination by a dissimilar color. For example, yellow would contaminate violet, since there is no yellow in pure violet; therefore, a violet with much yellow mixed in would exhibit a *low degree of saturation* (or intensity or chroma). Pure yellow, by contrast, has high intensity. By combining equal parts of the three primary colors, one produces a *neutral*—theoretically gray, but in practice often a muddy brown.

Color in Weaving   The textile arts are unique in their employment of many fine strands of color. Two or more colors woven intimately into a web tend to merge and blend at a distance. The equal distribution of two yarns that are pure but contrasting in color can result in a neutral color effect. For instance, if a warp is all of orange and a weft entirely blue, the completed fabric may give the impression of a neutral when viewed straight on, but turning the fabric slightly on the bias will cause either blue or orange to emerge as the dominant color. When the hues of warp and weft are vividly contrasting, the mixed color may sparkle and vibrate.

To the viewer with a trained eye, color can be observed in all but pure black and white. Dull colors or grays nearly always reflect some hue. We speak of "warm" grays that perhaps contain some yellow, or "cool" grays that show traces of green or blue. Neutrals are very important to the contemporary handweaver, but they are seldom mere grays and browns. Like the bark of a weathered tree, the soft neutrals, under close scrutiny, reveal the mellow tones of many colors.

Colors are almost magical in use. If we stare at something red for a few minutes and then look away toward a white surface, we see an afterimage that is green. This effect is produced because the eye becomes color fatigued. For much the same reason, yellow placed against green will not look the same as yellow placed against red.

When two closely related hues are laid side by side, the intensity of each is reduced by means of *simultaneous contrast*. Each original hue becomes cloaked in a veil of its complement and thereby is grayed to a certain extent. On the other hand, when two *contrasting* hues are adjacent to one another, each becomes more brilliant, because it has acquired a small portion of the other hue's complement. In general, black tends to make all hues appear more intense. Often, the use of several closely related hues can produce greater sparkle than a single color (Pl. 35, p. 303).

Everyone has intuitive and psychological reactions to color, and the designer can exploit these reactions in choosing the yarns for a particular project. Reds and yellows seem to suggest "warm," while blues and greens give one an impression of "cool" (Pl. 36, p. 303). Light values appear cooler than dark values. In general, warm colors seem more aggressive and advancing; cool colors tend to recede. Dark values are "heavier" than light values. Bright colors have a greater impact on the viewer than dull colors, so a relatively small proportion of bright color can be incorporated into a weaving, and the result will still be stimulating. The association of hues that are all of the same intensity creates the greatest possible force.

There are several ways that colors can be varied without actually changing their hue components. Chief among them is the alteration of surface texture to produce lights and shadows that subtly affect the color. A shiny surface reflects light, while a soft or pile fabric tends to absorb light, thus darkening the color.

The designer will find unlimited inspiration by observing the ways in which color and texture combine in nature. Perhaps the most important thing to know about color is that *any* hue can be employed successfully in a woven object and any two or more colors can be combined, provided their values, intensities, and proportional relationships are handled with sensitivity.

DESIGN PRINCIPLES

The principles of design are guidelines to be considered in developing a design. They are not rules, for there can be no rules governing imagination and ingenuity. In fact, the skilled designer may deliberately contradict some or all of these principles to create a particular effect. More often, the principles of design will be applied to a work by some critic or viewer *after* the work has been completed, for they are so much a part of the artist's training and background that he has unconsciously observed them in tracing his idea. The experienced craftsman does not mutter to himself, "Now I'm doing proportion," or "It's time to put in some balance." One is much more likely to hear the artist say, "Yes, that works," or "That doesn't work." Whether a design "works" is a highly subjective and empirical judgment based partly on such nebulous concepts as taste and aesthetic sensibility, as well as long observation of designs that *do* work. It would certainly be possible to formulate a design that embodies to perfection all the textbook principles, and yet produce an object that nobody would bother to look at. Nevertheless, virtually every work of art makes at least a token reference to the principles of design in either a positive or a negative manner. Works that attempt to shock, puzzle, astonish, or even repel the viewer in order to convey an idea do so because they violate conventions of "good" design. In fact, terms like "good" and "bad" are seldom used in relation to design, because they imply a universal standard that simply does not exist. Rather, one speaks of a design as being *effective* or *successful,* and any design is so when it satisfies the artist's aesthetic impulse and communicates with the audience he hopes to reach.

There is little agreement about just how many design principles there are. Some writers put the number at five, others at three or six. Actually, these differences are just a problem in semantics, for one authority will divide into two sections a concept that is lumped together by someone else. For purposes of this discussion, four seems an adequate and understandable number, those four being *proportion, balance, emphasis,* and *rhythm.*

Proportion

Proportion refers to the relationships of size or other measurable quantity among the elements in a design or between an object and its environment. For example, if the weaver plans to design an area rug, he must consider the proportion of the pattern or color areas to the overall size of the rug and—if its destination is known—the proportion of the whole rug to the part of the floor it will occupy. A related term, which is generally employed to indicate specific dimensions or a mathematical ratio, is *scale.* Almost everyone is familiar with the devices of *scale models* and *scale drawings,* which imply that regardless of the size of the finished product, the relationships of the individual members will remain the same. A tapestry cartoon that is scaled $1:2$ could be woven 1 foot by 2 feet, 2 feet by 4 feet, and so on. If the cartoon contains a figure that occupies half the space of the design, the same figure will always occupy half the space, even if the tapestry measures 50 by 100 feet.

The scale of any woven form must always be considered in relation to something else, for scale is a relative concept. For example, if one were to stand in front of Claire Zeisler's *Red Forest* (Fig. 552), the work would seem very large in scale compared to the human body. Yet if the same construction were hung inside a much larger enclosure, such as an airline terminal, it would be smaller in scale relative to its environment. Similarly, each individual yarn is small in scale compared to the knotting as a whole.

The term *out of proportion* has become part of our everyday vocabulary. When someone belabors a point that his companions deem trivial, they speak of his interest as being "out of proportion" to the significance of the subject. The same principle can be applied to a design. For example, if a small circle is placed in a very large square (Fig. 524), it seems out of proportion to the overall field of the design. However, if the little circle is repeated many times or is enlarged considerably, the proportion becomes more harmonious (Fig. 525). The forms in Figure 311 are very large, but their proportion to the overall size of the tapestry is elegant and satisfying. By contrast, a tapestry by Aurélie Nemours (Fig. 526), which is very similar in actual size, contains tiny squares and rectangles, but the repetition and variety of the forms creates a sense of proportion.

left: 524. If a small circle is placed in a very large square, it seems out of proportion to the overall field of the design.

right: 525. When the circle is enlarged or repeated many times, the proportion becomes more harmonious.

 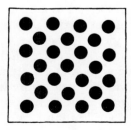

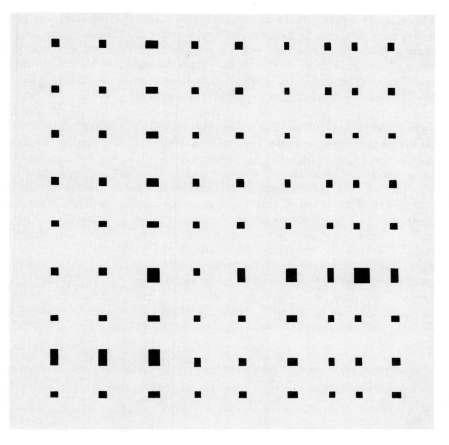

526. Aurelie Nemours design, executed at Aubusson by Atelier Picaud. *Acrux.* 1971. Tapestry of cotton and wool, 11'8" square. Mobilier National, Paris, courtesy International Biennial of Tapestries, Lausanne, 1971.

These two examples are fairly extreme. In most cases, the proportional relationships in a woven object are more subtle and complex: the proportion of one yarn to another; that of one color to a second, a third, a fourth, or more; the relationship between open areas and sections of solid weaving; the width of stripes or the scale of a plaid; the proportion of figures or patterns to each other and to the web as a whole—all these are important design considerations. Often, a slightly altered proportion can change the whole appearance of a design. A "sense of proportion" is largely intuitive and is frequently arrived at by trial and error. This is one instance in which predesigning on paper can be a real advantage to the weaver.

Balance

Balance is the condition that exists when all forces present are in a state of equilibrium. In a woven form, or in any work of art, balance is achieved when the *visual weight* of one side of the composition equals the visual weight of the other side. This concept of visual weight includes many factors: the colors (hues, values, and intensities), textures, sizes, shapes, and lines present in the various pattern areas. A large light area might be effectively balanced by two smaller dark areas, because the visual weights are equal.

A total absence of balance is comparable to the experience of singing "do-re-mi-fa-sol-la-ti . . . ." Most people feel a sense of incompleteness, even anxiety, and are literally forced to add the final "do." Some woven constructions take advantage of this phenomenon, deliberately leaving the viewer vaguely uneasy. But it is human nature to seek balance, and most weavers try to achieve it in their work.

Balance is often divided into two categories: symmetrical and asymmetrical. *Symmetrical* balance, occasionally called formal balance, refers to a composition in which the two sides form a mirror image of one another (Pl. 37, p. 304).

There is a tendency for symmetrically balanced designs to give the impression of calm, repose, even dignity, but of course this is not always the case. When a weaving contains energetic curves and lines or bold, vibrant colors, it will not be really restful no matter how perfect its symmetry.

A composition that exhibits *asymmetrical* or informal balance requires a bit more sophistication on the part of both designer and viewer. The two halves (or four quadrants, or whatever) of the work are not identical, yet their visual weights are sufficiently alike to balance the composition (Fig. 527). The effect is one of movement and spontaneity. This is not to say that asymmetrical balance is in any way "better" or more interesting, for extremely sensitive and challenging designs can be set within the limits of absolute symmetry. However, asymmetrical balance does present the designer with yet another problem to solve. The visual weights carried by the two sides of a design can be equalized by any number of devices—by adjusting color, texture, size, shape, or the placement of forms.

Without implying any criterion of effective design, it is safe to say that symmetrical balance is easier to do. One simply repeats in the second half of the design what one has done in the first. Like proportion, asymmetrical balance is largely a matter of intuition and judgment. The artist is not dealing with measurable quantities, such as "two small dark circles equal 27½ and one large red triangle equals 8 visual weights." After much experimentation the designer learns to sense when a composition is balanced, and in this case, too, designing on paper is very helpful.

Emphasis

Emphasis suggests that one particular part of a design catches and holds the viewer's eye more

left: 527. MILDRED FISCHER. *Panel.* 1958. Mixed yarns and mohair on linen, 45½ × 34″. Courtesy the artist.

below: 528. LARSEN DESIGN STUDIO. *Carrickmacross.* Double weave of wool in patterned Bawneen (Irish tweed), a traditional wool cloth of Ireland. Jack Lenor Larsen, Inc., New York.

than any other. One's attention is directed—either gradually or immediately—to some focal point or points and is held there.

A *repeat design* such as is found in most yardage, wallpaper, and upholstery fabric, has no real point of emphasis, except to a limited degree within each unit of the motif (Fig. 528). The size of the repeat can vary from a fraction of an inch to several square feet, but the principle remains the same—identical forms repeated over and over in a theoretically infinite space. Interest is created by the flow of rhythm from one motif to the next, so an exaggerated point of emphasis in each pattern area is unnecessary or undesirable. When a small-scale repeat design is viewed from a distance, it often gives the impression of overall texture, rather than discrete pattern.

A *unit design,* on the other hand, generally has some focal point and often subsidiary focal points. Most of the individual projects a weaver will undertake—wall hangings, sculptures, tap-

above: 529. Luis Feito, design, woven at the Atelier de Saint-Cyr. *Guadarrama.* 1971. Tapestry, 6′3″ × 8′5″. Collection La Demeure, Paris, courtesy International Biennial of Tapestries, Lausanne, 1971.

estries, place mats, pillow covers, rugs, even some garments—are based on the unit or self-contained design. The point of emphasis can be created by several means, including a dominant color, a change of texture, the convergence of sight lines, a contrasting shape or size, or an unexpected detail. The center of interest in Figure 529 is fairly obvious even to the casual observer; it is all but in the very center of the composition. Moreover, this focal placement is reinforced by the fact that the circle is the only classic form in the whole design. The opposing shapes embrace and direct attention to it. By comparison, the focal point in Ruben Eshkanian's *Haystack* (Pl. 21, p. 197) is masterfully subtle, because it is practically invisible. Only after the viewer has studied the tapestry for a while does he find his eye drawn back again and again to the tiny cluster of bright-colored pile yarns in the lower left corner.

The point of emphasis in a design allows the viewer's eye to rest momentarily and enriches by contrast the less demanding areas of the composition. In general, its strength is in proportion to the subtlety or impact of the design as a whole. Lacking a focal point, the unit design runs the risk of becoming mere background for something else that is more compelling.

Rhythm

Rhythm is a sense of continuity or recurrence, a succession of spaced intervals. In a visual design rhythm causes the eye to travel from one part of the composition to another until the entire work has been perceived.

In weaving rhythm can take a variety of forms, just as in music we recognize several kinds of rhythm—waltz, march, syncopated, and so on. The smooth flow of gently curved lines provides quite a different rhythm from the staccato of sharply angled turns or spaced individual forms (Pl. 37, p. 304). Rhythm helps to create the particular atmosphere or expression of any design.

Aside from these four principles, we could cite other factors that contribute to effective design, such as honesty of materials or relevance to one's time. For a weaver to copy any of the designs in Part I of this text would be no more appropriate than an Athenian temple constructed at the corner of Broadway and 42nd Street, or a rock group playing madrigals. Designs that are relevant to some period in history are useful for study or even experimentation, but they do not express the unique character, feeling, and experience of the 20th century.

In terms of weaving, honesty of materials suggests that a yarn is chosen for its own innate qualities, because it can best fulfill the requirements of a certain project. It does not make sense to use nylon yarns when wool would do a better job, simply because man-made yarns are "modern." Plastic that is made to look like wood remains imitation wood, but plastic used as plastic can be exciting and contemporary. The craftsman should acquaint himself thoroughly with all the available materials, so that he is in a position to choose the one that is best suited to his needs in any situation. Each provides its own kind of comfort, durability, and aesthetic potential, and each has its limitations.

All these guidelines and principles are worthless when one element is missing: the inspiration and imagination of the designer. That is the one quality we cannot categorize under neat headings and subheadings, yet somehow we always know when it is not there.

20 *Designing for the Loom*

All design, great or small, contains elements of compromise.

Dorothy Liebes in Craft Horizons,
March/April 1964

The preceding chapter explored design in terms of selected elements and principles. However, designing for the loom—as for any other medium—can also be considered as a series of *decisions:* decisions about the nature of the product to be woven; the fiber, color, and texture of the yarns; the form or pattern of the weaving (or both); the mechanics of the loom setup; and the final assembly of the woven fabric. Each of these decisions serves to limit the range of choices for those that follow. For example, the type of fabric to be woven determines, to some extent, the selection of a yarn; the characteristics of the yarn limit the form of the weaving or the other way around; the yarn and the pattern prescribe the loom setup; and all of the foregoing control the finished appearance of the web. From this point of view, design can be seen as an infinite range of choices, gradually narrowing until each element has been harmoniously incorporated into an end-product.

DESIGN DECISIONS

Choosing the Project

When a weaver is filling a commission, the nature of the product is determined for him. Often, the client will also have specific ideas about color, materials, size, shape, and other variables. However, the student or independent weaver, working to achieve his or her own expression, has no such guidelines. Obviously, the first group of projects to be eliminated from consideration are those that are beyond the weaver's level of experience or the complexity of the loom at his disposal. This still leaves a huge body of potential projects, some of which are described in the second section of this chapter. The weaver's own taste and preferences are perhaps the most compelling factors in this choice, but these preferences should be tempered by practicality.

A question that many weavers never grapple with is: What is the point of weaving this product by hand? The mere fact of being able to say "this is handwoven" seems hardly adequate when one realizes the great expenditure of labor involved in any handwoven object. There are,

315

in fact, many items that *can* be more efficiently produced by machine, and the simple duplication of power-loomed fabrics is not a worthy investment of the craftsman's time. The handmade product must exhibit some extra quality, some feature of design or execution that would be impossible to achieve on an industrial level.

Selecting the Yarns

Once the nature of the project has been established, the next step may be either selection of appropriate yarns or the creation of a pattern or form. One or the other can come first, or the two elements may be conceived simultaneously in the designer's mind.

When a utilitarian product is to be woven, the choice of yarns is often the first consideration, for questions of *suitability*—which seldom arise in sculpture or wall hangings—must be dealt with. A coarse, hairy yarn would not be suitable for a scarf or some other garment that will touch the wearer's skin, nor would a very fine, gossamer yarn be appropriate for a cloak that is meant to provide warmth. A tablecloth, place mat, or set of napkins must be constructed from yarns that are easily cleaned; a drapery fabric woven from flammable yarns would clearly be unsuitable.

After the specific requirements of the proposed fabric have been satisfied, one basic rule governs the selection of the materials: The weaver should employ the best-quality yarn he can afford. Labor is the most expensive ingredient in any handcrafted item, and the weaver's production time is the same regardless of whether he uses cheap materials or good ones. No matter how much skill and imagination the weaver contributes, the finished product will reflect the quality of its raw materials.

Deciding Upon Form or Pattern

The equivalent in weaving of an artist's sketchbook is the set of woven samples, carefully marked for loom setup and yarn types. A generous book of samples will provide endless inspiration, because in many cases a slight change of color, texture, or pattern will transform an insignificant design into something truly exciting. Perhaps a tiny corner of a sample could be expanded into a full-scale design. The weaver must

be willing to experiment, either on paper or on a sampling loom, until all the elements fall into place and the design fulfills his intentions. Of course, many designs are created in transit, so to speak—after the fabric is actually on the loom. The "happy accident" does occur—the slight mistake or sudden change of plans that turns out even better than the original design. But the weaver must have at least a rough idea of what he intends to do, or the results will nearly always be unsatisfactory. The design phase is the most truly creative part of the weaving.

So many options present themselves! Will the fabric be closely packed or loose and supple, solid or openwork, textured or smooth, shaped or rectangular, subtle in color or polychrome, two-dimensional or three, boldly patterned or simple? By weaving a sample or a series of samples with the projected end-product in mind, the designer will soon begin to narrow his range of choices. In the case of a large free-form structure, he may even wish to build a scale model before actually committing great quantities of yarn.

It is rare for the inventive weaver to sit down at the loom without an idea of what he intends to do. Simply by designing and weaving one fabric, he will think of two or five or a dozen other designs to try. Part of the challenge and fascination of weaving is that the craftsman's hands can seldom keep up with his head.

Setting Up the Loom

The choice of a pattern or form limits but does not always dictate the loom mechanics that will be employed to produce it. Often, the same result can be achieved in a variety of ways, and the weaver must decide upon the most economical method. For example, when the design calls for great color variation in one set of yarns, that variation can more easily be introduced in the warp, for after the loom has been dressed, weaving can proceed with a minimum of shuttle changes and references to the design plan. It is not uncommon for a weaver to spend more time in *planning* the loom setup than in actually weaving the web.

The amount of time and energy that will be expended in weaving the fabric is closely related to the complexity of the treadling. Numerous harnesses and shuttles slow the weaving process and also increase the chances of making a mistake. Of course, there are situations in which a very involved treadling pattern is required, but sometimes the desired effect can be produced more easily in some other way. A thorough knowledge of the loom and what it can do may save a great deal of time.

The manner in which the warp yarns are set up on the loom is so crucial to the appearance of the fabric that it deserves special mention. By spacing the warp yarns irregularly—that is, by uneven grouping in the reed—one can create a striped or ridged pattern that is particularly effective in fabrics that are exposed to light, such as room dividers, casements, and lamp shades. Sometimes very fine yarns can be made more versatile by an unusually close sett or even by threading two or three yarns through a single heddle. When highly elastic warp yarns are interspersed with dimensionally stable ones, the warp tension can be controlled fairly well.

In the following section considerations of loom setup and materials are discussed in relation to certain kinds of projects.

PLANNING SPECIFIC ITEMS

Almost anything that is typically made of fiber—and a few things that are not—can be handwoven on the loom. The list that follows presents only the broadest suggestion of potential projects for the handweaver and is in no way exhaustive of the possibilities.

Wall Hangings and Sculpture

It sometimes happens that the design for a wall hanging or sculpture will spring, fully conceptualized, into the weaver's mind. It is all there—motif, shapes and patterns, colors, size and proportions, even the yarn or yarns. All that is necessary is to fit the weave mechanics to this mental picture. On the other hand, the weaver may occasionally enter his studio with the intention of creating a wall hanging but not the slightest clue about how to begin. In most cases, however, the situation falls somewhere between these two extremes. The designer has a germ of an idea that must be expanded and developed into a full-scale plan for a wall hanging. Perhaps he has come upon a new yarn that intrigued him,

or been struck by a special combination of colors. Perhaps he has been inspired by the work of another craftsman, either contemporary or historical. Or, he may simply have noticed a pattern—in another art medium, in some object, in nature, in his immediate environment—that suggested the design for a wall hanging. Whatever the stimulus, this fragmentary idea must somehow be translated into warp and weft, into a satisfying combination of design *elements* that embodies, insofar as appropriate, the design *principles* outlined in the previous chapter.

The approximate size and shape of a wall hanging or sculpture are often among the first variables to be decided. It is difficult to visualize a design without forming some notion of its desirable proportions—a small oblong, a long narrow strip, a massive mural-size tapestry. The oblong shape—a rectangle that is longer in one dimension, hung either vertically or horizontally (Figs. 349, 556)—has long been popular for wall hangings. Yet virtually any size or shape can be worked into an effective design if the various elements are handled sensitively. Most weavers would faint at the suggestion they create a wall hanging nearly a football field long and less than 2 feet high, yet that is precisely what the designers of the *Bayeux Tapestry* (Fig. 74) accomplished nearly a thousand years ago. A three-dimensional sculpture presents the weaver with yet more decisions, for the size and shape must relate not only to a wall but to a whole environment.

The pattern or motif for a wall hanging is another major design question. It may range anywhere from a simply woven rectangle in which the major interest lies in color and shape relationships (Fig. 273) through an elaborate pictorial tapestry (Pl. 18, p. 162). If the weaver intends to plan a wall hanging around abstract or geometric shapes (Fig. 311), he may decide first to sketch the design on paper or even cut out the shapes and rearrange them until he arrives at the best combination. A pictorial design may be subjected to a long series of sketches before the weaver achieves precisely the effect he is seeking. Sometimes the pattern is determined first, and the weave mechanics must be adjusted to correspond; in other cases, the weave is chosen in advance, and only later does the designer consider what he will do with it. Either approach is equally valid. When a specific yarn, color, or

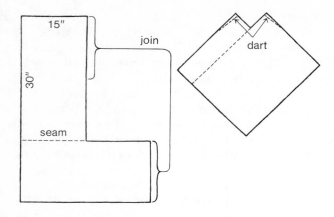

color relationship has been the initial stimulus, the weaver must determine above all how best he can exploit them.

A wall hanging or sculpture is an intensely personal expression on the part of the weaver. A glance at the illustrations in this book, as well as exposure to craft exhibitions and publications, will give the student weaver an idea of how other designer-craftsmen have interpreted fiber as an art medium.

Throughout history many cultures, including the Indians of Peru, have shaped garments on the loom, with a minimum of post-weaving construction—that is, cutting and sewing. The sari of India is an example of such a garment. Today, this practice is gaining new popularity with handweavers (Pl. 38, p. 337). Among the garments that can be fabricated in this manner are ponchos, shirts, scarves, vests, hats, mittens, belts, and neckties. Frequently, a seam or two is all that is needed before the article is ready to wear.

Figure 530 illustrates one method of constructing a poncho—a simple, blanketlike outer garment (Fig. 531). The plan calls for two lengths of fabric each about 15 inches wide and 30 inches long (finished dimensions). Only two seams are required to assemble the poncho, but

above left: 530. Plan for a loom-constructed poncho, based on two lengths of fabric each about 30 × 15″.

below: 531. Loom-constructed poncho with fringe, woven in two sections and seamed at the shoulders.

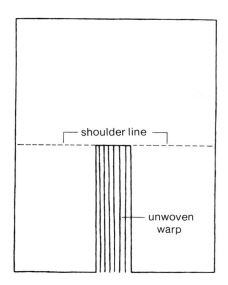

above: 532. A one-piece poncho can be constructed on the loom by leaving the warp yarns unwoven in one section for the neck opening. Button or tie closures at the neckline and under the arms complete the garment.

a dart at the shoulder enhances the fit. Some forethought is necessary to ensure that the design meshes properly when joined length to width. A plaid will be easier to match if it is square, and small patterns join more readily than large ones. A wider loom permits construction of a one-piece poncho (Fig. 532), with the warp yarns left unwoven in one section to allow for a neck opening. Button or tie closures at the neckline and under the arms complete the garment. The standard measurements can be adjusted to fit the intended wearer and could even be scaled down to make a baby's sweater. Wool and mohair yarns will produce a very warm covering (Fig. 533), while cotton or linen could be used for a lightweight summer wrap. By choosing the yarns and the weave draft with care, one can build a draping quality into the fabric, thus compensating for the loose fit.

A basic shirt or jacket can also be woven in one piece, but this construction requires a bit of

right: 533. Pisac-type poncho, Chahuaytiri, Peru. 1967. Wool, 4′6⅝″ × 4′1½″. American Museum of Natural History, New York (on loan from Grace Goodell). This poncho was made in two pieces and seamed down the center.

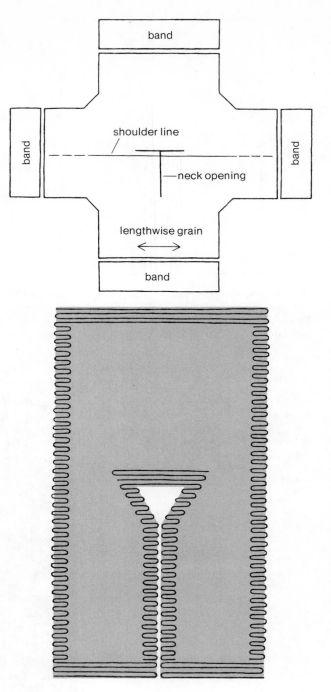

above: 534. Loom-constructed wool jacket with card-woven trim at neckline, front, and armholes.

above right: 535. Plan for a basic one-piece shirt or jacket with a decorative band around the bottom.

right: 536. Plan for a straight vest with a laid-in trim around all edges.

cutting and sewing (Fig. 534). The pattern in Figure 535 allows for a decorative band— perhaps card or inkle woven—around the bottom of the shirt, which improves the fit at the hipline. A T-shape slit is cut in the center for the neck opening.[1]

One of the simplest garments to make is a straight vest (Fig. 536), which is woven in one piece and reinforced around the edges with a laid-in technique (see pp. 168–170). The portion of the web that is intended for the neck opening is left unwoven, and the free warps are cut away after the weaving is completed. The sides can be laced or otherwise joined under the arms.

Pile weaves seem particularly appropriate for winter accessories such as hoods, mittens, and muffs, for they provide both actual and psychological warmth. A simple hood can be con-

structed from a rectangular length of fabric stitched in half at one selvedge to form the back seam. The chin ties are added separately.

Scarves, which are often left fringed at the ends, should be woven in such a way that they drape attractively. A tightly packed plain weave would probably result in a too-stiff fabric, unless

the yarns are very fine. Mohair yarns are soft and pleasant to the touch, so they are very popular in scarves. However, since they are elastic, they are easier to handle in the weft, with a more dimensionally stable yarn for the warp. The standard sizes include 15 by 48 inches, 8 by 36 inches, and 10 by 54 inches, not counting the fringe, if any.

Woven fabrics can often be successfully combined with other types of construction. Only the front of the sweater in Figure 537 is woven, in a dukagång pattern; the remainder is knit, with the flat knit material serving as background for the more decorative woven portion, as well as providing a better fit. The same yarn was used for the knitting as for the dominant color in the front. The woven portion is a continuous weft brocade threaded for honeycomb.[2]

Shoulder or hand bags in a wide variety of shapes and sizes can be woven in one piece, with handles added separately (Fig. 538). The bag can be a simple envelope or can be shaped with stiffeners and, if desired, lined on the inside. Tubular weave (see pp. 153–154) provides a very simple construction that is finished on three sides even before the fabric is removed from the loom. An allowance of 2 to 3 inches is left at the top for hemming. The straps could be braided, knotted, card woven, or inkle woven.

above: 537. Sweater of combined weaving and knitting techniques. The front is a dukagång warp brocade in wool.

right: 538. Shoulder bag with card-woven strap. Plain weave, looping, chaining, and overlaid techniques; linen warp, wool weft.

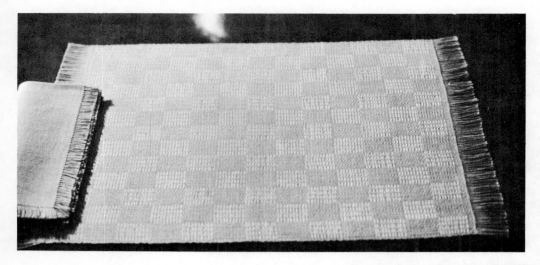

above: 539. RUTH DANIELS. Table mats with matching napkins. Linen, mat size 13 × 19″.

right: 540. Detail of table mat with widely spaced wool warp and corn husk weft.

below right: 541. DOROTHY LIEBES for Goodall Mills. Casement fabric of mohair and linen, powerloomed. Courtesy Dorothy Liebes Design, New York.

Table Linens

The term *linen* is a convention used to describe domestic textiles. Actually, tablecloths, napkins, and place mats can be woven from any flat, smooth fiber (Fig. 539). For a greater textural interest, a place mat can even be woven from raffia, grasses, or corn husks (Fig. 540), provided the surface is level. The only requirements are that the fabrics be rather firm and launder easily. The standard sizes for table linens are:

tablecloth: 52 inches square
                52 by 70, rectangular or oval
                60 by 84, rectangular or oval
                60 inches round

place mats: 13 by 19 inches

napkins: dinner, 18 inches square
              luncheon, 14 inches square
              tea, 12 inches square
              cocktail, 5 by 8 inches

Of course, these sizes can be adjusted to fit an unconventional table or preference. In all cases an allowance must be made for hems and—on the place mats—a fringe, if desired. Sets of napkins or place mats can be woven on a single continuous warp and cut apart after weaving. Place mats need not be identical in design to comprise a set; often they are woven from the same yarns but with a slightly different pattern. Clearly, a striking unit design would be wasted when the mat is covered by china, so the pattern is generally rather subdued, with color providing the major interest.

Yardage

Handwoven dress goods are no longer the major output of the loom, as was the case until the early part of this century, but many weavers still specialize in custom yardage. The fabric for men's garments is generally woven to between 27 and 30 inches in width (plus allowances for shrinkage and draw-in), while women's yardage is woven to 36 or 42 inches. It is a bit difficult to weave wool or other bulky yardage on a table loom, because the cloth beam will not accommodate great quantities of woven fabric. However, if a garment requiring many yards of wool material is planned, this difficulty can be overcome by laying out the pattern in advance and calculating manageable segments of fabric that correspond to the cutting arrangement. Each portion is then woven individually.

Drapery and Upholstery Fabric

Drapery fabric presents a unique challenge to the weaver: The material must be just as attractive when it is hung in multiple folds as when it is flat (Fig. 541). In addition to being relatively nonflammable and easy to clean, the casement or drapery fabric should offer special light-transmitting or light-blocking qualities, depending upon the use for which it is intended. Some drapery materials are designed to block out light altogether, while others merely screen the light and are either transparent or translucent. In the latter event, a subdued line or pattern can add visual interest while still maintaining the fabric's role as background for the more striking elements in the room. The drapery fabric should be sleyed as wide as possible on the loom, and particular attention must be paid to making the selvedges even and smooth.

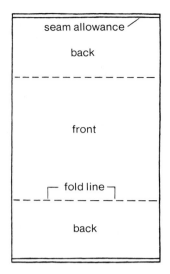

above: 542. Plan for a pillow cover seamed down the center of the back.

The finished width of upholstery fabric should be at least 32 inches, which is the standard size for cushions, including a seam allowance. Therefore, the web would be sleyed to about 36 inches to account for shrinkage and draw-in. A firm, compact, and abrasion-resistant fabric, with no long floats on the surface, will give the longest wear. Cotton is the most common warp material, but linen or certain man-made fibers might also be used successfully. Considerations of scale are important in designing fabric for a specific piece of furniture, because a large, bold pattern could easily overwhelm a delicate chair.

Home Furnishings

The handweaver will find ample grist for his mill in the area of home-furnishing accessories. Pillow covers, lamp shades, screens, dividers, throws, and rugs are only a few of the possibilities.

A pillow cover makes a good beginning project, but its design can be sophisticated enough to challenge even the most experienced weaver (Pl. 39, p. 337). Pillows can be woven flat and sewn to shape after weaving. In order to hide the seam on the reverse side, the weaving begins with a portion of the back, then proceeds through the front of the pillow cover to the remainder of the back (Fig. 542). Alternatively, a tubular weave (see pp. 153–154) can be employed, with ample

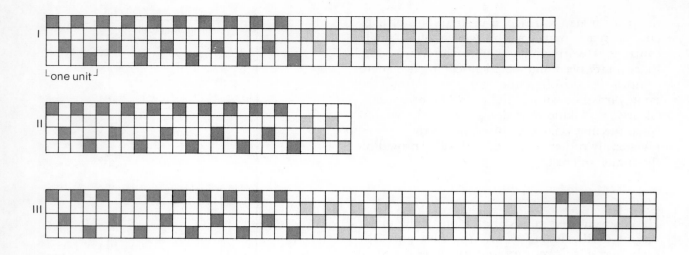

above: 543. Three versions of the summer-and-winter pattern in long-draft form. The draft is read from right to left.

below: 544. The profile drafts corresponding to the long drafts in Figure 543.

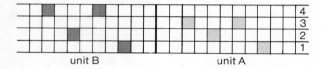

unit B   unit A

seam allowances at either end for turning in. Rug knots, lace weaves, or any other decorative device can be used with the greatest freedom. Since a pillow is by nature an accent, the design can be as bold, as amusing, even as eccentric as the weaver's taste allows.

THE PROFILE DRAFT

A profile draft is a short method of notation for unit pattern weaves. It is often used by designers to enlarge, scale down, or vary a pattern weave and is most helpful in creating original drafts.

The *summer-and-winter* weave is very easily adapted to this method of notation and can be employed to illustrate the concept of a profile draft. Like most unit pattern weaves, it is divided into two design blocks or units, which can be referred to as unit *A* and unit *B*. On a four-harness loom, the summer-and-winter pattern is based on a threading order of 1, 3, 2, 3 (unit *A*), followed by 1, 4, 2, 4 (unit *B*). Each of these units can be repeated as many times as desired before switching to the other unit—from summer to

winter, as it were—and thus pattern variation is achieved. Figure 543 shows three versions of the summer-and-winter threading pattern in the ordinary long-draft form. (The reader will note that the threading order is read from *right to left*—the opposite of the arrangement elsewhere in this text. Since many drafts, especially profile drafts, are read in this manner, the weaver should be able to interpret either system.) The *profile* threading draft that corresponds to all three of these long drafts is demonstrated in Figure 544. By comparing the two illustrations, one can see that in version I unit *A* is repeated five times, then unit *B* five times; in version II unit *A* is threaded only once, followed by five repeats of unit *B*; in version III the sequence is one unit *A*, one unit *B*, five times unit *A*, five times unit *B*. Obviously, these patterns could be varied in many other ways.

The weave draft or draw-down can also be reduced to a profile, which serves as a guide for the pattern arrangement without indicating either the placement or the precise number of individual yarns. Figure 545 shows both the profile draft and the long weave draft for the three threading arrangements given in Figure 543. In each case the profile draft indicates a *relationship*, and the long draft presents a *scale* based on that relationship.

Many pattern books, particularly those dealing with Early American designs, employ the profile system exclusively. The weaver who is interested in more intricate patterning should cultivate a facility in working with profiles.

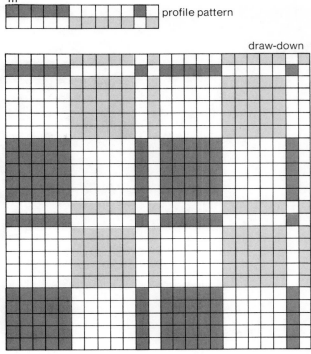

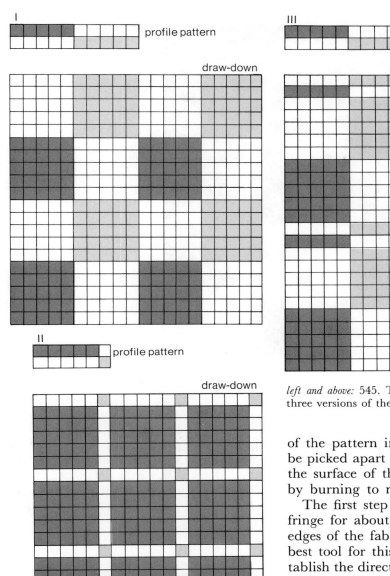

I   profile pattern

draw-down

II   profile pattern

draw-down

III   profile pattern

draw-down

left and above: 545. The long and profile weave drafts for three versions of the summer-and-winter pattern.

WEAVE ANALYSIS

Many designer-craftsmen are interested in historical weaves and like to copy all or a portion of an old pattern for adaptation in their own work. In addition, weavers are occasionally commissioned to replicate fabrics of the past for reconstruction of historical landmarks. It is necessary to have a sample of the original fabric that is large enough to provide at least three repeats of the pattern in both directions and that can be picked apart for analysis. Any pile or nap on the surface of the material should be removed by burning to reveal the underlying structure.

The first step in weave analysis is to ravel a fringe for about ¼ to ½ inch on two adjacent edges of the fabric. A strong yarn needle is the best tool for this purpose. Next, one should establish the direction of warp and weft. The warp yarn can usually be recognized, because it is the stronger, less elastic yarn, it is parallel to the selvedge, and it is more regular in placement.

Patterns are most often based on repetition of individual design units. A pin can be used to mark on the fabric the end points of two units of design in each direction. A corresponding area is then plotted on graph paper in the following manner. The first weft yarn is lifted to determine its horizontal arrangement across the warp within the two pattern units. Each time the warp appears *over* the weft, a mark is made on the paper. The same process is repeated with all the other weft yarns until the pattern area is complete. When very fine yarns are involved, a

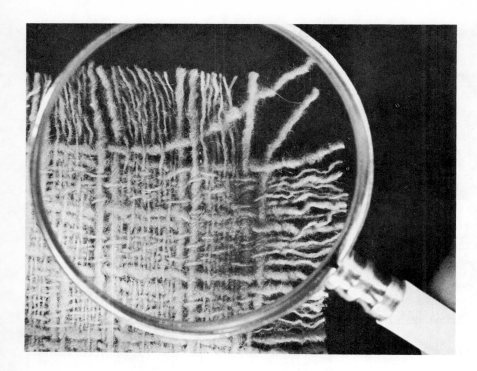

546. To analyze a weave from a sample, one must unravel a fringe on two adjacent edges of the fabric and then plot on graph paper the pattern of interlacement for one unit of the weave. A magnifying glass helps to sort out fine yarns.

magnifying glass will help (Fig. 546). It is wise to indicate the color, weight, and texture of the warp and weft yarns as the work progresses. For future reference a sample of each yarn can be cut and placed beside the graph. After the plotting is complete, the weave draft should resemble the pattern of the actual fabric. From this, a threading and treadling order can be derived.

Designing for the loom can be as simple or as complex as the weaver wishes to make it. Some designer-craftsmen work almost exclusively in plain weave, preferring to create a visual effect with color or texture. Others employ a limited range of yarns but seek ever more intricate patterning. Through constant experimentation, the weaver will eventually find his own direction.

21 *The Contemporary Fiber Craftsman*

The term *handweaving* or even *weaving* limits, to some extent, our comprehension of the work that is being done today in yarn interlacements and fabric construction. Perhaps it is more enlightening—and certainly it is more catholic—to describe individuals engaged in such enterprise as *fiber craftsmen,* a broad designation that embraces not only the handweaver who works with a conventional loom, but also the designer-consultant to industry, the craftsman whose medium is technically a nonwoven form, and the artist whose aesthetic works are based for the most part on fiber or yarn.

There is little agreement about what exactly constitutes a craft, as opposed to an art. Traditionally, media such as weaving, ceramics, glassblowing, metalwork, and so forth have been considered "minor arts," distinguishable from the "major arts" of painting and sculpture. However, many of the works reproduced in this book, though undeniably weaving, are closer to paint-

ing and sculpture than to the average person's notion of a handcrafted object. Similar difficulties arise in the other fields as well. If the construction of a stoneware pot is to be considered a craft, is the design of a large-scale architectural ceramic mural also a craft? If not, where precisely is the dividing line between art and craft? Questions of this nature have been raised time and again, but never answered in a manner that is generally satisfying. Many of the individuals whose work is illustrated in these pages would prefer to be called artists or artist-craftsmen. In the end, we have used the term "craftsmen" in the same sense that one describes a painter or sculptor as a craftsman—a serious worker who understands the tools and materials of his chosen medium and employs them to the best of his ability to create a product that is effective as a design and fulfills the purpose for which it was intended.

Fiber construction in the latter part of the 20th century is an enormous field. The designer-craftsman has at his disposal a plethora of new materials and techniques, while the potential of older, traditional materials and methods has been pushed to limits undreamed of a century ago. Weaving as a profession, as a viable life's-work, has been reestablished in a manner quite different from the guild weaving of three or four hundred years ago. Finally, the subject matter of weaving or of fiber construction in general has undergone a drastic reinterpretation. Indeed, the manipulation of fibers, yarns, and fabrics has undoubtedly changed more in the last two or three decades than it did in the previous two or three millennia.

INNOVATIONS IN FIBER CRAFT

New Materials

Fifty years ago the materials of weaving were essentially those that had been in use for fifty centuries: wool, linen, cotton, and silk. Since the 1920s a tremendous variety of new fibers and

yarns have been developed (Fig. 547), and the end is not in sight. Cecil Lubell, the executive editor of *American Fabrics,* has predicted that textile advances in the coming years will be even more extraordinary. He anticipates:

> More chemistry, more chemical refinement, less physical and psychological dependence on cotton and wool. Thermo-reactive materials which will be cool in summer, warm in winter. Chameleon materials which will change color under light. Fusable materials which can be connected without sewing. Soundproof materials which can be used for building. Impervious materials which can be cleaned by electronic or supersonic devices. Eternal materials with the performance of stainless steel and the aesthetics of textiles, materials which will be flameproof, stainproof, creaseproof, waterproof, antistatic, and will never wear out.[1]

The wonder fabrics and materials described by Lubell are not science fiction. In many cases the technology needed to produce them already exists, a side effect of space research. Even now, fabrics capable of conducting electricity are being woven from carbon/graphite yarns. The cloth has the hand and drape of fiber glass, but electrical power is distributed throughout by means of metallic conductors. The potential end-uses include bedding, heated clothing, and upholstery material for automobiles. In the Soviet Union electrically heated suits are manufactured for outdoor work in temperatures to $-75°F$. At the other extreme, garments fabricated from heat- or fire-resistant fibers are also a by-product of space exploration. A fabric made from graphite yarns, trademarked Thornel, is stronger than steel yet 40 percent lighter than the aluminum in jet airplanes. Thornel yarns are not practical for apparel, since they break when bent over a small radius, but they have many other potential applications.

Experimental Techniques

The search for new methods to fulfill the increasing needs of new forms has encouraged the contemporary designer-craftsman to tap many sources, both old and new. In some cases the

left: 547. ALICE EDELING. *Golden Gate,* sculpture-garment convertible from tunic to trouser-tunic. 1967. Metallic fabric of polyurethane and cotton. Courtesy the artist.

right: 548. A<small>NTONIN</small> K<small>YBAL</small>. Brown Cathedral. c. 1966. Art protis tapestry. Courtesy Art Centrum, Prague.

below right: 549. M<small>ILDRED</small> F<small>ISCHER</small>. Festival. 1970. Fabric fused to pulped linen, 34 × 24″. Courtesy the artist.

handweaver has borrowed a technique originally developed by and for industry; in others, he has reexamined traditional hand processes in light of their potential for 20th-century expression.

Mali   Often referred to as *stitch-knit,* Mali is a revolutionary new textile-manufacturing technique. The Mali machines began operating in East Germany in 1958 and have been described as an enormous boon to the textile industry. One Mali machine, functioning at its optimum efficiency, can produce as much fabric as twelve to sixty power looms in a comparable period of time.

The concept of the *Malimo* machine, one version of the process, is essentially quite simple. Two sets of yarns—a warp and a weft—are laid perpendicular to one another. However, rather than interlacing the two elements, the machine actually stitches them into position in the manner of sewing. Other Mali machines create pile fabrics, web textiles, and yarn.

The possibilities for adapting Mali principles to hand fiber craft were explored in a special tapestry exhibition held in Prague in the mid-1960s. All the tapestries in the show were created by laying yarns or fabric remnants on a heavy nonwoven backing and then stitching the various elements together (Fig. 548). The major advantage of this technique is that it permits a wide range of textural combinations. Furthermore, it overcomes many of the limitations encountered in conventional loom weaving; the designer can reproduce almost any pattern or effect he wishes. Both the design problems and the results are much like those of collage. A related technique was employed by Mildred Fischer in creating *Festival* (Fig. 549). The artist incorporated fragments of woven linen hangings, and fused these in a papermaking machine with pulped linen from warp thrums to form a single fiber sheet.

The Mali tapestries demonstrate one important aspect of 20th-century reality: The artist and the machine are *not* totally incompatible. Each has something to learn from the other. The Prague exhibition may inspire other artist-

craftsmen to experiment with thrums or short ends of yarn, plus fabric scraps, and the sewing machine (Fig. 550).

Knitting and Crocheting Both single-strand interlacements, knitting and crocheting have long been considered appropriate for the construction of utilitarian items, generally articles of clothing. Only recently has their great potential for nonfunctional works of art—sculpture, wall hangings, and tapestry—begun to be realized.

above left: 550. SHIRLEY E. HELD. Experimental fabric in handcrafted Mali technique.

left: 551. MARY WALKER PHILLIPS. Knit cover for a folding chair designed by EVA ZEISEL. 1964. Nub wool in a seed stitch. Courtesy the artist.

above: 552. WALTER G. NOTTINGHAM. *Fuses.* 1970–71. Crochet of Dacron and rayon, fused with heat; height 6′6″. Courtesy the artist.

Mary Walker Phillips has utilized her training as a weaver in designing large-scale knit wall hangings and upholstery fabric (Pl. 40, p. 338; Fig. 551). She often works in linen, rather than the classic wool, and blocks her finished work, thereby sacrificing the elastic quality normally characteristic of knit fabrics to emphasize the overall design.

Walter G. Nottingham is also a weaver, but he has explored many forms of nonwoven interlacement in his search for "the forms of things unknown." His three-dimensional sculpture *Fuses* (Fig. 552), composed of intermeshed crochet forms, is more than 6 feet high. Nottingham writes, "Fabric can and often does have within its aura a pent-up energy, an intense life of its own. I am not trying to make the visible seen, but the unseen visible."[2]

THE PROFESSIONAL WEAVER

The individual who earns a livelihood from weaving or some other fiber craft generally falls into one of three categories: the teacher; the workshop weaver, with or without apprentices or assistants; and the design consultant to industry. Some professional weavers actually fill all three roles, in addition to lecturing and giving demonstrations. The possibilities of a career in weaving are much greater now than they were a decade ago, but, as one might expect, the competition is also much greater.

The Workshop Weaver

The monumental yarn constructions of Claire Zeisler (Fig. 553) require a considerable amount of hand knotting and wrapping. In order to keep pace with the demand for her work, as well as with her own creative urge, Zeisler employs several assistants, who do most of the actual tying. The artist herself—thoroughly acquainted with the mechanics of yarn—designs the sculptures, supervises their execution, and makes whatever modifications are needed before each piece is finished. This workshop approach has provided Zeisler with a stimulating challenge. She writes, "I wanted the discipline which would be a necessity—the discipline involved in designing for others to carry out. I would have to stop improvising and formulate the idea clearly if assistants were to make the thing."[3]

553. CLAIRE ZEISLER. *Red Forest.* 1968. Square-knotted forms in dyed jute, height 8'. Collection First National Bank of Chicago.

above: 554. MAGDALENA ABAKANOWICZ. Environmental wall. 1971. Sisal, wool, and flax, especially spun for the project; 24'9" × 81'3". S'Hertogenbosch, Holland.

A similar approach is taken by Magdalena Abakanowicz (Fig. 554; see also Pl. 12, p. 94), whose massive environmental tapestries could not possibly be woven by a single person. The viewing public is occasionally shocked to learn that a work of art was actually executed by someone other than the artist whose name it bears, sometimes even without his or her direct involvement. Yet such a workshop situation has a very long precedent; great masters like Raphael and Rubens had assistants, and in some works only the principal figures were executed by the artist himself. Abakanowicz' medium—yarn and specifically sisal—and her forms are very much her own, and they express the artist's

hand as personally as though she had thrown each weft herself. As Figure 555 illustrates, Abakanowicz is thoroughly involved in the weaving process, and she supervises each work closely.

Sheila Hicks has established a number of workshops in the last several years, but their purpose and outlook are rather different from the shops of Zeisler and Abakanowicz. At the forefront of a trend that is becoming more and more common among prominent designer-weavers, Hicks has collaborated with native craftsmen in Chile, India, and most recently Morocco to revitalize the local weaving industries. The result is a superb blend of traditional cultural elements and the unerring design sense of the artist (Fig. 556). Not until she had thoroughly studied the country and its ancient weaving techniques did Hicks attempt to influence the Moroccan weavers. This symbiotic relationship between a 20th-century craftsman and a centuries-old craft tradition has benefited both, for the Moroccan weavers have been exposed to a fresh new outlook, while the artist has absorbed ideas that will remain forever a part of her total design concept.

There is some evidence that the medieval guild system of apprenticeship is gaining new popularity as a method for learning or perfecting the craft of weaving. In an apprentice situation the advanced student not only benefits from the direct one-to-one supervision of a master weaver but also gains practical experience by taking part in the execution of commissioned works. Furthermore, he has the unique ability, unknown in

the classroom, of observing the business end of a weaving shop—pricing, billing, packing, shipping, and so forth. There are obvious advantages to both master and apprentice.

Design for Industry

The textile industry is one of the largest in the world. In addition to clothing and home furnishings, textile manufacturers supply fabric for upholstery in cars, trains, planes, buses, and ships; for office and showroom decoration; for industrial purposes; even for sports equipment.

In the first flush of the Industrial Revolution there were no real designers in the great weaving mills. Rather, the emphasis was on imitating

left: 555. Environmental wall (Fig. 554) in progress on a custom-built frame. The artist is at center left.

above: 556. SHEILA HICKS. Wall rugs from the *Sejjada* series shown at the Galerie Bab Rouah, Rabat, Morocco, 1971. Height of each rug 7'7". Courtesy the artist.

designs from other sources, and as the machines became more sophisticated, there was a tendency to reproduce the most elaborate, fussy patterns, simply to demonstrate the marvels of the power loom. Even today, some textile mills do not employ staff designers. However, many hire as consultants skilled handweavers to supply designs.

The major problem confronting the industrial designer is machine-controlled efficiency. The power-loom operation is not financially successful unless the machine can be set to produce a large quantity of fabric with a minimum of human intervention. The manipulation of multiple harnesses and shuttles is time-consuming for the machine, just as it is for the hand loom; consequently, the power loom works best when the complexity of the design is warp-oriented. Industrial looms are becoming ever more automatic, and attempts are being made to utilize the computer in designing for the loom, as well as in controlling the weave mechanics.

Dorothy Liebes achieved her first success as a studio weaver (see Chap. 5), filling commissions for architects, decorators, and wealthy clients across the United States. Her involvement with industry began when she accepted a position with Goodall Mills in Maine. As stylist for home furnishings, Liebes strove to maintain a hand-loomed quality in the mass-produced fabrics (Fig. 557). Later, E. I. du Pont de Nemours & Co. assigned her the enviable task of experimenting with their new synthetic fibers. Until her death she served as design consultant for Bigelow-Sanford and Sears, Roebuck & Company. The experience of Dorothy Liebes proves that excellence of design is not incompatible with large-scale production. As Liebes herself said, "The craftsman-designer has to perform on a mass-culture level and within its limitations. It is foolish for him to resent the conditions of the market place."[4]

below left: 557. DOROTHY LIEBES for Goodall Fabrics, Inc. Drapery fabric, detail. 1946. Power loomed in an overshot technique with cut fringe; wool, cotton, and metallic fiber.

below: 558. BORIS KROLL. *Santa Fe.* 1972. Jacquard-loomed fabric in cotton and rayon with chenille yarn for the pattern; vertical repeat 14¼″, horizontal repeat 12¼″. Boris Kroll Fabrics, New York.

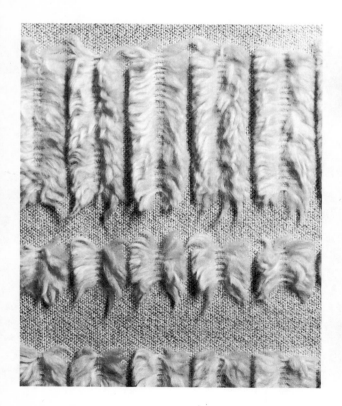

Jack Lenor Larsen operates his own fabric house in New York, from which he distributes power-loomed fabrics on a limited-production basis. By keeping his output relatively small, he has been able to create an incredibly diversified line and at the same time maintain a high level of quality in design (Pl. 41, p. 339). According to Larsen, "the power looming that my plant does—the turning out of one hundred yards of this and that—simply is not production to [the mass manufacturers]. It is using power tools but almost in a handcraft tradition. Mass production is for one man to watch sixty looms all going at once, all weaving the same thing without flaws."[5] Larsen's particular genius has been in adapting the power loom to a surprisingly wide range of design effects. Rather than forcing the design to conform to the needs of the machine, he has let the design come first and worried about the mechanics later.

In addition to the New York operation, Larsen maintains handweaving shops in nine countries, including Haiti, Colombia, Swaziland, and Mexico, all staffed with native weavers. Through these foreign branches he is able to renew his touch with the authentic character of the hand-loomed fabric.

Boris Kroll also directs his own textile firm, working primarily with Jacquard-loomed fabrics (Fig. 558). Kroll supervises every stage of the manufacturing process, from the spinning and blending of fibers into yarn, through the dyeing, to the actual fabric design. It is his conviction that the creation of a textile requires total design involvement, that the character of the yarn is just as important as the weaving pattern.

The cooperation of art and industry in the creation of fabric has proved so successful that one can expect to see more of it in the years to come. The industrial age can best fulfill its potential when machines provide the muscle and human beings supply the heart and soul.

WEAVING: ART AND CRAFT

Regardless of whether the weaver considers himself an artist or a craftsman, his work an art or a craft, many of the same standards apply: honesty of materials, effectiveness of design, care of execution, and fidelity to function, be it utilitarian or aesthetic. Weaving is such an enormous

field that there is room for all sorts of products; the craftsman is free to pursue his own bent.

Weaving as an Art Form

The outstanding weavers in the United States today are choosing the same paths as their counterparts in painting and sculpture. Neither size nor dimension is an obstacle in the creation of a form, and sedate squares and rectangles are no longer *de rigeur*.

To a certain extent weaving of the past two decades has tended to reflect contemporary trends in painting and sculpture. In the work of many prominent artist-weavers can be found elements of Pop Art (Fig. 559), a style that de-

559. RITZI and PETER JACOBI. *Armoir.* 1971. Mixed techniques, height 6'6". Courtesy Ruth Kaufmann Gallery, New York.

left: 560. EVELYN ANSELEVICIUS. *Linear Face II.* 1970–71. Tapestry of handspun wool, 6'6" × 7'6". Collection Mr. and Mrs. Robert Orchard, St. Louis, Mo.

below: 561. HERMAN SCHOLTEN. *Op en neer* (*Up and Down*). 1971. Tapestry of wool, sisal, and manille; 5'8" × 10'1". Courtesy the artist.

rives its forms and spirit from aspects of the mass culture; of Op (or optical) Art (Fig. 560), a form concerned with the response of the eye to visual stimuli often of an illusory nature; and of Minimal Art (Fig. 561), which attempts to limit art to the most basic elements of color, plane, and form. On the other hand, some critics would maintain that weaving as an art form has already moved into the mainstream, that fiber construction has begun to establish styles for the other media to imitate. A suggestion of this new identity is evident in the woven structures of

left: Plate 38. ANN-MARI KORNERUP. Tapestry-woven dress. Flax and wool. Courtesy Den Permanente, Copenhagen.

below: Plate 39. SUSAN GILMURRAY. Pillow covers. 1971. Monk's-belt weave with variations, including honeycomb; cotton and rayon warp, wool and synthetic-fiber weft; each pillow cover 22 x 24". Courtesy the artist.

Plate 40. Mary Walker Phillips. Knit hanging. 1971. Linen, 9′ x 4′5″. Courtesy the artist.

Plate 41. LARSEN DESIGN STUDIO. *Jubilee*. 1962. Power-loomed fabric with braid, soutache, and plied yarns of viscose and worsted. Jack Lenor Larsen, New York.

Plate 42. GRAU-GARRIGA. *Nisaga Decadent*. 1972. Tapestry of silk, cotton, wool, and rayon.
Courtesy Arras Gallery, New York.

340

Alice Adams (Fig. 562), and certainly of Magdalena Abakanowicz (Fig. 554). One particularly good example of the interplay between media is seen in the work of sculptor Barbara Chase-Riboud, whose elegant, sophisticated forms (Fig. 563) combine polished metal with silk yarns wrapped and braided in techniques learned from Sheila Hicks (Pl. 22, p. 198).

The tapestries of Grau-Garriga (Pl. 42, opposite) reflect a somewhat different trend. While adhering to the classic haute-lisse techniques, Grau-Garriga's work is thoroughly contemporary. Its brilliance of color, sensuality of line, and syncopation of texture speak always of yarn, never of paint on canvas.

In a 1970 issue of *Craft Horizons* Virginia Hoffman discussed the problem of weaving as an art form, as the intellectual and aesthetic equal of the so-called fine arts.

> As painting got off the easel, so weaving must get off the wall if it is to be sculptural, conceptually as well as physically. Woven forms must exist in space and relate to other three-dimensional forms in the environment rather than being isolated objects. . . . [Weaving] needs to cease being a spectator sport. It must bring forth significant responses and involvement on the part of the viewer. The primary motivation should be expression rather than decoration.[6]

Weaving as a Humanizer

The British psychologist Alexander Weatherson has written: "The nearer proximity of neighbors, packaged surroundings and the stereotyping of experience are paradoxically demanding greater

versatility in clothing and encouraging man to find his personality in the two areas left to him, dress and interior decoration."[7] If man is to seek his personal identity in the fabrics of everyday

below left: 562. ALICE ADAMS. Construction. 1965. Painted steel cable looped on a spiral. Courtesy the artist.

below: 563. BARBARA CHASE-RIBOUD. *Time Womb*. 1971. Aluminum and silk, height 4'8". Courtesy Betty Parsons Gallery, New York.

living, these items must be in some way unique, in some way more beautifully crafted or individually expressive than the mass-produced garments and furnishings of industry.

It is entirely possible for an article of clothing to be more-or-less conventional in design, yet display an artistry of fabric that sets it apart from the standardized product of the industrial mills (Fig. 564). The handweaver has great freedom to exercise his ingenuity in the creation of loom-constructed garments (see pp. 318–321) and yardage for clothing. Subtle decorative effects that would be impossible or prohibitively expensive on power equipment can imbue the hand-loomed fabric with rich, personal qualities.

Even greater impact is achieved by the garment that steps outside convention to create new lines and forms. Janet Decker's jacket (Fig. 565) was crocheted from wool, but it has little else

left: 564. BETTY KEELER. Dress, handwoven in a Finnish weave with attached top created on a hand knitting machine. Wool warp with man-made fiber weft. The weave employed is from *Handweaving Patterns from Finland,* by Helvi Pyysalo (Branford, 1958).

565. JANET DECKER. Jacket, hat, and mittens. 1971–72. Crochet of natural-dyed wool with textured fleece and leather. Courtesy the artist.

above: 566. DEBRA E. RAPOPORT. *Fibrous Raiment.* 1971. Knotted netting of video tape, 10 × 12'. Courtesy the artist.

right: 567. LOIS A. KNUDSEN. Woven panels. 1969. Linen, jute, mohair, and rayon with ceramic shapes; height of each panel 7'. Collection Dr. Alonzo Neufeld, Glendale, Calif.

in common with the apparel we are accustomed to seeing each day. Similarly, the "fibrous raiment" made of knotted netting by Debra Rapoport (Fig. 566) has a fluid, obviously hand-constructed quality that one expects from an "official" work of art, rather than a mere body covering. Such innovative designs make us question the standards and rules of dress that are normally adhered to. There is no reason why a garment must conform to a particular shape; as long as it performs its function—contributing to modesty, warmth, ease of movement, or whatever—it can be considered an effective design.

The same principles can be applied to interior decoration—upholstery fabric, room dividers, casement and drapery materials, accessories, and the like (Fig. 567). Dorothy Liebes designed all

the woven effects for the throne room of King Ibn Saud's land trailer (Fig. 568)—window blinds, upholstery, and bedspread. While the furnishings are simple and tastefully understated, there is an aura of elegance provided by the lush handwoven fabrics.

There is ample opportunity for the handcraftsman to express his individuality in the embellishment of his home. In Colonial times nearly all furnishings were home-made, and many families still treasure heirlooms meticulously crafted by great-grandparents. No machine can ever hope to duplicate the qualities of warmth and humanity—perhaps even of durability—inherent in an object patiently created by human hands.

Weaving as an Environment

The construction of a total environment from woven forms relates to Virginia Hoffman's plea for "involvement on the part of the viewer." The experience of standing, sitting, walking, *being* inside a woven environment is completely different from that of viewing a discrete form hung on the wall (Fig. 569). At any museum exhibition the largest crowd collects around the work of art that can be touched, crawled through, sat upon, and

below: 568. DOROTHY LIEBES. Handwoven fabrics for the Throne Room of the land trailer built for King Ibn Saud of Saudi Arabia. 1950. Blinds: oriental reeds, bamboo, and cotton; upholstery: cotton, raw silk, and metallic yarns; spread: loop fringe technique in cotton, raw silk, and metallic yarns. Commissioned by Spartan Aircraft Co.

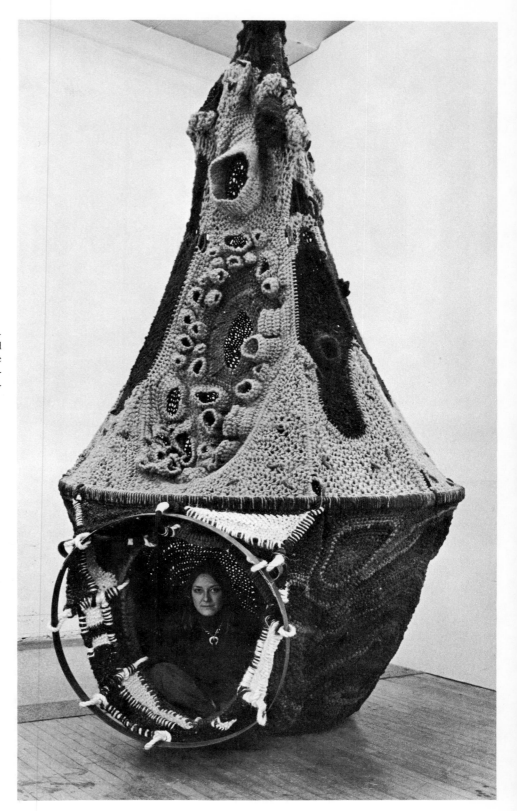

569. Barbara Shawcroft. *Arizona Inner Space*. Environmental woven structure of sisal and jute (photographed before completion of the 10′-long tunnel section). Courtesy the artist.

generally brought into direct contact with the viewer. One is instinctively drawn to an object that can be made a part of oneself and that one can be a part of. Many contemporary artists in various fields have been attracted by the concept of environment (Figs. 570, 571), for anything less than total immersion in the artist's form forces one's perception to be affected, often subliminally, by adjacent objects. The artist who creates an environment controls as fully as possible the viewer's aesthetic experience. And, in essence, any woven form, however small, however utilitarian, provides the observer with an aesthetic experience.

above: 570. GERHARDT G. KNODEL. Woven dining environment. 1970. Cotton, linen, and nylon, with glass mirror; 8 × 12 × 8′. Courtesy the artist.

right: 571. Detail of Figure 570, dining environment.

APPENDICES

appendix A Common Drafts
for the Four-harness Loom

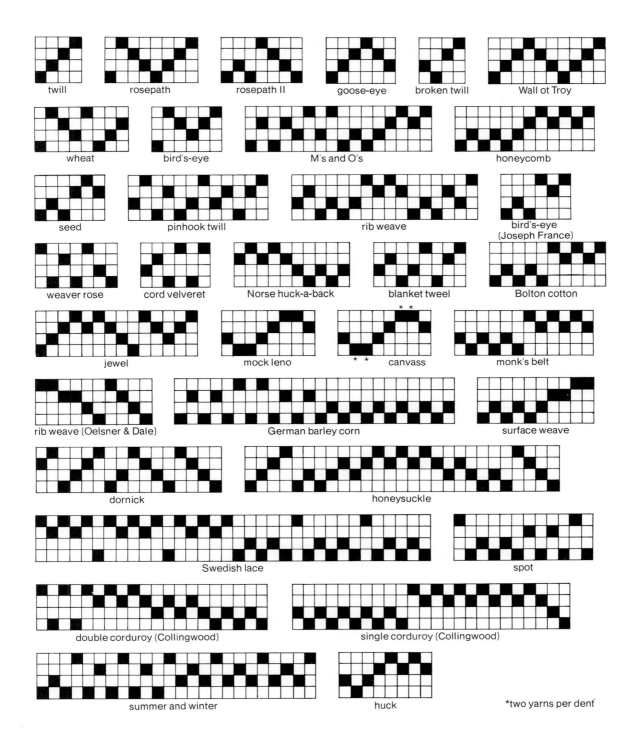

twill

rosepath

rosepath II

goose-eye

broken twill

Wall ot Troy

wheat

bird's-eye

M's and O's

honeycomb

seed

pinhook twill

rib weave

bird's-eye
(Joseph France)

weaver rose

cord velveret

Norse huck-a-back

blanket tweel

Bolton cotton

jewel

mock leno

canvass

monk's belt

rib weave (Oelsner & Dale)

German barley corn

surface weave

dornick

honeysuckle

Swedish lace

spot

double corduroy (Collingwood)

single corduroy (Collingwood)

summer and winter

huck

*two yarns per dent

Sample Yarn-calculation Form

Title/description of project _____

Finished length   _____

Allowance for warp take-up (10%)   _____

Allowance for shrinkage (10%)   _____

Allowance for loom waste   _____ ¾ yard _____

Allowance for hems   _____

     Total warp length   _____

Finished width   _____

Allowance for draw-in (10%)   _____

Allowance for shrinkage (10%)   _____

Allowance for hems   _____

     Width at reed   _____

Sett: $\dfrac{\text{ends per inch}}{} \times \dfrac{\text{width at reed}}{} = \dfrac{\text{total warp yarns}}{}$

Warp quantity: $\dfrac{\text{warp yarns}}{} \times \dfrac{\text{length of warp}}{} = \dfrac{\text{yards}}{}$

$\dfrac{\text{warp quantity}}{} \div \dfrac{\text{am't per spool/pound}}{} = \dfrac{\text{No. of spools/pounds}}{}$

Weft quantity: $\dfrac{\text{width at reed}}{} + \dfrac{\text{10\% take-up}}{} = \dfrac{\text{length of one weft}}{}$

$\dfrac{\text{weft yarns per inch}}{} \times \dfrac{\text{length of warp}}{} = \dfrac{\text{No. weft shots}}{}$

$\dfrac{\text{length of one weft}}{} \times \dfrac{\text{No. weft shots}}{} = \dfrac{\text{weft quantity}}{}$

$\dfrac{\text{weft quantity}}{} \div \dfrac{\text{am't per spool/pound}}{} = \dfrac{\text{No. of spools/pounds}}{}$

Sample Weaving Record

Title/description of project _____

Woven by _____ Date _____

	Warp	*Weft*

Yarn type _____ _____

Size   _____ _____

Color   _____ _____

Warp: No. warp yarns _____

       Order of warp _____

       Total yardage _____

       Total weight _____

       Finished length _____

Weft: Total yardage _____

       Total weight _____

       Finished width _____

Loom _____ Reed _____ E.P.I. _____

Draft name _____

No. harnesses _____ No. treadles _____

No. heddles: _____ _____ _____ _____ _____ _____ _____ _____

       frame 1   frame 2   frame 3   frame 4   frame 5   frame 6   frame 7   frame 8

Cost of project: _____ Selling cost: _____ _____

                                                    wholesale   retail

Comments _____

appendix C Sources of Materials and Equipment

LOOMS AND WEAVING EQUIPMENT— MANUFACTURERS AND DISTRIBUTORS

Gunnar Andersons, Vä vskedsverkstad, 792 00 Mora, Sweden

E. E. Gilmore, 1032 North Broadway, Stockton, Calif. 95205

Herald Looms, 118 Lee Street, Lodi, Ohio 44254

Kessenich Looms, 7463 Harwood Avenue, Wauwatosa, Wis. 53213 (looms for the handicapped available)

Walter Kircher, 355 Marburg/Lohn, Postfach 1408, Germany (available from Greentree Ranch, Route 3, Box 461, Loveland, Colo. 80537)

Lillstina, Inc., 66 Hawley Street, Binghamton, N.Y. 13901

L. W. Macomber, 166 Essex Street, Saugus, Mass.

Newcomb Loom, Co., Davenport, Iowa 52808

Nilus Leclerc, Inc., L'Isletville 6, Quebec, Canada (East Coast distributor: P. O. Box 491, Plattsburg, N.Y. 12901; West Coast distributor: P. O. Box 7012, Landscape Station, Berkeley, Calif. 94707)

Northwest Looms, Box 4872, Bainbridge Is., Wash. 98110 (Pioneer loom)

The Norwood Loom Company, Box 272, Baldwin, Mich. 49304

Pendleton Shop, Sedonia, Ariz. 86336

School Products Co., Inc., 312 East 23 Street, New York, N.Y. 10010 (Schacht, Leclerc, and Artcraft looms)

Structo Division, King-Seeley Thermos Co., Freeport, Ill.

DYES

Accolite Pigments, American Crayon Co., Sandusky, Ohio (Helizarin dyes)

Allied Chemical Corp, One Times Square, New York, N.Y. 10036, Att. Mrs. K. H. Jones, 6th Floor (acid dyes for wool and silk)

Bachmeier and Co., Inc., 154 Chambers Street, New York, N.Y. 10007 (acid, direct, aniline, benazel, chlorantine, and basic dyes)

C. D. Fitz Harding-Bailey, 15 Dutton Street, Bankstown, N.S.W. 2200, Australia (natural dyes)

Comak Chemicals Ltd., Swinton Works, Moon Street, London, N1, England (natural dyes)

Craftsman's Dyes, George Wells, The Ruggery, Glen Head, N.Y. 11545

W. Cushing and Co. Perfection Dyes, Kennebunkport, Maine 04046

Fab Dec, Box 3062, Lubbock, Tex. 79410

Glen Black Handwoven Textiles, 1414 Grant Avenue, San Francisco, Calif. 91433 (Procion dyes)

Handcraft Wools, Box 378, Streetsville, Ontario, Canada (Ciba dyes)

Kiehl Pharmacy, 109 Third Avenue, New York, N.Y. (natural dyes)

Nature's Herb Co., 281 Ellis Street, San Francisco, Calif. 94102

Old Fashioned Herb Co., 581 North Lake Avenue, Pasadena, Calif. 91100 (lump and powdered indigo root)

Putnam Fadeless Dyes, Monroe Chemical Co., 301 Oak Street, Quincy, Ill. 62302

Pylam Products Co., Inc., 95-11 218th Street, Queens Village, N.Y. 11429 (Procion dyes)

Harry E. Saier, Dimondale, Mich. 48821 (seeds for growing dye plants)

World-Wide Herbs, 11 Saint Catherine Street West, Montreal 18, Quebec, Canada

YARNS

J. Hyslop Bathgate and Co., Galashiels, Scotland (wool yarn and oddments)

Briggs and Little, York Mills, Harvey Station P. O., York County, New Brunswick, Canada

Charles Y. Butterworth, 2222 East Susquehanna Avenue, Philadelphia, Pa. 19128

William Condon and Sons, 65 Queen Street, P. O. 129, Charlottetown, P.E.I., Canada

Contessa Yarns, P. O. Box 37, Lebanon, Conn. 06249

Coulter Studios, 138 East 60 Street, New York, N.Y. 10022 (rya and other Scandinavian yarns)

Craft Yarns of Rhode Island, Inc., 603 Mineral Spring Avenue, P. O. Box 385, Pawtucket, R.I. 02862

Frederick J. Fawcett, Inc., 129 South Street, Boston, Mass. 02111

Greentree Ranch, Route 3, Box 461, Loveland, Colo. 80537

Handcraft Wools, Box 378, Streetsville, Ontario, Canada

House of Kleen, P. O. Box 224, North Stonington, Conn. 06359

Lily Mills, Shelby, N.C. 28150

Lundgren, Inc., 540 West Main Street, Northboro, Mass. 01532 (rya and other Swedish yarns, cow's hair, rya backing)

The Mannings, East Berlin, Pa. 17316

Oregon Worsted Co., P. O. Box 02098, Portland, Ore. 97202

Paternayan Brothers, Inc., 312 East 95 Street, New York, N.Y. 10028 (wholesale or large quantities)

Rammagerdin, Hafnar Straeti 5 & 17, Reyk Javik, Iceland (natural undyed wools)

Robin and Russ, 533 North Adams Street, McMinnville, Ore. 97128

Paula Simmons, Suquamish, Wash. 98392

Tinkler and Co., 237 Chestnut Street, Philadelphia, Pa. 19106

George Wells, The Ruggery, Glen Head, N.Y. 11545

Wettehoffin Katilollisuusopettajaopisto, Hämeenlinna, Finland

Clinton L. Wilkinson, 6429 Virginia Avenue, Charlotte, N.C.

The Yarn Depot, Inc., 545 Sutter Street, San Francisco, Calif. 94102

Yarn Primitives, Box 1013, Weston, Conn. 06880

SPINNING WHEELS AND EQUIPMENT

Albion Hills School of Spinning and Dyeing, Albion Hills, Ontario, Canada, Attention Edna Blackburn (wheels)

Anchor Chest Company, Box 107, Salem, Ohio 44460

Ashford Handicrafts Ltd., P. O. Box 121, Rakaia, New Zealand (wheels)

C. D. Fitz Harding-Bailey, 15 Dutton Street, Bankstown, N.S.W. 2200, Australia (wheels)

Colonial Textiles, The Sheldons, 2604 Cranbrook, Ann Arbor, Mich. (wheels and wool cards)

Cordarelle-Siminoff Studio, 573 Tenth Street, Richmond, Calif. 94801

E. B. Frye and Sons, Inc., Wilton, N.H. 03086

Greentree Ranch, Route 3, Box 461, Loveland, Colo. 80537

Handcraft Wools, Box 378, Streetsville, Ontario, Canada (wheels)

The Mannings, East Berlin, Pa. 17316

Lucien Quellet, Manufacturers Des Rouets, Village des Aulnais, Cite L'islet, Quebec, Canada

School Products, Co., Inc., 312 East 23 Street, New York, N.Y. 10010 (wheels and wool cards)

Paula Simmons, Suquamish, Wash. 98392 (carding and spinning oil)

Spincraft, c/o James A. Ronin, 611 Kirby Lane, Richardson, Tex. 75080

SPINNING MATERIALS—FIBERS

Cambridge Wools, Ltd., Box 2572, Auckland, New Zealand (scoured natural wools)

Davies-Watson, 15 Birdwood Road, Lower Hutt, New Zealand (wool)

Davis Cordage Co., 677 North Tillammok, Portland, Ore. 97227 (flax)

Greentree Ranch, Route 3, Box 461, Loveland, Colo, 80537 (wool and flax)

Handcraft Wools, Box 378, Streetsville, Ontario, Canada (all fibers)

Hidden Glen Farms, Mrs. Anita Schonsek, Hidden Glen, Meadowbrook, Pa. 19046 (wool)

Indiana Botanic Gardens, Inc., Hammond, Ind. 46325 (flax seed)

Sonya Johnson, 203 Paradise Street, Pullman, Wash. 99163 (wool)

Jones Sheep Farm, Peabody, Kan. 66866 (wool)

Soria Studio, 1454 Helvik 1, Bunnefjord, Norway (Norwegian Spelsau wool)

CHEMICALS

FMC Corporation, Inorganic Chemicals Division, 633 Third Avenue, New York, N.Y. 10017

Merck and Co., Inc., General Offices and Laboratories, Rahway, N.J.

Spectro Chem Inc., 1354 Ellison Avenue, Louisville, Ky. 40204

RUG HOOKING SUPPLIES

Craft Yarns of Rhode Island, Inc., 603 Mineral Spring Avenue, P. O. Box 385, Pawtucket, R.I. 02862

Norden Products, P. O. Box 1, Glenview, Ill. 60025

Rittermere Craft Studios Ltd., P. O. Box 240, Vineland, Ontario, Canada

George Wells, The Ruggery, Glen Head, N.Y. 11545

MACRAMÉ YARNS AND SUPPLIES

Craft Yarns of Rhode Island, Inc., 603 Mineral Spring Avenue, P. O. Box 385, Pawtucket, R.I. 02862

Dharma Trading Co., Box 1288, Berkeley, Calif. 94701

Frederick J. Fawcett, Inc., 129 South Street, Boston, Mass. 02111

P. C. Herwig Co., 264 Clinton Street, Brooklyn, N.Y. 11201

Lily Mills, Shelby, N.C. 28150

Macramé & Weaving Supply Co., 63 East Adams, Chicago, Ill. 60603

The Mannings, East Berlin, Pa. 17316

The Yarn Depot, Inc., 545 Sutter Street, San Francisco, Calif. 94102

BEADS

P. C. Herwig Co., 264 Clinton Street, Brooklyn, N.Y. 11201

Lemco, Box 40545, San Francisco, Calif.

Marion H. Mumby, Handmade Ceramic Beads, 206 Hanover Drive, Costa Mesa, Calif. 92626

Vicki Russell, P. O. Box 817, Whittier, Calif. 90601

Jean Simpson's Bead Tree, 1614 Ard Eevin Avenue, Glendale, Calif. 91202 (ceramic beads)

Walbead, Inc. 38 West 37th Street, New York, N.Y. 10018

FEATHERS

Gettinger Feather Co., 38 West 38th Street, New York, N.Y. 10018

PORCUPINE QUILLS

Pease Complex, Box 75, Chester, Mass. 01011

BOOK SUPPLIERS

Craft & Hobby Book Service, Box 626, Pacific Grove, Calif. 93950

K. R. Drummond, 30 Hart Grove, Ealing Common, London W.5, England

Museum Books, Inc., 48 East 43 Street, New York, N.Y. 10017

The Unicorn, Box 645 G, Rockville, Md. 20851

Wittenborn and Co., 1018 Madison Avenue, New York, N.Y.

appendix D Selected Yarn Designations

Common Yarn Count for Natural-fiber Yarns

cotton		worsted		wool or linen	
size	*yards per pound*	*size*	*yards per pound*	*size*	*yards per pound*
1	840	1	560	1	300
3/2	1260	6/1	3360	1½ lea	450
4/4	840	9/1	5040	5/1 (Scottish)	1500
4/12	280	10	5600	5½/1	1650
5/2	2100	10/2	2800	6/3	600
8/2	3360	10/4	1400	6/4 (Swiss)	450
8/4	1680	12/2	3360	7/2	1050
8/6	1120	12/3	2240	8/1 (dry spun)	2400
10	8400	15/2	4200	8/5 (Swedish)	450
10/2	4200	16/2	4480	9/3	800
10/3	2800	18/2	4800	10	3000
12/4	2520	20/2	5000	10/1 (dry spun)	2700
16/2	6720	22/2	6160	10/2 (wet spun)	1500
16/4	3280	26/2	7260	10/2 (dry spun)	1350
16/6	2240	32/2	8960	10/5	540
20/2	8400			12	3600
20/3	5600			14	4200
20/6 (floss)	2800			14/2	2100
24/2	10000			15/2	2250
24/3	6720			16	4800
30/2	12600			16/2	2400
34/2	14000			18/2	2700
50/3	14000			18/6	900
				18/8	675
				20	6000
				20/2	3000
				30	9000
				30/2	4500
				40/2	6000
				40/3	4000
				50/2	7500
				50/3	5000
				60/3	6000
				70/2	10500
				140/2	21000

Miscellaneous and Novelty Yarns

name	description	approximate yards per pound
macramé yarns		
English seating cord		250
8-cord cotton cable twist		920
jute cord	small	250
	medium	166
	large	100
jute-tone	2-ply	300
navy cord		420–440
nylon stitching twine	18/3	2200
seine cord, cotton	small	425
	large	207
nylon	#18	358
sisal	small	233
	large	100
cotton	lace yarn	1900
	3-cut cotton chenille	225–230
	6-cut chenille	425–450
	12-cut chenille	1200–1500
rayon flake		2500
linen	12-fold (parallel)	1450
silk		
douppioni (Scottish)	7/2	2100
	12/1	10000
silk tweed	14/1	11760
spun silk	60/2	12800
wool		
eiderdown		480
English Donegal tweed	singles	1850
loop or brushed mohair	large loop	1000
rug yarn, U.S.		400–500
Scandinavian	fine	600
	heavy	320
cowhair		680
acrylic, rug yarn	3-ply	560
	4-ply	440

Common Knitting Yarns

general name	yards per pound	fiber content
fingering	2720–2800	orlon and/or wool
pompadour	2160	wool
baby yarn	2240	wool
sport yarn	1600–2200	wool and/or nylon, acrylic
bulky	400–600	wool

Warp Densities (Yarns Per Inch)
In Order of Most Common Usage

reed size	sley 1,0	sley 1,1	sley 1,2	sley 2,2	sley 2,3	sley 3,3
12	6	12	18	24	30	36
15	$7\frac{1}{2}$	15	$22\frac{1}{2}$	30	$37\frac{1}{2}$	45
10	5	10	15	20	25	30
18	9	18	27	36	45	54
7	$3\frac{1}{2}$	7	$10\frac{1}{2}$	14	$17\frac{1}{2}$	21
9	$4\frac{1}{2}$	9	$13\frac{1}{2}$	18	$22\frac{1}{2}$	27
8	4	8	12	16	20	24

Warp Densities (Yarns Per Inch)
According to Yarn Sizes and Weaves

cotton yarns	twill	plain weave	pattern	fabric
50/3 or 30/2	45	42	40	
24/2	40	36	30	clothing accessories
20/2	36	32	30	most common cotton warp
10/2	27	24	$22\frac{1}{2}$	upholstery
8/2	27	24	20	
10/3	24	$22\frac{1}{2}$	20	double weave
20/6	24	$22\frac{1}{2}$	20	
5/2	20	18	15	
8/4	18	15	12	rugs
3/2	15	12	10	

linen yarns	firm	medium	open	fabric
50/2	45	40	36	luxurious
40/2	40	36	30	
18/1	36	30	27	
50/3	36	30	27	
12/1	30	24–27	$22\frac{1}{2}$	
20/2	27	24	20	medium-weight
10/1	24	$22\frac{1}{2}$–20	18	
14/2	$22\frac{1}{2}$	20	18	
7/1	$22\frac{1}{2}$	20	18	

appendix E Metric Conversion Tables

When dealing with foreign suppliers or consulting references printed abroad, the weaver should be able to convert readily from the American system of weights and measures to the metric system, employed by virtually every country outside the United States. The following tables provide multipliers for converting from metric to U.S. and the reverse; the multipliers have been rounded to the third decimal place and thus yield an approximate equivalent.

Metric to U.S.			U.S. to Metric		
to convert from:	to:	multiply the metric unit by:	to convert from:	to:	multiply the U.S. unit by:
length:					
meters	yards	1.093	yards	meters	.914
meters	feet	3.280	feet	meters	.305
meters	inches	39.370	inches	meters	.025
centimeters	inches	.394	inches	centimeters	2.540
millimeters	inches	.039	inches	millimeters	25.400
area and volume:					
square meters	square yards	1.196	square yards	square meters	.836
square meters	square feet	10.764	square feet	square meters	.093
square centimeters	square inches	.155	square inches	square centimeters	6.451
cubic centimeters	cubic inches	.061	cubic inches	cubic centimeters	16.387
liquid measure:					
liters	cubic inches	61.020	cubic inches	liters	.016
liters	cubic feet	.035	cubic feet	liters	28.339
liters	*U.S. gallons	.264	*U.S. gallons	liters	3.785
liters	*U.S. quarts	1.057	*U.S. quarts	liters	.946
weight and mass:					
kilograms	pounds	2.205	pounds	kilograms	.453
grams	ounces	.035	ounces	grams	28.349
grams	grains	15.430	grains	grams	.065
grams per meter	ounces per yard	.032	ounces per yard	grams per meter	31.250
grams per square meter	ounces per square yard	.030	ounces per square yard	grams per square meter	33.333

*The British imperial gallon equals approximately 1.2 U.S. gallons or 4.54 liters.
Similarly, the British imperial quart equals 1.2 U.S. quarts, and so on.

Bibliography

PART I: THE HISTORY OF FABRIC CONSTRUCTION

Ackerman, Phyllis. *Tapestry—The Mirror of Civilization.* New York: Oxford University Press, 1933.

Amsden, Charles Avery. *Navaho Weaving.* Albuquerque: University of New Mexico Press, 1949.

Atwater, Mary M. *The Shuttlecraft Book of American Handweaving.* New York: The Macmillan Company, 1956.

Baity, Elizabeth Chesley. *Man Is a Weaver.* New York: The Viking Press, Inc., 1949.

Birrell, Verla. *The Textile Arts.* New York: Harper & Brothers, 1959.

D'Harcourt, Raoul. *Textiles of Ancient Peru and Their Techniques.* Seattle: University of Washington Press, 1962.

Forbes, Robert J. *Studies in Ancient Technology,* Vol. 4, "Textiles." New York: W. S. Heinman, 1964.

Goodrich, F. L. *Mountain Homespun.* New Haven, Conn.: Yale University Press, 1931.

Hall, Eliza. *A Book of Handwoven Coverlets.* Boston: Little, Brown & Company, 1914.

Hoffman, Marta. *The Warp Weighted Loom.* Oslo: Oslo University Press, 1964.

Murray, Margaret. *Tomb of Two Brothers.* Manchester: Sherratt and Hughes, 1910.

Nordland, Odd. *Primitive Scandinavian Textiles in Knotless Netting.* Oslo: Oslo University Press, 1961.

O'Neale, Lila. *Textile Periods in Ancient Peru.* Berkeley, Calif.: University of California Press, 1930.

Roth, Ling H. *Studies in Primitive Looms.* Halifax: Sott Brothers, Ltd., 1950.

Threads of History. The American Federation of Arts, 1965.

Tidball, Harriet. *Thomas Jackson, Weaver.* Shuttle Craft Guild Monograph #13. Lansing, Mich.: Shuttle Craft Guild, 1964

Van Stan, Ina. *Problems in Pre-Columbian Textile Classification.* Tallahassee, Fla.: Florida State University Press, 1958.

Weigert, Roger-Armand. *French Tapestry.* Newton Centre, Mass.: Charles T. Branford Company, 1963.

White, Margaret. *The Decorative Arts of New Jersey.* Princeton N.J.: D. Van Nostrand Company, Inc., 1964.

PART II: HANDWEAVING ON THE LOOM

Flat Weaving

Albers, Anni. *On Weaving.* Middletown, Conn.: Wesleyan University Press, 1965.

Allen, Edith Louise. *Weaving You Can Do.* Peoria, Ill.: The Manual Arts Press, 1947.

Black, Mary E. *New Key to Weaving.* Milwaukee, Wis.: Bruce Publishing Company, 1957.

Blumenau, Lili. *The Art and Craft of Handweaving.* New York: Crown Publishers, Inc., 1955.

———. *Creative Design in Wall Hangings.* New York: Crown Publishers, Inc., 1966.

Brown, Harriette J. *Hand Weaving for Pleasure and Profit.* New York: Harper & Brothers, 1952.

Cyrus, Ulla. *Manual of Swedish Handweaving.* Newton Centre, Mass.: Charles T. Branford Company, 1956.

Davenport, Elsie. *Your Handweaving.* Pacific Grove, Calif.: Craft & Hobby Book Service, 1970.

Davison, Marguerite P. *A Handweaver's Pattern Book.* Swarthmore, Pa.: M. P. Davison, 1963.

Douglas, Harriet. *Handweavers' Instruction Manual.* Pacific Grove, Calif.: Craft & Hobby Book Service, 1949.

Emery, Irene. *Primary Structures of Fabrics.* Washington, D.C.: Textile Museum, 1966.

Engelstad, Helen. *Dobbeltvev i Norge.* Oslo: Gyldendal Norsk Forlag, 1958.

Francisco, Irene. *Opening a Door to Two-Harness Techniques.* Shelby, N.C.: Lily Mills Company, 1960.

Frey, Berta. *Seven Projects in Rosepath.* Berta Frey, 1959.

Gallinger, Osma. *Joy of Weaving.* Scranton, Pa.: International Textbook Company, 1950.

Greer, Gertrude. *Adventures in Weaving.* Peoria, Ill.: Chas. A. Bennett Company, Inc., 1951.

Hooper, Luther. *Handloom Weaving.* London: Sir Isaac Pitman & Sons, Ltd., 1934.

House, Florence. *Notes on Weaving Techniques.* New York: Elizabeth Salisbury, 1964.

Kirby, Mary. *Designing on the Loom.* London and New York: The Studio Publications, Inc., 1953.

Nye, Thelma M., ed. *Swedish Weaving.* New York: Van Nostrand-Reinhold Company, 1972.

Overman, Ruth, and Lula Smith. *Contemporary Handweaving.* Ames, Iowa: Iowa State University Press, 1955.

Plath, Iona. *Handweaving.* New York: Charles Scribners Sons, 1964.

Pyysalo, Helvi. *Handweaving Patterns from Finland.* Newton Centre, Mass.: Charles T. Branford Company, 1958.

Selander, Malin. *Swedish Handweaving.* Goteborg: Wazäta, 1959.

———. *Weaving Patterns.* Goteborg: Wazäta, 1956.

Steedsman, Nellie E. *Patterns on a Plain Weave.* N. E. Steedsman, 1959.

Thorpe, Azalea Stuart, and Jack Lenor Larsen. *Elements of Weaving.* Garden City, N.Y.: Doubleday & Company, 1967.

Thorpe, Heather G. *A Handweaver's Workbook.* New York: The Macmillan Company, 1966.

Tidball, Harriet. *Double Weave: Plain & Patterned.* Pacific Grove, Calif.: Craft & Hobby Book Service, 1960.

———. *Two-Harness Textiles: Loom Controlled.* Pacific Grove, Calif.: Craft & Hobby Book Service, 1967.

————. *The Weaver's Book: Fundamentals of Handweaving*. New York: The Macmillan Company, 1962.

————. *Woolens and Tweeds*. Pacific Grove, Calif.: Craft & Hobby Book Service, 1961.

Tovey, John. *The Technique of Weaving*. New York: Reinhold Publishing Corporation, 1966.

West, Virginia. *Finishing Touches for the Handweaver*. Newton Centre, Mass.: Charles T. Branford Company, 1967.

Worst, Edward. *How to Weave Linens*. Milwaukee, Wis.: Bruce Publishing Company, 1926.

Zielinski, Stanislaw A. *Encyclopedia of Hand-Weaving*. New York: Funk & Wagnalls Company, 1959.

Znamierowski, Nell. *Step-by-Step Weaving*. New York: Golden Press, Inc., 1967.

Tapestry

Beutlich, Tadek. *The Technique of Woven Tapestry*. New York: Watson-Guptill Publications, 1971.

Kahlenberg, Mary Hunt, and Anthony Berlant. *The Navajo Blanket*. New York: Frederick A. Praeger, Inc., 1972.

Kaufmann, Ruth. *The New American Tapestry*. New York: Reinhold Publishing Corporation, 1968.

Tidball, Harriet. *Contemporary Tapestry*. Pacific Grove, Calif.: Craft & Hobby Book Service, 1964.

Weigert, Roger-Armand. *French Tapestry*. Newton Centre, Mass.: Charles T. Branford Company, 1963.

PART III: OTHER CONSTRUCTION METHODS

Pile Weaves

Allard, Mary. *Rugmaking: Techniques and Design*. Philadelphia: Chilton Book Company, 1963.

Collingwood, Peter. *The Techniques of Rug Weaving*. New York: Watson-Guptill Publications, 1968.

Grierson, Ronald. *Woven Rugs*. Leicester, England: Dryad Press, 1960.

Ingers, Gertrud. *Nya Mattor*. Vasteras, Sweden: ICA Publishing Company, 1959.

Laury, Jean Ray, and Joyce Aiken. *Handmade Rugs from Practically Anything*. Philadelphia: Countryside Press, 1972.

Lewes, Klares, and Helen Hutton. *Rug Weaving*. Newton Centre, Mass.: Charles T. Branford Company, 1962.

Seagroatt, Margaret. *Rug Weaving for Beginners*. New York: Watson-Guptill Publications, 1972.

Sylwan, Vivi. *Svenska Ryor*. Stockholm: Bokforlaget, 1934.

Tod, Osma Gallinger, and Josephine Couch Del Deo. *Rug Weaving for Everyone*. New York: Bramhall House, 1957.

Willcox, Don. *The Technique of Rya Knotting*. New York: Van Nostrand-Reinhold Company, 1971.

Zarbock, Barbara J. *The Complete Book of Rug Hooking*. New York: Golden Press, Inc., 1972.

Znamierowski, Nell. *Step-by-Step Rugmaking*. New York: Golden Press, Inc., 1972.

Simple Looms and Nonloom Techniques

Alexander, Marthann. *Simple Weaving*. New York: Taplinger Publishing Company, Inc., 1969.

Atwater, Mary Meigs. *Byways in Handweaving*. New York: The Macmillan Company, 1967.

————. *Guatemala Visited*. Pacific Grove, Calif.: Craft & Hobby Book Service, 1946.

Beitler, Ethel. *Create with Yarn: Hooking, Stitchery*. Scranton, Pa.: International Textbook Company, 1964.

De Dillmont, Therese. *Encyclopedia of Needlework*. Mulhouse, Alsace, France: DMC Library.

Dendel, Esther Warner. *Needleweaving: Easy as Embroidery*. Philadelphia: Countryside Press, 1972.

Graumont, Raoul, and Elmer Wenstrom. *Square Knot Handicraft Guide*. Cambridge, Md.: Cornell Maritime Press, 1949.

Gubser, Elsie H. *Bobbin Lace*. McMinnville, Ore.: Robin and Russ Handweavers.

Harvey, Virginia I. *Macramé: The Art of Creative Knotting*. New York: Van Nostrand-Reinhold Company, 1967.

Harvey, Virginia, and Harriet Tidball. *Weft Twining*. Pacific Grove, Calif.: Craft & Hobby Book Service, 1969.

Kroncke, Grete. *Weaving with Cane and Reed*. New York: Van Nostrand-Reinhold, Company, 1968.

Lundback, Maja, and Marta Rinde-Ramsback. *Small Webs*. Vasteras, Sweden: ICA Publishing Company, 1959.

Marein, Shirley. *Off the Loom: Creating with Fibre*. New York: The Viking Press, Inc., 1972.

May, Florence Lewis. *Hispanic Lace & Lace Making*. New York: Hispanic Society of America, 1939.

Meilach, Dona Z. *Macramé—Creative Design in Knotting*. New York: Crown Publishers, Inc., 1971.

Nordland, Odd. *Primitive Scandinavian Textiles in Knotless Netting*. Oslo: Oslo University Press, 1961.

Phillips, Mary Walker. *Creative Knitting*. New York: Van Nostrand-Reinhold Company, 1971.

————. *Step-by-Step Knitting*. New York: Golden Press, Inc., 1967.

————. *Step-by-Step Macramé*. New York: Golden Press, Inc., 1970.

Rainey, Sarita. *Weaving Without a Loom*. Worcester, Mass.: Davis Publications, Inc., 1966.

Wilson, Jean. *Weaving Is for Anyone*. New York: Van Nostrand-Reinhold Company, 1967.

PART IV: SPINNING AND COLORING

Spinning

Davenport, Elsie. *Your Handspinning*. London: Sylvan Press, 1964.

Fannin, Allen. *Handspinning: Art & Technique*. New York: Van Nostrand-Reinhold, 1970.

Grasett, K. *Complete Guide to Handspinning*. London: London School of Weaving.

Holding, May. *Notes on Spinning and Dyeing Wool*. London: Skilbeck Brothers, Ltd., 1949.

Kluger, Marilyn. *The Joy of Spinning*. New York: Simon and Schuster, Inc., 1971.

Yarn Dyeing

Adrosko, Rita J. *Natural Dyes and Home Dyeing*. New York: Dover Publications, Inc., 1971.

Bolton, Eileen. *Lichens for Vegetable Dyeing.* Newton Centre, Mass.: Charles T. Branford Company, 1960.

Brooklyn Botanical Garden. *Dye Plants and Dyeing—A Handbook.* Brooklyn, N.Y.: Brooklyn Botanical Garden, 1964.

Colton, Mary-Russell Ferrell. *Hopi Dyes.* Flagstaff, Ariz.: Northland Press for Museum of Northern Arizona, 1965.

Conley, Emma. *Vegetable Dyeing.* Penland, N.C.: Penland School of Handicrafts, Inc.

Dana, Mrs. William Starr. *How to Know the Wild Flowers.* New York: Dover Publications, Inc., 1963.

Davenport, Elsie. *Your Yarn Dyeing.* Pacific Grove, Calif.: Craft & Hobby Book Service, 1970.

Davidson, Mary. *The Dye Pot.* Middleboro, Ky.: Mary Davidson.

Kierstead, Sally. *Natural Dyes.* Boston: Branden Press, Inc.

Leechman, Douglas. *Vegetable Dyes.* New York: Oxford University Press, 1943.

Leggett, William E. *Ancient and Medieval Dyes.* New York: Chemical Publishing Company, 1944.

Lesch, Alma. *Vegetable Dyeing.* New York: Watson-Guptill Publications, 1970.

Mairet, Ethel. *Vegetable Dyes.* London: Faber and Faber, 1946.

Thurston, Violetta. *Use of Vegetable Dyes.* Leicester, England: Dryad Press, 1943.

Tidball, Harriet. *Color and Dyeing.* Pacific Grove, Calif.: Craft & Hobby Book Service, 1965.

PART V: DESIGN IN FABRIC CONSTRUCTION

Albers, Anni. *On Designing.* Middletown, Conn.: Wesleyan University Press, 1961.

Albers, Josef. *The Interaction of Color.* New Haven, Conn.: Yale University Press, 1963.

Biegeleisen, J. I., and J. A. Cohn. *Silk Screen Techniques.* New York: Dover Publications, Inc., 1958.

Beitler, Ethel J., and Bill C. Lockhart. *Design for You.* New York: John Wiley & Sons, Inc., 1969.

Bevlin, Marjorie E. *Design Through Discovery.* New York: Holt, Rinehart and Winston, Inc., 1970.

Frey, Berta. *Designing and Drafting: Basic Principles of Cloth Construction.* New York: The Macmillan Company, 1958.

Hartung, Rolf. *Creative Textile Design: Thread and Fabric.* New York: Van Nostrand-Reinhold Company, 1964.

Itten, Johannes. *The Art of Color.* New York: Van Nostrand-Reinhold Company, 1966.

Oelsner, G. H. *Handbook of Weaves.* New York: Dover Publications, Inc.

Posselt, Emanuel A. *Technology of Textile Design.* Philadelphia: Textile Publishing Company.

Scheidig, Walther. *Crafts of the Bauhaus.* New York: Van Nostrand-Reinhold, 1967.

PERIODICALS

American Fabrics, 24 East 38 Street, New York, New York 10016.

Craft Horizons, published by the American Crafts Council, 16 East 52 Street, New York, New York 10022.

Creative Crafts. This publication is out of print, but back copies are available from libraries.

Form, Swedish Society for Industrial Design, Svenska Slojd-föreningen, Box 7047, S-103 82, Stockholm 7, Sweden.

Handicrafter. This publication is out of print, but back copies are available from libraries.

Handweaver & Craftsman, 220 Fifth Avenue, New York, New York 10001.

Quarterly Journal of the Guilds of Weavers, Spinners and Dyers. Subscriptions available through: Mary Barker, 1 Harrington Road, Brighton 6, England.

Shuttle, Spindle and Dyepot, Handweavers Guild of America, 339 North Steele Road, West Hartford, Connecticut 06117.

Webe Mit. Subscriptions available through: 705 Baiblingen bei Stuttgart, Postfach 65, Germany.

Copies of *Ciba Review,* a trade journal published in Basle, Switzerland, are available in most large libraries. The following issues may be of special interest:

#1	*Medieval Dyeing*
#2	*India, Its Dyers, and Its Colour Symbolism*
#4	*Purple*
#5	*Tapestry*
#7	*Scarlet*
#8	*The Dressing of Hides in the Stone Age*
#9	*Dyeing and Tanning in Classical Antiquity*
#10	*Trade Routes and Dye Markets in the Middle Ages*
#12	*Weaving and Dyeing in Ancient Egypt and Babylon*
#14	*Clothing Making in Flanders*
#15	*Pile Carpets of the Ancient Orient*
#16	*The Loom*
#18	*Great Masters of Dyeing in 18th Century France*
#20	*The Development of the Textile Crafts in Spain*
#21	*Weaving and Dyeing in North Africa*
#23	*The European Carpet*
#24	*The Basle Ribbon Industry*
#27	*The Textile Trades in Medieval Florence*
#28	*The Spinning Wheel*
#29	*Venetian Silks*
#30	*The Essentials of Handicrafts and the Craft of Weaving among Primitive People*
#33	*Bark Fabrics of the South Seas*
#34	*The Development of Footwear*
#35	*The Hat*
#36	*Indian Costumes*
#37	*Textile Ornament*
#38	*Neckties*
#39	*Madder and Turkey Red*
#40	*Turkestan and Its Textile Crafts*
#44	*Ikats*
#45	*The Crafts of the Puszta Herdsman*
#54	*Basketry and Woven Fabric of European Stone and Bronze Age*
#58	*Batiks*
#59	*The Reel*
#63	*Basic Textile Techniques*
#68	*Dyeing among Primitive Peoples*
#76	*Early American Textiles*
#84	*Maori Textile Techniques*
#85	*Indigo*

#88	*Swedish Peasant Dress*		1965/1	*Nonwovens*
#110	*Damask*		1965/2	*Flax*
#117	*Tablet Weaving*		1965/3	*Yarn and Thread*
#133	*Coptic Textiles*		1967/1	*Animal Motifs on Fabrics*
#136	*Peruvian Textile Techniques*		1967/4	*Japanese Resist-dyeing Technique*
1961/3	*Gold and Textiles*		1968/2	*Textiles in Biblical Times*
1963/2	*Early Chinese Silks*		1969/2	*Greek Contemporary Handweaving*
1964/6	*Knitting Techniques*		1969/3	*Bamboo*

Notes to the Text

CHAPTER 1

1. Will Durant, *Story of Civilization,* Part I, "Our Oriental Heritage" (New York: Simon and Schuster, 1954), p. 1.

CHAPTER 3

1. "Warp and Weft in Eastern Symbolism," *Ciba Review,* #16.
2. Robert J. Forbes, *Studies in Ancient Technology,* Vol. 4, "Textiles" (New York: W. S. Heinman, 1964), p. 229.
3. Forbes, p. 160.
4. *Histories,* Book III.
5. C. J. Lamm, *Tilskueren* (Copenhagen, 1938), p. 338
6. *Ibid.*
7. Forbes, p. 236.

CHAPTER 4

1. (New York: Vintage, 1954), p. 112.
2. Richard Winston, *Charlemagne from the Hammer to the Cross* (New York: Vintage, 1954), p. 112.
3. William Holmes, *Textile Fabrics of Ancient Peru* (Bureau of Ethnology, Smithsonian Institution, Bulletin #7, 1889).
4. Richardson Wright, *Hawkers and Walkers in Early America* (Philadelphia, 1926), pp. 104–5.
5. Mary M. Atwater, *The Shuttlecraft Book of American Hand-weaving* (New York: Macmillan, 1956), p. 6.
6. Margaret White, *The Decorative Arts of New Jersey* (Princeton, N.J.: Van Nostrand, 1964), p. 56.
7. *Ibid.*

CHAPTER 5

1. Nikolaus Pevsner, *Pioneers of Modern Design* (Middlesex, Eng.: Penguin, 1960), p. 22.
2. Gillian Naylor, *The Bauhaus* (London: Studio Vista, 1968).
3. *Anni Albers: On Weaving* (Middletown, Conn.: Wesleyan, 1965), p. 79.
4. *Craft Horizons,* XXX (December 1970), p. 5.
5. *Ibid.*

CHAPTER 7

1. Leslie J. Clarke, *The Craftsman in Textiles* (New York: Praeger, 1968), pp. 52–55.

CHAPTER 9

1. (Middletown, Conn.: Wesleyan, 1965), p. 45.

CHAPTER 11

1. "Helena Barynina Hernmarck," *Craft Horizons,* XXX (March/April 1970), p. 20.

CHAPTER 17

1. William Jaggard, ed., *Dyes and Dyeing Natures Fadeless Colours,* reprinted from a text of 1705.
2. *The Dier's Assistant in the Art of Dyeing Wool and Woollen Goods,* ext. from the works of Ferguson, Dufay, Hellot, Geoffrey, and Colbert (London: Paraclete Potter, 1813).
3. Jaggard.

CHAPTER 18

1. The material dealing with ikat printing techniques has been excerpted from Mary I. Ehlers, "Some Experimentation in Resist and Discharge Processes: Batik, Ikat, Resist and Direct Dye, Resist and Direct Discharge," (Unpublished thesis, Iowa State University, 1970).

CHAPTER 20

1. Jean Scorgie, "Handweaver's Designs for Contemporary Garments in Loom and Nonloom Techniques" (Unpublished thesis, Iowa State University, 1969).
2. *Ibid.*

CHAPTER 21

1. Cecil Lubell, "The Materials," *Body Covering* (New York: Museum of Contemporary Crafts, 1968), p. 5.
2. Quoted in Lee Nordness, *Objects: USA* (New York: Viking, 1970), p. 335.
3. *Craft Horizons,* XXVIII (September/October 1968), p. 12.
4. *Craft Horizons,* XXIV (March/April 1964), p. 23.
5. *Ibid.,* p. 24.
6. *Craft Horizons,* XXX (August 1970), p. 19.
7. Alexander Weatherson, "Body Covering: Psychological Aspects," *Body Covering* (New York: Museum of Contemporary Crafts, 1968), pp. 7–8.

Glossary

Terms italicized in the definitions are themselves defined within the glossary.

adjective dye   A dye that requires a *mordant* to produce fast color.

apron   A canvas fabric nailed to the *cloth beam* and *warp beam* on some *looms*. The aprons help to maintain the *warp* in its proper position.

back beam   Part of the framework of a *loom;* a rigid beam at the back of the loom that supports the *warp* and maintains its horizontal position.

back stitch   See *Brook's Bouquet.*

backstrap loom   A simple horizontal *loom* on which *warp tension* is maintained between a stationary object and the body of the weaver.

balanced weave   A *weave* in which the number of *warp* yarns per inch is equal to the number of *weft* yarns per inch.

bark cloth   See *tapa cloth.*

basic weave   A specific system of yarn interlacement not derived from any other system. The basic weaves are usually considered to be *plain weave, twill,* and *satin.*

basket weave   A *derivative* of *plain weave* created by consistently interlacing two or more *warp* yarns with two or more *weft* yarns.

basketry   A *weaving* technique that employs semirigid materials to create a self-supporting object.

basse lisse   A *tapestry* woven on a conventional horizontal *loom.*

bast fiber   A woody *fiber* from a plant such as jute, flax, sisal, or hemp.

batten   See *beater.*

beaming   The process of winding the *warp* yarns onto the *warp beam.*

beater   The framework that supports the *reed* on a *loom.* The beater swings freely to pack the *weft* yarn into position.

bight   See *bout.*

blanket   In *weaving,* a trial *web* or sampler.

block   A pattern unit or section of a *weave.*

blocking   A finishing process applied to *fabrics* to make them conform to a desired shape.

bobbin   A spool around which the *weft* yarn is wrapped for *weaving.* Often, the bobbin fits into a larger *shuttle.* Also, a yarn-carrying tool for lacemaking, *tapestry,* and several other techniques.

bobbin lace   A form of *lace* worked with several individual threads each wrapped around a spool or bobbin.

bobbin winder   A simple hand-cranked or electric machine for winding *yarn* onto a *bobbin,* spool, or *quill.*

bottom mordanting   The application of a *mordant* to a material before it is dyed.

bouclé yarn   A looped *novelty yarn* similar to a *ratiné.*

bout   In weaving, a group of *warp* yarns treated alike.
  1. One complete circuit of yarn on the *warping frame.*
  2. One group of yarns tied together at the *cloth stick.*
  3. One group of yarns *warped* and *chained* together.

braiding   A simple *finger weave* used to create decorative bands.

breast beam   Part of the framework of a *loom;* a rigid beam at the front of the loom that supports the *warp* and maintains its horizontal position.

brocade   A three-element construction in which a decorative yarn is added to a *plain-weave* or other simple ground. Brocades can be *loom-controlled* or *discontinuous.*

Brook's Bouquet   A *lace weave* in which the *weft* yarn is wrapped around several *warps* to draw them together.

butterfly shuttle   A miniature skein of *weft* yarn wound around the fingers, used for *tapestry* or other *finger weaves.*

cable yarn   A *yarn* composed of two or more *ply yarns* twisted together.

card clothing   A set of wires or spikes protruding from a foundation, used in *carding.*

card sliver   A thick strand of partially aligned *fibers;* the product of the *carding* operation.

card weaving   A simple *weaving* technique in which hole-punched cards or tablets, through which the *warp* yarns are threaded, take the place of a *loom* and *harnesses.* The result is a narrow band of *warp-face fabric.*

carding   The process of separating and partially aligning loose *fibers* in preparation for *spinning.*

cartoon   A preliminary sketch used as a guide for pattern *weaving,* especially for *tapestry* or *rya.*

castle   The uppermost part of the *loom* framework, which supports the *harnesses.*

chaining   A *weaving* technique in which the *weft* yarn is looped around groups of *warp* yarns to form a surface *pile.*

chaining the warp   The process of looping the *warp* upon itself to prevent tangling during the transfer from the *warping frame* to the *loom.*

chiné   See *ikat.*

choke ties   Lengths of cord wrapped tightly around the *warp* yarns to maintain their order during transfer to the *loom.*

chroma   See *intensity.*

cloth beam   A cylindrical member at the front of the *loom* around which the woven *fabric* is wound.

cloth stick   A rod attached to the *cloth beam* upon which *warp* yarns are mounted.

clove hitch   One of the principal knots used in *macramé.*

combing   A process by which loose *fibers* are straightened and sorted for length prior to *spinning* according to the *worsted system.*

cord yarn   See *cable yarn.*

corduroy   In handweaving, a *weave* that provides for long *weft floats* on the surface of the *fabric,* which are cut after weaving to create a *pile.*

corkscrew yarn A *novelty yarn* created by twisting together *yarns* of different diameters, sizes, or *fiber* contents, or by varying the speed or direction of twist.

counterbalance loom A floor *loom* in which the *harnesses* operate in tandem. As one harness is raised, the connecting one is lowered.

crepe yarn A highly twisted *yarn*.

crimp The waviness of a *fiber*.

crochet A single-element construction in which a *yarn* is looped upon itself by means of a notched hook to create *fabric*.

cross The point at which the *warp* yarns are alternated around pegs on the *warping frame* or reel during the *warping* operation. The cross maintains the correct sequence of yarns. Also called the *lease*.

cross ties Preliminary ties made in the *warp* yarn to maintain the *cross* until the *lease sticks* are inserted.

damask A reversible patterned *fabric* created from a combination of *satin* and *sateen* weaves.

Danish medallion A *lace weave* in which the *weft* yarn departs from its horizontal orientation to create a loop on the surface of the *fabric*.

denier The basic unit of size of a *filament yarn,* equal to the weight in grams of 9000 meters of yarn.

dent One space in the *reed* of a *loom*.

derivative weave A modification of a *basic weave*.

design The ordered arrangement of parts to make a whole; loosely, a pattern or motif.

discontinuous weave Any *weave* in which some of the *weft* yarns do not run from *selvedge* to selvedge but appear only in certain portions of the *web*.

double weave A *weave* that produces two distinct layers of cloth simultaneously, often connected or interpenetrating at some point.

double-face fabric Any *fabric* with two structurally identical sides.

draft A graphic representation of the appearance and/or mechanics of a particular *weave*.

drafting In spinning, the process of compressing and extending loose *fibers* into *yarn*.

draw The *draft* of a threading pattern for the *loom;* the order in which the *warp* yarns are threaded through the *heddles*.

draw-down The graphic representation of a *weave* on paper; a weave *draft*.

draw-in The tendency for a *web* to narrow on the *loom* during the *weaving* process.

dressing The preparation of the *loom* for *weaving,* which includes: *beaming,* threading the *heddles,* sleying the *reed,* and tying on to the *cloth stick*.

dukagång A Scandinavian *laid-in weave* in which the decorative yarn *floats* over three consecutive *warp* yarns and is tied down by the fourth.

dyestuff Any material, natural or synthetic, that can be used for imparting color to an absorptive subject, such as a *yarn*.

eccentric weft A *weaving* technique in which the *weft* yarn departs from its horizontal orientation to move in arcs or at acute angles to the *warp*.

embroidery Ornamental stitchery applied with a needle to a *fabric* ground.

ends Individual *warp* yarns.

fabric A construction made from *fibers;* a *textile*.

felt A nonwoven *fabric* constructed by interlocking loose *fibers* through a combination of heat, moisture, and pressure or friction.

fiber A material, either man-made or derived from natural sources, capable of being spun into *yarn* or thread.

filament fiber A *fiber* that can be measured in yards or miles. Silk and all the man-made fibers are filament length. Compare *staple fiber*.

filler See *weft*.

finger weave A *weave* created through the direct intervention of the weaver by manipulation of individual *warp* yarns with the fingers or a *pickup stick*.

flake yarn A *yarn* to which small tufts of *fiber* have been added at irregular intervals.

float Any portion of a *warp* or *weft* yarn that extends without intersection over two or more units of the opposing set of yarns.

flossa See *rya*.

flyer wheel A *spinning* device that *drafts* and twists the *fibers* simultaneously. Power is supplied by a foot treadle.

frame loom Any simple square or rectangular *loom,* usually lacking *harnesses* and a *beater*.

gamp A trial *web* or sampler.

gating The process of adjusting the *loom* after it has been *dressed* but before *weaving* begins.

gauze weave A *lace weave* created by crossing or twisting selected *warp* yarns before inserting the *weft*.

Ghiordes knot A classic knot used to create *pile* rugs and for *rya* weaving.

God's-eye A diamond-shape emblem worked by wrapping *yarn* continually around two crossed sticks; a ritual symbol in Latin America.

guide string A preliminary measuring cord used to establish the correct *warp* length and pattern of winding on the *warping frame* or reel.

guimpe yarn See *ratiné yarn*.

hand The touch or feel of a *fabric*.

handspindle The simplest *spinning* device consisting of a disc-shaped weight centered on a long notched shaft.

hank A unit of measure for cotton, wool, and silk *yarns*. A hank of cotton or silk yarn equals 840 yards; a hank of worsted yarn equals 560 yards; a hank of woolen yarn equals either 300 or 1600 yards.

harness A frame that supports a group of *heddles* on the *loom*.

haute lisse A *tapestry* woven on a vertical *tapestry loom*.

heddle A wire, strip of metal, or cord with an eye in the center. One (or more) *warp* yarns are threaded through each heddle to control the separation of the warp and create a *shed*.

heddle frame See *harness*.

heddle rod A device that performs the function of a *harness* on simple *looms*.

herringbone A *derivative* of the *twill* weave.

high wheel A *spinning* device that drafts and twists the fiber in two operations. Power is supplied by manually turning the large drive wheel.

hooking The process of forcing loops of *yarn* through a previously woven backing to create a *pile* fabric.

hue The pure state of any color.

ikat The process of *resist* dyeing portions of a *warp* or *weft* (or both) before *weaving* to create a pattern.

inkle loom A simple *loom* used for *weaving* narrow bands of *warp-face fabric*.

inlay, inlaid See *laid-in weave*.

intensity The relative purity or grayness of a color.

jack loom A floor *loom* in which each *harness* operates independently.

Jacquard loom A complex power *loom* capable of producing elaborate pattern *weaves*.

jaspé See *ikat*.

kasuri, kashiri See *ikat*.

kilim A classic Polish form of *tapestry*.

knitting A single-element construction in which a *yarn* is continually looped upon itself by means of needles to create *fabric*.

knob yarn See *nub yarn*.

lace A decorative openwork *fabric* created by twisting fine threads together to form a pattern. See also *needle lace, bobbin lace*.

lace weave An openwork *weave* usually characterized by a distortion from the parallel of *warp* or *weft* yarns.

laid-in weave A *finger weave* in which decorative *weft* yarns are added to a *plain-weave* ground in selected portions of the *web*.

lamb's wool Wool clipped from sheep less than eight months old.

lamm, lam A bar that connects the *harnesses* to the *treadles* on a floor *loom*.

lary sticks Temporary supports fastened between the *breast beam* and the *back beam* of a *loom*, used by some weavers during the loom-*dressing* operation.

lea A unit of measure for linen *yarn*, equal to 300 yards.

lease, leish, leash See *cross*.

lease sticks A pair of smooth, flat sticks used to maintain the *cross* in the *warp* yarns before and during *weaving*.

leno A *lace weave* created by crossing selected *warp* yarns in a certain pattern prior to inserting the *weft*.

line Flax (linen) *fibers* longer than 12 inches.

linsey-woolsey A Colonial expression referring to *fabric* woven from a linen *warp* and a wool *weft*.

linters Waste *fibers* that are too short for *spinning*. Linters are used in the manufacture of rayon, a *synthetic fiber*.

lockstitch A *weaving* technique in which the *weft* wraps tightly around several *warp* yarns to draw them together and create an openwork effect.

loom Any device used for *weaving* that performs the minimum function of holding the *warp* yarns taut and in their proper positions.

loom-controlled weave Any *weave* that is created solely through the interaction of the *heddles* and *harnesses* on a *loom*. Compare *finger weave*.

loop yarn A *novelty yarn* in which a curling effect yarn is held in place around a core by a binder yarn.

looping A high-*pile weave* in which loops of *weft* yarn are left on the surface of the *fabric*.

macramé A technique in which a set of parallel yarns are knotted together to create a decorative *fabric*.

Mali An industrial *fabric*-construction process—with applications for handweaving—in which two sets of *yarns*

or yarns and pieces of fabric are stitched together in the manner of sewing.

man-made fiber A *fiber* created in the laboratory that contains no natural ingredients; loosely, any nonnatural fiber. Compare *synthetic fiber*.

matting The process of constructing a nonwoven *fabric* from pounded mulberry bark. See also *tapa cloth*.

mercerization A finish applied to cotton to improve its luster, strength, and dyeability.

merino yarns *Yarns* spun from a mixture of wool and cotton in any proportion.

Mexican lace A variation of *leno*.

mock double cloth A three-element *weave* composed of two sets of *weft* yarn but only one *warp*. The *fabric* resembles both *brocade* and *tapestry*.

monofilament yarn A *yarn* composed of only one *fiber filament*.

mordant A chemical substance that combines with a *dyestuff* to enhance absorption of the color and to make the color fast.

multifilament yarn A *yarn* composed of two or more *fiber filaments*.

multiharness loom Any *loom* with more than four *harnesses*.

natural fiber Any *fiber* derived from plant or animal sources. The four most common natural fibers are cotton, linen, wool, and silk.

needle lace A form of *lace* composed of stitches and knots made with a single continuous thread in a needle.

netting A looping and knotting technique worked on a single continuous strand to produce openwork *fabric*.

novelty yarn A complex *yarn* characterized by irregularities of size, twist, or effect.

nub yarn A *novelty yarn* in which a decorative strand is wrapped repeatedly around a core to form an enlarged segment.

overshot A *weave* characterized by *weft floats* on a *plain-weave* ground.

paddle, warping paddle A flat tool with a handle and two parallel rows of holes or slots, used for measuring several *yarns* at once on the *warping frame* or reel.

paddle warping The process of measuring several *warp* yarns simultaneously with the aid of a paddle.

Persian knot See *Sehna knot*.

pick See *weft*.

pick count The number of *weft* yarns per inch in a woven *fabric*. Compare *sett*.

picking 1. In *weaving*, the act of throwing or passing the *weft* yarn through a *shed* in the *warp*. 2. In *spinning*, a hand operation in which the compact mass of *fibers* is initially opened and blended prior to *carding*.

pickup stick A narrow pointed needle or rod used for manipulating the *warp* yarns for a *finger weave*.

pile weave A *weave* characterized by strands or loops of *weft* yarn protruding from the surface of the *fabric*.

plain weave A *basic weave* created by consistently interlacing one *warp* yarn with one *weft* yarn.

plaiting A simple *finger weave* used primarily to create decorative bands.

ply yarn A *yarn* in which two or more single strands are twisted together.

primary color   A color that cannot be mixed from other colors.

profile draft   An abbreviated method of graphic notation for unit pattern weaves; a short *draft*.

quill   The shaft around which the *weft* yarn is wound in a *bobbin* or *shuttle*.

raddle   See *spreader*.

ratchet   A braking device on both the *warp beam* and the *cloth beam* of a *loom*, which prevents them from turning and holds the *warp* under *tension*. The ratchet is released to roll the warp forward.

ratiné yarn   A *novelty yarn* in which a bulky yarn is looped around a core yarn and held in place with a binder.

raw silk   Silk that has not been degummed and still contains the serecin secreted by the silkworm.

reed   A comblike device set into the *beater* on a *loom*. The reed helps to maintain the horizontal position of the *warp* yarns and also beats each new *weft* yarn into position.

reed hook   See *sley hook*.

rep weave   A derivative of *plain weave* in which the pattern of interlacement is extended either vertically or horizontally.

reprocessed wool   Wool that has been reclaimed from *fabric* scraps that were never used.

resist   Any material that is applied to a surface before dyeing or printing to prevent absorption of ink or dye in the area covered.

reused wool   Wool reclaimed from used *fabric*.

rib weave   See *rep weave*.

rölakan   A classic Scandinavian form of *tapestry*.

roving   1. An untwisted *yarn*. 2. A condensed mass of *fibers* ready for *spinning* into yarn.

rya   A Scandinavian *pile weave* based on the *Ghiordes knot*.

ryijy   The Finnish name for *rya*.

sateen   A *weave* similar to *satin* but with *floats* in the *weft* direction.

satin weave   A *basic weave* characterized by long *floats* on the surface of the *fabric*.

saturation   See *intensity*.

scaffold yarns   Extra *yarns* added temporarily to a *warp* or weft on the *loom* to contribute color, density, texture, or some special effect.

scouring   A cleaning bath that removes dirt and natural oils from wool *fibers, yarns,* or *fabrics*. Vegetable fibers are also scoured before dyeing.

secondary color   The product of two *primary colors*.

sectional warp beam   A *warp beam* divided into 2-inch segments, essential for *sectional warping*.

sectional warping   A method of measuring the *warp* yarns directly on the *loom*, thus combining the *warping* and *beaming* operations.

seed yarn   Similar to a *nub yarn*, but with smaller segments.

Sehna knot   A classic knot used to create *pile* rugs, especially in Persia.

selvedge, selvage   The lengthwise or *warp*wise edge of a woven *fabric*; the point at which the *weft* yarns bind the warp to form a finished edge.

sericulture   The cultivation of the silkworm for the production of silk.

sett, set   The density of a *fabric*; the number of *warp* yarns per inch, especially as *sleyed* at the *reed*.

shag weave   Any *weave* that incorporates a long, cut *pile*.

shed   The space between separated *warp* yarns through which the *weft* yarn is passed. A shed is created by raising one or more *harnesses* or *heddles*.

shed sword   A flat stick used for creating a *shed* on simple *looms*.

shedding   The process of creating a *shed* in the *warp* by manipulation of *harnesses* or *heddles* on the *loom*.

shoddy   See *reused wool*.

shot   One passage of the *weft* yarn through a *shed*; also, one weft yarn.

shuttle   A tool on which the *weft* yarn is wrapped so it can be passed through a *shed* in the *warp*.

shuttle race   An extension at the base of the *reed* which supports the *shuttle* as it moves across the *warp*.

silk-screen printing   A form of *stencil printing* in which dye is squeezed through a stretched mesh of silk that has been painted with a *resist* in the areas that are not to print.

singles yarn   A *yarn* composed of only one strand.

sizing   A finishing process applied to *yarns* to make them stronger and more compact.

skeleton yarns   See *scaffold yarns*.

sley hook   A tool for threading *warp* yarns through the *dents* in a *reed* prior to *weaving*.

sleying   The process of drawing the *warp* yarns through the *reed* on a *loom*.

slit   A vertical opening in a *web*, especially in *tapestry*, created at the juncture of two pattern areas.

slit tapestry   A form of *tapestry* in which long slits or openings are created in the *fabric* by *weaving* sections of the *warp* independently.

slot knitting   A *knitting* process worked through an opening in a board to create flat *fabric*.

slub yarn   A *novelty yarn* that is left untwisted at intervals to produce bulky areas.

solution dyeing   The process of introducing color into the liquid solution for *synthetic fibers* before they are extruded.

soumak   A low-*pile weave* in which the *weft* yarn is wrapped around a *warp* yarn or a group of warp yarns according to one of several patterns.

Spanish knot   A classic knot used to create *pile* rugs.

Spanish lace   A *lace weave* in which segments of the *warp* are woven individually.

spinning   The process of drawing out and twisting loose *fibers* to form a continuous strand of *yarn*.

spool knitting   A *knitting* process worked on a thread spool or disc to create a cylindrical *fabric*.

spool rack   An upright frame used to hold spools or cones of *yarn* during the measuring or for *sectional warping*.

sprang   A single-element construction in which a set of stretched *warp* yarns are twisted upon one another to form a symmetrical pattern.

spreader   A flat stick with nails or spikes protruding at one-inch intervals; used to distribute the *warp* yarns evenly on the *loom*.

square knot   One of the principal knots used in *macramé*.

square knotting   See *macramé*.

squirrel cage reel   See *swift*.

staple fiber A short *fiber* that can be measured in inches or fractions of inches. All *natural fibers* except silk are staple length. Compare *filament fiber*.

stencil printing A method of transferring an image or design to surface by tracing around a precut pattern.

stretcher A device for maintaining consistent width of *fabric* on the *loom*.

string heddle A *heddle* made of linen cord.

substantive dye A dye that is permanent when heated alone with the material to be colored; a *dyestuff* that does not require a *mordant*.

swift A device used to hold a skein of *yarn* while it is wound onto spools or *shuttles*, or to wind a skein from a cone or spool.

synthetic fiber A *fiber* made by chemical means but composed partly of vegetable materials; loosely, any non-natural fiber. Compare *man-made fiber*.

tabby See *plain weave*.

tablet weaving See *card weaving*.

takeup The extra *yarn* allowance needed for lacing over and under the opposing set of yarns in *weaving*.

tapa cloth A nonwoven *fabric* once common in Africa, Hawaii, and the South Pacific, made by pounding bark from the paper mulberry tree.

tapestry A *weft-face plain-weave fabric* in which the *weft* yarns are *discontinuous;* usually decorative or expressive.

tapestry fork A tool that takes the place of a *beater* and *reed* in *tapestry* weaving.

tapestry loom A vertical two-*harness loom* used primarily for *finger weaves*. *Tapestries* woven on such a loom are referred to as *haute lisse*.

tela se lengua A Spanish form of *ikat* printing, usually in blue dye on white yarns.

temple, template See *stretcher*.

tension In *weaving*, the tautness of *warp* yarns during the measuring process and when stretched on the *loom*.

tension box A machine used to maintain uniform *tension* in the *warp* yarns during *sectional warping*.

tertiary color A color produced by combining adjacent *primary* and *secondary* colors.

textile A construction made from *fibers;* often used to refer specifically to woven *fabric*.

thread count The number of *warp* and *weft* yarns per inch in a woven *fabric*.

thrums The unweavable portion of the *warp* yarns required for tying on to the *loom*. Also called *loom waste*.

tie-up The connections between the *harnesses* and the *lamms* and between the lamms and the *treadles* on a floor *loom*. Also, the process of making such connections for a particular *weave*.

top A thick strand of long, partially aligned *fibers;* the product of the *combing* operation.

top dyeing The process of dyeing a second color over a previous one.

top mordanting The application of a *mordant* to a material after it has been dyed.

tow Flax (linen) *fibers* shorter than 12 inches.

treadle A foot lever that controls the raising of *harnesses* on a floor *loom*.

tromp as writ A term signifying that a *weave* is to be *treadled* in the same order as the *harnesses* are threaded.

tubular double weave A *weave* that produces two distinct layers of *fabric* connected at both *selvedges*.

tufting An industrial form of *hooking*.

Turkish knot See *Ghiordes knot*.

Tussah silk Silk from cocoons of uncultivated silkworms.

twill A *basic weave* characterized by diagonal lines.

twining A two-element construction in which two or more *weft* yarns are twisted around one another as they interlace with the *warp*.

ultimates Short lengths of flax *fiber* ready for *spinning*.

umbrella swift See *swift*.

unbalanced weave A *weave* in which either the *warp* yarns or the *weft* yarns are more concentrated. Compare *balanced weave*.

value The lightness or darkness of a color.

virgin wool New wool that has never before been made into *yarn*.

warp A set of yarns that are parallel to one another and to the *selvedge* or longer dimension of a woven *fabric:* the lengthwise element in a woven construction.

warp beam A cylindrical member at the back of a *loom* around which the unwoven *warp* yarns are wound.

warp stick A rod attached to the *warp beam* upon which *warp* yarns are mounted.

warp-face Describes a *fabric* or *weave* in which the *warp* yarns predominate or cover the *weft* completely.

warping The process of preparing the *warp* yarns for the loom: measuring, establishing the *cross, chaining*.

warping comb See *spreader*.

warping creel See *spool rack*.

warping frame, warping reel Simple devices for measuring the *warp* yarns prior to *weaving*. Both make provision for establishing a *cross* in the yarns.

warp-weighted loom An upright *loom* used by many ancient cultures, in which the *warp* yarns are suspended from a horizontal bar and weighted at the bottom.

weave A particular pattern or order of interlacement for *warp* and *weft* yarns.

weaving The process by which two sets of threads of any substance are interlaced at right angles to form a continuous *web*.

web The *fabric* created by interlacing *warp* and *weft;* the product of the *loom*.

weft A set of yarns or other material perpendicular to the *selvedge* or longer dimension of a woven *fabric;* the crosswise element in a woven construction.

weft-face Describes a *fabric* or *weave* in which the *weft* yarns predominate or cover the *warp* completely.

wild silk See *Tussah silk*.

woof See *weft*.

woolen system A *spinning* process wherein relatively short, un*combed* wool or flax *fibers* are made into *yarn*.

worsted system A *spinning* process wherein long, *combed* wool or flax *fibers* are made into yarn.

yarn A continuous strand of material spun from drawn-out and twisted *fibers*.

yarn count The size or relative coarseness or fineness of a *yarn*. *Filament fiber* yarns are measured in *deniers;* the greater the number, the coarser the yarn. *Staple fiber* yarns are measured in *hanks* (cotton, wool, and silk) or *leas* (linen); the greater the number, the finer the yarn.

Index

References are to page numbers, except for color plates and black-and-white illustrations, which are identified by figure and plate numbers.

Abakanowicz, Magdalena, *Abakan Red III,* Pl. 12, p. 94; environmental wall, 332, Figs. 554, 555

Adams, Alice, construction, 341, Fig. 562

Albers, Anni, 72, 73, 136, 158, 221; Bauhaus tapestry, 73, Fig. 118; *La Lux I,* 169, Fig. 296; *Tikal,* 158, Fig. 273; *With Verticals,* 73, Fig. 120

Albers, Josef, 73

Al-Hilali, Neda, decoration on vest, Pl. 37, p. 304; *Nar,* Pl. 23, p. 231

American Crafts Council, 74–75

American Fabrics, 328

Anselevicius, Evelyn, *Linear Face II,* tapestry, 336, Fig. 560

appliqué, ancient Egyptian, 28; on felt, 12, Fig. 15

Arkwright, Richard, spinning machine, 250, Fig. 458

Arts and Crafts Movement, England, 71

asbestos fiber, 85, Fig. 136

Atwater, Mary Meigs, 73–74, 219; *Crackle Weave,* 73, Fig. 119

back stitch, 160

backstrap loom, 95–96, 209–213, Figs. 150, 151, 377–383

balanced weave, 133, Fig. 221

Baldishol Tapestry, 50, Pl. 6, p. 41

Bandol, Jean de, *The Apocalypse,* tapestry, 48, Fig. 75

Baroque period in Europe, handweaving, 65–67, Figs. 109–112; Flanders, 65–66, Figs. 109, 110; France, 67, Fig. 112

basket weave, 141, Fig. 236

basketry, 4, 14–15, Figs. 1, 21–24; contemporary, 15, Fig. 24; Egyptian, 14, Fig. 22; Pomo Indian, 15, Fig. 23; Wappo Indian, 14–15, Fig. 21

Bataille, Nicolas, *The Apocalypse,* tapestry, 48, 49, Fig. 75; *King Arthur,* from *Christian Heroes,* tapestry, 48, Fig. 76

Bauhaus School of Design, 71–72, 302

Bayeux Tapestry, 47, 50, 317, Fig. 74

beam, back, 90; breast, 90; cloth, 90–91; warp, 90

beaming, 119–122, Figs. 199–203

beaters, 92, Fig. 147; types of, 102

beating, 131; loom mechanism, 92

Beaumetz, Pierre de, 48

Becherer, Thelma, wall hanging, 87, Fig. 140

Bellini, Jacopo, 64

Beni Hassan, wall paintings, 27, 249, Fig. 48

Berger, Otti, 72

binding fabric edges, 182, Fig. 323

binding points, 140

blanket stitching, 181, Fig. 320

blocking, 186, Fig. 335

Blumenau, Lili, 73–74; *Transparent and Opaque,* 73, Fig. 121

bobbin quills, 130, Fig. 216

bobbin winder, 104, 130, Figs. 163, 164, 215

bobbins, 103, 130, 172, Fig. 217; historical, 23, Fig. 40, tapestry, 103, 172, Fig. 302

Bodlaender, Hesi, macramé necklace, 228, Fig. 413

Bonchon, Basile, 98

Börner, Hélène, 71

bouclé yarns, 84, Fig. 133

braided fringe, 182–184, Figs. 330, 331

braiding, 238, Figs. 436, 437

brocade, 155, 168–169, Figs. 266–268, 295, 296; continuous (loom-controlled), 155, Figs. 266–268, Pls. 14–16, p. 128; discontinuous (weaver-controlled), 168–169, Figs. 295, 296; Japanese, 58, Figs. 95, 96; warp, 155, Figs. 266, 267, Pls. 14, 15, p. 128; weft, 155, Figs. 266, 268, Pl. 16, p. 128

Broederlani, Melchior, *Annunciation,* tapestry, 62, Fig. 99

Bronzino, Agnolo, *Eleanora of Toledo and Her Son Giovanni de' Medici,* 65, Fig. 107

Brook's Bouquet, 160, 164, Figs. 278, 280

butterfly shuttle, 157, Fig. 269

Byzantine Empire, handweaving in, 37–38, Figs. 64–67

cable (cord) yarn, 83, Fig. 131

cabling, 267

Carcher, Nicolaus, 65

card weaving, 241–244, Figs. 446–452, Pl. 24, p. 231

carding, 45, 256–258, Figs. 72, 469–474; hand, 256–258, Figs. 469–473; machine, 258, Fig. 474; tools for, 253–254, Figs. 465, 466

carpets, *see* rugs

castle, 91

chaining, 191, Figs. 338, 339

Chancay weaving, Peru, 54–55, Figs. 86, 88

Chang, Karen, ikat, 294, Pls. 30–32, p. 285

Chase-Riboud, Barbara, *Time Womb,* 341, Fig. 563

chenille yarns, 84, Fig. 133

Chilkat Indians, 16, 192; twining, 16, Figs. 26, 27

Chimu weaving, Peru, 54

China, handweaving in, 33–35, 56–57, Figs. 54–59, 90–93

Chinese draw loom, Minko, woodcut, 98, Fig. 156

chinoiseries, 66, 67, Fig. 112

Chojnacka-Gantarska, Maria, *Le Son,* looped tapestry, 193, Fig. 349

choke ties, 116

chroma, 308

cloth of gold, 47, 61, Fig. 98

clove hitch (double half hitch), 183–184, 224–226, Figs. 405–409; diagonal, 225, Figs. 406, 407; for finishing a handwoven fabric, 183–184, Figs. 330, 331; horizontal, 225, Fig. 405; vertical, 225–226, Fig. 408

Cohen, Ahza, *Arrow in Four Parts,* tapestry, 305, Fig. 519

Colbert, Jean Batiste, 23, 67

Collingwood, Peter, 203; corduroy rug, 203, Fig. 365; sprang screen, 17, Fig. 30

Colonial America, weaving in, 67–69, Figs. 113–115

color, design element, 308–309; hue, 308, Fig. 523; intensity, 308–309; in weaving, 309, Pls. 35, 36, p. 303; primary, 308; secondary, 308; tertiary, 308; value, 308, Pl. 34, p. 303

combing, 83, 258–259, Figs. 475–477

combs, worsted, 254, Fig. 467

Coptic weaving, 35–37, 194, Figs. 60–63, Pl. 4, p. 39

corduroy, 203–205, Figs. 365–369

core yarn, 83, 267, Fig. 491

corkscrew yarns, 84, Fig. 133

corrective heddle, 91, Fig. 144

cotton fiber, 79, Fig. 125; mordanting, 276–277; perle, 84; scouring, 274–275

count, yarn, 86

counterbalance loom, 91, 100, 102, Figs. 144, 158

coverlets, Early American, 68–69, Figs. 113–115

Craft Horizons, 75

crocheting, innovations in, 330–331, Fig. 552

Crompton, Samuel, 69, 250

cross, 111, Figs. 181, 182

cross ties, 116, Figs. 189, 190

cross-stitching, 180, 181, Fig. 319

Cságoly, Klára, *Vollkommenheit,* tapestry, 176, Fig. 313

Curtis, Luke, multiple God's-eye, 240, Fig. 443

cutwork embroidery, 19

Daniels, Ruth, table mats, 322, Fig. 539

Danish medallion, 159–160, 165, Figs. 276, 277, 282

Decker, Janet, jacket, hat, and mittens, 342, Fig. 565

demi-line flax fibers, 83

design, 301–314; decorative, 301; drapery fabric, planning, 323; elements of, *see* elements of design; for textile industry, 333–335, Figs. 555–558; for the loom,

design (*continued*)
315–326; garments and accessories, planning, 318–321, Figs. 530–538; home furnishings, planning, 323–324; principles of, *see* principles of design; profile draft, 324, Figs. 543–545; repeat, 313, Fig. 528; sculpture, planning, 317–318; structural, 301; table linen, planning, 322–323, Figs. 539, 540; unit, 313, Fig. 529; upholstery fabric, planning, 323; wall hangings, planning, 317–318; weave analysis, 325–326, Fig. 546; yardage, planning, 323

Di Mare, Dominic, *Sculptural Form,* 87, Fig. 139

double half hitch, *see* clove hitch

double knot, 181, Fig. 327

double weaves, 152–155, 166–168, Figs. 258–265, 289–294; double-width cloth, 152, 153, Fig. 259; pattern, 166–168, Figs. 289–294; reverse, 154–155, Figs. 264–265; tubular, 153–154, Figs. 260–262, Pl. 13, p. 127

Dourdin, Jacques, 48, 49

dovetailing, 174, Fig. 306

draft, 136–139, 324–325; comprehensive, 138, 139, Figs. 233, 234; profile, 138, 324–325, Figs. 543–545; threading, 136–137, Figs. 227–229; tie-up, 137, Fig. 230; treadling, 137, Fig. 231; weave, 137–139, Fig. 232

drafting, in spinning, 247, 260, 261, Figs. 480, 483

drapery fabric, Liebes, 334, Fig. 557

draw, 136–137, Figs. 227–229; pointed, 137, Fig. 228; straight, 136–137, Fig. 227

draw, 98, Fig. 156

draw-in of web, 110

dressing the loom, 117–126, Figs. 192–211; errors, checking loom for, 125; heddles, threading, 122–123, Figs. 204–209; lease sticks, inserting, 117–118, Figs. 192, 193; reed, sleying, 123–124, Figs. 207, 208; sectional warping, 121–122, Figs. 202, 203; warp, spreading, 118–119, Figs. 194, 195; warp, winding, 119–121, Figs. 198–201; warp ends, tying at front of loom, 124–125, Fig. 209

Duderstadt, Bruce, hooked rug, 206, Fig. 371

dukagång, 169–170, Figs. 297–299

dyeing, yarn, 268–289; history of, 268–270, Fig. 493; Egypt, ancient, 28; equipment for, 272–273, Fig. 496; materials for, 272–273; natural dyestuffs, 278–289, Fig. 503; piece, 268, Pl. 26, p. 266; process of, 271–279

dyeing process, 271–279; dye bath, 277–278, Fig. 501; dye procedures, special, 278–279, Figs. 502, 503; equipment for, 272–273, Fig. 496; extraction of the dye, 273–274, Figs. 497, 498; materials for, 272–273; mordanting, 275–277; natural materials, gathering, 271–272, Fig. 495; results, documenting, 279, Pl. 25, p. 265; scouring, 274–275

dyes, adjective, 271; extraction of, 273–274, Figs. 497, 498; history of, 268–270; procedures, special, 278–279, Figs. 502, 503; substantive, 271, Fig. 494

eccentric weft, in tapestry, 173

Edeling, Alice, metallic dress, 328, Fig. 547

edge finishes, 180–185; binding, 182, Fig. 323; braided fringe, 182–184, Figs. 330, 331; hemming, 181–182, Figs. 321, 322; knotted fringe, 182–184, Figs. 325–329; stitching, 180–181, Figs. 317–320; woven fringe, 184–185, Figs. 332–334

Egypt, ancient, handweaving in, 26–28, Figs. 45–49

Egyptian plaitwork, 16–17

elements of design, 302–309; color and light, 308–309; line, 302–305, Figs. 518, 519; shape, 302; space, 305–306, Fig. 520; texture, 306–307, Figs. 521, 522

Elliott, Lillian, *Tribal Cloth,* card weaving, 244, Pl. 24, p. 232

embroidered net panel, 20, Fig. 39

embroidery, ancient Egyptian, 28

England, handweaving during Renaissance, 63–64, Fig. 104

Entanglements, 306, Fig. 520

Eshkanian, Ruben, *Haystack,* pile tapestry, 203, 313, Pl. 21, p. 197

Europe, handweaving in, Baroque period, 65–67, Figs. 109–112; Middle Ages, 45–51, Figs. 72–79; Renaissance, 61–65, Figs. 98–108

Fannin, Allen and Dorothy, 247; *Stairwell,* casement fabric, 264, Fig. 488

Far East, handweaving in, 33–35, 56–59; China, 33–35, 56–57, Figs. 54–59, 90–93; Japan, 57–59, Figs. 94–97

feather mantle, Chancay, 55, Fig. 88

Feito, Luis, *Guadarrama,* tapestry, 313, Fig. 529

felting, 5–6, 11–12, Fig. 13

fiber preparation for handspinning, 255–260, Figs. 468–479; carding, 256–258, Figs. 469–474; combing, 258–259, Figs. 475–477; picking, 255–256, Fig. 468; roving, forming, 259–260, Figs. 478, 479; scouring, 256; sorting, 255

fibers, 79; animal (protein), 80; asbestos, 85, Fig. 136; characteristics of, 81; classification of, 80–81; combed, 83; filament, 82; flax, 83; hair staple, 83; man-made, 80–81; mineral, 80; natural, 80; principal, 75, Figs. 125–128; silk, 83; staple, 83; synthetic, 80, 81, 86; wool, 251, Fig. 459; vegetable (cellulosic), 80

Field of the Cloth of Gold, 61, Fig. 98

filament fibers, 82

filament-fiber yarns, 86, Fig. 137

filler, *see* weft

finger weaves, *see* weaver-controlled weaves

finishing procedures, 180–186

Fischer, Mildred, *Elokuu,* 88, Fig. 142; *Festival,* woven fragment fused to pulped linen, 329, Fig. 549; *Panel,* 312, Fig. 527

flake yarns, 84, 264, Figs. 133, 489

Flanders, handweaving in, Baroque, 65–66, Figs. 109, 110; Middle Ages, 49, Fig. 77; Renaissance, 61–63, Figs. 100–103

flax (linen) fibers, 83

flossa knot, 201–203, Figs. 358–363; *see also* rya

flyer wheel, 252–253, 261, Figs. 462, 463, 482

frame looms, historical, 96–97, Figs. 154, 155; permanent, 213–214, Figs. 384–387; reusable, 215–220, Figs. 388–395; square, 216–217, Figs. 390–392

France, handweaving, in, Baroque, 67, Figs. 111, 112, Pl. 9, p. 60; Middle Ages, 47–49, Figs. 74–76; Renaissance, 64, Fig. 105

fringe, braided, 182–184, Figs. 330, 331; knotted, 182–184, Figs. 325–329; woven, 184–185, Figs. 332–334

Frost, Robert, of Nottingham, 23

Fruytier, Wilhelmina, tapestry, 177, Fig. 314

functional finishes, 180, 186; blocking, 186, Fig. 335; cleaning, 186

fustian, 46

gauze weave, 156

Ghiordes knot, 199–202; continuous, 200, 203, Fig. 353; individual, 199, 202, Figs. 352, 358–362

Gilmurray, Susan, woven pillow covers, Pl. 39, p. 337

Glauber's salts, 277

Gobelin overcast, 173, Fig. 305

Gobelins workshops, Paris, 67

God's-eye, 240–241, Figs. 443–445

Goya, Francisco de, *Queen Maria Luisa,* 13, Fig. 19

Grau-Garriga, *Écuménisme,* tapestry, 74, 172, Figs. 122, 303; *Nisaga Decadent,* tapestry, 341, Pl. 42, p. 340

Greece, classical, handweaving in, 31–32, Fig. 52

Greek soumak, 166, Fig. 340

Grenier, Pasquier, 62

griffe, 98

ground looms, 96, Figs. 152, 153

Gropius, Walter, 71

Grossen, Françoise, *Contact,* 228, Fig. 414

guide string, wrapping, 111–112, Figs. 179, 180

guimpe yarns, 84

half knot, 223–224, Figs. 400, 401

Hallman, Ted, *Albe's Tree,* 14, Fig. 20; woven meditation environment, 214, Fig. 385

handspindle, 248–249, 251–252, 263, Figs. 454, 460, 486, 487

handspinning, *see* spinning

Handweaver & Craftsman, 75

Hargreaves, James, 69, 250

harnesses, 91, 92, Fig. 146; number of, 101

Harvey, Virginia, macramé hanging, 222, Fig. 396

Hebrews, ancient, handweaving among, 29–31

heddle frame, *see* harness

heddle rod, 210, 211, Fig. 380

heddle transfer rods, 104

heddles, 91, Fig. 145; corrective, 91, Fig. 145; kind of, 102; metal, 91, Fig. 145; slot-and-eye, 210, Figs. 378, 379; string, 91, 211–212; Figs. 145, 146, 380, 381; threading, 122–123, Figs. 204–209

Held, Shirley E., Mali technique, 330, Fig. 550; silk-screen hanging, 298, Fig. 517

hemming, 181–182, Figs. 321, 322; start of the web, 132

hems, 110

hemstitching, 180–181, Fig. 317

Hernmarck, Helena Barynina, 179; *Little Richard,* tapestry, 179, Pl. 18, p. 162

Herodotus, 29, 32, 33, 95, 249

herringbone twill, 142, Fig. 242

Heyerdahl, Thor, 51

Hicks, Sheila, 208, 332–333; *Barber's Pole,* 208, Pl. 22, p. 198; wall rugs, 332–333, Fig. 556; *White Letter,* 85, Fig. 135

high wheel, spinning, 252, 262, Figs. 461, 484

high-pile weaves, 189, 193–208; corduroy, 203–205, Figs. 365–369; hooking, 205–208, Figs. 370–376; looping, 193–199, Figs. 348–351; rug knots, 199–201, Figs. 352–356

Hispano-Moresque weaving, 44, Pl. 5, p. 40

Hoffman, Virginia, 341, 344

Holbein, Hans, the Younger, *Penelope at the Loom,* 97, Fig. 154; *Portrait of George Gisze of Danzig,* 190, Fig. 337

honeycomb pattern, 122, Fig. 204

honeysuckle pattern, 138

hooked rug, Duderstadt, 206, Fig. 371

hooking, 205–208, Figs. 370–376; frame, 206–207, Fig. 372; tools, 207, Figs. 373–375

Hornby, Anne, flossa rug, Pl. 20, p. 196

hue, 308, Fig. 523; contrasting, 309, Pls. 35, 36, p. 303

Hunt of the Unicorn, The, tapestry, 64, Fig. 105

Ica weaving, Peru, 54–55, Fig. 87

I-form looms, 215–216, Figs. 388–389

ikat, 290–296, Figs. 504–514

Inca weaving, Peru, 54–55, Fig. 89

indigo, 269, 278–279, Figs. 492, 502

Industrial Revolution, 23, 69, 71, 75, 250, 333

inkle looms, 218–220, Fig. 394

Islamic weaving, 43–44, Figs. 68–71

Italy, handweaving in, Middle Ages, 50–51, Fig. 79; Renaissance, 64–65, Figs. 106–108

jack loom, 100–102, Fig. 159

Jacobi, Ritzi and Peter, *Armoir,* 335, Fig. 559

Jacquard, Joseph Marie, 99

Jacquard loom, 98–99, Fig. 157

Japan, handweaving in, 57–59, Figs. 94–97

Johnson, Hannah, 205–206; bed rug, 206, Fig. 370

Josephine knot, 226, Fig. 410

Jürgen, Johann, 250

Justinian I, and silk cultivation, 37

kasuri (kashiri), 291, Fig. 506; *see also* ikat

Kay, John and Robert, 98

King Arthur, from *Christian Heroes,* tapestry, 48, Fig. 76

knitting, innovations in, 330, Fig. 551, Pl. 40, p. 338; slot, 239–240; spool, 239

knob yarns, 84

Knodel, Gerhardt, G., woven dining environment, 346, Figs. 570–571

knotless netting, 16–17

knots, clove hitch, 224–226, Figs. 405–409; Josephine, 226, Fig. 410; half, 223–224, Figs. 400, 401; lark's-head, 119, 218, 227, Fig. 197; macramé, 223–226, Figs. 400–410; overhand, 226, Fig. 411; rug, 199–201, Figs. 352–356; square, 224, 227, Figs. 402–404

Knudsen, Lois A., woven panels, 343, Fig. 567

Kornerup, Ann-Mari, tapestry-woven dress, Pl. 38, p. 337

K'o-ssu silks, 56–57, Pl. 8, p. 59

Krank, Wolfram, *Vase with Outriding Strings,* 15, Fig. 24

Krejci, Luba, lace panel, 24, Fig. 44

Kroll, Boris, *Santa Fe,* Jacquard-loomed fabric, 334, 335, Fig. 558

Kybal, Antonin, *Brown Cathedral,* tapestry, 329, Fig. 548

lace, bobbin, 19–20, Figs. 37, 38; bone, 19; free, 20, Fig. 38; needle, 19, Fig. 35; pillow, 19, 24, Figs. 42, 43; straight, 20, Fig. 37

lace weaves, 156–165; Brook's Bouquet, 160, 164, Figs. 278, 280; Danish medallion, 159–160, 165, Figs. 276, 277, 282; leno, 156–158, 163, Figs. 271, 272, 279; Mexican lace, 158, 165, Figs. 274, 283; sampler, 160–165, Figs. 279–283; Spanish lace, 158, 159, 164, Figs. 275, 281

lacemaking, 19–24

laid-in weave, 168–170, Figs. 295–299; discontinuous brocade, 168–169, Fig. 295; dukagång, 169–170, Figs. 297–299; mock double cloth, 170, Fig. 299

lamm cord, 129, Fig. 213

lark's-head knot, 119, 218, 227, Fig. 197

Larsen, Jack Lenor, 75, 335; *Jubilee,* power-loomed fabric, Pl. 41, p. 339

lease sticks, 107, Fig. 175; inserting, 117–118, Figs. 192, 193

lease ties, 116

LeBrun, Charles, 67; *Life of the King,* tapestry, 67, Pl. 9, p. 60

leno weave, 156–158, 163, Figs. 271, 272, 279

Leonardo da Vinci, 249; design for hand-driven spinning machine, 250, Fig. 457

letting off (from the warp beam), 131–132

Liebes, Dorothy, 74, 315; blinds, detail, 74, Pl. 11, p. 94; casement fabric, 322, Fig. 541; drapery fabric, 334, Fig. 557; fabric for King Saud's land trailer, 343–344, Fig. 568

Life of the King, The, tapestry, 67, Pl. 9, p. 60

linen fiber, 79, Fig. 126; mordanting, 276–277; scouring, 274–275

linters, 83

locked loops, 183, Fig. 329

lockstitch, 166, Fig. 284

loom bench, 102, 103, Fig. 161

loom waste, 109

loom-constructed garments, 318–321, Figs. 530–537, Pl. 38, p. 337

loom-controlled weaves, 140–155; basic, 140–142, Figs. 235–243; basket, 141, Fig. 236; brocade, 155, Figs. 266–268; double, 152–155, Figs. 258–265; plain (tabby), 140–141, Figs. 236, 237; rep, 141, Fig. 237; sampler, 142–152, Figs. 244–257; satin, 142, Fig. 243; twill, 141–142, Figs. 238–242

looms, 6, 90–102; accessories, 102–104; adjusting, 129–130, Fig. 214; beating mechanism, 92, 102, Fig. 147; backstrap, 95–96, 209–213, Figs. 150, 151, 377, 382, 383; basic, parts of, 90–92, Fig. 144; cost of, 102; counterbalance, 91, 100, 102, Figs. 144, 158; designing for, 315–326; draw, 98, Fig. 156; dressing, 117–125; evolution of, 92; fabric from, removing, 135; fabric on, protecting, 133; fixed-warp, 216–217, Fig. 390; frame of, 90–91, 102; hand, 50, 67, 99–100; horizontal frame, 96–97; horizontal ground, 96, Figs. 152, 153; I-form, 215–216, Figs. 388, 389; inkle, 218–220, Fig. 394; jack, 100–101, 102, Fig. 159; Jacquard, 98–99, Fig. 157; long-web tapestry, 217–218, Fig. 392; Ojibway, 192, 218, Fig. 393; permanent frame, 213–214, Fig. 386; pit, 96, Fig. 152; power, 69; reusable frame, 215–220, Figs. 388–395; selecting, 100, 101, Fig. 159; setting up, 316–317; shedding mechanism, 91–92; short-web tapestry, 217, Fig. 391; simple, 209–220; slot, 240, Figs. 441–442; square frame, 216–217; table, 100, 101, 102, Fig. 160; tripod, 96, 97, Fig. 153; type of, 100–101; warp-weighted, 8, 16, 92–95, 192, Figs. 7, 27, 149; warping aids, 104–107

loop yarns, 84, Fig. 133

looping, 193–199, Figs. 348–351

low-pile weaves, 189, 191–193; chaining, 191, Figs. 338, 339; soumak, 192–193, Figs. 344–347; twining, 192, Figs. 340–343

Lubasin S, 293

Lubell, Cecil, 328

Lurçat, Jean, *The Apocalypse,* tapestry, 175, Fig. 310; *Liberty,* tapestry, 175; *Man,* tapestry, 175

MacGilchrist, Bonnie, *Soft Fireplace,* 85, Fig. 136

macramé, 17–19, 76, 183, 222–233, Figs. 396–420, Pl. 2, p. 22, Pl. 23, p. 231; chair, Thompson, 230, Fig. 419; cords, measuring, 222–223; designing for, 229–233, Figs. 413–420, Pl. 23, p. 231; equipment, 222, 223, Fig. 398; hanging, Paque, 229, Fig. 415; knots, basic, 223–226, Figs. 400–410; materials, 222, 223, Fig. 397; necklace, Bodlaender, 228, Fig. 413; sampler, 226–228, Fig. 412

madder, 278

Mali, 329–330, Figs. 548–550

Manufacture Royale des Meubles de la Couronne, 67

Marein, Shirley, scarf, 220, Fig. 395

Matthews, Mary Ehlers, double ikat hanging, 296, Fig. 514

matting, 5–6, 10–11, Fig. 12, Pl. 1, p. 21

Meredith, Dorothy L., ikat hanging, 185, Fig. 332

Mesopotamia, handweaving in, 28–29, Fig. 50

Mexican lace, 158, 165, Figs. 274, 283

Middle Ages in Europe, handweaving, 45–51, Figs. 72–79; Flanders, 49, Fig. 77; France, 47–49, Figs. 74–76; Italy, 50–51, Fig. 79; Norway, 49–50, Fig. 78

Middle East, ancient, handweaving, 26–31, Figs. 45–51; Egypt, 26–28, Figs. 45–49; Hebrews, 29–31; Mesopotamia, 28–29, Fig. 50; Persian Empire, 31, Fig. 51, Pl. 3, p. 39

mineral fibers, 80, 81

Minimal Art, 336, Fig. 561

Minko, Tachibana, Chinese draw loom, woodcut, 98, Fig. 156

mock double cloth, 170, Fig. 299

Moholy-Nagy, László, 301, 302

monofilament yarns, 82

mordanting, 269, 275–277, Fig. 500

Morris, William, 70–71; *Woodpecker,* tapestry, 71, Pl. 10, p. 93

Morton, Alastair, 203

Mountains and Birds, silk damask, 35, Fig. 57

Muche, Georg, 71

multifilament yarns, 82

mummy cloth, 27, Fig. 47

Munoz, Aurelia, *Tres Personnages,* macramé, 230, Figs. 417, 418

Munsell, Albert, 308

Museum of Contemporary Crafts, New York, 74

Navajo weaving, 51, 174, Pl. 17, p. 161

Nazca weaving, 53, Figs. 80, 83, 84

Nemours, Aurelie, *Acrux,* tapestry, 310–311, Fig. 526

neolithic knot, 183, Fig. 328

netting, 12–14, 236–237, Figs. 17, 18, 431–433, 566; embroidered, 20, Fig. 39; knotless, 16–17

Nissen, Nana, *Vector Equilibri Um,* wool yarn over bamboo frame, 213, Fig. 384

Noh robe, Japan, 58, Fig. 96

nonloom techniques, 10–24, 221–244; basketry, 14–15, Figs. 21–24; braiding, 238, Figs. 436, 437; card weaving, 241–244, Figs. 446–452; felting, 11–12, Fig. 13; God's-eye, 240–241, Figs. 443–445; lacemaking, 19–24, Figs. 35–44; macramé, 17–19, 222–233, Figs. 32–34, 396–420; matting, 10–11, Fig. 12, Pl. 1, p. 21; netting, 12–14, 236–237, Figs. 17–20, 431–433; plaiting, 237–238, Figs. 434, 435; slot knitting, 239–240, Figs. 441, 442; spool knitting, 239, Figs. 438–440; sprang, 16–17, 233–236, Figs. 28–30, 421–430; twining, 15–16, 192, Figs. 25–27, 340–343

Norway, handweaving, Middle Ages, 49–50, Fig. 78

Nottingham, Walter G., *Fuses,* crochet, 330, 331, Fig. 552

novelty yarns, 83–84, Figs. 132, 133

nub yarns, 84, Fig. 133

nylon, 86

Ojibway Indian loom, 192, 218, Fig. 393

Op Art, 336, Fig. 560

Oseberg burial ship, 49–50; textile from, 50, Fig. 78; weaving tablets from, 241, Fig. 446

Ouchi, Michi, *Blue and Purple,* weaving and macramé, 233, Fig. 420

overcasting, 180, 181, Fig. 318

overhand knot, 226, Fig. 411

paddle warping, 114–116, Figs. 183–188

Pannemaker, Pieter, 62

Paque, Joan Michaels, macramé hanging, 229, Fig. 415

Paracas weaving, Peru, 52–54, Figs. 81, 82, Pl. 7, p. 42

Parrott, Alice, *God's Eye Hanging,* 241, Fig. 445

patchwork, 76, Fig. 124

pattern double weave, 166–168, Figs. 289–294

pattern weaves, 324–325

Perkins, Sir William H., 270

perle cotton, 84

Persian Empire, ancient, handweaving in, 31, Fig. 51, Pl. 3, p. 39

Persian knot, *see* Sehna knot

Philippine edge, 181, Fig. 326

Phillips, Mary Walker, knit cover for chair, 330, Fig. 551; hanging, 330, Pl. 40, p. 338

pick, *see weft*

pick count, 133

picking, 255–256, Fig. 468

pile weaves, 189–208; chaining, 191, Figs. 338, 339; corduroy, 203–205, Figs. 365–369; hooking, 205–208, Figs. 370–376; looping, 193–199, Figs. 348–351; rug knots, 199–201, Figs. 352–356; soumak, 192–193, Figs. 344–347; twining, 192, Figs. 340–343

pillow covers, Gilmurray, Pl. 39, p. 337; plan for, 323, Fig. 542

pit loom, 96, Fig. 152

Pizarro, Francisco, 55, 291

plain weave, 129, 140–141, Figs. 235–237

plaiting, 6, 237–238, Figs. 434, 435

plaitwork, Egyptian, 16–17

Plictho, The, Rosetti, 269–270, Fig. 493

ply yarns, 82–83, Fig. 131

plying, 263–267, Figs. 490, 491

Poliakoff, Serge, *Formes,* tapestry, 176, Fig. 311

Polo, Marco, 46, 50, 51, 56

Pomo Indians, basketry, 15, Fig. 23

Pop Art, 335, Fig. 559

Powys, Marian, *Fawns,* pillow lace, 24, Fig. 42

pre-Columbian weaving, 51–55, Figs. 80–89, Pl. 7, p. 42

primary colors, 308

principles of design, 309–314; balance, 311–312, Fig. 527, Pl. 37, p. 304; emphasis, 312–314, Figs. 528, 529; proportion, 310–311, Figs. 524–526; rhythm, 314, Pl. 37, p. 304

printing, yarn, *see* yarn printing

profile draft, 138, 324–325, Figs. 543–544

pull-in, of the web, 110

quills, bobbin, 130, Fig. 216

raddle, 107

Rapoport, Debra E., *Fibrous Raiment,* knotted netting, 343, Fig. 566

Raphael, cartoon for *The Miraculous Draught of Fishes,* watercolor, 63, Fig. 102

ratchet, 90

ratiné yarns, 84, Fig. 133

rayon, 86

reed, 92, Fig. 147; sleying, 123–124, Figs. 207, 208

reed hook, 106, Fig. 172

reels, warping, 104–105, 111–112, Figs. 167, 168, 179, 189

Renaissance Europe, handweaving in, 61–65, Figs. 99–108; England, 63–64, Fig. 104; Flanders, 61–63, Figs. 99–103; France, 64, Fig. 105; Italy, 64–65, Figs. 106, 107; Spain, 64–65, Fig. 108

rep weaves, 141, Fig. 237

repeat design, 313, Fig. 528

reverse twill, 142, Fig. 241

Rogers, Ezekiel, 68

rölakan weaving, 174

Rome, classical, handweaving in, 32–33, Fig. 53

Rosetti, Gioanventura, 268–269; *The Plictho,* 269–270, Fig. 493

Rossbach, Ed, *Construction with Newspaper and Plastic,* 88, Fig. 143; silk screen, 298, Pl. 33, p. 286

roving, in spinning, 259–260, Figs. 478, 479

Rubens, Peter Paul, 65–66; *The History of Constantine,* tapestry, 66, Figs. 109, 110

rug knots, 199–203, Figs. 352–356, 358–363

rug shuttle, 103

rug weaves, *see* pile weaves

rugs, 189–208; pillar, 57, Fig. 93; tapestry-woven, 28, Fig. 49

rya, 201–203, Figs. 358–364; Hornby rug, Pl. 20, p. 196; knots, 202, Figs. 358–362; stick, 203, Fig. 364; Swedish rug, 202, Pl. 19, p. 195; weaving techniques, 202–203

Sadley, Wojciech, *Sleepless Night,* pile tapestry, 201, Fig. 357

Saga of Jourdain de Blaye, tapestry, 49, Fig. 77

samplers, knotted and braided, 18, Fig. 34; lace weaves, 160–165, Figs. 279–283; loom-controlled weaves, 142–151, Figs. 244–257; macramé, 226–228, Fig. 412; Naxca, 53, Fig. 84

Samson and the Lion, silk compound twill, 38, Fig. 65

Sassanian weaving, Persia, 31, 43–44; *Cock,* 31, Pl. 3, p. 39

satin weaves, 142, Fig. 243

scale, 310

Schira, Cynthia, *Ikat with Walnut,* 294, Fig. 510

Scholten, Herman, 176, 179; *Light and Water,* tapestry, 178, Fig. 315; *Op En Neer (Up and Down),* 336, Fig. 561

Schroeder, Frances, weaving on permanent metal hoop frame, 215, Fig. 387

scouring, yarn, 256, 274–275

secondary color, 308

sectional warping, 121–122, Figs. 202–203

seed yarns, 84, Fig. 133

Sehna knot, 199–200, Figs. 354, 355

Sekimachi, Kay, *Marugawa V, VI, VII,* card-weaving, 244, Fig. 452; *Nagore III,* 82, Fig. 129

selvedge, 25, 131, 184, Fig. 219; even, maintaining, 132–133, Fig. 220; in weft ikat printing, 295, Fig. 511

sericulture, 33–34, 37–38, Figs. 54, 55, 64

sett, calculating, 110, Fig. 178

Shapira, Nathan, *Galaxy,* hand print on satin, 306–307, Fig. 522

Shawcroft, Barbara, *Arizona Inner Space,* environmental woven structure, 344–345, Fig. 569; interchangeable forms, 306, Fig. 521

shedding mechanism of the loom, 91–92

shedding sequence, 131

Sheldon, William, 63; tapestry map of Worcestershire, 64, Fig. 104

shrinkage of fabric, 110

shuttle race, 102

shuttles, 103, Fig. 162; butterfly, 157, Fig. 269; filling, 130–131, Figs. 215–217; flat, 103; fly, 98; ski, 103; stick, 103; throwing, 131

silk fibers, 34, 79, 83, Fig. 128; manufacture, 66, 67, Fig. 111; production, 33–34, 37–38, Figs. 54, 55, 64; raw, 85; tussah, 85; wild, 85; yarns, 85

silk screen, 296–298, Figs. 515–517, Pl. 33, p. 286

Skowronski, Hella, *Sprang No. 6,* 236, Fig. 430

sley hook, 106, Fig. 172

sleying the reed, 123–124, Figs. 207, 208

slip knot, 123, Fig. 206

slit tapestry, 174–175, Figs. 308–309

slits, in tapestry weaving, 173–174, Figs. 305–307

slot knitting, 239–240, Figs. 441, 442

slot-and-eye heddle, 210, Figs. 378, 379

slub yarns, 84, Fig. 133

Smith, Mary Alice, 75

Solomon Islands hand loom, 92, Fig. 148

soumak, 192–193, Figs. 344–347

Southern Highlands, U.S., craft revival in, 75–76

Spain, handweaving during Renaissance, 64–65, Fig. 108

Spanish knot, 199–201, Fig. 356

Spanish lace, 158–159, 164, Figs. 275, 281

spindle, hand, 248–249, 251–252, 263, Figs. 454, 460, 486, 487

spinning, 247–267; ancient Egyptian, 27; equipment, 251–253, Figs. 460–463; fiber preparation equipment, 253–254, Figs. 464–467; fiber preparation, 255–260, Figs. 468–479; history of, 248–250, Figs. 454–458; materials for, 251, Fig. 459; planning the yarn, 254–255; process of, 260–263, Figs. 480–487; yarn design, 263–267; Figs. 488–491

spinning machine, 250, Figs. 457, 458

spool knitting, 239, Figs. 438–440

spool rack, 106, Fig. 171

sprang, 16–17, 76, 233–236, Figs. 28–30, 421–430

spreader, 107, Fig. 176

square knot, 224, 227, Figs. 402–404

squirrel cage reel, 106, 107, Fig. 174

Stamsta, Jean, *Serpentine,* Pl. 13, p. 127

staple fibers, 83

staple-fiber yarns, 86, Fig. 138

Stölzl, Gunta, 71; slit Gobelin wall hanging, 71, Fig. 117

Story of Alexander the Great, tapestry, 61–62, Fig. 100

straight twill, 141–142, Figs. 238–240

stretcher, 104, Fig. 165

string heddle, 91, Figs. 145–146; for simple looms, 211–212, Figs. 380, 381

S-twist, 267, Fig. 490

summer-and-winter weave, 324, Figs. 543–545

Sutherland, Graham, *The Eagle: Emblem of St. John,* detail of *Christ in Glory,* tapestry, 176, Fig. 312

swift, 106

sword (shed stick), 210, 211, Fig. 380

Taaniko twining, Maori, 15, Fig. 25

tabby, *see* plain weave

table loom, 100–101, Fig. 160

tablet weaving, *see* card weaving

taking up (onto the cloth beam), 131–132

tapa cloth, 5, 10–11, Fig. 12, Pl. 1, p. 21

tapestry, 170–179, Figs. 300–316; basse-lisse (low warp), 171; bobbins, 103, 172, Fig. 302; cartoon, 172; contemporary, 175–179, Figs. 309–316, Pl. 18, p. 162; eccentric weft, 173; equipment, 171–172, Figs. 300–302; fork, 171, Fig. 301; Gobelin, 173; haute-lisse (high-warp), 171; historical, 47–50, 61–67, Figs. 75–78, 99–102, 104, 105, 109, 110, Pl. 6, p. 41; Pl. 9, p. 60; Pl. 10, p. 93; kilim, 173; looms, 171, 217–218, Figs. 300, 391, 392; materials, 171; Navajo, 174, Pl. 17, p. 161; rölakan, 174; simple looms for, 216–218, Figs. 390–392; slit, 174–175, Figs. 308, 309; slits, methods of dealing with, 173–174, Figs. 304–307; weaving techniques, 172–174, Figs. 303–307

Tawney, Lenore, *Ark Curtain,* 174, 175, Fig. 309

tela se lengua ikat, 291, Pl. 28, p. 283

tension box, 105, Fig. 170

Thompson, Joanne Asher, macramé chair, 230, Fig. 419

Thompson, Susan R., *Blazing Star,* warp ikat, 294, Pl. 29, p. 284

threading draft, 136–137, Figs. 227–229

throw shuttle, 103

thrums, 109

Tiahuanaco weaving, Peru, 54, Fig. 85

tie-up, 126–129; draft, 137, Fig. 230; preparing, 126, Figs. 212–214

Toth, Sandor, hanging, 305, Fig. 518

treadle cord, 129, Fig. 213

treadles, 126, 129, 137, Fig. 212

treadling draft, 137, Fig. 231

tripod loom, 96, 97, Fig. 153

tubular double weave, 153–154, Figs. 260–262, Pl. 13, p. 127

tufting, 205; *see also* hooking

Turkish knot, *see* Ghiordes knot

twill weaves, 141–142; herringbone, 142, Fig. 242; reverse, 142, Fig. 241; straight, 141–142, Figs. 238–240

twining, 15–16, 192, Figs. 340–343; braided-weft, 192, Fig. 342; Chilkat, 16, Figs. 26, 27; looped, 192, Fig. 343; Maori, 15–16, Fig. 25; three-strand, 192, Fig. 341; two-strand, 192, Fig. 340

umbrella swift, 106, Fig. 173

unbalanced weave, 133, Fig. 222

Unicorn in Captivity, The, tapestry, 64, Fig. 105

unit design, 313, Fig. 529

Utamaro, Kitagawa, *Reeling of Silk,* woodcut, 34, Fig. 54; *Weaving of Silk,* woodcut, 34, Fig. 55

Van Aelst, Pieter, 62; *The Miraculous Draught of Fishes,* 63, Fig. 101

Van Eyck, Jan, 50

Vaňková, Marie, *Space Lace Form,* pillow lace, 24, Fig. 43

Van Meckenem, Israhel, the Elder, *Woman Spinning,* 249, Fig. 456

Vaucanson, Jacques de, 98–99

Verecundus, Vercilius, shop sign of, 32, Fig. 32

Vermeer, Jan, *The Lacemaker,* 19, Fig. 36

Vogel, Ludwig, *Two Women Weaving,* 97, Fig. 155

wadmal, 45, 46, Fig. 73

warp, 25; broken, correcting, 134, Figs. 223, 224; length and width of, calculating, 109–111; measuring, 111–116, Figs. 179–190; spreading, 118–119, Figs. 194, 195; tying ends at front of loom, 124–125, Fig. 209; width of, 110; winding, 119–121, Figs. 199–201

warp takeup, 109–110, Fig. 177

warp wrapping, 165–166, Figs. 284–288

warp yarns, 137; choosing, 108–109; total quantity of, calculating, 111

warp-face fabric, 133

warping, 111–116, Figs. 179–191; cross, 111–113, Figs. 181, 182; equipment for, 104–106, Figs. 166–171; guide string, 111–112, Figs. 179, 180; paddle, 114–116, Figs. 183–188; primitive, 111, Fig. 8; sectional, 121–122, Figs. 202, 203

warping creel, 105, Fig. 171

warping frame, 104–105, 112–113, Figs. 166, 180, 182, 189

warping reel, 104–105, 111–113, Figs. 167, 168, 179, 190

warp-weighted loom, 32, 92, 95; Chilkat, 16, Fig. 27; Egyptian, Fig. 48; Greek, Figs. 7, 52; Icelandic, 95, Fig. 149

Weatherson, Alexander, 341

weave analysis, 325–326, Fig. 546

weave draft, 137–138, Fig. 232; deriving, 138–139

weaver-controlled weaves, 156–179; lace weaves, 156–165, Figs. 271–283; laid-in weave, 168–170, Figs. 295–299; pattern double weave, 166–168, Figs. 289–294; tapestry, 170–179, Figs. 300–316; warp wrapping, 165–166, Figs. 284–288

Weavers' Guild, 46

weaves, basic, 140–142, Figs. 235–243; basket, 141, Fig. 236; brocade, 155, 168–169, Figs. 266–268, 295, 296, Pls. 14–16, p. 128; double, 152–155, Figs. 258–265; finger, 157, Fig. 270; herringbone twill, 142, Fig. 242; high-pile, 189; lace, 156–165; laid-in, 168–170, Figs. 295–299; loom-controlled, 140–155; low-pile, 189, 191–193; pattern double, 166–168, Figs. 289–294; plain (tabby), 140–141, Figs. 236, 237; rep, 141, Fig. 237; reverse double, 154–155, Figs. 264, 265; reverse twill, 142, Fig. 241; satin, 142, Fig. 243; straight twill, 142, Figs. 238–240; tapestry, 170–179; twill, 141–142, Figs. 238–242; tubular double, 153–154, Figs. 260–262, Pl. 13, p. 127; warp wrapping, 165–166, Figs. 284–288; weaver-controlled, 156–179

web, hemming the start of, 132; measuring, 133–134; removing from the loom, 134–135, Figs. 225–226

Webb, Aileen Vanderbilt, 74

weft, 25; eccentric, 173

weft yarns, changing, 132, Fig. 219; choosing, 108–109; quantity, calculating, 111

weft-face fabric, 133

Weitzman, Susan, *Tapestry for Frances Lynn*, 84, Fig. 134, *Unwoven Tapestry*, 247, Fig. 453

Willis, Sweenie, mat, 5, Fig. 2

woof, *see* weft

wool fibers, 79, Fig. 127; grades of, 251, Fig. 459; lamb's, 84; mordanting, 275–276; reprocessed, 84; reused, 84; scouring, 274; virgin, 84

woolen system of spinning, 254

woolen yarns, 83–84, 86

World Crafts Council, 75

worsted, spinning system, 254; yarn, 86

yarn calculation, 108–111

yarn design, 263–267, Figs. 488–491

yarn printing, 290–298

yarns, 79–86; bouclé, 84; cable (cord), 83; chenille, 84; construction of, 82–84; cork-screw, 84; decorative, 83; degree of twist, 82, Fig. 130; dyeing, *see* dyeing, yarn; effect, 83; filament, 86, Fig. 137; flake, 84; guimpe, 84; handspinning of, *see* spinning; knob, 84; loop, 84; long-staple, 83; monofilament, 82; multifilament, 82; novelty, 83–84, Figs. 132–133; nub, 84; planning, for handspinning, 254–255; ply, 82–83, Fig. 131; properties of, 84–86; ratiné, 84; seed, 84; selecting, 316; short-staple, 83; silk, 85; sizes of, 86; thrown silk, 85; staple-fiber, 86, Fig. 138; warp, *see* warp yarns; warping, 112–116; weft, *see* weft yarns; wool, 83–84; worsted, 85

Young Bear, John, slot-and-eye heddle, 210, Fig. 378

Zachai, Dorian, 302; *Lady Performing*, tapestry, 178, 179, Fig. 316

Zeisler, Claire, *Red Forest*, 310, 331, Fig. 533; *Red Madagascar*, 229, Fig. 416; *Red Wednesday*, Pl. 2, p. 22

Z twist, 267, Fig. 490

Photographic Sources

References are to figure numbers unless indicated Pl. (plate).

Alinari–Art Reference Bureau, Ancram, N.Y. (19, 53, 77, 100–101, 107, Pl. 3); American Crafts Council, New York (121, 396); American Museum of Natural History, New York (3, 13, 16); Ancillotti Fotografie, Milan (551); Anderson–Art Reference Bureau, Ancram, N.Y. (106); Gunnar Anderssons Vävskedsverkstad, Oxberg, Sweden (163, 171–172); Archives Photographiques, Paris (36, 74–75); Ashe, Alan W., Asheville, N.C. (123); Avila, Adam, Los Angeles (Pl. 12); Baldwin, Joel, New York (124); Boesch, Ferdinand, New York (385); Ciba-Geigy Limited, Basel (10–11, 17, 29, 64); Cooper, A. C., Ltd., London (98); Cordry, Donald, Cuernavaca (151); Crane, Tom, New York (414, 560); Cyr, Don, New Haven (460–462, 466, 482, 484, 486, 495–501); Dovydenas, Jonas, Chicago (416); E. I. DuPont de Nemours & Company, Wilmington (125–128); Éditions Hoa-Qui, Paris (1); Éditions Paroissiales d'Assy (310); Foster, Jack, Cincinnati (142, 527, 549); Freeman, John R., & Co. Ltd., London (Pl. 10); Gilchrist, Martine, New York (531, 534, 564); Gilmore, Paul T., Seattle (430); Giraudon, Paris (50–51); Gross, Richard, Los Angeles (136, 569); Hallman, Ted, Berkeley (20, 427); Hanson, Bob, New York (521); Harvey, Virginia, Seattle, and William Eng (330); Held, Shirley E., Ames, Iowa (38, 47, 80, 333, 439, 504, 509, 512–514, 517, 537, 540, 546); Hirmer Fotoarchiv, Munich (22); Index of American Design, National Gallery of Art, Washington, D.C. (115); Ruth Kaufmann Gallery, New York (309); Kester, Bernard, Los Angeles (520); King, Alex, New York (488); Knapp, Tamarra, S. Aceworth, N.H. (316); Knudsen, Walter P., Pacoima, Calif. (567); Langlois, Suzy, Paris (Pl. 22); Larsen, L., Copenhagen (5, 73); Lauros-Giraudon, Paris (67); Nilus/Leclerc Inc., L'Isletville, Quebec (300); Lewandowska, Emanuela, and Authors' Agency Ltd., Warsaw (357); Dorothy Liebes Design, Inc., New York (568); Los Angeles County Museum of Art (Pl. 17); Makinem, Eino, Copyright © National Museum of Finland, Helsinki (363); Metropolitan Museum of Art, New York (52); Münchow, Ann, Aachen (66); Museum of Modern Art, New York (296); Nelson, O. E., New York (Pl. 2); Nordahl, Jan, Sodertalje, Sweden (554); Lee Nordness Gallery, New York (129, 552); Novosti Press Agency, Moscow (15, 57); Perron, Robert, New York (63); Pollitzer, Eric, Garden City Park, N.Y. (44, 133, 145, 162, 169, 174–176, 259, 262, 264, 289, 291, 294, 301–302, 321–324, 331, 335, 339, 347, 351, 355, 397–399, 401, 403, 412–413, 443, 451, 538, 550, Pls. 13–16, 26, 40); Pottinger, Robert, Chicago (120); Rampazzi Ferruccio, Turin, and Soprintendenza alle Antichità Egittologia, Turin (49); Riboud, Marc, Magnum, Paris (556, 563); Rosso, Foto, Turin, and Soprintendenza alle Antichità Egittologia, Turin (45); Schopplein Studio, San Francisco (Pl. 29); Service de Documentation Photographique de la Réunion des Musées Nationaux, Paris (Pl. 9); Sexton, Mark, Salem, Mass. (Pl. 1); Smith, J. Douglas, Lancaster, Pa. (Pls. 30–32); Soprintendenza ai Monumenti ed alle Gallerie dell'Umbria, Perugia (90); Steinkopf, Walter, West Berlin (337); Stone & Steccati, San Francisco (452, Pl. 24); Teigens Fotoatelier, Oslo (Pl. 6); Thompson, P. W. & I., Coventry (312); *Time Canada*, Montreal (Pl. 18); Uht, Charles, New York (12); United States Department of the Interior, Indian Arts and Crafts Board, Washington, D.C. (2); Van-Cols of Colchester Limited (365); Van Wageningen, Ton, Amsterdam (561); Varela, O. L., Washington, D.C. (93); Vine, David, New York (141, 247, 249, 255, 257, 279–283); Wyatt, A. J., Philadelphia (59).

Fig. 157 from *Historic Textile Fabrics* by Richard Glazier (London: B. T. Batsford Ltd., 1923). Fig. 503 from *The New Britton & Brown Illustrated Flora* by Henry A. Gleason (New York: New York Botanical Garden, 1952). Fig. 156 from *Traditional Crafts of Japan* by Charles Pomeroy (New York and Tokyo: John Weatherhill, Inc., 1967–68). Figs. 148 and 153 from "Studies in Primitive Looms" by H. Ling Roth, from Royal Archaeological Institute Journal, #47–48, 1917–18. Pls. 19, 38 from *New Design in Weaving* by Donald J. Willcox (New York: Van Nostrand Reinhold, 1970).

Works by Lurçat and Poliakoff: Permission A.D.A.G.P. 1973 by French Reproduction Rights, Inc.